Child's Play

Critical Issues in Sport and Society

Michael Messner and Douglas Hartmann, Series Editors

Critical Issues in Sport and Society features scholarly books that help expand our understanding of the new and myriad ways in which sport is intertwined with social life in the contemporary world. Using the tools of various scholarly disciplines, including sociology, anthropology, history, media studies and others, books in this series investigate the growing impact of sport and sports-related activities on various aspects of social life as well as key developments and changes in the sporting world and emerging sporting practices. Series authors produce groundbreaking research that brings empirical and applied work together with cultural critique and historical perspectives written in an engaging, accessible format.

Jules Boykoff, *Activism and the Olympics: Dissent at the Games in Vancouver and London*

Diana T. Cohen, *Iron Dads: Managing Family, Work, and Endurance Sport Identities*

Jennifer Guiliano, *Indian Spectacle: College Mascots and the Anxiety of Modern America*

Kathryn Henne, *Testing for Athlete Citizenship: The Regulation of Doping and Sex in Sport*

Michael A. Messner and Michela Musto, eds., *Child's Play: Sport in Kids' Worlds*

Jeffrey Montez de Oca, *Discipline and Indulgence: College Football, Media, and the American Way of Life during the Cold War*

Stephen C. Paulson, *Why Would Anyone Do That?: Lifestyle Sport in the Twenty-first Century*

Child's Play

Sport in Kids' Worlds

EDITED BY MICHAEL A. MESSNER
AND MICHELA MUSTO

RUTGERS UNIVERSITY PRESS
NEW BRUNSWICK, NEW JERSEY, AND LONDON

Library of Congress Cataloging-in-Publication Data
Names: Messner, Michael A., editor. | Musto, Michela, editor.
Title: Child's play : sport in kids' worlds / edited by Michael A. Messner and Michela Musto.
Description: New Brunswick, New Jersey : Rutgers University Press, [2016] | Series: Critical issues in sport and society | Includes bibliographical references and index.
Identifiers: LCCN 2015028619 | ISBN 9780813571461 (hardback) | ISBN 9780813571454 (pbk.) | ISBN 9780813571478 (e-book (web pdf)) | 9780813572918 (e-book (epub))
Subjects: LCSH: Sports for children. | Sports for children—Social aspects. | Sports for children—Psychological aspects. | BISAC: SPORTS & RECREATION / General. | PSYCHOLOGY / Developmental / Adolescent. | SOCIAL SCIENCE / Children's Studies. | SOCIAL SCIENCE / Gender Studies. | SOCIAL SCIENCE / Ethnic Studies / General.
Classification: LCC GV709.2 .C474 2016 | DDC 796.083—dc23
LC record available at http://lccn.loc.gov/2015028619

A British Cataloging-in-Publication record for this book is available from the British Library.

Visit our website: http://rutgerspress.rutgers.edu

Manufactured in the United States of America

For Barrie Thorne
In appreciation for her groundbreaking research on children,
and her decades of inspiration and mentorship

Contents

PART II

Fields of Play: Kids Navigating Sport Worlds

Child's Play

Introduction

KIDS AND SPORT

Michael A. Messner and Michela Musto

Millions of kids play sports. Everybody knows this. But only recently has the general public started to consider critical questions about youth sports. One bundle of questions concerns unequal access: who gets to play sports, and who does not? Up until the fairly recent and dramatic influx of girls, youth sports were for the most part set up by men, for boys. Middle-class kids in the suburbs, disproportionately white and native-born, continue to enjoy easier access to sport participation than do immigrant kids, urban poor kids, and kids of color. Questions of unequal access, while important, often raise deeper questions: how, when, and under what conditions do youth sports enhance the health and social and emotional development of kids?

Questions of unequal access and concerns about the positives and negatives of aspects of youth sports are important areas of public debate. In assessing any such public concern, we need strong and reliable scholarly research, rather than unfounded assumptions or ideology. For instance, in recent years media pundits, documentary filmmakers, and politicians have sounded the alarm of an "obesity epidemic" among youth, a fear fueled in part by cultural images of inactive kids glued to electronic screens while hoovering down sugary soft drinks and fat-laden fast foods. There are good reasons to encourage kids to engage in healthy eating and regular exercise, but the cultural fears surrounding the image of the lazy, fat child tends to obscure a parallel empirical reality: kids are playing organized sports today in huge numbers. But we don't really know whether or to what extent youth sports participation is part of the problem or part of the solution when it comes to concerns about children and health. One reason for this lack of understanding is that scholars of sport have largely ignored kids as active participants—as athletes and fans—and have mostly failed to study the ways in which sport, both for good and for ill, is so often an important and meaningful part of the larger landscape of childhood. With the original works of research collected in *Child's Play*, we broaden and deepen the scholarly study of children and sport and provide a road map for future studies.

In this introduction, we document what we see as a paradox: the relative silence among sport sociologists concerning kids and sport, against a backdrop of massive youth sport participation. Then, drawing from the emergent scholarly study of children and youth (both as a growing subfield within sociology and as an interdisciplinary domain), we argue that a deep and critical research engagement with kids and sport not only will yield insights that are relevant to people's everyday concerns, but also can contribute to central scholarly questions about embodiments, violence and health, social inequality and mobility in schools, neighborhoods, and families, and consumption and audience reception of mass media as well as engagements with new media.

Youth Sports: The Hidden Part of the Iceberg

Our hunch was that sport studies scholars have mostly ignored the topic of kids and sport. To test this assumption, we examined all of the articles published in the past decade within the *Sociology of Sport Journal, Journal of Sport and Social Issues,* and *International Review for the Sociology of Sport* and found that scholars devote a tremendous amount of attention to studying sports media (21.3 percent of all of the articles), professional sports (10.7 percent), elite amateur sports (8.6 percent), sport organizations (6.3 percent), and collegiate sports (5.8 percent). We believe that comparing this percentage distribution to the image of an iceberg is useful here, if not in exact numerical proportions, then at least metaphorically. About 11 percent of an iceberg, we are often told, is generally visible above the waterline; the rest lies below the surface. Scholars of sport have spent a huge proportion of time observing, analyzing, and writing about the most publicly visible "tip" of sport: college, professional, and elite amateur sports, and their coverage in print, electronic, and new media. Combined, these topics constitute nearly half (46.4 percent) of the articles published within sport journals in the past ten years.

Like the hidden parts of an iceberg, aspects of sport that have larger numbers of participants—such as youth sports—are less frequently the subject of sociologists' attention. Over the decade of journals that we analyzed, only 3.4 percent of the articles focused on teenagers in high school sports, such as Laura Azzarito and Louis Harrison's (2008) examination of the naturalization of racialized discourses within physical education classes or Kathleen E. Miller et al.'s (2005) investigation of differences between jocks' and non-jocks' behavior within high schools. And during this same ten years only eight articles—approximately 1 percent of the total sample—focused primarily on kids' sports up to age fourteen (Cooky and McDonald 2005; Dagkas and Quarmby 2012; Grasmuck

2003; King-White 2010; Light 2010; McHale et al. 2005; Wachs and Chase 2013; Wheeler 2012).

Examinations of kids in scholarly sport books fare no better. Of the twenty-seven books published in the State University of New York Press series on "Sport, Culture, and Social Relations" between 1993 and 2012, only one, *Paradoxes of Youth and Sport*, a collection of essays that focused minimally on children, considered kids or youth sports (Gatz, Messner, and Ball-Rokeach 2002). Similarly, none of the fourteen books published between 2004 and 2013 in the Routledge "Critical Studies in Sport" series focused primarily on kids or youth sports. *Child's Play* is the first book to contemplate kids and sport in the still-young Rutgers University Press "Critical Issues in Sport and Society" series. Of the twenty-one annual book awards given by the North American Society for the Sociology of Sport since 1990, two went to books focused on kids or youth sports—Sherri Grasmuck's (2005) *Protecting Home*, a fine ethnographic study of Little League baseball in Philadelphia, and Emily Chivers Yochim's (2009) *Skate Life*, a study of skateboarders mostly in their mid- to late teens.

A small number of book-length studies by sport sociologists skirt the edges of kids' experiences with sport: Michael Messner's (2009) study of community-based Little League and AYSO leagues focused not on kids but on adults' experiences in youth sports. One chapter of Leslie Heywood and Shari L. Dworkin's (2003) book on cultural images of women athletes examined children's views of women athletes. Although Hilary Levey Friedman's (2013) *Playing to Win* did not focus exclusively on sports, it examined the experiences of parents, coaches, and children involved in youth soccer and other competitive youth activities, such as chess and dance. But for the most part, going back to Gary Alan Fine's (1987) *With the Boys* and stretching through political scientist Jennifer Ring's (2009) *Stolen Bases*, sociologists of sport have primarily left the writing of books on kids and sport to scholars outside of their field or to journalists. For example, Eileen McDonagh and Laura Pappano's influential book about sex segregation in youth sports, *Playing with the Boys* (2008), was coauthored by a political scientist and a journalist. Similarly, journalists have also written books such as *Little Girls in Pretty Boxes* (Ryan 1996), *Until It Hurts* (Hyman 2009), *Concussions and Our Kids* (Cantu and Hyman 2012), and *The Most Expensive Game in Town* (Hyman 2012).

That journalists and scholars from other fields are taking on the topic of kids and sport is not bad but in fact a welcome sign that "sport studies" is becoming less insular as an academic field, and thus more broadly relevant to scholars, popular social critics, and practitioners. But we contend that the scholarly study of kids and sport, and the interface between scholarship and popular journalistic treatments of the topic, will be greatly enhanced if and when sport sociologists move kids to the center of their research agenda. Thus far however—be it in research articles in scholarly journals or book-length monographs—scholars who define themselves partly or primarily as sport sociologists and publish their work in sport sociology venues have been largely silent when it comes to studying the topic of kids and sport.

Ignoring what is below the surface of the most publicly visible manifestations of sport has important implications for the field of sport studies. The part of an iceberg that lies below the water's surface may be less visible to the naked eye, but it is also the largest portion of the mass and serves to keep the tip of the iceberg afloat and visible above the water. Although it is difficult to accurately estimate the number of children involved in youth sports annually, huge numbers of youth in the Canada and the United States appear to participate in sports each year.[1] For example, a 2008 Canadian longitudinal survey found that 71 percent of kids aged six to nine and 84 percent of kids aged ten to thirteen reported participating in sports at some level (Clark 2008; Guèvremont, Findlay, and Kohen 2008). The same year, a nationally representative survey in the United States found two-thirds of youth reported being currently involved in at least one organized or team sport, and those who were involved reported that, on average, they had played on 2.1 sports teams over the past year. Moreover, the study found that an additional 16 percent of kids had at one time participated in an organized or team sport, leaving only 17 percent of respondents who said that they had never been involved in an organized or team sport (Sabo and Veliz 2008).

The Canadian and US national surveys hint at the massive numbers of kids who play at least some organized sports during their formative years. Still, researchers leading these studies asked broad questions that may have included many forms of exercise that some may not consider within the category of "organized sports," so the number of kids aged roughly six to fourteen who play organized sports is difficult to tally in the aggregate. However, the numbers reported by some of the largest US youth sports organizations also hint at children's large participation levels: USA Hockey reports that 355,000 boys and girls (107,000 of them eight years old and younger) played in their youth division in 2012 (USA Hockey 2012). Pop Warner claims 250,000 football players and 180,000 cheer and dance participants in forty-two states and several countries in 2010 (Pop Warner 2013). American Youth Soccer Organization (AYSO) currently claims to have 50,000 teams, with 600,000 players, who are supported by 250,000 adult volunteers, mostly within the United States, but also in Moscow, the US Virgin Islands, and Trinidad and Tobago (AYSO 2013). In 2012, Little League Baseball and Softball sponsored 7,006 programs in seventy-nine countries. From their "T-ball" for the youngest players, through Junior Leagues for thirteen- through fourteen-year-olds, Little League boasts 37,632 baseball teams with 574,450 players, plus 9,041 softball teams with 135,765 players (Little League 2013). The US Tennis Association (USTA) claims expanding programs for kids and juniors (USTA 2013), while US Kids Golf holds summer camps for young golfers, aged six through twelve (US Kids Golf 2013). USA Swimming and USA Track & Field report 300,000 and 170,000 members as young as age eight, respectively (USA Swimming 2013; USA Track & Field 2013).

It hardly takes a detailed statistical profile to understand that there are massive numbers of kids who participate in organized sports; we can see this in our daily lives, just being around kids, families, schools, neighborhoods, community parks, and recreation centers, in addition to seeing the numbers of kids included as spectators at major commercial sporting events. The kids who play and watch sports today supply the demographic buoyancy for the future of sport: they will become the high school, college, and adult athletes; the referees; the sportswriters and commentators; the coaches, trainers, and managers; the sports fans and consumers; as well as the volunteer parents who sustain youth sports teams and leagues.

But it would be a mistake to study kids simply in terms of ways that they constitute "the future of sport"—a construction of children that is front and center on the websites of national sport organizations that fear the withering and eventual extinction of their sport if they fail to aggressively recruit and retain kids. Instead, and following the lead of the burgeoning field of the sociology of childhood and youth, we argue that it is crucial for sport scholars to study kids not simply as future adults, but as active subjects who create their own social worlds (Corsaro 2003; Fine 1987; Prout and James 1990; Pugh 2014; Thorne 1993). Deploying this approach will allow critical scholars of sport to add important depth and critical dimension to the study of kids and sport, moving us beyond statistical profiling that, while interesting and important, may be most useful for those who market conventional sports and athletic products to kids.

We offer five possible reasons why sport scholars have largely ignored kids' sports. First, most scholars of sport teach and conduct research on college campuses, where (at least in the United States) sports are an integral component—highly popular, but also a source of problems—of the very institutions in which we work. It makes sense to study what's under our noses; in fact, some administrators on our campuses recruit sport scholars to do research on student athletes, NCAA compliance, and other issues related to college sport. Second, some scholars of sport receive funding to study adult sports, sport organizations, or mass media coverage of sports; perhaps less research funding is available to study kids and sports—especially for the "critical" sorts of sport research many of us do.

Third, researchers who study kids and sport close-up, as participant observers, ethnographers, or in-depth interviewers, might balk at studying kids, for fear that university institutional review boards will put up roadblocks to research. There appears to be a widespread belief among researchers that there is a daunting gantlet of gatekeepers—university IRBs, sport organizations, school administrators and teachers, and parents—who make direct research access to kids difficult, if not impossible. Fourth, sport scholars may view children and childhood from an "adult ideological perspective," where children are primarily seen as the next generation of adults. Within this perspective, children's activities—such as their involvement within youth sports—are often trivialized as "play," and not taken seriously by adults or considered worthy topics of scholarly investigation (Speier 1990; Thorne 1993). Finally—and we wonder if this might not be the most important reason—many sport scholars engage most readily with research on elite sports or on mass-mediated sports because, admit it or not, we are fans. Just as with the tip of an iceberg, for many of us the high-profile elite sports are the most visible and attractive part to observe. We read newspaper sports pages and magazines, watch live broadcasts of our favorite sports, and catch televised or Internet sports highlights regularly, perhaps daily. In a repetitive sort of loop, there they are right before our eyes; we see them (and enjoy them), therefore we study them.

In what follows, we briefly review the burgeoning interdisciplinary and sociological field of children and youth studies as a foundation for developing a research agenda on kids and sport.

Learning from Children and Youth Studies

An emergent paradigm for studying children and adolescents has developed within sociology and the social sciences more broadly (Corsaro 2003; Prout and James 1990; Thorne 1993). Unlike psychological and developmental approaches to childhood, which assume that kids passively assimilate into existing social structures as they grow older, the sociology of childhood paradigm argues that children and youth actively construct and contest adult-based meanings and understandings during group-based interactions (Corsaro 1979, 2003; Fine 1987; Hardman 1973; Prout and James 1990; Thorne 1993; Willis 1977). Although kids' cultures are certainly related to and overlap with the adult world, scholars of childhood argue that children's cultures must be conceptualized as "worthy of study in their own right, independent from the perspective and concern of adults" (Prout and James 1990, 8).

When studying children and youth, scholars like Matthew Speier (1990) and Barrie Thorne (1993) have cautioned against considering children from an "adult ideological perspective," which imposes adult concepts and concerns onto children's and teenagers' lives. However, based on our review of the past ten years of articles within *SSJ, JSSI,* and *ISSR,* many articles recently published by sport sociologists have mostly emphasized future-oriented outcomes when studying youth sports. For example, sociologists often examine whether youth sports promote "positive development" among children and teenagers (see Coakley 2011 for a review). By deploying variables such as children's and teenagers' academic outcomes (Miller et al. 2005), popularity in school (Shakib et al. 2011), or their likelihood of engaging in behavior adults might consider to be "deviant" (Denham

2011; Sabo et al. 2005) quantitative youth sports research has allowed us to make large-scale, systematic comparisons between children—especially across social categories such as race, class, and gender. But by framing studies of children in terms of their "development," we miss important opportunities to theorize how children actively construct and negotiate their lives *together*, as a part of group-based interactions that occur within their peer cultures (Corsaro and Eder 1990; Ferguson 2001; Thorne 1993).

Although gatekeepers such as the IRB, parents, coaches, and kids themselves may slow the process of gaining access to field sites and potential interview participants, a multitude of studies employing the sociology of childhood paradigm demonstrates that adult researchers can and do get access to children's worlds (Ferguson 2001; Friedman 2013; Lareau 2011; Lewis 2003; Morris 2012; Pascoe 2007; Pugh 2009; Thorne 1993). Entrance into children and teenagers' peer groups is often facilitated when researchers are able to present themselves as an "atypical, less power adult" in comparison to parents, teachers, and other adult authority figures (Corsaro 2003; Corsaro and Molinari 2008, 239; Fine and Sandstrom 1988; Mandell 1988; Thorne 1993). Many ethnographers avoid assuming an authoritative or disciplinarian relationship toward students in classrooms (Bettie 2003; Corsaro 2003; Hadley 2007; Perry 2002; Thorne 1993). One's clothing and hairstyle can also help differentiate adult researchers from other authority figures (Bettie 2003; Pascoe 2007; Perry 2002). Although it takes commitment, time, and creativity to gain access to kids' groups, by taking kids' cultures seriously, scholars have illuminated how aspects of children's social relations are integral to processes that maintain inequality. It is likely that dominant patterns of social relations are created, maintained, and potentially challenged within many aspects of youth sports, but remain undertheorized within existing sports literature.

Toward a Sociology of Kids and Sport

Drawing from the burgeoning field of the sociology of children and youth, we introduce five broad potential topics of research, some of which are taken up by the chapters in this book, which we hope will stimulate sociological studies of kids and sport: kids' experiences of play; kids who do not play sports; kids as sport consumers; kids' sport as a locus of intersectional social inequalities; and kids' health and injuries in sport.

Play, Sport, and Kids' Agency

A common starting place in sociology of sport introductory courses and texts is to juxtapose "sport"—narrowly defined as institutionalized, rationalized, rule-bound, and record-keeping forms of competition—with views of "play"—defined as more creative and spontaneous activities, less bound by formal rules, "an expressive activity done for its own sake" (Coakley 2009, 7). Parents today—even as they ferry their kids from one organized activity to another—often bemoan the ways in which the formal organization of their kids' lives, including youth sports, suppresses opportunities for creative play. However, no matter how organized and routinized the lives of kids, there is always time and space for creativity, for "the play element" in daily life. Put in the language of social theory, social structure does not imply an erasure of active agency; instead, kids are always active social agents in the creation of their worlds, and their daily actions exist along a continuum of reproductive and resistant agency.

Studies of sport too can benefit from this perspective on kids' creative agency within adult-created institutionalized sport, but also in spaces and during times when kids are relatively free from adult supervision and control. Some kids play self-organized pickup sports, as well as self-created and "alternative" sports. The often troubled relationship between kid-created sport cultures like skateboarding and adult systems of authority (schools, police, parents) who might fear these kids as deviant or dangerous can be a fruitful field of inquiry (Atkinson and Young 2008; Beal 2008; M. K. Donnelly 2008). In addition, researchers have begun to explore how commercial sport organizations and sports media have at times routinized, rationalized, and commercialized kid-created street sports and youth nonsport leisure activities (Friedman 2013; Heino 2000; McKendrick, Bradford, and Fielder 2000; Wheaton 2004). These moments are opportune sites for researchers to explore classic scholarly questions of play and sport, agency and structure, creativity and rationalization. They are also sites for contributing to an expanding field of inquiry in cultural studies, studying ways through which kids' creativity is potentially commodified (Banet-Weiser 2007; Buckingham 2011; Cook and Kaiser 2004; France 2007; Livingstone 2002; McNeal 1992).

Dropouts, Failures, and Refuseniks

A key element of a research agenda on kids and sport would focus on kids who do not, cannot, or will not play sports. Focusing exclusively on kids who play sports—especially those who come to identify as athletes—risks falling into what Thorne (1993, 98) calls "the Big Man Bias" in social research—the tendency of researchers to focus on the most visible and high-status central players in a social setting, thus skewing or missing altogether the experiences and meanings of those at the margins and at the bottom of hierarchies. Paying attention to those who do not play is especially important given the participation disparities that currently exist within youth sports. The 2008 US and Canadian surveys we referenced earlier demonstrate that white, suburban kids have easier access to youth sports than do poor, urban, and kids of color. Moreover, when compared to boys, girls start playing sports at a later age and quit playing earlier (Clark 2008; Guèvremont, Findlay, and Kohen 2008; Sabo and Veliz 2008). These survey data can generate research questions aimed at exploring the social processes through which race, class, and gender inequalities differentially constrain and enable access to as well as experiences within youth sports (Cooky 2009; Messner 2002). After all, a key observation of intersectional feminist sociology is that the standpoint of marginalized groups can supply researchers with an invaluable critical understanding of the workings of power, privilege, and subordination (Collins 1986; Smith 1987).

But research on kids who don't play sports should not focus exclusively on access and attrition. To do so, we argue, risks colluding with an ascendant popular health discourse that uncritically promotes sports participation as always good and healthy for kids. Within this framework, nonsporty kids are defined either through a conservative lens as lazy couch potatoes, dropouts, and losers, or through a liberal lens as underprivileged, "at-risk" kids who lack social support to play sports. Following Thorne (1993) and sport sociologists who are critical of the "positive development" narratives about sport, we argue that an understanding of nonparticipating kids' experiences and views of sport can yield insights that will fuel a critical understanding of institutionalized sport. There are kids who hate sports and sports culture, probably for good reasons: kids who have been alienated by PE teachers, coaches, athletes, and sports culture; kids who found early on that they lacked the skills, emotional predispositions, or body types to excel in sports (or even to fit in competently in ways that avoided humiliation); kids who hate competition; kids who may not have time to play sports, either because they work (Estrada and Hondagneu-Sotelo 2011; Kwon 2014) or pursue other extracurricular activities (Friedman 2013). Understanding these kids' lives can helps us to move beyond liberal scholarly frameworks that emphasize better and more democratic access to existing institutionalized youth sport, toward imagining alternatives to sport that emphasize inclusiveness, lifelong physical activity and health, and building cooperative relationships and skills. An exemplary model for this sort of critical research is Michael Atkinson and Michael Kehler's (2010, 73) examination of young Canadian boys who are "developing decisively anti-sport and PE attitudes" and are "choosing to withdraw from gym class as soon as they are institutionally allowed." Learning from the critical, resistant agency of these boys, Atkinson and Kehler argue that researchers can contribute to efforts to decenter and replace forms of sport and PE that have enforced and rewarded a singular and oppressive form of masculinity. "This must begin," the researchers conclude, "by changing the pedagogy of physical education" (2010, 85).

Kids as Fans and Consumers of Sport

Kids not only play sports in great numbers, but watch sports and consume sports products too. A 1999 national survey of US youth aged eight to seventeen found that 98 percent of boys and 90 percent of girls reported using some sort of sports media (including television, movies and videos with sport themes, video games, newspapers, books, magazines, the Internet, and radio). One in three kids said they did so daily, and 71 percent said they did so at least weekly (Amateur Athletic Foundation of Los Angeles 1999). A content analysis of the TV sports programs that boys watch most found that viewers are fed a steady package of programming and commercials that, together, amounts to a "televised sports manhood formula" expressing values of aggression, violence, militarism, the erasure of women, and consumption of car-related products and snack foods (Messner, Dunbar, and Hunt 2000).

These studies may now be dated, but they suggest that kids are major consumers of sports media, and they hint at what these kids are seeing and hearing as they watch. But they don't tell us much of anything about the meanings that kids make of sports entertainment: What do kids do when they watch or listen? Is sports consumption for kids an act of individual escape? Is it a means of connecting symbolically or, in the words of cultural critic Timothy Beneke (1997), of "BIRGing" or "Basking In Reflected Glory" of one's favorite sports team or athlete? Is the consumption of sports knowledge or the wearing of elite sports team clothing a resource for kids in building their own peer communities, much in the same way that Allison Pugh (2009) sees consumption in general as a way that youth shape identities and forge meaningful connections with peers? Under what conditions does consumption of sports reinforce or even amplify actual participation in sports, and under what conditions does it serve as a substitute or escape from physical activity (perhaps research on sports video games would be most fruitful here)? Cutting across all of these questions, how does an intersectional (race, class, gender, sexuality) perspective on kids inform our understanding of the shifting contextual meanings of kids' sports consumption? And more broadly, how does sport entertainment and brand culture make claims about contemporary notions of citizenship and meanings related to membership, community, and individualism for children and youth? One of the few articles on kids that appeared in the sport journals we examined was an exemplary examination of the ways in which white middle-class girls, aged eleven to fourteen, make meaning out of their own sport experiences. This study illuminated the contradictory dynamics of sport in girls' worlds, in particular how their narratives reflect liberal feminist corporate slogans from Nike, simultaneously reproducing and challenging intersectional inequalities (Cooky and McDonald 2005).

Intersectional Inequalities and Social Mobility

Social inequalities of gender, race, and class are not simply "reflected," but actively created and at times contested in sport. Recent decades have seen a huge influx of girls into sports, but national youth sports surveys show that "never participated" rates are still higher for girls—21 percent to boys' 13 percent—and drop-out rates for preadolescent girls are much higher than for boys. We are just beginning to understand the broad social processes—in families, schools, peer groups, media, and youth sports organizations—that tend still to limit and in some ways marginalize girls in sport (Cooky 2009).

Rich yet mostly untapped research questions surround the issue of sex-segregation versus integration of youth sports. While some have argued that sex segregation of youth sports inherently re-creates and naturalizes gender hierarchies, others have expressed caution that a forced integration of youth sports might push thousands of girls away from participating (McDonagh and Pappano 2008; Travers 2008). Research on adult coed sports shows how even in contexts where men and women play a sport together, supposedly as equals, assumptions of male superiority and male-dominated interactional patterns intrude in ways that tend to re-create gender hierarchies (Wachs 2002). What meanings do kids make from their experiences in sex-segregated versus sex-integrated sports? How do gender-nonconforming kids experience sport institutions that are routinely divided in binary sexes, and how will a growing visibility of transgender kids affect youth sports (Travers 2008)? How do kids make sense of the very stark gender divisions of labor and power they tend to experience among adult coaches, managers, and team parents in youth sports and school sports (Chafetz and Kotarba 1995; Coakley 2006; Messner 2009; Thompson 1999). The fact is, we just don't know that much about the ways that kids experience and make gender meanings in youth sports.

Issues of race and class in youth sports are equally vexing, and present a fascinating blank slate for researchers. Again, the survey research hints at big questions: Don Sabo and Phil Veliz (2008) found in their national youth sports survey that the more privileged the family is, the more likely it is that the children will be involved in organized sports. The same national study found that white children are more likely to be participants in sports than are children of color, as are kids who live in suburban (versus rural or urban) areas, those who live in families with two parents at home, and those whose parents are college-educated, with higher family incomes. Clearly, class and race privilege make it more likely that families will have access to youth sports, and will also have the kinds of resources (such as transportation) necessary to participate.

Poor kids and kids of color are increasingly defined as "at risk" within a social context of declining public support for schools and for poor families. Douglas Hartmann's (2001) research on "midnight basketball" is useful here for asking critical research questions: as sport is increasingly marked by advocacy organizations as a positive and healthy thing for "at-risk" kids, as a "solution" for poverty or as an alternative to gang activity, how do kids experience and make meanings of these sport programs (Coakley 2002)? Researchers too can ask fresh and important questions about immigrant kids and sport: How do they "fit in" (or not) to existing youth sports and school sports organizations (King-White 2010)? Do immigrant kids bring different orientations to sport, and even different sports, to US and Canadian contexts? If so, how do youth sports organizations respond? Under what conditions might native-born kids' xenophobia be challenged, and tolerance and respect amplified when they team up with kids from Mexico, China, or South Asia? And, how might we think of sport broadly, as a realm of children's rights and social justice in an increasingly globalizing world (P. Donnelly 1997; Grenfell and Rinehart 2003; Weber 2009)?

Research questions on kids and social inequalities should also focus on the connections between youth sports and families (Wheeler 2012). Sabo and Veliz (2008) found in their survey that 95 percent of parents in the United States believe that sports participation helps raise their child's self-esteem and 68 percent believe it improves their child's grades. Messner (2009, 2011) found that professional-class parents use youth sports to amplify an ascendant gender ideology of "soft essentialism," positioning girls as flexible choosers and boys as linear creatures, naturally destined for competition in public life. But kids don't passively absorb adults' belief systems. How do kids understand, reproduce, or resist adult divisions of labor, power, and ideology at the nexus of work, family, and youth sports? Are these gender ideologies played out in similar or different ways in poor and working-class families? Sociologist Annette Lareau (2011) argues that professional-class families engage in a process of highly organized, structured, and goal-oriented "concerted cultivation" of their children, while working-class parents more commonly subscribe to a less-structured practice of "natural growth" for their kids. By studying upper-middle-class kids' competitive activities, Friedman (2013) similarly argues that activities like soccer allow children to acquire "competitive kid capital," which may advantage them later in life, such as when applying to and entering elite colleges.

Comparative research on kids' sports in communities with different socioeconomic bases could illuminate the extent to which these classed patterns are also evident in youth sports. Are professional-class kids more likely to view sport participation as a future data point on a competitive résumé for admission to a top college? Are working-class or poor kids more likely to engage in sport for its own sake, or perhaps to see an athlete identity as a direct avenue to college athletic scholarship (and perhaps a pro career)? How do kids imagine this?

Health and Injuries

We know very little about kids, sport, and health. However, the growing body of research on teens, sport, and health correlates is suggestive: Kathleen Miller and her colleagues, in several national studies of youth, adolescence, and sports, found differences between teens who played some sports and those who were "highly involved" in sports. Teenaged boys and girls appear to derive some health benefits from playing sports: they are statistically less likely than nonathletes to use illicit drugs, drink alcohol, smoke cigarettes, or attempt suicide. In addition, girls who played sports were found to have more positive body images than girls who did not play sports, and were more likely to use seatbelts when riding in cars. On the other hand, "highly involved athletes" were found to be *more* involved in dangerous risk taking and unhealthy practices: they were more likely to use anabolic steroids, more likely to binge drink, and twice as likely to be suicidal. Highly involved girl athletes were also more likely than nonathletes to use dieting and exercise to control their weight, and to use extreme forms of weight control like vomiting and laxatives (Miller et al. 1999, 2001, 2005, 2006).

The findings of Miller and her colleagues' national studies converge with those of journalists Joan Ryan (1996) and Mark Hyman (2009), whose work emphasizes the health dangers and risks that inhere when families and communities overemphasize sports for kids. For this reason, research on kids' sports should explore the hypothesis that—for girls and for boys—*playing sports* can be a very good thing; however, becoming a highly involved *athlete* may not be a very good thing. Sport organizations, as well as schools, the mass media, and many families, often operate on a taken-for-granted assumption that the goal of youth sports is the creation of athletes; it is possible that the potential health (and other developmental) benefits of playing sports may actually be lost or worse when kids pour too much into sport identities, practices, and goals.

The growing controversy around head injuries in football and other sports is an opportunity for research on pain, injury, and risk in youth sports. How are youth sports organizations responding? In 2013, Hockey Canada banned body checking for Pee Wee (up to age twelve) participants (Gretz 2013). On the Pop Warner Football website in 2012, and in the midst of revelations about widespread concussions in football, Pop Warner's executive director cheerily reassured readers (many of them presumably parents) that although concussions do occur in football at older age levels, Pop Warner's rules and protective equipment make the game safe for kids: "We've been growing each year. This is the twenty-second season for which we have data, and we've been up nineteen of those twenty-two years. This year was about flat. So under the circumstances, that's not bad. . . . I think football is not going to go away." Are families reassured by this, or are they steering their kids away from tackle football or other combat and collision sports? A 2013 national poll in the United States found that 33 percent of parents say that their knowledge of head injury dangers makes them now less likely to allow their kids to play football (Marist Poll 2013). If this is a trend, then which families are and which are not opposed to their kids playing football (Dagkas and Quarmby 2012)? And more generally, how is a "no pain no gain" values system being deployed, incorporated, and embodied, or resisted in kids' sports today?

Another pertinent body of research might bring empirical observations to bear on the current scholarly chasm between the two currently prominent perspectives on childhood health, obesity, and sport. On the one side, we have epidemiological research and public programs that fuel fears of growing levels of childhood obesity, and posit youth sports and physical activity as a key element of a solution. On the other, cultural critics argue that the "obesity epidemic" is a construction of a bipartisan neoliberal political spectrum and a burgeoning social problems industry that views sport and exercise as a convenient means to individualize "solutions" to health problems. Given their complex etiology, cultural critics argue, such health problems would be better addressed with massive social programs that provide decent jobs, housing, schools, and healthy and affordable food for people and their kids who are currently marginalized and limited by class and racial inequalities (Campos et al. 2006; Wachs and Chase 2013). What is currently missing from this debate is an understanding of how kids experience being at the nexus of these debates, targeted by social policies (including sport and exercise) aimed at getting them to "take responsibility" for their own health and bodies. Under what conditions is this healthism-through-sport empowering for kids (and for which kids)? Under what conditions does it deflect attention away from awareness of social inequalities, or when might it spark a critical understanding and progressive action?

THIS VOLUME

Not only is sport an important area in many kids' lives, but it is also becoming a field of public policy debate related to schools, health, violence prevention, gender equality, and class and racial mobility. We have argued here that most sociologists have been slow to focus on children and sport. However, studying youth sports will contribute to the rich and growing field of children and youth studies. We believe that the works in *Child's Play* will inspire other researchers to pursue these and other questions. In particular, we hope that the methodological range of the works in this book—including survey research, participant observation, focus groups, individual interviews, critical cultural and media studies—will provide foundations for examining kids and sport from multiple vantage points.

We have organized the book in two sections. Part I, "Playing Fields," features essays that examine the landscape of youth sports from broad structural and cultural perspectives. These chapters illuminate how gender, race, social class, and immigration inequalities structure the sports worlds that children enter, and show how the organization of youth sports both reflects and reinforces adult values and concerns about kids. In chapter 1, Donald Sabo and Philip Veliz draw from national surveys of US children and families to provide a picture of who plays sports and who doesn't, and to hint at the benefits and dangers of sport participation. In chapter 2, Douglas Hartmann and Alex Manning examine how racial inequalities structure both unequal access to and unequal treatment within youth sport. Next, in chapter 3 Cheryl Cooky and Lauren Rauscher draw from analyses of sports media events. They critically examine how the racialization of high-profile female athletes amplifies barriers to sport participation for girls of color. In chapter 4, Toben Nelson deploys epidemiological research on exercise, food consumption, and health to challenge the common assumption that youth sports participation is always a healthy counterforce against childhood obesity. Jeffrey Montez de Oca, Jeffrey Scholes, and Brandon Meyer close this section with a critical analysis of the National Football League's media and school-based strategies to turn kids into avid football fans.

Part II, "Fields of Play," goes inside kids' worlds to see how they actively navigate and contest adult meanings in sport. In chapter 6, Michela Musto uses ethnographic observation and interviews with boys and girls on a swim team to show how kids construct gender boundaries that are very different in the structured context of the pool versus during free time on the deck. Next, in chapter 7 Murray Drummond deploys a unique method of conducting longitudinal focus group interviews with boys, shedding light on how boys' meanings of masculinity, sport, and health shift over time. In chapter 8, Chelsey Thul, Nicole LaVoi, Torrie Hazelwood, and Fatimah Hussein use interviews and participant advocacy research to illuminate how Muslim East African immigrant girls negotiate severe cultural constraints to participate in sport. Next, in chapter 9, Ann Travers examines how a growing population of transgender youth and their parents navigate the constraints of youth sport organizations premised on a binary separation of boys' and girls' sports. In chapter 10, Michael Kehler looks at the dynamics inside boys' locker rooms. He argues that the narrow conceptions of masculinity constrain and do violence to boys, and also shows how nonconforming boys creatively deploy survival strategies in locker rooms. In chapter 11, James McKeever takes us full circle, drawing from interviews and autoethnography to show how a community park in a poor, multiracial Los Angeles neighborhood creates the possibilities for adult coaches to mentor kids in ways that usher them in to long-term commitments as future mentors in the park. Finally, an afterword from distinguished sociologist of childhood William Corsaro concludes the collection.

NOTE

1. For sports that involve older athletes, organizations such as the NCAA and the National Federation of State High School Associations compile and publish statistics on the number of athletes involved annually. However, no central organization collects information on children, making the number of children playing sports less clear.

REFERENCES

Amateur Athletic Foundation of Los Angeles. 1999. *Children and Sports Media*. Los Angeles: AAFLA.

American Youth Soccer Organization. 2013. "About AYSO." http://ayso.org/AboutAYSO.aspx.

Atkinson, Michael, and Michael Kehler. 2010. "Boys, Gyms, Locker Rooms, and Heterotopia." In *Boys' Bodies: Speaking the Unspoken*, edited by Michael Kehler and Michael Atkinson, 73–90. New York: Peter Lang.

Atkinson, Michael, and Kevin Young. 2008. *Deviance and Social Control in Sport*. Champaign, IL: Human Kinetics.

Azzarito, Laura, and Louis Harrison. 2008. "'White Men Can't Jump': Race, Gender, and Natural Athleticism." *International Review for the Sociology of Sport* 43.4: 347–364.

Banet-Weiser, Sarah. 2007. *Kids Rule! Nickelodeon and Consumer Citizenship*. Durham, NC: Duke University Press.

Beal, Becky. 2008. "Skateboarding." In *Battleground: Sports*, edited by Michael Atkinson, 383–389. Westport, CT: Greenwood.

Beneke, Timothy. 1997. *Proving Manhood: Reflections on Men and Sexism*. Berkeley: University of California Press.

Bettie, Julie. 2003. *Women without Class: Girls, Race, and Identity*. Berkeley: University of California Press.

Buckingham, David. 2011. *The Material Child: Growing Up in Consumer Culture*. Malden, MA: Polity.

Campos, Paul, Abigail Saguy, Paul Ernsberger, Eric Oliver, and Glenn Gaesser. 2006. "The Epidemiology of Overweight and Obesity: Public Health Crisis or Moral Panic?" *International Journal of Epidemiology* 35.1: 55–60.

Cantu, R. C., and M. Hyman. 2012. *Concussions and Our Kids: America's Leading Expert on How to Protect Young Athletes and Keep Sports Safe*. Boston: Houghton Mifflin Harcourt.

Chafetz, Janet Saltzman, and Joseph A. Kotarba. 1995. "Son Worshippers: The Role of Little League Mothers in Re-creating Gender." *Studies in Symbolic Interaction* 18: 217–241.

Clark, Warren. 2008. "Kids' Sports." 11–008. Component of Statistics Canada Catalogue. Canadian Social Trends. http://www.statcan.gc.ca/pub/11–008-x/11–008-x2008001-eng.htm.

Coakley, Jay. 2002. "Using Sports to Control Deviance and Violence among Youths: Let's Be Critical and Cautious." In *Paradoxes of Youth and Sport*, edited by Margaret Gatz, Michael A. Messner, and Sandra Ball-Rokeach, 13–30. Albany: State University of New York Press.

———. 2006. "The Good Father: Parental Expectations and Youth Sports." *Leisure Studies* 25.2: 153–163.

———. 2009. *Sport in Society: Issues and Controversies*. New York: McGraw-Hill.

———. 2011. "Youth Sports: What Counts as 'Positive Development?'" *Journal of Sport and Social Issues* 35.3: 306–324.

Collins, Patricia Hill. 1986. "Learning from the Outsider Within: The Sociological Significance of Black Feminist Thought." *Social Problems* 33.6: 14–32.

Cook, Daniel Thomas, and Susan B. Kaiser. 2004. "Betwixt and Be Tween: Age Ambiguity and the Sexualization of the Female Consuming Subject." *Journal of Consumer Culture* 4.2: 203–227.

Cooky, Cheryl. 2009. "'Girls Just Aren't Interested': The Social Construction of Interest in Girls' Sport." *Sociological Perspectives* 52.2: 259–283.

Cooky, Cheryl, and Mary G. McDonald. 2005. "'If You Let Me Play': Young Girls' Insider-Other Narratives of Sport." *Sociology of Sport Journal* 22.2: 158–177.

Corsaro, William A. 1979. "'We're Friends, Right?' Children's Use of Access Rituals in a Nursery School." *Language in Society* 8.2–3: 315–336.

———. 2003. *We're Friends, Right? Inside Kids' Culture*. Washington, DC: Joseph Henry Press.

Corsaro, William A., and Donna Eder. 1990. "Children's Peer Cultures." *Annual Review of Sociology* 16: 197–220.

Corsaro, William A., and Luisa Molinari. 2008. "Entering and Observing in Children's Worlds." In *Research with Children: Perspectives and Practices*, edited by Pia Christensen and Allison James, 239–259. New York: Routledge.

Dagkas, Symeon, and Thomas Quarmby. 2012. "Young People's Embodiment of Physical Activity: The Role of the 'Pedagogized' Family." *Sociology of Sport Journal* 29.2: 210–226.

Denham, Bryan E. 2011. "Alcohol and Marijuana Use among American High School Seniors: Empirical Associations with Competitive Sports Participation." *Sociology of Sport Journal* 28.3: 362–379.

Donnelly, Michele K. 2008. "Alternative and Mainstream: Revisiting the Sociological Analysis of Skateboarding." In *Tribal Play: Subcultural Journeys through Sport*, edited by Michael Atkinson and Kevin Young, 197–214. Bingley: Emerald.

Donnelly, Peter. 1997. "Child Labour, Sport Labour: Applying Child Labour Laws to Sport." *International Review for the Sociology of Sport* 32.4: 389–406.

Estrada, Emir, and Pierrette Hondagneu-Sotelo. 2011. "Intersectional Dignities: Latino Immigrant Street Vendor Youth in Los Angeles." *Journal of Contemporary Ethnography* 40.1: 102–131.

Ferguson, Ann Arnett. 2001. *Bad Boys: Public Schools in the Making of Black Masculinity*. Ann Arbor: University of Michigan Press.

Fine, Gary Alan. 1987. *With the Boys: Little League Baseball and Preadolescent Culture*. Chicago: University of Chicago Press.

Fine, Gary Alan, and Kent L. Sandstrom. 1988. *Knowing Children: Participant Observation with Minors*. Vol. 15. Newbury Park, CA: Sage.

France, Alan. 2007. *Understanding Youth in Late Modernity*. New York: McGraw-Hill.

Friedman, Hilary Levey. 2013. *Playing to Win: Raising Children in a Competitive Culture*. Berkeley: University of California Press.

Gatz, Margaret, Michael A. Messner, and Sandra Ball-Rokeach. 2002. *Paradoxes of Youth and Sport*. Albany: State University of New York Press.

Grasmuck, Sherri. 2003. "Something about Baseball: Gentrification, 'Race Sponsorship,' and Neighborhood Boys' Baseball." *Sociology of Sport Journal* 20.4: 307–330.

———. 2005. *Protecting Home: Class, Race, and Masculinity in Boys' Baseball*. New Brunswick, NJ: Rutgers University Press.

Grenfell, Christopher C., and Robert E. Rinehart. 2003. "Skating on Thin Ice: Human Rights in Youth Figure Skating." *International Review for the Sociology of Sport* 38.1: 79–97.

Gretz, Adam. 2013. "Hockey Canada Votes to Ban Body Checking at Pee-Wee Level." *CBS Sports*, May 25. http://www.cbssports.com/nhl/eye-on-hockey/22302086/hockey-canada-votes-to-ban-body-checking-at-pee-wee-level.

Guèvremont, Anne, Leanne Findlay, and Dafna Kohen. 2008. "Organized Extracurricular Activities of Canadian Children and Youth." *Health Reports* 19.3: 82–003-X.

Hadley, Katherine Gold. 2007. "Will the Least-Adult Please Stand Up? Life as 'Older Sister Katy' in a Taiwanese Elementary School." In *Representing Youth: Methodological Issues in Critical Youth Studies*, edited by Amy L. Best, 157–181. New York: New York University Press.

Hardman, Charlotte. 1973. "Can There Be an Anthropology of Children?" *Journal of the Anthropological Society of Oxford* 4.2: 85–99.

Hartmann, Douglas. 2001. "Notes on Midnight Basketball and the Cultural Politics of Recreation, Race, and at-Risk Urban Youth." *Journal of Sport and Social Issues* 25.4: 339–371.

Heino, Rebecca. 2000. "New Sports: What Is So Punk about Snowboarding?" *Journal of Sport and Social Issues* 24.2: 176–191.

Heywood, Leslie, and Shari L. Dworkin. 2003. *Built to Win: The Female Athlete as Cultural Icon*. Minneapolis: University of Minnesota Press.

Hyman, Mark. 2009. *Until It Hurts: America's Obsession with Youth Sports and How It Harms Our Kids*. Boston: Beacon, 2009.

———. 2012. *The Most Expensive Game in Town: The Rising Cost of Youth Sports and the Toll on Today's Families*. Boston: Beacon, 2012.

King-White, Ryan. 2010. "Danny Almonte: Discursive Construction(s) of (Im)migrant Citizenship in Neoliberal America." *Sociology of Sport Journal* 27.2: 178–199.

Kwon, Hyeyoung. 2014. "The Hidden Injury of Class in Korean-American Language Brokers' Lives." *Childhood* 21.1: 56–71.

Lareau, Annette. 2011. *Unequal Childhoods: Class, Race, and Family Life*. Berkeley: University of California Press.

Lewis, Amanda. 2003. *Race in the Schoolyard: Negotiating the Color Line in Classrooms and Communities*. New Brunswick, NJ: Rutgers University Press.

Light, Richard L. 2010. "Children's Social and Personal Development through Sport: A Case Study of an Australian Swimming Club." *Journal of Sport and Social Issues* 34.4: 379–395.

Little League. 2013. "Little League around the World." http://www.littleleague.org/learn/about/historyandmission/aroundtheworld.htm.

Livingstone, Sonia. 2002. *Young People and New Media: Childhood and the Changing Media Environment.* London: Sage.

Mandell, Nancy. 1988. "The Least-Adult Role in Studying Children." *Journal of Contemporary Ethnography* 16.4: 433–467.

Marist Poll. 2013. "Youth Football Takes Hard Hit . . . One-Third of Americans Less Likely to Allow Son to Play Football because of Head Injury Risk." October 23. http://maristpoll.marist.edu/1023-youth-football-takes-hard-hit-one-third-of-americans-less-likely-to-allow-son-to-play-football-because-of-head-injury-risk/.

McDonagh, Eileen, and Laura Pappano. 2008. *Playing with the Boys: Why Separate Is Not Equal in Sports.* New York: Oxford University Press.

McHale, James P., Penelope Vinden, Loren Bush, Derek Richer, David Shaw, and Brienne Smith. 2005. "Patterns of Personal and Social Adjustment among Sport-Involved and Noninvolved Urban Middle-School Children." *Sociology of Sport Journal* 22.2: 119–136.

McKendrick, John H., Michael G. Bradford, and Anna V. Fielder. 2000. "Kid Customer? Commercialization of Playspace and the Commodification of Childhood." *Childhood* 7.3: 295–314.

McNeal, James U. 1992. *Kids as Customers: A Handbook of Marketing to Children.* New York: Lexington Books.

Messner, Michael A. 2002. *Taking the Field: Men, Women, and Sports.* Minneapolis: University of Minnesota Press.

———. 2009. *It's All for the Kids: Gender, Families, and Youth Sports.* Berkeley: University of California Press.

———. 2011. "Gender Ideologies, Youth Sports, and the Production of Soft Essentialism." *Sociology of Sport Journal* 28.2: 151–170.

Messner, Michael A., Michele Dunbar, and Darnell Hunt. 2000. "The Televised Sports Manhood Formula." *Journal of Sport and Social Issues* 24.4: 380–394.

Miller, Kathleen E., Merrill J. Melnick, Grace M. Barnes, Michael Farrell, and Don Sabo. 2005. "Untangling the Links among Athletic Involvement: Gender, Race, and Adolescent Academic Outcomes." *Sociology of Sport Journal* 22.2: 178–193.

Miller, Kathleen E., Merrill J. Melnick, Michael P. Farrell, Donald F. Sabo, and Grace M. Barnes. 2006. "Jocks, Gender, Binge Drinking, and Adolescent Violence." *Journal of Interpersonal Violence* 21.1: 105–120.

Miller, Kathleen E., Donald F. Sabo, Michael P. Farrell, Grace M. Barnes, and Merrill J. Melnick. 1999. "Sports, Sexual Behavior, Contraceptive Use, and Pregnancy among Female and Male High School Students: Testing Cultural Resource Theory." *Sociology of Sport Journal* 16.4: 366–387.

Miller, Kathleen E., Donald F. Sabo, Merrill J. Melnick, Michael P. Farrell, and Grace M. Barnes. 2001. *The Women's Sports Foundation Report: Health Risks and the Teen Athlete.* East Meadow, NY: Women's Sport Foundation.

Morris, Edward W. 2012. *Learning the Hard Way: Masculinity, Place, and the Gender Gap in Education.* New Brunswick, NJ: Rutgers University Press.

Pascoe, C. J. 2007. *Dude, You're a Fag: Masculinity and Sexuality in High School.* Berkeley: University of California Press.

Perry, Pamela. 2002. *Shades of White: White Kids and Racial Identities in High School.* Durham, NC: Duke University Press.

Pop Warner. 2013. "About Us." http://www.popwarner.com/About_Us.htm.

Prout, Alan, and Allison James. 1990. "A New Paradigm for the Sociology of Childhood? Provenance, Promise, and Problems." In *Constructing and Reconstructing Childhood: Contemporary Issues in the Sociological Study of Childhood,* edited by Allison James and Alan Prout, 7–34. London: Falmer Press.

Pugh, Allison. 2009. *Longing and Belonging: Parents, Children, and Consumer Culture*. Berkeley: University of California Press.

———. 2014. "The Theoretical Costs of Ignoring Childhood: Rethinking Independence, Insecurity, and Inequality." *Theory and Society* 43.1: 71–89.

Ring, Jennifer. 2009. *Stolen Bases: Why American Girls Don't Play Baseball*. Champaign: University of Illinois Press.

Ryan, Joan. 1996. *Little Girls in Pretty Boxes: The Making and Breaking of Elite Gymnasts and Figure Skaters*. New York: Doubleday.

Sabo, Don, Kathleen E. Miller, Merrill J. Melnick, Michael P. Farrell, and Grace M. Barnes. 2006. "High School Athletic Participation and Adolescent Suicide: A Nationwide US Study." *International Review for the Sociology of Sport* 40.1: 5–23.

Sabo, Don, and Philip Veliz. 2008. "Go Out and Play: Youth Sports in America." East Meadow, NY: Women's Sport Foundation.

Shakib, Sohaila, Philip Veliz, Michele D. Dunbar, and Don Sabo. 2011. "Athletics as a Source for Social Status among Youth: Examining Variation by Gender, Race/Ethnicity, and Socioeconomic Status." *Sociology of Sport Journal* 28.3: 303–328.

Smith, Dorothy E. 1987. *The Everyday World as Problematic: A Feminist Sociology*. Boston: Northeastern University Press.

Speier, Matthew. 1990. "The Adult Ideological Viewpoint in Studies of Childhood." In *Rethinking Childhood Perspectives on Development and Society*, edited by Arlene S. Skolnick, 168–186. Boston: Little, Brown.

Thompson, Shona M. 1999. *Mother's Taxi: Sport and Women's Labor*. Albany: State University of New York Press.

Thorne, Barrie. 1993. *Gender Play: Girls and Boys in School*. New Brunswick, NJ: Rutgers University Press, 1993.

Travers, Ann. 2008. "The Sport Nexus and Gender Injustice." *Studies in Social Justice* 2.1: 79–101.

United States Tennis Association. 2013. "About Us." http://www.usta.com/About-USTA/?intloc=headernav.

USA Hockey. 2012. "USA Hockey 2011–2012 Annual Report." http://www.usahockey.com/about_usa_hockey/Annual_Report.aspx.

USA Swimming. 2013. "What Is USA Swimming?" http://www.usaswimming.org/DesktopDefault.aspx?TabId=1398&Alias=Rainbow&Lang=en.

USA Track & Field. 2013. "Young Athletes." http://www.usatf.org/Youth.aspx.

US Kids Golf. 2013. "About Us." http://www.uskidsgolf.com/about-us.

Wachs, Faye Linda. 2002. "Leveling the Playing Field Negotiating Gendered Rules in Coed Softball." *Journal of Sport and Social Issues* 26.3: 300–316.

Wachs, Faye Linda, and Laura Frances Chase. 2013. "Explaining the Failure of an Obesity Intervention: Combining Bourdieu's Symbolic Violence and the Foucault's Microphysics of Power to Reconsider State Interventions." *Sociology of Sport Journal* 30.2: 111–131.

Weber, Romana. 2009. "Protection of Children in Competitive Sport: Some Critical Questions for London 2012." *International Review for the Sociology of Sport* 44.1: 55–69.

Wheaton, Belinda. 2004. "Selling Out? The Globalization and Commercialization of Lifestyle Sports." In *Global Politics of Sport: Sport in the Global Society*, edited by Lincoln Allison, 127–146. London: Routledge.

Wheeler, Sharon. 2012. "The Significance of Family Culture for Sports Participation." *International Review for the Sociology of Sport* 47.2: 235–252.

Willis, Paul E. 1977. *Learning to Labor: How Working Class Kids Get Working Class Jobs*. New York: Columbia University Press.

Yochim, Emily Chivers. 2009. *Skate Life: Re-imagining White Masculinity*. Ann Arbor: University of Michigan Press.

PART I

Playing Fields

THE SOCIAL LANDSCAPE
OF YOUTH SPORTS

CHAPTER 1

Surveying Youth Sports in America

WHAT WE KNOW AND WHAT IT MEANS FOR PUBLIC POLICY

Don Sabo and Philip Veliz

Former NBA basketball player and New Jersey senator Bill Bradley liked to quip that "the most popular sport in America is jumping to conclusions." In the United States, adults often approach youth sport from a polarized, "all bad" or "all good" perspective (Eitzen 2003). Coaches are lauded or vilified. Competition is good or bad for kids. Sport enhances kids' health or endangers it. Sport provides kids from different races, socioeconomic backgrounds, and genders an opportunity to get ahead in life or it re-creates social inequalities. But the reality is that members of the general public and research communities have only a modicum of facts and analyses to inform their assessments of youth sport. In this chapter we draw from survey research to shed light on the role of sport in kids' lives, while pointing to new puzzles that can be explored with future research.

Sport sociology has grown since its inception during the 1970s, and yet, as Michael Messner and Michela Musto observed in their introduction, comparatively few sociologists focus on youth sports. This chapter provides an overview of what survey research reveals about US kids and sport. First, we describe participation patterns in competitive organized youth sports, focusing on variations by gender, race, and ethnicity, socioeconomic status, grade level, family characteristics, and type of community. Second, we summarize recent national data that confirm that children leave organized sports in droves as they age—a pattern that is especially prevalent among girls and kids of color. In this regard, we point to the decline in the number of US public and private schools—especially those schools with higher proportions of girls and racial/ethnic minorities—that provide interscholastic sports to their students. Third, we evaluate research on the links between youth athletic participation and educational achievement across all sport. Fourth, we examine research on links between athletic participation and adolescent health, such as illicit drug and alcohol use, physical activity involvement, sexual risk taking, and pregnancy prevention. Finally, we identify emerging areas in which sport survey research is needed, such as children with special needs, poor kids, children in immigrant families, and GLBT youth.

Participation: Who and How Many?

Social scientists recognize that millions of American youth play sports, and that youth sports have grown tremendously, particularly since the passage of Title IX in 1972 (Stevenson 2007). Less is known about why children get involved, stay involved, play multiple sports, quit one sport to explore another, leave sport altogether, or never play sports in the first place. Even fewer studies have considered how or why schools and communities provide differing levels of participation opportunities to young people. Are girls, kids from poor or working-class families, or racial and ethnic minorities provided the same level of opportunities as boys, well-to-do kids, and whites? Does youth sport function as an "equal opportunity" sector in America, or does it reflect (and maybe reproduce) inequalities between rich and poor, whites and minorities, boys and girls?

Counting the number of kids involved with sports is an important but daunting task. Sports governing bodies, coaches, educators, child and teen health advocates, parent-teacher organizations, and public health providers use overall participation rates and subgroup comparisons to guide policy and action. Social scientists who use survey research to study youth sports have tapped large government-sponsored databases to assess participation patterns and trends.[1] Some data sets measure athletic participation in general, meaning they ask teenagers how many sports they participated in during the past year in their school and community. Some government school-based surveys gather information about involvement with specific sports like basketball, cheer, football, lacrosse, swimming, or volleyball (Johnston et al. 2014). Although data gathered from government surveys are often nationally representative, and have sophisticated sampling designs and high response rates, not all school officials comply. The effort to clearly understand complex realities involving millions of kids remains a work in progress.

Despite these flaws in the data, it is clear that lots of kids play sports. In collaboration with the Women's Sports Foundation, during 2007 we conducted two nationwide surveys of kids and parents in order to better understand intersections among families, schools, and communities, and US children's involvement with sport. We commissioned the Harris Interactive to conduct a school-based survey of youth from a random selection of about one hundred thousand public, private, and parochial schools in the United States. The final sample consisted of 2,185 third through twelfth grade girls and boys. We also conducted phone interviews with a national cross-section of 863 randomly selected parents of children in grades three through twelve. African American and Hispanic parents were oversampled in order to enhance understanding of the needs and experiences of underserved girls, boys, and their families. We outline some key findings from this Go Out and Play survey later (Sabo and Veliz 2008).

Nearly three-quarters of youth reported playing an organized or team sport, while fully 84 percent were currently playing or were past participants when asked. Only 15 percent said they have never participated in a sport. As figure 1.1 shows, nearly equal percentages of girls and boys reported currently playing organized and team sports (69 percent and 75 percent, respectively). Just 18 percent of girls and 13 percent of boys reported never participating in a sport at all, and high percentages of US children were involved with at least one sport across all grade levels. Participation rates varied a great deal, however, by grade level and type of community. Figure 1.2 demonstrates that when considering students involved with at least one sport, for example, participation was most prevalent among suburban elementary school students and also among children in urban middle schools. And yet, in urban communities, only 59 percent of third to fifth grade girls were involved with sports, compared to 80 percent of boys. The widest participation gap, between ninth through twelfth grade girls and boys, also occurred in urban communities (59 percent and 68 percent). Furthermore, despite the fact that large percentages of children participate in sport at some point in their lives, girls enter sports at a later age than boys (7.4 years old, on average, compared to

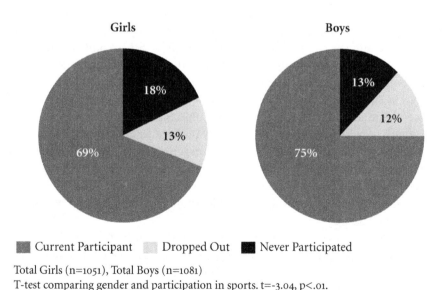

Total Girls (n=1051), Total Boys (n=1081)
T-test comparing gender and participation in sports. t=-3.04, p<.01.

Figure 1.1. Participation in organized and team sports. Source: Go Out and Play survey (Sabo and Veliz 2008).

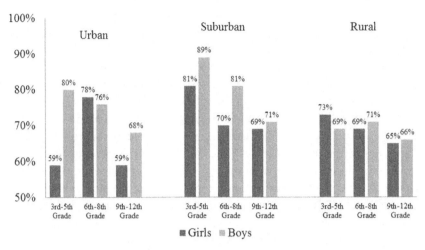

T-tests comparing gender and athletic participation by grade and place of residence.
3rd–5th Grade—Urban: t=3.93, p<.001; Suburban: t=1.56, p=.119; Rural: t=-.074, p=.482.
6th–8th Grade—Urban: t=-.0290, p=.772; Suburban: t=2.36, p=.019; Rural: t=.311, p=.756.
9th–12th Grade—Urban: t=1.12, p=.264; Suburban: t=.595, p=.552; Rural: t=.086, p=.932.

Figure 1.2. Percentage of students who are involved in at least one organized sport. Source: Go Out and Play survey (Sabo and Veliz 2008).

6.8 years old), and this gender gap is widest in urban communities (girls 7.8 and boys 6.9 years old).

Economic disparities and racial inequalities often mediate gender gaps in sport. High involvement with sports was more typical if kids came from wealthier, more affluent communities. Overall, kids from richer communities were more apt to play three or more sports. And yet the results in figure 1.3 reveal that for both white girls and white boys the percentages of highly involved athletes grew as family median income increased. In contrast, among children of color, boys outnumbered girls as highly involved athletes across all the income groups. For girls of color, the percentages of highly involved female athletes declined in the upper-middle and well-to-do income categories ($50,000–65,000 and above $65,000). In short, a rough gender equity exists for highly involved white girl and boy athletes from the above-$65,000 income group, yet girls of color from all income levels showed lower rates of participation in US youth sports than their male counterparts.

Gender, race, and class also influence kids' drop-out rates. Girls and boys tend to leave sport at increasing rates as they move from elementary school to high school. Suburban girls, however, are the one exception to this trend—their drop-out rate remains steady at 6 percent from third through eighth grades. Whereas the drop-out rates of suburban and rural girls and boys in middle schools were comparable, the rate for urban girls in middle schools was four times higher than

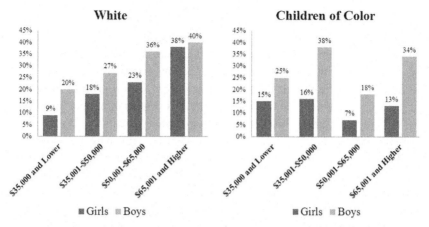

Chi-Square tests comparing differences among the percentages of students participating in three or more sports and the median income level of the school community.

White-$35,000 and lower: $\chi2=2.97$, p=.085; $35,001–$50,000: $\chi2=4.65$, p<.05; $50,001–$65,000: $\chi2=6.94$, p<.01; $65,001 and higher: $\chi2=.095$, p=.758.
Nonwhite-$35,000 and lower: $\chi2=6.87$, p<.01; $35,001–$50,000: $\chi2=13.83$, p=.001; $50,001–$65,000: $\chi2=2.96$, p=.086; $65,001 and higher: $\chi2=8.21$, p<.01.

Figure 1.3. Highly involved athletes by race, gender, and income. Source: Go Out and Play survey (Sabo and Veliz 2008).

that for suburban girls (24 percent and 6 percent) and twice as high as for rural girls (13 percent).

The findings raise important questions about girls' experiences with sport. Why, for example, do so many urban girls leave sport during the middle school years? A three-year program evaluation study conducted by the Boston Girls Sports and Physical Activity Project sheds light on this issue (Women's Sports Foundation 2007). Urban communities often provide more athletic opportunities to third through fifth grade boys than girls, which means that for many girls it is not until middle school (sixth–eighth grades) that they have real options to get involved with sport. As a result, urban girls are more likely than boys to start sport during middle school. The Boston evaluation revealed that because of the comparatively later start, many urban girls did not develop the physical literacy or athletic skills as boys their age. Girls' fewer athletic options translated into a lack of athletic self-confidence, less fun, and feeling clumsy and out of place. Finally, some urban girls who tried sports but quit during middle school did so because they were needed at home after school to care for siblings while their single parents worked. Boys weren't expected to fill these child care roles.

The Go Out and Play telephone survey with parents also generated information about youth sports and family life. For example, we found that children's involvement with sports was associated with higher levels of family satisfaction.

Youth sports helped build communication and trust between many parents and children. Sports provided a vehicle for parents and kids to spend time together, to have conversations, or to practice together, both in dual-parent families and single-parent families. While a majority of parents said they want similar levels of athletic opportunity for their daughters and sons, 39 percent of moms and 37 percent of dads believed that their community offered more sports programs for boys than for girls. Moreover, 32 percent of white parents felt this way, compared to 51 percent and 49 percent of Black and Hispanic parents, respectively. And finally, 53 percent of low-income parents shared this perception, compared to just 31 percent of high-income parents. Furthermore, while mothers and fathers provided similar levels of encouragement and support for both their daughters and sons, girls were often shortchanged by dads, who seemed to channel more energy into mentoring sons. While many fathers endorsed "fairness" and equal support for girls as well as boys, results from the student survey showed that whereas 46 percent of boys ranked dads as number one on their list of mentors who "taught them the most" about sports and exercise, dads ranked third on girls' list, coming in at 28 percent. Mothers ranked fifth at 23 percent.

Michael Messner's (2009) and Tom Farrey's (2008) respective books on youth sports have helped fill the "sport and family" research void, but there clearly remains a great deal to learn about the role of youth sports in families. In the Go Out and Play study (Sabo and Veliz 2008) we suggested that sports often act as "part of a wider convoy of social support" (7) that may bring children into closer contact and communication with their parents. However, more nuanced qualitative studies of specific sports in a variety of community settings and interviews with parents who represent the range of parental involvement in youth sport are sorely needed. Just as there is no such thing as the "American family," there is no typical or overarching template surrounding family life and youth sport involvement. The challenge for researchers is to better understand the complex processes that surround youth sport and family life.

ATTRITION: KIDS' MOVEMENTS IN, OUT, AND BETWEEN SPORTS

The range of athletic options has grown in recent decades. Gone are the "old days" when boys' football, basketball, baseball, and track and field were the only games in town. Previous thinking around kids' participation in sport was often simplistic—kids either "played" or "dropped out" of sport. However, the "in and out" dichotomy tells only part of a more complex story of youths' participation in sport. Later in the chapter we discuss a recent survey that documents some of the complexity that enables kids' movements in, out, and between various sports (Sabo and Veliz 2014a).

Monitoring the Future (MTF) provides perhaps the richest trove of data on teen athletic participation in a variety of sports (Johnston et al. 2014). About fifty thousand students are surveyed every year (eighth-, tenth-, and twelfth-graders) and pertinent information is gathered pertaining to sports participation as well as educational outcomes, health behaviors, social engagement, and substance use. The large sample sizes and troves of information enable researchers to examine participation rates among eighth grade, tenth grade, and twelfth grade students in a variety of sports.[2] Since 2006, respondents have been able to specify baseball, basketball, cross-country, field hockey, football, gymnastics, ice hockey, lacrosse, soccer, swimming, tennis, track and field, volleyball, weight lifting, wrestling, and "other sports." We believe that the "other sports" category provides a general vehicle to capture participation data on the profusion of athletic opportunities such as Ultimate Frisbee, cycling, flag football, double Dutch, martial arts, downhill skiing, skateboarding, surfing, or rock climbing. In order to measure the ebbs and flows of sports participation and attrition, we combined multiple nationwide samples of US adolescents who participated in MTF surveys between 2006 and 2012.

First, figures 1.4 and 1.5 show participation rates for eighth and twelfth grade students in fifteen different sports between 2006 and 2012. Traditional sports (basketball, football, and baseball) had high participation rates among boys, with a solid showing of "other sports" at 24 percent. Among the girls, participation was highest in "other sports," followed by basketball, volleyball, baseball, and

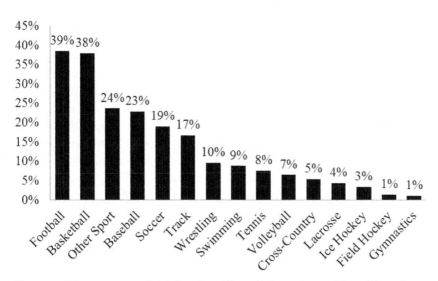

Figure 1.4. The percentage of eighth and twelfth grade boys who participated in each sport, 2006–2012. Source: Data provided by the Monitoring the Future Study.

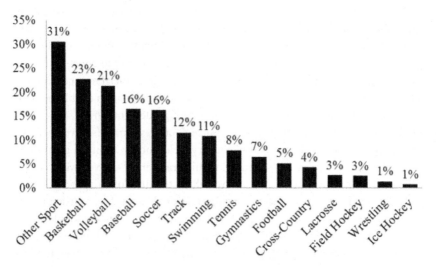

Figure 1.5. The percentage of eighth and twelfth grade girls who participated in each sport, 2006–2012. Source: Data provided by the Monitoring the Future Study.

soccer. Participation rates are similar for boys and girls in some sports like swimming (9 percent and 11 percent, respectively), tennis (8 percent for both genders), and cross-country (5 percent and 4 percent, respectively).

We also traced how participation rates in each of the fifteen sports fluctuated between eighth and twelfth grades. We discovered and documented startlingly high attrition rates in almost every sport. The percentage of attrition ranged between lows of–2 percent in cross-country to–68 percent in field hockey (the statistical analyses generated an average–32 percent attrition rate across all sports).[3] We also assessed whether the attrition rates were higher, lower, or the same between boys and girls, between racial and ethnic groups, and for families at different socioeconomic levels. Comparing figures 1.6 and 1.7, the attrition rates among girls between eighth and twelfth grade in all sports were two to three times higher than those among boys. In basketball, for example, the attrition rates were–64 percent for girls and–36 percent for boys. The respective rates in lacrosse were–42 percent and–13 percent, for soccer–53 percent and–31 percent.

Our statistical analyses also revealed that the sports with a larger percentage of racial and ethnic minorities also had high rates of attrition between eighth and twelfth grades (Sabo and Veliz 2014a). Conversely, sports with a higher percentage of white participants had low overall rates of attrition between eighth and twelfth grades. Specifically, for each 1 percent increase in the percentage of white participants in a given sport, there was a corresponding 1.5 percent decrease in the sport's attrition rate.

Lots of teens, we learned, are exploring the growing array of "other sports." Overall participation in "other sports" ranked second highest (27 percent)

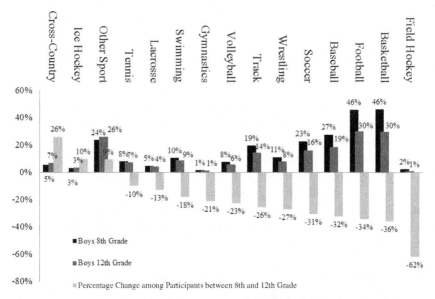

Figure 1.6. Percentage change among participants between eighth grade and twelfth grade boys, by sport. Source: Data provided by the Monitoring the Future Study.

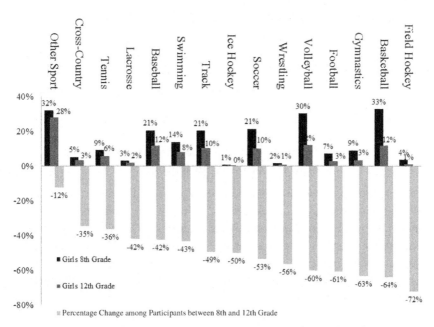

Figure 1.7. Percentage change among participants between eighth grade and twelfth grade girls, by sport. Source: Data provided by the Monitoring the Future Study.

among eighth- and twelfth-graders, third among boys (24 percent), and first (31 percent) among girls. And yet "other sports" were not as much of a refuge from attrition among girls as they were for boys. While boys' rate of participation in "other sports" increased by 9 percent between eighth grade and twelfth grade, girls' percentage decreased by 12 percent. Why are so many more girls leaving sports than boys? Why are organized schools and community sports failing to provide equitable access and opportunity across genders, racial and ethnic groups, and family income levels? While survey research can help expose and describe these differences, it cannot explain them. Multiple methods and interdisciplinary research are needed to investigate this line of research.

It makes good policy sense to recognize the complexity of kids' movements in, out, and between sports. First, research can inform efforts to increase physical literacy among young children as part of a wider strategy for healthy youth development. Second, national sport governing board leaders can use reliable participation and attrition data to evaluate and improve programs. Third, adolescent health advocates, physical activity promoters, and medical professionals may find participation and attrition data useful for planning purposes. Also, as parents learn more about the elevated risks for concussion and serious injury in contact sports like football, they may find it inspiring that so many kids appear to be experimenting with a growing array of sport alternatives. Finally, among kids themselves, our unearthing of the widespread movements of kids in, out, and between sports may help displace the long-standing "quitter" stigma with an "explorer" identity. A marketplace metaphor may help explain some of the navigation in and across "other sports," where kids are "consumers" and sports are "commodities" generated by schools and communities. As the marketplace of "other sport" opportunities and options expands, consumer kids try more products, especially those whose families have more resources and institutional options available to invest.

THE PERSISTENCE OF STRUCTURED INEQUALITY IN US HIGH SCHOOL SPORTS

One big question in youth sport that emerges from the historical backdrop of the women's movements and passage of Title IX in the 1970s is, "Have we got gender equity yet?" Our research indicates the answer is "no"! In order to assess gender inequities in adolescent athletic participation across historical time, we analyzed longitudinal survey data from the Department of Education's Office for Civil Rights Data Collection. We wanted to know whether the allotment of athletic opportunities to boys and girls in US high schools had changed during the decade between 2000 and 2010. We drew on a matched sample of 7,254 public four-year high schools that participated in the Civil Rights Data Collection during both the 1999–2000 and 2009–2010 school years (Sabo and Veliz 2012).

During a decade of expanding athletic participation opportunities across US high schools, boys continued to receive more opportunities than girls, and boys' opportunities grew faster than those of girls. By 2009–2010, fifty-three athletic opportunities were offered for every one hundred boys, compared with forty-three opportunities for every one hundred girls. Even after controlling for students' socioeconomic status, the opportunity gap between girls and boys continued to increase. Furthermore, by 2009–2010, boys still received disproportionately more athletic opportunities than girls in all community settings—urban, suburban, towns, and rural communities. The evidence debunks long-standing claims by many men's sport leaders that the increasing allocation of athletic opportunities for girls leads to a loss of opportunities for boys.

Some schools reported dropping their sports programs during this decade. In 2000, 8.2 percent of schools offered no sports programs. The percentage had nearly doubled by 2010, rising to approximately 15 percent. Contributing to the existing gender disparities, schools with disproportionately higher female enrollments (i.e., the student body is 56 percent female or higher) were more likely to have dropped interscholastic sports between 2000 and 2010. The bottom line is that institutional cuts in high school sport programs hit girls harder than boys. Such results also raise an important question: if the same decadelong trend in dropped athletic programs persisted for the next ten years, how many kids would be affected? Seven percent of public schools lost sports programs between 2000 and 2010, while fewer than one percent added sports to their academic portfolio. Extrapolating this same trend, by 2020, an estimated 27 percent of US public high schools (4,398 schools) will be without *any* interscholastic sports. This means an estimated 3.4 million young Americans (1,658,046 girls and 1,798,782 boys) will not have any school-based sports activities to participate in by 2020, if the current trend continues.[4]

EDUCATIONAL ACHIEVEMENT

Journalist Amanda Ripley's "The Case against High School Sports" appeared as a feature article in the October 2013 issue of the *Atlantic*. She was dismayed by international data that showed US teens were behind many other nations in various measures of academic performance. Whereas test scores in critical thinking in mathematics placed South Korean fifteen-year-olds fourth in the world, for example, their US counterparts ranked thirty-first in the hierarchy. Ripley's effort to locate the culprit responsible for "America's international mediocrity in education" resulted in an indictment of high school sports. To make such claims, she drew upon work conducted by sociologist James Coleman (1961), who, based on a mixed-method study of ten Chicago high schools conducted more than a half-century ago, concluded that American school sports were a detriment to boys' academic achievement. Ripley bolstered her polemic against the corrosive influence of sport on educational achievement with a variety of observations: American teens spend more time playing sports than kids from other nations; school districts spend more money on sports, equipment, coaches, and athletic administrators than on math classes; American kids love sports and participate in droves. But just *how* these factors lead to mediocre educational outcomes among both US boys and girls was not spelled out or backed by research evidence. Rather, she bolstered her argument with a case study of the Premont Independent School District, from Texas, in which the school principal eliminated all sports programs as part of comprehensive reforms designed to save money, enhance academic performance, and avert imminent closure. She averred that Premont's excessive focus on sports—especially football—contributed to its slack educational standards and outcomes. But one fundamental social scientific question that emerges from this magazine piece is whether or not Premont High School is representative of the forty-two thousand public and private high schools in the United States. What does existing research have to say?

Coleman's (1961) conclusion that sports eroded *boys'* academic performance was later echoed in the 1960s by sociologist Harry Edwards, who described sports (and again he meant *boys'* sports) as a "treadmill to oblivion" for young Black males (Edwards 1984). He argued that Black males chased unrealistic athletic dreams and as a result crashed and burned academically and in life. Coleman's insights and conclusions, however, were based on a small regional sample of schools. Edwards's contentions derived from an overarching sociological and historical analysis of racial inequality that was often applied to understanding race relations in Olympic, intercollegiate, and high school sports. In contrast, more recent and nationally representative social science research comes to the opposite conclusion. For example, after reviewing the research on high school sport participation and educational attainment, Hartmann (2008, 3) concluded, "Research has time and again demonstrated a strong and positive correlation between high school sports participation and academic achievement." Several similar reviews also found that participation in sports is positively associated with a variety educational outcomes (Farb and Matjasko 2012; Feldman and Matjasko 2005; Holland and Andre 1987).

In an effort to throw new empirical light on these issues, during the late 1980s, Don Sabo, Merrill Melnick, and Beth Vanfossen (1989) initiated a nationwide longitudinal analysis of the role of sport in the lives of America's minority youth—both girls and boys—and for the first time, Hispanics and Blacks, as well as whites. Using data from the US Department of Education High School & Beyond study (a database generated by the National Center for Education Statistics) we followed an initial sample of more than thirty thousand high school sophomores (1980) through their senior year (1982) and two and four years beyond high school (1984; 1986). The results showed that the "dumb jock" stereotype proved to be false. Minority athletes actually fared better academically than nonathletes from the same groups. African American and Hispanic athletes—among both boys and girls—scored higher on standardized reading, vocabulary, and mathematics tests than their nonathletic counterparts. Sports involvement lowered the drop-out rate among some minorities in suburban and rural schools, though not in urban schools. Indeed, depending on school location (i.e., urban, suburban, and rural) some racial and ethnic minorities seemed to benefit more academically from sports involvement, such as Hispanic female athletes in rural and suburban schools, while Black females and males in urban schools showed the least favorable educational benefits.

More recent survey research points to both the reality and complexity of links between sport involvement and educational achievement. Generally, student athletes in high school tend to do better academically over time (Crosnoe 2002; Eccles and Barber 1999; Marsh and Kleitman 2002; Videon 2002). Naomi Fejgin's (1994) longitudinal study of 22,696 high school students in 1,052 schools found that both female and male athletes had higher grades, higher educational aspirations, and less school-related discipline problems than nonathletes. At the school level, higher sports participation rates for girls and boys across US public high schools were associated with higher AP math, AP science, AP foreign language, and overall AP enrollment rates (Veliz and Shakib 2014). Moreover, schools with higher sport participation rates for girls and boys reported significantly fewer suspensions during the school year and fewer crimes on school grounds (Veliz and Shakib 2012).

With respect to the differences in academic outcomes across specific types of sports, a nationwide study of eighth-, tenth-, and twelfth-graders found that participants in tennis and soccer were more likely to report an A as their average grade, study for ten or more hours during a typical week, and have strong aspirations to graduate from college when compared to their peers who did not participate in these sports (Sabo, Veliz, and Rafalson 2013). However, the same report found that participants in wrestling were less likely to report an average "A" grade, less likely to study for ten or more hours during a typical week, and less likely to have strong aspirations to graduate from college when compared to their peers who did not participate in this sport. Some studies find that football players have higher suspension and expulsion rates than nonathletes and participants in other sports (Sabo, Veliz, and Rafalson 2013), yet more research is needed to unearth the complexity of relationships between youth sport involvement and educational advantages.

Youth Sports and Health

The elevated risks for concussion and head injury among football players have rightfully grabbed headlines in recent years. One reality is that the American public is rarely informed of the health impacts of youth sport, and a key reason for the information void is that there is so little research being done. Why so little focus? While today we take for granted that smoking is a health hazard, it took more than fifty years of cumulative research to soundly confirm that smoking was a source of disease and for laws and public health campaigns to encourage smoke-free lifestyles (Brownlee 2007). In contrast, the amount of research that takes a public health approach to youth sport is accurately described as "neonatal" in scope and results. One obvious question is, since millions of kids play sports in America, doesn't it make sense to learn more about their associated health risks and protective assets?

While some research finds that sports involvement can benefit adolescent health (Diehl et al. 2012; Lisha and Sussman 2010; Pate et al. 1996, 2000), other studies identify different types of health-compromising behaviors (Denham 2011; Kreager 2007; Veliz, Boyd, and McCabe 2013a, 2013b). Our assessment is that the majority of research confirms that sport is a positive asset in the lives of youth (Farb and Matjasko 2012; Feldman and Matjasko 2005). For instance, one recent study found that participation in competitive sports kept adolescents physically active during eighth through twelfth grades, a period when physical activity significantly declines (Sabo and Veliz 2014b). Accordingly, the study found that when compared to adolescents who do not participate in sports, adolescents who participated in at least one competitive sport during the past year engaged in 1.5 days more of physical activity for at least sixty minutes during the past week. Moreover, participation in competitive sports was found to be a stronger factor among twelfth-graders (when compared to eighth- and tenth-graders) to maintain appropriate levels of physical activity throughout the week. This finding is significant in that US federal physical activity guidelines call for youth to engage daily in at least sixty minutes of aerobic, muscle-strengthening, or physical activity (US Department of Health and Human Services 2010).

Although sport participation can play a positive role in adolescents' lives, sport also introduces a variety of health risks—particularly with respect to certain types of substance use (Lisha and Sussman 2010). While most studies find sports participation helps lower cigarette and illicit drug use, athletes are more likely to drink alcohol and engage in problem drinking (Lisha and Sussman 2010). Moreover, certain types of sports participation increase the risk of alcohol consumption, marijuana use, and nonmedical use of prescription medications (Veliz, Boyd, and McCabe 2013a, 2013b, 2015). For instance, a recent study using MTF survey data (see Veliz, Boyd, and McCabe 2013b) found that adolescents who participated in any competitive sport (i.e., participated in at least one competitive sport) had similar odds of engaging in nonmedical opioid use when compared to nonparticipants. Generally, then, no association was detected between sports participation and nonmedical opioid use. However, when the same association was tested within *specific types* of sport, adolescents who participated in football and wrestling had higher odds of nonmedical prescription opioid use than adolescents who did not participate in these sports. Put another way, wrestlers and football players were more likely than nonathletes and athletes in other sports to abuse nonmedical opioids.

Among US adolescents between age ten and twenty-four, "unintentional injuries" constitute the leading cause of death, accounting for 48 percent of mortality (Blum and Qureshi 2012). The lack of seatbelt use is often implicated in these deaths. During the latter 1990s, a group of researchers set out to assess the relationships between sports and adolescent health. Using data from the 1997 Youth Risk Behavior Surveillance Survey, a national survey of more than sixteen thousand US public and private high school students, the authors explored associations between past-year athletic participation and regular seatbelt omission (Melnick et al. 2010). After the researchers controlled for the effects of gender, age, race, parental education, and school urbanicity, they found that student athletes were significantly more likely than nonathletes to report seatbelt use. Separate gender-specific analyses showed that this effect was significant for girls but only marginally significant for boys. In addition, the effect was strongest for adolescents who participated in three or more school or community sports teams. Perhaps future research will unravel how or why athletes—especially girls—tend to buckle up more so that nonathletes.

Alongside the recognition that sport can be a threatening environment for girls and women, being an athlete can be socially and emotionally empowering for girls. Survey research, for example, has analyzed the relationship between athletic participation on sexual behavior and pregnancy risk (Sabo et al. 1999; Miller et al. 2000). Findings indicated that female athletes were less likely to get pregnant than their nonathletic counterparts. Nationally, female athletes were less than half as likely to get pregnant as female nonathletes (5 percent and 11 percent, respectively). Reduced pregnancy rates were found in African American, white, and Hispanic female athletes. Female athletes were also more likely than their nonathletic counterparts to report not having intercourse, first having intercourse later in adolescence, having sex less often, and being more likely to use contraceptives. Other research, moreover, examined whether athletic participation helped protect female athletes from sexual "victimization" through a variety of social-psychological mechanisms such as team membership, physical strength, and self-confidence (Fasting et al. 2012). Among US college students of traditional undergraduate age (aged eighteen through twenty-four), student athletes were significantly less likely to report sexual victimization during their late high school and early college years than their nonathletic counterparts.

Conclusion

We began this chapter by noting the dichotomous, good-versus-bad discourses that often characterize youth sports. We have shown, using survey research, that there are also many babies in the bathwater of contemporary youth sport in America, which is to say that not all sports are alike. Sport often plays a positive role in kids' lives, but it does not do so equally, across the board, for all kids. Furthermore, there are some youth sport programs with poor coaches, bloated budgets, and subcultures that foster lousy behavior, poor study habits, and negative health outcomes. The subcultures and social networks of tennis, basketball, lacrosse, and track and field are often very different from those of football, rugby, or wrestling. And there are schools in which football is fetishized and overfunded at the expense of girls' sports and lesser-status boys' sports. Nationally, the vision of gender, race, or class equity among US teens in sport has not been fulfilled, especially in urban schools and communities.

While positive synergies between athletic experiences and academic performance exist, they are not the same across all sport subcultures. Does it make sense to generalize about the educational and health correlates of all sports across all schools, somehow superimposing a "one theory fits all" explanatory framework? And there are certainly well-adjusted, healthy high school kids who invest more identity, energy, and aspirations in algebra, physics, or poetry. In addition, youth athletic participation is not confined to school sports, but increasingly spills over into community-based programs, particularly among kids who play more than one sport. Finally, given the powerful influence of social inequality on educational outcomes in US schools, does it make sense to claim that sports somehow uniformly erode kids' development across all schools and communities?

Surveys conducted through the Center for Research on Physical Activity, Sport & Health have generated findings that cry out for more research. For example, while immigrants compose a substantial portion of the US population, only a smidgeon of formal research focuses on athletic participation among immigrant children or parental attitudes toward girls' and boys' sport involvement (Sabo and Veliz 2008). We also learned that about nine out of every one hundred US families have a child who has a disability that can interfere with sports and exercise. These children are often interested in sports and exercise, and many of their parents want to see more programs offered in schools and communities. There is also a gender gap in sports and exercise activity among children with disabilities—surprisingly, it is *boys* who are less physically active than girls. But the amount of sport research devoted to children with disabilities and their families is minimal. Similarly bullying, sexual assault, and dating violence are part of adolescent life—in communities, schools, gangs, and also sport. GLBT youth also remain an underserved and underresearched group of kids in sport.

Public health agencies and officials uniformly call for more physical activity among youth and young adults. Commercial and nonprofit community sports programs are mushrooming across the United States. Researchers need to affiliate with local community sports programs and nonprofits to assess which sports or physical activities foster preventive health behaviors and greater levels of physical literacy among elementary and middle school kids. The LAUSD/Beyond the Bell/LA84 Middle School Partnership After-School Sports program is doing just this: engaging and assessing more than twelve thousand kids' involvement in Los Angeles after-school sport programs (LA84 Foundation 2013). In short, the social worlds of youth sport are expanding and becoming much more complex. It remains to be seen whether sport researchers keep pace with the variegation or merely observe it from the theoretical grandstands.

Presuming that there is both good and bad in youth sports, the survey findings reviewed in this chapter tilt toward the former but certainly do not exclude the latter. Quantitative research is sometimes caricaturized as an exercise in scientific or statistical certainty. This is rarely if ever the case. The findings and associations discussed in this chapter help reveal some of the complex social, cultural, and developmental landscapes that make up youth sport in America. The evidence shows that while millions of kids are involved in one or more sports, many eventually leave during adolescence. For lots of kids, certainly not all, the evidence suggests that sports involvement can go hand in hand with personal and social empowerment. In contrast to generalizations that sport is "good for kids" or "bad for kids," our sport-by-sport analyses show that different sport experiences influence kids in different ways. And substantial evidence shows that kids' athletic experiences are influenced by wider institutional forces linked to gender, race and ethnicity, and income inequality. Youth sports are clearly not an equal opportunity playing field. We've just begun to understand how these larger forces intersect with kids' personal development, family life, educational outcomes, health behaviors, and sexual choices.

NOTES

1. Some examples of nationally scaled survey data sources on youth sports participation are the National Longitudinal Study of Adolescent Health; the Centers for Disease Control and Prevention's Youth Risk Behavior Surveillance Survey; the US Department of Education's Monitoring the Future Study; and the Center for Research on Sport, Physical Activity, and Health's "Go Out and Play" survey data. For discussion, see Staurowsky et al. (2015).

2. The primary question posed to respondents that addressed athletic participation was "In which competitive sports (if any) did you participate in during the LAST 12 MONTHS? Include school, community, and other organized sports. (Mark all that apply.)"

3. Participation and attrition rates in this study were defined and measured as percentages. For example, if the participation rate for baseball/softball among eighth-graders was 10 percent (ten baseball/softball participants in the eighth grade divided by one hundred students in the eighth grade) and the participation rate among twelfth-graders was 5 percent (five baseball/softball participants in the twelfth grade divided by one hundred twelfth-graders), then the attrition rate between eighth and twelfth grade would be–50 percent. In short, the participation rate in twelfth grade is half the participation rate in eighth grade.

4. It should be noted that, despite the existing mandate from the US Department of Justice, not all schools provide the federal government with accurate information on whether they offer sports or not. The lack of information and the noncompliance are regrettable in that effective evaluation is made more difficult.

REFERENCES

Blum, Robert, and Farah Qureshi. 2012. "Morbidity and Mortality among Adolescents and Young Adults in the United States." John Hopkins Bloomberg School of Public Health. http://www.jhsph.edu/research/centers-and-institutes/center-for-adolescent-health/az/_images/us%20fact%20sheet_final.pdf.

Brownlee, Shannon. 2007. *Overtreated: Why Too Much Medicine Is Making Us Sicker and Poorer*. New York: Bloomsbury.

Coleman, James S. 1961. *The Adolescent Society: The Social Life of the Adolescent and Its Impact on Education*. New York: Free Press.

Crosnoe, Robert. 2002. "Academic and Health-Related Trajectories in Adolescence: The Intersection of Gender and Athletics." *Journal of Health and Social Behavior* 43.3: 317–336.

Denham, Bryan E. 2011. "Alcohol and Marijuana Use among American High School Seniors: Empirical Associations with Competitive Sports Participation." *Sociology of Sport Journal* 28.3: 362–379.

Diehl, Katharina, Ansgar Thiel, Stephan Zipfel, Jochen Mayer, David G. Litaker, and Sven Schneider. 2012. "How Healthy Is the Behavior of Young Athletes? A Systematic Literature Review and Meta-Analyses." *Journal of Sports Science and Medicine* 11.2: 201–220.

Eccles, Jacquelynne S., and Bonnie L. Barber. 1999. "Student Council, Volunteering, Basketball, or Marching Band: What Kind of Extracurricular Involvement Matters?" *Journal of Adolescent Research* 14.1: 10–43.

Edwards, Harry. 1984. "The Collegiate Athletic Arms Race: Origins and Implications of the 'Rule 48' Controversy." *Journal of Sport and Social issues* 8.1: 4–22.

Eitzen, Stanley D. 2003. *Fair and Foul: Beyond the Myths and Paradoxes of Sport*. Lanham, MD: Rowman & Littlefield.

Farb, Amy Feldman, and Jennifer L. Matjasko. 2012. "Recent Advances in Research on School-Based Extracurricular Activities and Adolescent Development." *Developmental Review* 32.1: 1–48.

Farrey, Tom. 2008. *Game On: The All-American Race to Make*. New York: ESPN Books.

Fasting, Kari, Celia H. Brackenridge, Kathleen E. Miller, and Don Sabo. 2008. "Participation in College Sports and Protection from Victimization." *International Journal of Sport and Exercise Psychology* 6.4: 427–441.

Fejgin, Naomi. 1994. "Participation in High School Competitive Sports: A Subversion of School Mission or Contribution to Academic Goals?" *Sociology of Sport Journal* 11.3: 211–230.

Feldman, Amy, and Jennifer L. Matjasko. 2005. "The Role of School-Based Extracurricular Activities in Adolescent Development: A Comprehensive Review and Future Directions." *Review of Educational Research* 75.2: 159–210.

Hartmann, Douglas. 2008. "High School Sports Participation and Educational Attainment: Recognizing, Assessing, and Utilizing the Relationship." LA84 Foundation. http://www.la84foundation.org/3ce/HighSchoolSportsParticipation.pdf.

Holland, Alyce, and Thomas Andre. 1987. "Participation in Extracurricular Activities in Secondary School: What Is Known, What Needs to Be Known?" *Review of Educational Research* 57.4: 437–466.

Johnston, Lloyd D., Patrick M. O'Malley, Jerald G. Bachman, John E. Schulenberg, and Richard A. Miech. 2014. "Monitoring the Future National Survey Results on Drug Use, 1975–2013: Volume 1, Secondary School Students." Ann Arbor: Institute for Social Research, University of Michigan.

Kreager, Derek A. 2007. "Unnecessary Roughness? School Sports, Peer Networks, and Male Adolescent Violence." *American Sociological Review* 72.5: 705–724.

LA84 Foundation. 2013. "RSS Research Brief." www.LA84.org.

Lisha, Nadra E., and Steve Sussman. 2010. "Relationship of High School and College Sports Participation with Alcohol, Tobacco, and Illicit Drug Use: A Review." *Addictive Behaviors* 35.5: 399–407.

Marsh, Herbert W., and Sabina Kleitman. 2002. "Extracurricular School Activities: The Good, the Bad, and the Nonlinear." *Harvard Educational Review* 72.4: 464–502.

Melnick, Merrill J., Kathleen E. Miller, Don Sabo, Grace M. Barnes, and Michael Farrell. 2010. "Athletic Participation and Seatbelt Omission among U.S. High School Students: A National Study." *Health Education & Behavior* 37.1: 23–36.

Messner, Michael A. 2009. *It's All for the Kids: Gender, Families, and Youth Sports*. Berkeley: University of California Press.

Miller, Kathleen, Don Sabo, Michael Farrell, Grace M. Barnes, and Merrill Melnick. 2000. "Sports, Sexual Behavior, Contraceptive Use, and Pregnancy among Female and Male Adolescents: Testing Cultural Resource Theory." *Sociology of Sport Journal* 16.4: 366–387.

Pate, Russell R., Gregory W. Heath, Marsha Dowda, and Stewart G. 1996. "Association between Physical Activity and Other Health Behaviors in a Representative Sample of US Adolescents." *American Journal of Public Health* 86.11: 1577–1581.

Pate, Russell R., Stewart G. Trost, Sarah Levin, and Marsha Dowda. 2000. "Sports Participation and Health-Related Behaviors among US Youth." *Archives of Pediatrics & Adolescent Medicine* 154.9: 904–911.

Ripley, Amanda. 2013. "The Case Against High School Sports." *Atlantic*, October.

Sabo, Don, Merrill Melnick, and Beth Vanfossen. 1989. "The Women's Sports Foundation Report: Minorities in Sports." East Meadow, NY: Women's Sports Foundation.

Sabo, Don, Kathleen Miller, Michael Farrell, Grace Barnes, and Merrill Melnick. 1999. "High School Athletic Participation, Sexual Behavior and Adolescent Pregnancy: A Regional Study." *Journal of Adolescent Health* 25.3: 207–216.

Sabo, Don, and Philip Veliz. 2008. "Go Out and Play: Youth Sports in America." East Meadow, NY: Women's Sports Foundation.

———. 2012. "Decade of Decline: Gender Equity in High School Sports." Ann Arbor, MI: SHARP Center for Women and Girls.

———. 2014a. "Mapping Attrition among U.S. Adolescents in Competitive, Organized School, and Community Sports." Buffalo, NY: Center for Research on Physical Activity, Sport & Health.

———. 2014b. "Participation in Organized Competitive Sports and Physical Activity among U.S. Adolescents: Assessment of a Public Health Resource." *Health Behavior and Policy Review* 1.6: 503–512.

Sabo, Don, Philip Veliz, and Lisa Rafalson. 2013. *More Than a Sport: Tennis, Education, and Health*. White Plains, NY: USTA Serves.

Staurowsky, Ellen J., Mary Jane De Souza, Kathleen E. Miller, Don Sabo, Sohaila Shakib, Nancy Theberge, Philip Veliz, A. Weaver, and Nancy I. Williams. 2015. *Her Life Depends on It III*. East Meadow, NY: Women's Sports Foundation.

Stevenson, Betsey. 2007. "Title IX and the Evolution of High School Sports." *Contemporary Economic Policy* 25.4: 486–505.

US Department of Health and Human Services. 2010. "Healthy People 2010: Understanding and Improving Health." http://www.healthypeople.gov/2010/Document/tableofcontents .htm#volume1.

Veliz, Philip, Carol Boyd, and Sean E. McCabe. 2013a. "Adolescent Athletic Participation and Nonmedical Adderall Use: An Exploratory Analysis of a Performance-Enhancing Drug." *Journal of Studies on Alcohol and Drugs* 74.5: 714–719.

———. 2013b. "Playing through Pain? Sports Participation and Nonmedical Use of Opioid Medications among Adolescents." *American Journal of Public Health* 103.5: e28–e30.

———. 2015. "Competitive Sport Involvement and Substance Use among Adolescents: A Nationwide Study." *Substance Use and Misuse* 50.2: 156–165.

Veliz, Philip, and Sohaila Shakib. 2012. "Interscholastic Sports Participation and School-Based Delinquency: Does Participation in Sport Foster a Positive High School Environment?" *Sociological Spectrum* 32.6: 558–580.

———. 2014. "Gender, Academics, and Interscholastic Sports Participation at the School Level: A Gender-Specific Analysis of the Relationship between Interscholastic Sports Participation and AP Enrollment." *Sociological Focus* 47.2: 101–120.

Videon, Tami M. 2002. "Who Plays and Who Benefits: Gender, Interscholastic Athletics, and Academic Outcomes." *Sociological Perspectives* 45.4: 415–444.

Women's Sports Foundation. (2007). "Boston Girls Sports and Physical Activity Project." Unpublished report. East Meadow, NY: Women's Sports Foundation.

CHAPTER 2

Kids of Color in the American Sporting Landscape

LIMITED, CONCENTRATED, AND CONTROLLED

Douglas Hartmann and Alex Manning

In the United States, as in many countries around the world, competitive athletics are often thought of as an unparalleled arena of opportunity and mobility for children and youth from disadvantaged backgrounds. There is obviously some truth to this, especially given patterns of racial discrimination and disparities in other social domains, and that helps explain why sport is often so popular in many communities of color. However, while opportunities for fun, fitness, socialization, development, and even mobility in and through sport do exist for American kids of color, they also face challenges of access and issues of treatment that are unique, uneven, and unequal when compared to the typical experience of white, middle-class children and youth. And these differences and disparities can, we believe, both compromise the benefits and accentuate the problems of all youth sport and athletic involvement. This chapter provides an overview of some of the ways in which race structures physical activity and athletic participation for children and youth from communities of color. We believe that these unique experiences and challenges have significant implications for how sport is experienced and understood by young people of color in the United States.

We begin by providing a brief overview of rates of sports participation and physical activity for young people of color across the country. Then, we discuss some of the factors that help explain the uneven and unequal rates of participation, focusing on the obstacles that stand in the way of young people of color's full and equal access to sport and the ways these youth are channeled toward some sports more than others. In the third section we argue that the challenges kids of color face in the athletic arena not only are about unequal access, but also involve differential treatment in the activities and programs in which they actually do participate. Drawing respectively from Hartmann's research on sport-based crime prevention (2015, 2012, 2001) and Manning's work (2014) on USA Soccer's new national development model, two different dimensions of differential treatment are highlighted: (1) how young people of color are specifically targeted for development and high performance in certain, elite-level athletic programs and sporting organizations; and (2) how sport is disproportionately understood and used as a form of social control of kids of color. Consistent with the larger thrust of this volume, we conclude the chapter by presenting some preliminary interview data that suggest some of the potential contributions of taking parents and kids of color more seriously as agents in the production, reproduction, and potential contestation of the material patterns and cultural forces that structure sport participation and physical activities in the contemporary United States.

PARTICIPATION RATES

When we started doing background research for this chapter, we assumed that young people of color in the United States faced significant, systematic inequities when it came to physical activity and athletic participation. After all, for decades sport researchers have claimed that racial and ethnic minorities participate in youth sports at lower rates overall when compared to their white peers (Ewing and Seefeldt 2002). And with all of the persistent racial gaps in areas such as wealth and poverty, education, health care, and criminal justice in society as a whole (for a comprehensive overview, see Carter and Reardon 2014), we saw no reason that these patterns would have shifted appreciably.

In many respects, it does appear that youth and young people of color continue to be underrepresented in sports. For example, we learned that white youth are more likely to participate in youth sports from grades three through eight than any other racial group (Physical Activity Council 2013). We also found that the mean age for African American and Latino/a kids entering organized sports is significantly higher than that for white kids. Anglo children are, on average, 6.6 years of age when they begin to participate in sports, as compared with 7.7 years of age for African American kids and 8.2 years for Latino/a youth (Aspen Institute 2015). Studies have found Latino American students are less likely to participate in sports in comparison to white American students (Davalos, Chavez, and Guardiola 1999; Feldman and Matjasko 2007), and Asian American youth appear to have the lowest rates of sports participation of any racial community in the United States (Darling 2005; Faircloth and Hamm 2005; Feldman and Matjasko 2005).

However, the current research and evidence on racial disparities were more equivocal and mixed than we anticipated. For one thing, there are some real limitations in the data. National and even state-level data are essentially nonexistent for Native American children (Stick and Schaeffer 2014), and we know next to nothing about athletic participation among ethnic and racial subgroups and new immigrant communities. Second, there are some distinctive variations in racial patterns when we take gender into account. Proportionally fewer girls of color are involved with sports than white girls, and girls of color are also much more likely than their male counterparts to be non-athletes. However, the same discrepancies across racial and ethnic groups do not exist among boys and young men of color (Sabo and Veliz 2008).

Third, and perhaps most important, youth sports are actually quite racially and ethnically diverse. According to Donald Sabo and Philip Veliz (2008), 15 percent of all girls and 16 percent of all boys who participate in sports are African American, numbers that compare quite favorably to the overall population (approximately 14 percent nationally). Similarly, 17 percent of female athletes and 15 percent of male athletes are Hispanic. Participation rates for African American youth are particularly strong. Some of the most systematic sociological research that has been conducted suggests that Black/African American youth are more likely to participate in sports than youth from any other racial or ethnic group (Feldman and Matjasko 2005, 2007). Kathleen E. Miller and colleagues (2005) found similar patterns of sports participation for Black/African American and white youth. Randall Brown and William P. Evans (2002) reported that "African American students play more sports than Latino and Asian American students" (Peguero et al. 2013). Here it is also worth noting that while white youth are the most likely to participate in sports in grades three through eight, their rates of participation fall off dramatically beginning at age twelve and continuing into high school, the reverse pattern holds for African American kids. More than half (52 percent) of African American youth, both boys and girls, begin to participate in sports only around eighth grade.

At least two additional clarifications and qualifications are in order. First, racial participation in different sporting activities is particularly mixed and uneven, with minority groups being significantly overrepresented in some sports and underrepresented in others. Demographic statistics from the US Tennis Association show that white adolescents tend to be overrepresented in noncontact sports like tennis, golf, or swimming, while Latino/as and African Americans are overrepresented in contact sports. More specifically, white adolescents are almost twice as likely to participate in tennis (9 percent) as African American or Latino/a youth (5 and 4 percent, respectively). Overall, according to the association, 77 percent of participants in youth tennis are white (compared with 9 and 14 percent African American and Latino/a).

On the other hand, African American males are almost 43 percent more likely to play football than other sports, and 68 percent more likely to take up basketball. By comparison, they are less likely to play baseball, soccer, wrestle, or swim.[1] The one noncontact sport they are more likely (35 percent) to engage is track. By way of comparison, Latino boys are most likely to play soccer (68 percent) and less likely to wrestle or swim or, perhaps surprisingly, to play baseball. African American females are more likely to play basketball or run track, but less likely to play softball or lacrosse, swim, or run cross-country; for Latinas, the most likely sports are soccer and track, with softball, lacrosse, swimming, and cross-country being less likely. Importantly, Black girls are 11 percent less likely to play any sport, with Latina girls being 31 percent less likely (Sagas and Cunningham 2014).

The second additional point to make is that all of the statistics we have presented are for organized, competitive athletic pursuits—"sports" in the most common usage of the term. What is not captured in these numbers are rates of participation in less competitive, more recreational athletic pursuits and physical activities (e.g., in recreational settings, physical education classes, or other movement-oriented activities). This is a crucial point because there is a tremendous amount of evidence in the area of public health that poorer, low-income children, who we know come disproportionately from communities of color in the United States, suffer the health consequences of much lower levels of physical activity (Halpern 2006). Put somewhat differently, the fact that patterns of participation in organized, competitive sports may be more equitable than we have sometimes realized may actually blind us from the fact that rates of activity among the masses not involved in these more intensive, higher level pursuits are the far bigger issue and problem.[2]

In sum, then, the most basic and important general point about race and youth sports is that children of color are unevenly and often unequally represented in the youth sporting landscape. The net result of these unequal patterns of participation is clear: children and youth of color have less access to the purported benefits of athletic competition and physical activities—higher levels of fitness, greater opportunities to experience the social benefits of competition, socializing with others, and having role models, or even the most basic, elemental benefits of recreation, fitness, and fun.

ACCESS ISSUES

Some of the patterns of uneven and unequal athletic participation among youth of color in the United States may be explained by cultural differences between racial communities. For example, many researchers and community members alike believe that African Americans are disproportionately drawn to basketball more than other sports; a similar dynamic is believed to hold for Latino/as when it comes to soccer. Conversely, our interviews and fieldwork in the Twin Cities of Minnesota provide anecdotal evidence that some new immigrant families and parents (Hmong and Laotian immigrants in this case and, to a lesser extent, Somali) are not as drawn to sport in the first place, preferring their children to focus on schoolwork and family responsibilities over sports (or any other extracurricular activities for that matter). Obviously, these cultural preferences and tastes could play an important role in influencing the sports and physical activities these children end up playing.

As sociologists, however, we tend to focus less on individual choices and general cultural preferences than on the broader social structures and organizational factors that might provide barriers or obstacles to some activities, while encouraging entry or involvement into others. And one of the first and most basic sets of factors we would highlight in this regard has to do with the economic marginalization and class disadvantage that so often is associated with minority status in the United States.

There is a large and well-established sociological literature on economic barriers to social inclusion in sport (Collins 2003). In fact, when one surveys research and reports on youth participation rates in sport, the clearest, most consistent patterns are those related to class and economics. According to the Physical Activity Council (2013), for example, kids from wealthier families tend to start playing sports earlier (family incomes over $100,000 at age 6.3, below $35,000 at 8.1 years of age, almost two years later). Similarly, the Aspen Institute's (2015) Play Project reports that the 20 percent of US households that take in over $100,000 in income per year account for 33 percent of kids actively involved in competitive youth sports. Moreover, kids in richer neighborhoods and school districts participate at consistently higher rates as compared with those in less well-off areas. The same study found that in "low socio-economic schools" (that is, schools in areas of limited school funding), 24.6 percent of eighth-graders participate in sports. In contrast, 30.9 percent of students in "middle socio-economic schools" participate in athletics and 36.9 percent in the richest school districts.

Our point is that the economic and material challenges of access are accentuated and intensified for those in communities of color who are disproportionately poorer and less stable financially. Part of this is simply economic. Significant resources are required to play sport across childhood into the teenage years, especially as young athletes develop and the competition gets more intensive and expensive, requiring additional and often specialized training and development. This is where the intersections of race and class need to be considered—or, put more precisely, where the fact that there is significant overlap between racial background and economic status such that people in communities of color tend to be have lower levels of employment, higher rates of poverty, less access to good schools, community facilities, and after-school programs, and so on.

And when we talk about class and economics, it is not just the cost of playing sports that is problematic for minority kids and their families. For example, as Michael Messner shows in *It's All for the Kids* (2009), class and racial privilege often translates into robust adult volunteer participation and other levels of support for youth sports in well-to-do suburban areas. Other material factors that impact participation levels are unequal neighborhood and community resources as well as high levels of reliance on public programs and facilities like those associated with parks and recreation departments. The problem with publicly funded athletic opportunities and facilities is that they have actually been declining since the 1980s, with cutbacks in governmental resources and more reliance upon the market and private organizations (Crompton 1998; Crompton and McGregor 1994).

Access and opportunity are also strongly impacted by the programs and facilities offered in schools. Youth from nonwhite backgrounds tend to be much more prevalent or represented in "school-sponsored" athletic activities than in private, "agency-sponsored" programs (Ewing and Seefeldt 2002). Over the past couple of decades, scholastic athletic programs have been cut back dramatically in elementary and middle schools, high school programs have become more fee-based, and physical education has been slashed dramatically—less than a day or two a week in many districts, if students are lucky. Today, it is estimated that over 70 percent of parents pay a hundred dollars or more for their children to participate in sports through their schools (Show 2009). According to the Aspen Institute (2015), the differential resources and opportunities available through schools are pivotal factors in racial inequalities, even when sports are provided for free or for a nominal fee in the educational context. Studies of after-school intramural athletic involvement show a similar pattern: low-income and African American students are much more likely to participate in these school-based programs (Edwards et al. 2011; Kanters et al. 2013).

One final, very important factor to consider in explaining the differential rates of access and participation among children of color in the United States involves cultural labeling and the concentration of nonwhite youth in a select set of high-profile, racialized sports. In the wake of the civil rights movement, a fairly well-developed literature on racial "stacking" in sport emerged. Stacking was the idea that African American athletes were channeled only into certain positions in the sports they played (Eitzen and Sage 1992; Frey and Eitzen 1991; Lapchick 1999; Margolis and Piliavin 1999; Smith and Leonard 1997). In tackle football, for example, African American boys were directed to play running back, wide receiver, or defensive back rather than quarterback or offensive line. While such practices may not be quite so pronounced today, our argument extends a similar logic to suggest that kids of color are identified and targeted for specific sports (and at elite levels) and discouraged from playing others.

Practices of micro-level racial stereotyping by coaches, leagues, organizations, and whole systems can manifest themselves within specific sports at various levels of competition. Such patterns reveal larger racial and classed assumptions and stereotypes in operation at the level of youth sports, even when organizations try to address issues of athletic access and support. For example, in his preliminary fieldwork on elite youth soccer in the United States, Alex Manning has found that some elite-level youth coaches within the academy system implement such racial and class rhetoric when envisioning an ideal boys' soccer team. During a conversation about the racial and class demographics of a particular academy team (in this case mostly white and middle- to upper-middle-class) the coach joked that "we don't have any Allen Iversons" and wished for a multicultural team that had "big, strong, and fast African strikers, technical and quick Latino midfielders, and well-positioned, composed, and determining white defenders" (Manning 2014).

While USA Soccer does not use such explicit racial language, the federation has recently targeted its elite youth development program specifically at urban areas and other communities with larger communities of color where athletic talent is believed to be concentrated and underdeveloped (Borden 2012; Laroue 2012). We will return to this development in the next section.

Differential Treatment

The challenges that kids of color face in the American athletic arena are not only about unequal access and opportunity. They also involve differential treatment in the activities and programs and even specific sports in which they actually do participate. These differences manifest themselves in one of two very different ways. One extends from the ways in which kids of color appear to be channeled into some sporting activities and away from others. It involves the ways in which young people of color are often targeted for athletic development and high performance by elite-level programs and sporting organizations. The second is how sport is disproportionately understood and utilized as a means of social containment and control for youth and young people of color.

Manning's (2014) research on USA Soccer's new development program is a powerful illustration of the former. In an attempt to make elite men's soccer more accessible for urban immigrants and racial minorities (and thus more competitive internationally), the US Soccer Federation (USSF) and Major League Soccer (MLS) have created eighty development academies for boys ages twelve through eighteen across the United States. This soccer development policy is geared toward increasing the male professional talent pool in US soccer. Academies affiliated with professional clubs (sixteen in the United States) have been championed by leaders and coaches within the soccer community because they provide the coaching, facilities, and, for a few, housing and financial support for families that have been underrepresented in high levels of youth soccer (Borden 2012).

The words of Jürgen Klinsmann, the head coach and technical director of the US Men's National Team, speak to the classed and racial assumptions that inform the conception of the ideal professional soccer player. "Soccer is very similar to basketball, you need [players] out of the lower class environment and soccer worldwide is a lower class environment sport. We all [came] out of moderate families and fought our way through . . . so we need to keep this hunger throughout out life. I compare it to basketball here, because I look at these guys and they are coming from inner cities. So we need to find ways to connect, however that could be, to connect with Hispanics, to connect with everybody in the soccer environment in the U.S., and to get kids who are really hungry, to get kids on technical level to perform [at a world class and professional level] and what I mean is first touch" ("Future for U.S. Soccer" 2010).[3]

These cultural assumptions directly influence current elite youth soccer policy and practice, which target young people of color for athletic development and elite-level performance. The notion that elite and future professional soccer success requires more access for urban kids of color from working-class backgrounds is rooted in the idea that there is an untapped and plentiful source of soccer talent in communities of color all across the United States. In addition to racial assumptions about innate athletic talent, Klinsmann's class-based logic about "really hungry" kids reflects the popular US sporting narrative of a desperate, resource-deprived person (most often a person of color) investing all of his or her effort into a sport as a way of escaping hardship and rising to the top of professional athletics. From this perspective, the reason that elite American soccer has not been successful previously is because soccer in the United States has been culturally classified as essentially a "white, middle-class, and suburban sport" littered with moms, minivans, and orange slices (Andrews et al. 2006; Hersh 1990).

Klinsmann's class and racial diagnosis of America's soccer flaws is more than just a personal quirk. This rhetoric is prevalent and has had significant policy implications in the highest levels youth soccer in the United States (see the creation of the Developmental Academy System).[4] Participants in the field of elite youth soccer adopt elements of this rhetoric when discussing their own experiences and soccer clubs. In interviews with two coaches of two different US Soccer Development Association teams that are not affiliated with MLS teams, both coaches lamented the fact that their clubs could not take in kids from poorer communities or communities of color because of cost barriers. As one of the coaches put it, "The hardest thing, I guess, for me is that there are kids out there who would be worthwhile for us to bring in, but we just financially can't afford it. We bring 'em in, we test 'em out, we think they have the potential to grow, but we can't save 'em all. We can't bring 'em all in" (Manning 2014).

These coaches are concerned about access (but only at the most elite level) and profess a desire to coach more inclusive teams. They see socioeconomic and racially diversity as an important component of an ideal, successful, and extremely talented soccer academy. However, this form of elite athletic inclusiveness/

diversity and support does not address concerns of access and support for soccer at a more local and recreational level. Their concern, in short, is to create a pipeline for elite-level competition.

Such a targeted approach to recruitment of racial minorities, immigrants, and the working classes into elite soccer spaces has consequences beyond rhetoric employed by coaches. For example, conversations with coaches and players at different soccer clubs reveal that registration fees for younger less elite teams were being used to subsidize one or two scholarship funds for older players at the elite academy level (Manning 2014). Furthermore, such targeted recruitment of racial minorities can produce significant labor and stress for parents and players. In an interview with a current college soccer player, who played for an elite pay-to-play academy in his youth, the racial and classed dimensions of the "undiscovered" ideal soccer player intersected with the daily life. Devin shared the following story with me about the college recruitment cycle and recruiting a talented Latino player. "When the college push happened, we had a stud from a neighboring town who had played in academies in South America. He didn't have a car and his parents were working during practice, so my dad and I would drive an hour out of our way to pick him up, take him to practice, and sometimes feed him" (Manning 2014). In this conversation, Devin also made clear that his academy team often cycled through a number of immigrant and lower-class players (who rarely stuck with the team due to costs, travel, and transportation) as they looked to bolster their status and competitive success. Such stories speak to the patterns and possible negative consequences of targeting marginalized populations.

The other kind of athletic endeavor in which children of color appear to be channeled and concentrated is programs directed toward social intervention and control. The belief that sport is an important and almost uniformly positive arena of socialization, education, and opportunity for youth and young people has a long history that goes back to the origins of modern sport itself. However, these notions of sport as a tool for social development are often believed to hold particular, unique significance for young people from marginalized and disadvantaged backgrounds. Indeed, these ideas originally took shape in the United States during the play movement of the early 1900s, which was promoted by progressive reformers who believed that the development of parks and recreation programs and provision of access to sport was a way to socialize and "Americanize" the waves of working-class immigrant, ethnic, and racial minorities moving into American cities, especially in the North (Cavallo 1981).

In the late 1990s and the early part of the new millennium, the more controlling face of youth sport and physical activity reasserted itself with the emergence and proliferation of youth sports initiatives that took crime control, risk prevention, and public safety as their primary focus (Cole 1996; Pitter and Andrews

1997; see also Carrington and McDonald 2008). Midnight basketball, researched by Hartmann (forthcoming; see also 2001) was as an extreme and thus revealing case: it was almost exclusively about social containment and control, less oriented to the desires and needs of young people themselves than to the perceived public need to contain, control, resocialize, and reeducate its target population of young, African American males. While such initiatives are often well intentioned and can benefit participants if properly implemented (Hartmann 2012), they often play off of racialized stereotypes and have meant that the experience of programming for youth of color looks very different (being controlled rather than having fun or staying fit) from that of mainstream, middle-class youths' experiences in sport (Andrews et al. 2003; Lareau 2011). More generally, it is also worth noting that this strategy of using sport to regulate and control poor boys and young men of color appeals widely across the political spectrum partly because it allows mainstream America to say that it is doing something good for otherwise disadvantaged populations while skirting public discussion of more substantial, meaningful public investment in communities and schools, jobs, health care, and housing. This is just one of the more pronounced ironies of sport policy for youth in the context of curtailed and privatized social services of the neoliberal era described previously.

The Experience and Understanding of Young People and Their Parents

Often missing from the research on race and youth sport in the United States is an understanding of how (or to what extent) the deeply racialized structures of the youth sports world are understood and experienced by kids of color themselves and their parents. Are these folks aware of these inequities and disparities? Do they see barriers and obstacles? How do they see and experience the different ways they are treated? These are important questions because we know that kids of color (and their families) do not always have the same motivations and assumptions and experiences as their white counterparts. One example of such contrasts has to do with the issue of retention and dropouts. In 1992, Vern Seefeldt, Martha Ewing, and Stephan Walk found that the main reasons African American and Hispanic youth gave for dropping out of sports were "too much emphasis on winning," "needing more time for school," and "ineffective coaching." These stood in contrast to those of white youth, who were more likely to cite "no longer having fun" (see also Weiss and Ferrer-Caja 2002). Do these patterns still hold today? Are resources or access part of the problem for kids of color? What about differential treatment from coaches or league organizers? Has burnout or injury become a factor? And how do they compare or contrast with the reasons white youth give when they drop out?

These are important questions because we have found, in a series of preliminary interviews, evidence that parents from communities of color are actually quite interested in and aware of the racial composition and dynamics of the various activities, programs, leagues, and teams that their children participate in. An interview with a middle-class Black mother we call Valerie about frustrations with her fourteen-year-old son's participation in club soccer highlights this awareness. "In general, these are not my social group of folks. I wouldn't want to hang out with these people. . . . I don't want him to think that in order to be or have something that you have to be white or white like and so that's why I was like is it the wrong message [having him play for a travel soccer team]." Valerie's explanations for removing her boy from a predominately white and upper-middle-class travel soccer club demonstrate the quiet ways soccer clubs can exclude and the importance of racial composition for parents of color as they navigate youth sports with their children. They also suggest that parents of color may have different motivations for their kids' participation. They are interested in having their kids play sports not only because of the various developmental and health benefits that may accrue but also because they see sport as an arena for racial socialization—that is, for exposing their children to racial groups and situations they might not otherwise encounter in their regular, daily lives.

Sometimes these experiences are integrated and diverse, in other cases they may involve being in white-majority settings or, conversely, settings that are "majority-minority." For example, from an interview with a Black father from a middle-class background with five kids involved in various organized activities, it was clear that participation in various sports had visible racial dimensions. This dad, whom we call Rob, said that "race is always on my mind" when thinking about getting his kids involved in certain sports. Rob viewed sports like soccer and wrestling as more racially inclusive and diverse; in contrast, he saw baseball, softball, and hockey as essentially white games, and with regard to hockey he made it clear that he would allow his kids to join such activities only if they knew some of the kids or parents beforehand. For this father, fear of racial isolation for his kids in certain sports played a significant role in how he approached his children's participation in sports.

Parents of color appear to be very much aware of and attentive to these racial dynamics and see physical fitness and all manner of athletic activities as a unique space and opportunity to encounter and learn about the dynamics of racial identity and interaction in contemporary America. Rob's son's experience with wrestling highlights this possibility. When describing wrestling, Rob said, "You know, I thought wrestling was more of a white sport, but when my son started I was pleasantly surprised at how many kids of color were doing it." This racial diversity surprised Rob and challenged his own assumptions about certain sports. Such an experience speaks to the possibility and opportunity for more positive racial interactions and environments in different youth sporting environments.

Parental attentiveness to the racial dynamics of youth sports has implications for ethno-racial socialization as well. The notion of ethno-racial socialization focuses on the messages and strategies parents of color use to teach their children about their respective culture, prepare them for potential experiences with racism and prejudice, and promote healthy mistrust of out-groups (Hughes et al. 2006; Peters and Massey 1983; Suarez-Rozco 2001; Tatum 1987; Winkler 2012; see also Hughes 2003; Hughes and Chen 1999). In addition, there has been much attention given to how ethno-racial socialization relates to outcomes for children along dimensions of racial identity (Anglin and Whaley 2006; McHale et al. 2006), self-esteem (Constantine and Blackmon 2002; Goodstein and Ponterotto 1997), mental health (Scott 2003), and academic achievement and engagement (Grantham and Ford 2003; Smalls 2009). The key point here is that sport offers several ways for parents to socialize their children racially and ethnically.

First, athletic activities are significant places where children can develop ideas about race outside of families or the school, which ethno-racial socialization has claimed as the most critical agent in racial socialization (Boykin and Ellison 1995; Hughes 2003; McHale et al. 2006). Youth sports offer a window into how children, their peers, and their parents understand and learn about race, thus adding to a more comprehensive understanding of ethno-racial socialization and the racial dimensions of youth sports. Erin Winkler's (2012, 7) comprehensive racial learning framework is particularly useful for understanding how race and socialization intersect within youth sports. Comprehensive racial learning is a "process through which children negotiate, interpret, and make meaning of various and conflicting messages they receive about race, ultimately forming their own understandings of how race works in society and their lives." This framework pays attention to multiple influences (family, media, peers, teachers, activities), while recognizing the role of the child in developing ideas about race (Winkler 2012; see also Van Ausdale and Feagin 2001). Sport, simply put, is a rich site where multiple messages about race are transmitted, contested, and interpreted by parents and children alike.

Parents and other adults often make many assumptions about the attractiveness of youth sports and athletic participation for kids, and the larger benefits of these activities. But we should also not forget that kids and young people themselves may have their own unique interests and ideas about all of this. One example of this comes from the ethnographies of high school basketball conducted by Reuben May (2008) and Scott Brooks (2009), which help us see how sport can be a unique, subcultural site for collective identity and community building among young African American men. Another illustration comes from Hartmann's research with teenagers and young men of color involved with midnight basketball leagues. Hartmann (forthcoming) found that while these programs were often justified as "crime prevention" programs, participants in them did not see themselves as potentially unlawful or prone to crime as the program funders and supporters believed. Instead, these midnight basketball participants (admittedly at the high end of the age spectrum we are dealing with here) were looking for facilities and programs that offered them the opportunity to play basketball at a fairly organized, high-quality level in a city that had few such public programs available. In other words, these program participants simply wanted to have fun, stay fit, and socialize with their friends and teammates.

These various motives and desires are not all that different from the reasons that youth and young people from all racial groups and ethnic backgrounds want to play sports. They also serve as a hedge against the beliefs that kids of color are uniquely obsessed with or overinvested in sports. And yet we may know less about the attitudes and understandings of sport among kids of color than anyone else in the sports world. Losing sight of these realities—that is, failing to appreciate the most basic human needs and desires that draw young people to sports and physical activity—may be one of the most demoralizing and dehumanizing problems with our sport system, if not of sport studies itself.

CONCLUSION

In a society marked by persistent racial inequities and obstacles, sport can serve as a unique arena of enjoyment, socializing, and opportunity for youth and young people of color. However, these positive outcomes are not automatic, and sport itself is far from immune to the deleterious effects of race and racism. Indeed, our primary and most basic point is that if the benefits of youth sports are to be fully realized for children of color, we must attend to the racial realities and obstacles that constitute the American youth sporting landscape. That is, we must understand the barriers to access and equal opportunity that confront youth and young athletes of color; we must try to avoid treating kids of color in stigmatizing and dehumanizing ways; and we must try to take advantage of the opportunities that are available while counteracting the barriers and stigmas of race. The imperatives here involve both proper comprehension and intentional action.

And when it comes to acting and understanding, we must also not forget to take seriously the agency and subjectivity of kids of color and their parents. These folks, after all, are the ones whose lives and life worlds are most directly and decisively impacted by the structures of race in the athletic arena. As we've suggested, they might not always have the same views of the obstacles they face or be motivated by the same goals and objectives as program organizers, other parents, or idealistic social scientists. All of this is crucial if we are to continue to make good on the history and promise of sport as a positive, progressive racial force in contemporary social life.

NOTES

1. The odds of African American and Latino youth for participating in various sports were generated in comparison to their Anglo counterparts, controlling for family structure, parental education, place of residence, school performance, and age.

2. Similar patterns of unequal and uneven access and involvement in all manner of out-of-school-time activities and programs apply all across the country (Feldman and Matjasko 2007; Moore et al. 2014).

3. See "Future for U.S. Soccer" (https://www.youtube.com/watch?v=0706qsZT71c).

4. MLS and the US Men's National Team (USMNT) have traditionally relied on private club teams and universities as a talent pool to select from, but due to international competition and a burgeoning professional league, MLS and US Soccer have begun to adopt the top-down developmental approach of the international sporting world. In 2007, the US Soccer Federation (USSF) created official legislation that forces youth soccer players who play on MLS-operated youth clubs and other US Soccer Development Association (USSDA)–licensed academies to commit to a yearly ten-month soccer schedule with regional and national travel (Borden 2012). Youth players in development academies are not allowed to play for their high school, and the ten-month schedule is indicative of the commitment of players, families, and franchises (Bell 2012; Laroue 2012). USSF/USSDA officials consistently evaluate academy players and coaches based on a set of soccer development criteria that are supposed to engender a plethora of professionally talented US soccer players for MLS clubs and the USMNT. There are currently eighty USSF-sanctioned development academies across the United States; sixteen are directly associated with MLS franchises and are free for players. The nonaffiliated clubs are often still pay-to-play due to a lack of financial support.

REFERENCES

Andrews, David. 2006. *Sport–Commerce–Culture: Essays on Sport in Late Capitalist America.* New York: Peter Lang.

Andrews, David L., Robert Pitter, Detlev Zwick, and Darren Ambrose. 2003. "Soccer, Race, and Suburban Space." In *Sporting Dystopias: The Making and Meanings of Urban Sport Cultures,* edited by Ralph C. Wilcox, David L. Andrews, Robert Pitter, and Richard L. Irwin, 197–220. Albany: State University of New York Press.

Andrews, David L., Michael Silk, and Robert Pitter. 2008. "Physical Culture and the Polarized American Metropolis." In *Sport and Society: A Student Introduction,* 2nd ed., edited by Barrie Houlihan, 284–304. London: Sage.

Anglin, Deidre, and Arthur Whaley. 2006. "Racial/Ethnic Self-labeling in Relation to Group Socialization and Identity in African-Descended Individuals." *Journal of Language and Social Psychology* 25.4: 450–463.

Aspen Institute. 2015. "Sport for All. Play for Life." http://www.aspeninstitute.org/publications/sport-all-play-life-playbook-get-every-kid-game.

Bell, Arch. 2012. "Claudio Reyna's U.S. Soccer Vision." ESPN.com, April 16. http://espn.go.com/sports/soccer/story/_/id/7790903/us-soccer-claudio-reyna-vision-fixing-us-youth-soccer-arch-bell.

Borden, Sam. 2012. "High School Players Forced to Choose in Soccer's New Way." *New York Times,* March 3. http://www.nytimes.com/2012/03/04/sports/soccer/soccers-all-year-model-forces-high-school-players-to-choose.html?_r=1&hp.

Boykin, Wade, and Constance Ellison. 1995. "The Multiple Ecologies of Black Youth Socialization: An Afrographic Analysis." In *African-American Youth: Their Social and Economic Status in the United States,* edited by Ronald L. Taylor, 93–128. Westport, CT: Praeger.

Brooks, Scott N. 2009. *Black Men Can't Shoot.* Chicago: University of Chicago Press.

Brown, Randall, and William P. Evans. 2002. "Extracurricular Activity and Ethnicity: Creating Greater School Connection among Diverse Student Populations." *Urban Education* 37: 41–59.

Carrington, Ben. 2010. *Race, Sport, and Politics: The Sporting Black Diaspora.* London: Sage.

Carrington, Ben, and Ian McDonald. 2008. "The Politics of 'Race,' and Sports Policy in the United Kingdom." In *Sport and Society: A Student Introduction*, 2nd ed., edited by Barrie Houlihan, 230–254. London: Sage.

Carter, Prudence L., and Sean F. Reardon. 2014. "Inequality Matters." New York: William T. Grant Foundation.

Cavallo, Dominick. 1981. *Muscles and Morals: Organized Playgrounds and Urban Reform, 1880–1920.* Philadelphia: University of Pennsylvania Press.

Cole, Cheryl L. 1996. "American Jordan: P.L.A.Y., Consensus, and Punishment." *Sociology of Sport Journal* 13: 366–397.

Collins, Michael F. 2003. *Sports and Social Exclusion.* London: Routledge.

Constantine, Madonna G., and Sha'Kema Blackmon. 2002. "Black Adolescents' Racial Socialization Experiences: Their Relations to Home, School, and Peer Self-Esteem." *Journal of Black Studies* 32.3: 322–335.

Crompton, John L. 1998. "Forces Underlying the Emergence of Privatization in Parks and Recreation." *Journal of Park and Recreation Administration* 16.2: 88–101.

Crompton, John L., and B. McGregor. 1994. "Trends in the Financing and Staffing of Local Government Park and Recreation Services." *Journal of Park and Recreation Administration* 12.3: 19–37.

Darling, Nancy. 2005. "Participation in Extracurricular Activities and Adolescent Adjustment: Cross-Sectional and Longitudinal Findings." *Journal of Youth and Adolescence* 34.5: 493–505.

Davalos, Deana B., Ernest L. Chavez, and Robert J. Guardiola. 1999. "The Effects of Extracurricular Activity, Ethnic Identification, and Perception of School on Student Dropout Rates." *Hispanic Journal of Behavioral Sciences* 21.1: 61–77.

Edwards, Michael B., Jason N. Bocarro, Michael A. Kanters, and Jonathan M. Casper. 2011. "Participation in Interscholastic and Intramural Sport Programs in Middle Schools: An Exploration of Race and Gender." *Recreation Sports Journal* 35: 157–173.

Eitzen, D. Stanley, and George Harvey Sage. 1982. *Sociology of American Sport.* Dubuque, IA: Wm. C. Brown.

Ewing, Martha E., and Vern Seefeldt. 2002. "Patterns of Participation in American Agency-Sponsored Youth Sports." In *Children and Youth in Sport*, 2nd ed., edited by Frank L. Smoll and Ronald E. Smith, 39–56. Dubuque, IA: Kendall/Hunt.

Faircloth, Beverly S., and Jill V. Hamm. 2005. "Sense of Belonging among High School Students Representing Four Ethnic Groups." *Journal of Youth and Adolescence* 34.4: 293–309.

Feldman, Amy F., and Jennifer L. Matjasko. 2005. "The Role of School-Based Extracurricular Activities in Adolescent Development: A Comprehensive Review and Future Directions." *Review of Educational Research* 75.2: 159–210.

———. 2007. "Profiles and Portfolios of Adolescent School-Based Extracurricular Activity Participation." *Journal of Adolescence* 30: 313–332.

Frey, James, and D. Stanley Eitzen. 1991. "Sport and Society." *Annual Review of Sociology* 17: 503–522.

"Future for U.S. Soccer." 2010. YouTube video, June 27. https://www.youtube.com/watch?v=0706qsZT71c.

Goodstein, Renee, and Joseph Ponterotto. 1997. "Racial and Ethnic Identity: Their Relationship and Their Contribution to Self-Esteem." *Journal of Black Psychology* 23.3: 275–293.

Grantham, Tarek, and Donna Ford. 2003. "Beyond Self-Concept and Self-Esteem: Racial Identity and Gifted African American Students." *High School Journal* 87.1: 18–29.

Guest, Andrew M. 2013. "Cultures of Play during Middle Childhood: Interpretive Perspectives from Two Distinct Marginalized Communities." *Sport, Education, and Society* 18.2: 167–183.

Halpern, Robert. 2006. "Critical Issues in After School Programming." In *Monographs of the Herr Research Center for Children and Social Policy*, edited by Frances Stott, 1–141. Chicago: Erikson Institute.

Hartmann, Douglas. 2001. "Notes on Midnight Basketball and the Cultural Politics of Recreation, Race and At-Risk Urban Youth." *Journal of Sport and Social Issues* 25: 339–372.

———. 2012. "Rethinking Community-Based Crime Prevention through Sports." In *Sport for Development, Peace, and Social Justice*, edited by Robert Schinke and Stephanie J. Hanrahan, 73–88. Morgantown: West Virginia University Press/Fitness Information Technologies.

———. 2015. "Sport and Social Intervention." In *Sociology of Sport Handbook*, edited by Richard Guilianotti, 335–344. London: Routledge.

———. Forthcoming. *Midnight Basketball, Race, and Neoliberal Social Policy: The History and Significance of a Sporting Innovation.* Chicago: University of Chicago Press.

Hersh, Phillip. 1990. "Soccer in U.S. at Crossroads: World Cup Seen as Last Resort to Stir Fan Support." *Chicago Tribune*, June 3, C1.

Hughes, Diane. 2003. "Correlates of African American and Latino Parents' Messages to Children about Ethnicity and Race: A Comparative Study of Racial Socialization." *American Journal of Community Psychology* 31: 15–33.

Hughes, Diane, Meredith Bachman, Diane Ruble, and Andrew Fuligini. 2006. "Tuned In or Tuned Out: Children's Interpretations of Parents' Racial Socialization Messages." In *Child Psychology: A Handbook of Contemporary Issues*, edited by Lawrence Balter and Catherine S. Tamis-Lemonda, 591–610. Philadelphia: Psychology Press.

Hughes, Diane, and Lisa Chen. 1999. "The Nature of Parents' Race-Related Communications to Children: A Developmental Perspective." In *Child Psychology: A Handbook of Contemporary Issues*, edited by Lawrence Balter and Catherine S. Tamis-Lemonda, 467–490. Philadelphia: Psychology Press.

Kanters, Michael A., Jason N. Bocarro, Jonathan M. Casper, Michael B. Edwards, and Myron F. Floyd. 2013. "School Sport Participation under Two School Sport Policies: Comparisons by Race/Ethnicity, Gender, and Socioeconomic Status." *Annals of Behavioral Medicine* 45.1: 113–121.

Kelley, Bruce, and Cari Carchia. 2012. "Hey, Data Data—Swing! The Hidden Demographics of Youth Sport." Sport and Fitness Industry Association. http://espn.go.com/espn/story/_/id/9469252/hidden-demographics-youth-sports-espn-magazine.

Lapchick, Richard. 1999. "Crime and Athletes: The New Racial Stereotypes of the 1990s." Boston: Northeastern University, Center for Study Sport and Society. http://www.sportinsociety.org.

Lareau, Annette. 2011. *Unequal Childhoods: Class, Race, and Family Life.* Berkeley: University of California Press.

Laroue, Jimmy. 2012. "Richmond Kickers Make Developmental Academy Free for 2012–2013 Season." *Potomac Soccer Wire*, February 20. http://www.potomacsoccerwire.com/news/458/20694.

Manning, Alex. 2014. "Elite Organized Sports and Development: The Case of U.S. Soccer." Paper presented at the annual meeting of the North American Society for the Sociology of Sport, Portland, OR, November 7.

Margolis, Benjamin, and Jane Allyn Piliavin. 1999. "'Stacking' in Major League Baseball: A Multivariate Analysis." *Sociology of Sport Journal* 16: 16–34.

May, Reuben. 2008. *Living through the Hoop.* New York: New York University Press.

McHale, Susan, Ann Crouter, Ji-Yeon Kim, Linda Burton, Kelly Davis, Aryn Dotterer, and Dena Swanson. 2006. "Mothers' and Fathers' Racial Socialization in African American Families: Implications for Youth." *Child Development* 77.5: 1387–1402.

Messner, Michael. 2009. *It's All for the Kids: Gender, Families, and Youth Sports*. Berkeley: University of California Press.

Miller, Kathleen E., Merrill J. Melnick, Grace M. Barnes, Michael P. Farrell, and Don Sabo. 2005. "Untangling the Links among Athletic Involvement, Gender, Race, and Adolescent Academic Outcomes." *Sociology of Sport Journal* 22.2: 78–193.

Moore, Kristin, David Murphey, Tawana Bandy, and Mae Cooper. 2014. "Participation in Out-of-School Time Activities and Programs." Bethesda, MD: Child Trends. http://www.childtrends.org/wp-content/uploads/2014/03/2014–13OutofSchoolActivities1.pdf.

Peguero, Anthony, Ann Marie Popp, Zahra Shekarhkar, T. Lorraine Latimore, and Dixie J. Koo. 2013. "Punishing Racial and Ethnic Minority Student Athletes." *Justice Policy Journal* 10.2: 1–27.

Peters, Mary F., and Grace Massey. 1983. "Mundane Extreme Environmental Stress in Family Stress Theories: The Case of Black Families in White America." *Marriage and Family Review* 6: 193–218.

Physical Activity Council. 2013. "2012 Participation Report. Physical Activity Council Annual Study Tracking Sports, Fitness, and Recreation Participation in the USA." http://physicalactivitycouncil.com/PDFs/2012PacReport.pdf.

Pitter, Robert, and David L. Andrews. 1997. "Serving America's Underserved Youth: Reflections on Sport and Recreation in an Emerging Social Problems Industry." *Quest* 49: 85–99.

Sabo, Donald, and Philip Veliz. 2008. "Go Out and Play: Youth Sports in America." Meadow, NY: Women's Sports Foundation.

Sabo, Donald, Philip Veliz, and Lisa Rafalson. 2013. *More Than a Sport: Tennis, Education, and Health*. White Plains, NY: USTA Serves.

Sagas, Michael, and George Cunningham. 2014. "Sports Participation Rates among Underserved American Youth." Aspen Institute's Project Play: Reimagining Youth Sports in America. http://www.aspeninstitute.org/sites/default/files/content/docs/education/Project_Play_Underserved_Populations_Roundtable_Research_Brief.PDF.

Schultz, Lorina E., John L. Crompton, and Peter A. Witt. 1995. "A National Profile of the Status of Public Recreation Services for At-Risk Children and Youth." *Journal of Park and Recreation Administration* 13.3: 1–25.

Scott, Lionel D. 2003. "The Relation of Racial Identity and Racial Socialization to Coping with Discrimination among African Americans." *Journal of Black Studies* 33.1: 520–538.

Seefeldt, Vern, Martha Ewing, and Stephan Walk. 1992. "Overview of Youth Sports Programs in the United States." Washington, DC: Carnegie Council on Adolescent Development.

Show, Jon. 2009. "Basketball Still Tops in Youth Sport Participation." *Sports Business Daily*, August 17. http://www.sportsbusinessdaily.com/Journal/Issues/2009/08/20090817/SBJ-In-Depth/Basketball-Still-Tops-in-Youth-Participatio.aspx.

Smalls, Ciara. 2009. "African American Adolescent Engagement in the Classroom and Beyond: The Roles of Mother's Racial Socialization and Democratic-Involved Parenting." *Journal of Youth and Adolescence* 38: 204–213.

Smith, Earl, and Wilbert M. Leonard. 1997. "Twenty-Five Years of Stacking Research in Major League Baseball: An Attempt at Explaining This Reoccurring Phenomenon." *Sociological Focus* 30.4: 321–331.

Stick, Christina, and Madison Schaeffer. 2014. "The Native Strong Project Research Protocol. Healthy Kids, Healthy Futures Grant Program." Denver, CO: Notah Begay III Foundation.

Suarez-Orozco, Carola, and Marcelo Suarez-Orozco. 2001. *Transformations: Immigration, Family Life, and Achievement Motivation among Latino Adolescents*. Stanford, CA: Stanford University Press.

Tatum, Beverly. 1987. *Assimilation Blues: Black Families in a White Community*. Westport, CT: Greenwood.

Van Ausdale, Debra, and Joe R. Feagin. 2001. *The First R: How Children Learn Race and Racism*. Lanham, MD: Rowman & Littlefield.

Weiss, Maureen R., and Emilio Ferrer-Caja. 2002. "Motivational Orientations to Youth Sports." In *Advances in Sport Psychology*, 2nd ed., edited by T. Horn, 101–183. Champaign, IL: Human Kinetics.

Winkler, Erin. 2012. *Learning Race, Learning Place. Shaping Racial Identities and Ideas in African American Childhood*. New Brunswick, NJ: Rutgers University Press.

CHAPTER 3

Girls and the Racialization of Female Bodies in Sport Contexts

Cheryl Cooky and Lauren Rauscher

During the 2012 summer Olympic Games, the US women's gymnastics team, dubbed "The Fierce Five," captured America's hearts, as well as the social and news media spotlight, with their awe-inspiring performance and dramatic "comeback" as the first to win the team gold medal for the United States since 1996. One member of the team, sixteen-year-old Gabrielle (Gabby) Douglas, made history becoming the first American, the first African American woman, and the first woman of color to win both the team and individual all-around competitions (Singh 2013). Given her success, it is perhaps unsurprising that Gabby Douglas even "out-trended" Michael Phelps, the American gold-medal swimmer who held the title for most Olympic gold medals, on Twitter at one point during the Olympic Games (Jordan-Zachary 2013).

Another young teenager also captured the media spotlight during the 2012 summer Olympic Games. Missy Franklin, a member of the US women's swim team, became the first American woman to swim seven events, winning four gold medals and a bronze. She broke the world record in the 200-meter backstroke event, doing so just minutes after competing in another event. Those inside and outside the swimming community deemed her the "Next Big Thing" in swimming, a timely honor given the previous "Next Big Thing" in swimming, Michael Phelps, had announced his retirement at the end of the 2012 games. Franklin, seventeen years old at the time, was anointed "America's Sweetheart" and framed as such in both mainstream news media and on social media (Crouse 2014). Franklin also unofficially holds the world-record title for appearances in fans' "selfies" (Crouse 2014).

One might expect that Douglas's outstanding accomplishments would garner respectful news media coverage and accolades in social media as had Franklin's accomplishments. However, the dominant media frame for Gabby Douglas's groundbreaking Olympic achievements centered not on her history—and record-making performance—but instead on her appearance, specifically her hair. In the context of the white-dominated sport of gymnastics, the importance of appearance for judges is paramount, and standards of appropriate appearance reflect hegemonic white ideals of femininity and beauty. Many gymnastics teams opt for the same leotard, the same color hair ribbons, and the same hairstyle. For Black gymnasts, this requires the adoption of hairstyles that are most easily achieved by those with hair texture most common among their white teammates (e.g., straight, relatively smooth, and thin). The controversy surrounding Gabby Douglas centered on her inability to fully achieve the slicked-back, high ponytails of her white teammates (all of whom were teenagers). The mainstream media devoted a good deal of attention to a Twitter discussion (or feud, depending on the account) among Black women regarding Douglas's "unkempt" hair (see Singh 2013). According to these mainstream media accounts, some Black women tweeted about what they viewed as Douglas's inability to tame her unkempt hair, while other women rushed to her defense.

Racialized and politically contested hair controversies are quite common when considering the media coverage of Black female athletes, particularly when they occur within white-dominated sporting spaces or when Black female athletes are contrasted with or compared to white female athletes. For instance, five years prior to the controversy surrounding Gabby Douglas, Don Imus sparked media "frenetic inaction" (Wachs et al. 2012) when he referred to the 2007 NCAA championship runner-up Rutgers women's basketball team as "nappy-headed ho's." The racist slur and its aftermath garnered more attention, and in some news media outlets two to three times as much coverage, as the entire two weeks of the women's NCAA championship tournament (Cooky et al. 2010). Notably, Imus's commentary compared Rutgers to the "cute girls" from Tennessee, a comment that critics argue was a representative illustration of who could "'pass' as part of mainstream [white] culture" (Knapp 2007: B1, as cited in Cooky et al. 2010, 151). Nearly a decade prior to Imus's comments, Venus Williams's braided hair generated controversy during the 1999 Australian Open quarterfinals when the beads from her braids fell out during a match. Mainstream media referred to this incident as a "bad hair day" (Clarey 1999) and the event made it to an ESPN-generated "Top 10 Williams' sisters controversies" list in 2004.

As feminist sport studies scholars, these media events lead us to question how girls negotiate such representations in ways that shape the current racial disparities in girls' sport participation. We draw insights from feminist media studies and the sociology of childhood to address this concern. We then extend the literatures on media coverage of female athletes to critically interrogate the hegemonic representational strategies within mainstream media outlets that position white female athletic bodies as normative, desirable, and empowered despite the fact that this empowerment is often constructed through hypersexualized imagery. Using critical race theory and feminist intersectional frameworks, we turn our focus to discuss the two main ways in which racialization of female athletes occurs in cultural discourses: (1) when women of color are represented in the media, they are portrayed in ways consistent with controlling images used to marginalize women of color in a desegregated, "postracial" society; and (2) the ways in which female athletes are represented often rely upon and reproduce discursive whiteness, which silences, erases, and excludes female athletes of color while simultaneously upholding white privilege. We interrogate the following concerns: In what ways do the racialized controlling images amplify the structural barriers that girls of color, and in particular Black girls, encounter in their sport participation? Both images of white female athletes and images of female athletes of color are racialized; however, we suggest that the ways in which these images are racialized differs, and shapes girls' understandings of female athleticism in important ways. We conclude this chapter with a discussion of the implications of these representational strategies on the structural realities of girls sport participation and offer suggestions for future empirical work to explore these dynamics. In doing so, we hope to inspire research inquiry on how girls' reproductive and resistant agentic negotiations of mediated cultural discourses of female athleticism and cultural discourses of Black femininity/womanhood shape and inform racialized disparities in girls' sport participation.

RACIAL DISPARITIES IN GIRLS' SPORT PARTICIPATION

Title IX is credited with improving the contemporary landscape of girls' participation in the United States. Title IX (Title IX of the Education Amendments of 1972) states that "no person in the United States shall, on the basis of sex, be excluded from participation in, be denied the benefits of, or be subjected to discrimination under any educational program or activity receiving Federal financial assistance" (Title IX, 20 USC §1681 *et seq.*). Since Title IX's passage, high school girls' interscholastic sports participation has increased from 294,015 in 1971–1972 to over 3.2 million in 2012–2013 (National Federation of High School Associations 2012–2013).

Despite conventional wisdom that Title IX has successfully leveled the playing field for girls in sport, along with the empirical data showing that girls' participation in sport has reached record numbers, a gender gap in youth sport persists (Hanson 2005; Sabo and Veliz 2008, 2011). Using a nationally representative sample of high school students and a variety sport participation measures, Sandra L. Hanson (2005) finds that girls are less likely than boys to participate in sport across racial/ethnic groups, including Blacks, Latinas, and Asian Americans (for a review, see Hanson 2005). A recent national study conducted by the Women's Sports Foundation found that the percentage of sport opportunities for high school boys was 26 percent higher than that for girls, and this gap is echoed in specific community-level analyses: boys living in urban, suburban, town, and rural areas received a larger proportion of athletic opportunities than did girls in those communities (Sabo and Veliz 2011). The lowest percentage of opportunities existed in urban schools for both boys and girls, but the availability of athletic opportunities was lowest for urban girls (25 percent compared to 35 percent for urban boys) (Sabo and Veliz 2011). When broadening the definition of sport participation to include a variety of measures of organized sports activity or physical education in school (not solely high school sport), researchers found that girls from urban and rural communities were less involved than their male peers (Sabo and Veliz 2008). The findings led the authors to describe urban girls as the "have-nots" in sports and physical education.

Furthermore, important race- and class-based disparities exist among girls with respect to opportunity and participation in sport and physical activity (LaVoi and Thul forthcoming). Latinas and Black girls (Hanson 2005; Kimm et al. 2002; Taylor et al. 2000), immigrant girls (Thul and LaVoi 2011), girls from low-income families and communities (Sabo and Veliz 2011), and girls who reside in urban areas are significantly less likely to participate in organized youth sport and physical activity than their white, middle-class, and suburban counterparts (Sabo and Veliz 2008; Sabo et al. 2004). However, Asian American girls—especially those in higher socioeconomic status (SES) families, who attend private schools, and who live in rural areas—mirror white girls' sport participation rates, exceeding the rates of both Black and Hispanic girls (Hanson 2005), demonstrating that race and class intersect in shaping participation.

Individual, structural, and cultural-level factors collectively contribute to the disparities among girls' sport and physical activity participation (Cooky 2009; LaVoi and Thul forthcoming; Messner 2002; Tucker Center for Research on Girls & Women in Sport 2007). At the individual level, research documents that social support from family, coaches, peers, and physical education teachers; value, interest, and enjoyment of physical activity; self-esteem; and girls' perceptions of their physical competencies influence the likelihood of girls' sport participation (Tucker Center 2007). Several studies suggest that these factors are key to understanding the racial disparities in girls' sport involvement (LaVoi and Thul forthcoming). In another study, Asian Pacific girls from high socioeconomic backgrounds reported higher levels of positive feelings about sport and athletic activities than their middle and low-income counterparts (Erkut et al. 1996). East African immigrant girls reported that they enjoyed culturally relevant activities, such as swimming in girl-only spaces and dance, over more conventional and available competitive sports, such as soccer and basketball (Thul and LaVoi 2011). Mira Grieser et al. (2008) found that both Black and Hispanic girls reported less enjoyment in physical activity and that they perceived less support from teachers, boys, and families compared to white girls. Given the support for girls and women's sports in Black communities historically (Cahn 1994; Messner 2002), these findings may be surprising; however, this shift may be the result of the racial integration of schools wherein physical activity contexts are organized along white, normative values, which inadvertently lead to exclusions among marginalized groups (Azzarito 2005).

On a structural level, girls' sport participation is shaped by access to opportunity and distribution of resources, including cost, transportation, and safety (LaVoi and Thul, forthcoming; Sabo and Veliz 2008; Staurowsky et al. 2009). Given the patterns of residential segregation in the United States (Massey and Denton 1998), these factors contribute to lower physical activity levels among girls in low-income families, many of whom are girls of color, particularly for those who live in high-density urban areas and neighborhoods lacking in community safety. More specifically, as the rate of neighborhood poverty, population density, and underemployment/unemployment increase, the availability of safe public parks within walking distance of one's home decreases considerably (Babey, Hastert, and Brown 2007). Amy V. Reis and colleagues (2008) found that the physical environment of recreation centers impacts physical activity rates for African American youth, in terms of proximity, hours of operation, level of maintenance, as well as contributing to family concerns regarding the safety of their girls and the risk of sexual assault. Last, some low-income recent immigrant families rely upon their daughters to contribute to the household in meaningful ways through employment or significant domestic and child care responsibilities (Jamieson et al. 2005; Thul and LaVoi 2011), which creates barriers for Latina girls to participate in school-sponsored organized sports or after-school physical activity programming.

Cultural factors, such as gender stereotypes about femininity; gender-based expectations from parents, coaches, and teachers; and other cultural and religious norms, also shape the extent to which girls participate in sport and physical activity (LaVoi and Thul forthcoming; Tucker Center 2007). For instance, Taylor et al. (2000) found that Latinas and Black girls worried about sweating during physical education classes because it would affect their hair and makeup. East African immigrant girls value modesty and privacy, and covering their bodies according to cultural and religious tradition makes it prohibitive to participate in some sports (Thul and LaVoi 2011).

In the following section, we extend the discussion on cultural factors that shape girls' sport involvement by focusing on racialized cultural representations of female athletes. These representations and how girls interpret and make meaning of them illustrate another important dimension for understanding the ways in which individual, structural, and cultural factors collectively and simultaneously operate to impact the racial disparities in girls' sport participation.

"If You Can't See It, You Can't Be It":
Media Images and Girls' Sport Participation

The politically charged media accounts surrounding Black female athletes' hair that we described at the outset of this chapter raise the following questions: How do girls understand and make sense of representations of female athletes? In what ways does race shape the way girls negotiate media images and discourses? How do girls reproduce, negotiate, and challenge these cultural representations? To what extent do girls' interpretations of racialized media representations of female athletes help us more fully understand racial disparities in girls' sport participation? In this section, drawing from the extant literature, we offer theoretical linkages between cultural representations and empirical trends in youth sport and physical activity that illustrate the complex dynamics between girls' athletic desires/aspirations, the levels of social support they receive from significant others, structural opportunities afforded to them, and the larger cultural context of gender and sport.

Media discourses shape and impact how girls and women see themselves and their position in broader societal gender relations (Driscoll 2002; McRobbie 1991). The social media campaign, originating from the documentary film *Miss Representation*, "If you can't see it, you can't be it," addresses the lack of positive media representations of women and female role models for young girls, and situates these concerns within the broader context of a lack of women in leadership and decision-making positions in politics, business, and other institutions, such as sports. While the documentary film draws upon a diverse set of statistics and trends to make an advocacy-driven argument regarding the role of the media in perpetuating institutional sexism, we assert that the dearth of respectful representations of girls and women in the media, and in particular sports media, is problematic on many levels but raises particular concerns for the lives of girls. Adolescence is commonly understood as a time wherein cultural proscriptions of emphasized femininity become magnified. It is also a time when girls drop out of organized sports (Tucker Center 2007). To what extent do media framings, images, and representations contribute to, or shape, these trends?

While the importance of positive images of women in sport to provide role models for young girls has been documented in the literature (Adriaanse and Crosswhite 2008; Harrison and Frederickson 2003; Krane et al. 2011), the silence, trivialization, sexualization, and racialization of female athletes and women's sports are pervasive. Through social and cultural experiences of sexual objectification, girls and women are encouraged to treat themselves as objects to be gazed at, or to engage in what researchers refer to as self-objectification (Harrison and Frederickson 2003). In the context of sport, Elizabeth Daniels (2009) argues that sexualized images of female athletes enable girls' self-objectification. When shown sexualized images of female athletes, teenage girls and young college women were more likely to describe themselves in terms of their physical appearance when compared to girls and women who were shown images of female athletes performing a sport. Conversely, girls and women shown images of female athletes playing a sport were more likely to use self-descriptions that focused on their physical abilities (Daniels 2009). This research is important for demonstrating that *how* female athletes are portrayed matters to girls' embodied self-perceptions.

At the same time, third-wave feminist sports studies scholars have critiqued the second-wave feminist objectification thesis, arguing that the "image of the female athlete can function in positive ways," serving as a source of empowerment for girls and young women by challenging the conventional gender binary that situates femininity and athleticism in oppositional ways (Heywood and Dworkin 2003, 5). Empirical research offers support for this claim: Johanna A. Adriaanse and Janice J. Crosswhite (2008) found that girls were more likely to adopt sport role models when the athlete exhibited "feminine" qualities such as being kind, modest, caring, and fair. Yet, for other feminist scholars, women's sports organizations, and girl advocacy groups, representational strategies that focus on female athletes' sexuality and sexual appeal are problematic, especially as they contradict how girls and female athletes wish to be represented (Kane, LaVoi, and Fink 2013; Krane et al. 2011) and often do not appeal to sports fans and nonfans alike (Kane and Maxwell 2011).

Vikki Krane and colleagues conducted focus groups with preadolescent, white middle-class athletes on what types of images of female athletes they preferred and why. While the girls differed as to which images they preferred, the reasons for liking or disliking an image were similar. Girls liked images of female athletes that illustrated "authenticity," in other words athletes were featured in uniform, in the context of their sport, and were ready or intent to play, or conveyed a passion for their sport. Girls disliked images where girls were outside the context, not in legitimate athletic poses, or images where athletes were perceived to be a "poor sport." Krane et al. (2011) interpreted the girls' negotiations as illustrating the value system of white, middle-class girls; female athletes should not show off or be arrogant about their abilities. The white girls of Krane et al.'s study exhibited what Darnell Hunt (1997, 403) has termed "raced ways of seeing." Krane et al. (2011, 765) found that the girl participants described a Black track and field athlete as "depressed, mad, sad, and having a bad day whereas a similarly posed white track and field athlete was described as determined, concentrated, and focused." The researchers called for future research that explores how whiteness frames girls' sport experiences and perceptions.

Drawing from Hunt's conceptualization of "raced ways of seeing," which refers to the ways in which race informs how individuals both see and come to understand social reality as well act upon that reality, we add that researchers should consider how raced ways of seeing, and the racialized social contexts in which images and meanings are struggled for and against, inform how girls make meaning of the hegemonic media images of female athletes. There are a few studies that offer insights into these concerns. In *Built to Win*, Leslie Heywood and Shari L. Dworkin's (2003) groundbreaking work on third-wave feminism in sport, the authors conducted focus groups with boys and girls to explore how they negotiated the seemingly empowering iconic imagery of female athletes. The authors found that when shown an image of Marion Jones, young participants simultaneously ascribed both empowering and disempowering qualities to Jones. The comments were infused with critiques of Jones's body as too tall, too powerful, and ugly, and despite the feminine codes in the image (Jones was featured in a formal evening gown wearing makeup), some students remarked she was "ugly" and "frightening" yet other students thought she was "glamorous" and "strong and pretty" (Heywood and Dworkin 2003, 154). Heywood and Dworkin argued that how boys and girls negotiated images of female athletes was shaped by their social locations, as well as the social locations occupied by the female athlete. These findings demonstrate the need for research that goes beyond media effects studies, which often assume a deterministic socialization model whereby girls (and boys) internalize media messages. Instead, contemporary theories of interpretive reproduction recognize that kids are active media consumers (and producers) and call for ethnographic research that can uncover how children negotiate images and make meaning of media content (Cosaro 2010).

Ethnographic feminist media studies research demonstrates that audiences/viewers/consumers, including girls, actively engage with cultural meanings and representations (Currie 1999; Driscoll 2002; McRobbie 1991). When considering the sociocultural context in which media consumption takes place, engaging the media is both a collective and an individual act (Milestone and Meyer 2011). In other words, young girls (and audiences in general) make meaning of media texts through social interactions situated in specific social contexts, both of which must be taken into consideration when examining how girls negotiate and actively construct meanings (Milestone and Meyer 2011; Pugh 2009). Moreover, media texts shape our racialized, gendered, and classed identities as we negotiate the meanings of a text with our own experiences and interpersonal relationships (Milestone and Meyer 2011). Our social locations also shape the ways in which we as viewers negotiate meanings embedded in media texts (Hunt 1997; Hunt and James 2008), and as such negotiations are fluid, contextual, and contested (Gannon, Byers, and Gonick 2014).

Researchers in sports studies have recently begun examining images of female athletes using audience reception theories and methodologies (Fissette and Walton 2014; Kane, LaVoi, and Fink 2013; Krane et al. 2011). This research, often employing focus group methodologies, demonstrates the reproductive and resistant agency of young girls and college-aged female athletes to negotiate and challenge the hegemonic cultural representations of female athleticism, as discussed earlier. These studies are important in addressing how media images shape and impact the lives of girls and offer insights on how girls negotiate cultural representations of female athleticism. In another study, when adolescent girls were asked to rate images of models on their "attractiveness" (which could include both internal and external indicators), the athletic models received the lowest attractiveness scores across all groups in the sample (Bissell and Hays 2010), although girl athletes were more favorable in their assessments of athletic models than girls who did not play sport, and Black girls had more favorable assessments of the athletic models than white girls (Bissell and Hays 2010). Given that young girls engage media in ways that shape the construction of their identities, and for our purposes, their identities as female athletes, we turn our attention in the following section to examining the hegemonic cultural representations of female athletes in the media.

Cultural Representation of Female Athletes: Silence, Trivialization, and Sexualization

Extensive research documents the ways in which women's sport and female athletes are silenced, trivialized, and sexualized in mainstream media. Silence refers to the ways in which the media ignore or do not cover women's sports in their programming and broadcasts or silence the perspectives of women/female athletes within their sports broadcasts. One of the consistent findings in the literature on gender and the media is the silencing of female athletes, specifically the lack of respectful, serious coverage of women's sport. This trend emerges in a variety of media platforms including print and televised news media (Adams and Tuggle 2004; Cooky, Messner, and Hextrum 2013; Eastman and Billings 2000; Kian, Vincent, and Modello 2008; Lumpkin 2009; Pratt et al. 2008). For example, in longitudinal research on the televised news media coverage of sport, the time networks spent covering women's sport declined over the twenty-year period and was at its lowest ever—2 percent (Cooky, Messner, and Hextrum 2013). Although some research demonstrates a shift toward more respectful representation of women's sports (Kane and Buysse 2005; McKay and Dalliere 2009), these patterns are typically observed in smaller media markets or in niche markets.

Trivialization refers to media images or frames wherein the accomplishments, achievement, physicality, prowess, and competitive ethos of female athletes are downplayed, for example, by using female athletes as the target of humor, featuring athletes in ambivalent ways, or focusing on their fashion sensibilities. One way the media trivialize women's sports and female athletes is by focusing more prominently on what female athletes do, or who female athletes are, off the court.

Media portrayals of female athletes as wives, mothers, or girlfriends of famous male athletes or celebrities or fashion models may seem to be a "positive" representation. However, given the persistent homophobia in women's sport and the overall lack of coverage of women in competitive events, this representation serves to downplay women's strength, athleticism, and physicality by positioning female athletes in conventional feminine roles, reassuring audiences that these are heterosexual "real" women, not "mannish lesbians" (Cahn 1994).

Sexualization of female athletes refers to imagery that features female athletes' bodies as objects of sexual pleasure and has been examined thoroughly in the literature (Daniels and LaVoi 2012). This research demonstrates how female athletes often are featured in hypersexualized and objectified ways. Female athletes regularly appearing in *Sports Illustrated*'s annual swimsuit issue as bikini models constitutes a contemporary example of trend. The swimsuit issue is the primary way female athletes receive coverage in the magazine, as research demonstrates coverage on women's sports rarely appears in the actual sports content pages (Bishop 2003; Lumpkin 2009). Researchers find that female athletes' sexuality rather than their athleticism is emphasized in the swimsuit issue, suggesting that female athletes' marketability lies in their sexuality, not in their athleticism (Kim, Sagas, and Walker 2010).

While we can point to several contemporary high-profile girl athletes who have captured the attention of mainstream and social media (Mo'ne Davis, Sam Gordon, as well as Missy Franklin and Gabby Douglas), often "the girl athlete as cultural icon" garners significant media attention during Olympic years (as with Franklin and Douglas) or when a girl athlete is exceptional or extraordinary (as was the case with Davis and Gordon). Although there is little media attention devoted specifically to girls' sport participation (media silencing of girls' sport), both Davis and Gordon entered the media spotlight as girl athletes competing in and delivering dominating performances all-male teams/leagues, Little League baseball and football, respectively. Some feminist sport studies scholars argue that had these girls participated in an all-girls baseball league or an all-girls football league, they likely would not have received the same media attention and achieved popular culture significance (Mary Jo Kane, email to the first author, 2014). Mo'ne Davis, thirteen at the time, was the first Little League player to grace the cover of *Sports Illustrated* and, given our discussion, is one of only a handful of female athletes to grace the magazine's cover not wearing a swimsuit. At nine years old, Sam Gordon made history becoming the first female football player to appear on a Wheaties cereal box. Gordon also made an appearance on the television program *NFL GameDay Morning*, a program dominated by men, in both content and delivery. Despite these girl icons, it is rare that girl athletes occupy meaningful spaces in the culture, and in particular sports media, which speaks to girls' marginalization in sports contexts. As such, existing scholarship on race and gender in media images of female athletes tends to focus on young women or adult female athletes, and examines media images from a Black/white binary. Therefore, our discussion will be limited by the extant literature.

In the following section, we examine the racialized processes of sexualization of female athletes in the media. We focus on what cultural discourses circulate in and through the media and popular culture that girls may be engaging, negotiating, and resisting as they make meanings of their own sport participation experiences, and as they come to understand themselves as female athletes.

The Good, the Bad, and the Controlling: Racialized Images of Female Athletes

Despite the extensive body of literature on gender, sport and the media, there is a relatively small number of scholars who examine the racialization of female athletic bodies and interrogate how racialized meanings shape the ways we see and think about female athletes in our culture, especially how these meanings are constitutive of and constituted by whiteness (Douglas 2005, 2012; McDonald 2000; McDonald and Cooky 2013; Meân 2013; Schultz 2005). While silence, ambivalence, and sexualization are trends in the way female athletes are represented in the media, how these manifest—and the meanings they convey— differ for white female athletes and female athletes of color.

As discussed earlier, silence is the most common form of media representation for female athletes. Yet, when female athletes are featured in media, differing images and messages are constructed that are racialized. In contrast with the cultural imagery of white female athletes, which relies upon and reproduces the "good white girl construct" (McDonald 2009) and the ideal of "true womanhood" wherein white female athletes are represented as good wives, mothers, and citizens (Banet-Weiser 1999; McDonald 2000, 2009), the cultural imagery of Black female athletes relies upon and reproduces "controlling images," of Black women such as the Jezebel and the Black Lady, which describe images employed to subjugate women of color and to justify their oppression (Collins 2009; Douglas 2012). Patricia Hill Collins (1998, 32) argues that contemporary images of Black women are part of the "new politics of containment" designed to control Black women in the current context of desegregated, color-blind racism.

In the context of sport, the media discursively position female athletes of color, primarily Black female athletes, in a variety of contradictory and overlapping ways that are fluid and contested. Black female athletes exist in a precarious position, always at risk of becoming a "fallen hero" with the slightest indiscretion, such as wearing a provocative tennis outfit or not having "fixed" hair. Cultural images and discourses that portray Black female athletes as "respectable," "young ladies of class" (Cooky et al. 2010, 153), a "racially neutralized American goddess" (Meân 2013, 79), or as sexually attractive to men (Collins 2005) exist alongside portrayals Black female athletes as "bad girls" (McDonald and Cooky,

2013, 199), "nappy-headed ho's" (Cooky et al. 2010, 140), "sexually grotesque" (McKay and Johnson 2008, 500), "animalistic" (Schultz 2005), or "too muscular" (Cooky, Dycus, and Dworkin 2013).

The sexualization of Black female athletes takes two forms, the first of which portrays women athletes as sexual objects attractive to men, which functions to assert and affirm their presumed heterosexuality and to deflect the threat of lesbianism (Collins 2005; McDonald 2000). Early media framings of Women's National Basketball Association (WNBA) players (Banet-Weiser 1999; McDonald and Cooky 2013) and Olympic track star Marion Jones (Meân 2013) illustrate this pattern. These particular athletes have been celebrated as heroes, superstar athletes, morally superior, respectable, engaged in the community, and role models for girls (Banet-Weiser 1999; Meân 2013). Their marital and motherhood status, conformity to white, middle-class normative standards of beauty, and off-the-court roles as fashion models or "fashionistas" are emphasized (Banet-Weiser 1999; Meân 2013). These discursive strategies situate Black female athletes within normative discourses of gender, race, and sexuality, thereby reassuring audiences and fans of their "good girl" status (particularly in contrast to "bad boy" NBA players) and enhancing their marketability and accessibility to the predominantly white sport audiences, consumers, and fans (Banet-Weiser 1999).

These representations not only uphold heteronormativity, but also mirror the Black Lady controlling image (Collins 1998, 2005), whereby Black women's race is minimized or erased. According to Collins, the "Black Lady" is free from the constraints of racism; she effortlessly combines marriage, motherhood, and a successful career all while embodying traditionally white, middle-class standards of beauty and comportment (Collins 1998; see also Banet-Weiser 1999). Notably, respectability is central to the "Black Lady" controlling image (Collins 1998). Black women must be respectable "ladies" in order to achieve middle-class status and to avoid the representations of promiscuity, hypersexuality, and bitchiness (e.g., Jezebel) that often subjugate poor and working-class Black women (Collins 2005). For example, in response to Don Imus's comment about the Rutgers University women's basketball team as "nappy-headed ho's," the team's coach, journalists, and the governor of New Jersey defended the players and repeatedly described them as "young ladies of class" (Cooky et al., 2010, 151), thus evoking the Black Lady controlling image.

Yet, the Black Lady controlling image, while on the surface a "positive" representation, is elusive and fleeting for Black female athletes. For instance, prior to the 2000 Summer Olympic Games, American track and field gold medal Olympian Marion Jones was framed in media narratives in ways typical for white female athletes. Her race was largely erased as she was positioned as the "superstar next door" and "Jones's exceptional ability was juxtaposed by everyday references to her everyday, ordinary (mainly white) femininity" (Meân 2013, 79). Yet, once she was found guilty of using performance-enhancing drugs, the media framed her as a "seductress, liar, and cheat" (Meân 2013, 82), whereby she thus became repositioned within racialized discourses of deviant, criminal Black womanhood.

The second strategy that sexualizes Black female athletes is one that demonizes Black female athletes as sexually deviant, transgressing normative (i.e., white) standards of femininity. Imus's racist remarks regarding the Rutgers team emerged from a larger cultural context whereby Black women are deemed immoral, uncivilized, and sexually deviant (Collins 1998, 2005, 2009). The derogatory remark, "nappy-headed ho's," illustrates the interconnected imagery of Black women as sexually deviant with undisciplined bodies who exist outside of normative femininity (Cooky et al. 2010). This representation is consistent with the Jezebel controlling image used to portray poor and working-class Black women as deviant, hypersexual, and "freaky" (Collins 2005). In their study of media representations of tennis superstars Serena and Venus Williams, James McKay and Helen Johnson (2008, 500) argue that the Williams sisters were subjected to such imagery and discursive strategies that situate Black women's bodies as less desirable, downright ugly, and sexually grotesque. The hypersexualization of the Williams sisters as "exotic/erotic yet deviant and repulsive, athletic yet animalistic and primitive, unfeminine yet hyperfeminine, muscular yet threateningly hyper-muscular" pathologizes Black women's bodies and reinscribes the stellar athletic accomplishments within a narrative framework that resonates a racist, colonialist past (McKay and Johnson 2008, 500). Specifically, the media representations of the Williams sisters have historical roots in the nineteenth century, when Scottish doctors put Sartjee "Sarah" Baartman on display as the "Hottentot Venus," making a spectacle of her body, specifically her genitalia (McKay and Johnson 2008).

The ways cultural images of white female athletes are positioned and understood, however, often attribute empowerment—not deviance—to the sexualized imagery of white female athletes (Cooky 2010). Journalist Ariel Levy (2006), in her discussion of "raunch culture," critically interrogates the "pornification" of popular culture and raises important questions regarding the cultural discourses that link commercialized hypersexuality with (sexual) empowerment for women. Yet, many professional white female athletes, such as Alex Morgan, Amanda Beard, and Danica Patrick, will anecdotally assert that appearing in "lad" magazines, like FHM (For Him Magazine), Maxim, Playboy, or Sports Illustrated's "Swimsuit Issue," in sexually suggestive or provocative poses, is empowering as they are able to counter stereotypical notions of female athletes (presumably the "mannish lesbian" stereotype) and conventional ideas of femininity (Branded 2013; Media Coverage & Female Athletes 2013). These images challenge the traditional perception of female athletes and allow female athletes to demonstrate they can be physically strong and powerful while also remaining heterosexually attractive and feminine.

Sexualized imagery however, has a problematic history for women of color, in particular for Black women, whose sexuality has been controlled by white men culturally, structurally, and interpersonally (Collins 2009). And while white women's sexuality has also been controlled by white men, white women's racial and class privilege affords them a degree of "agency" to embrace their sexuality (both culturally and structurally) in ways that might be problematic for girls and women of color, given the dynamics of institutional and interpersonal racism. Often the empowerment potential embedded in the contemporary sexualized imagery of female athletes is a potential that is more readily realized by girls and women who occupy various privileged social locations (race, class, and sexuality) within the matrix of domination.

It is not our intent to position sexuality/sexualization as necessarily "bad," or to engage in moral debates regarding media imagery or the choices women make to coproduce or consume sexualized media images. Rather, we wish to contextualize the discussion within the larger structural context in which cultural imagery is produced, read, and negotiated. Given the ways in which the sports that occupy the "center" of our culture are masculine-identified, male-dominated, and male-controlled, along with the dearth of images of female athletes, and especially of female athletes as athletically competent, we must consider sexualized imagery within this broader context of sport, and the gender and race relations that reside within (Messner 2002).

We must also consider the culture of sexualization and how arguments regarding the empowering potential of sexualized imagery of female athletic bodies in particular, and of women's bodies in general, often ignore sexism, racism, homophobia, and other axes of oppression (Gill 2012), particularly as they shape the lived realities of girls and women of color, whose bodies have historically been understood to be sexually deviant, lascivious, and dangerous (Collins 2009; Dagbovie-Mullins 2013). In her essay on the sexualization of culture debate, Rosalind Gill (2012, 737) cogently argues, "Despite the language of empowerment, discussion of power seems curiously absent." Extending Gill's argument to the images of female athletes, we argue considerations of power (cultural, structural, and interpersonal), and how power is always infused in not only how images are produced but also how they are read, must be at the center of any discussion of the meanings and implications of sexualization for female athletes. As Gill (2012, 741) explains, "sexualization does not operate outside of processes of gendering, racialization and classing, and works within a visual economy that remains profoundly ageist, (dis)ablest and heteronormative."

Much of the extensive literature on the media coverage of female athlete lacks a connection to critical whiteness studies and a feminist intersectional analysis. Drawing upon critical whiteness studies would enable feminist scholars to interrogate how images of white female athletes are racialized and often rely upon the reproduction of whiteness and white privilege, rather than situating considerations of racialized imagery primarily, if not entirely, within discussions of female athletes of color. Without placing a critical examination of whiteness on how the media and cultural outlets represent female athletes, whiteness retains its power by remaining unmarked and normative (Frankenberg 1993; McIntosh 1988). White privilege itself gets unknowingly reproduced in much of the scholarship on gender and the media, as whiteness is central to the representational strategies employed by corporations and media outlets that profit and benefit directly from these strategies (Kusz 2007).

A few recent studies that examine media portrayals of male athletes from a whiteness studies approach provide insights as to what we might find when analyzing the representation of female athletes. Kelly Poniatowski and Erin Whiteside (2012, 7) found that coverage of the predominantly white Canadian National Hockey team at the 2006 Winter Olympics portrayed the players as "prime examples of not only how to look, but how to act" given their embodiment of heroic masculinity, exceptional physicality, intellect, and moral righteousness on and off the ice. Similarly, Michael Butterworth (2007, 235) found that media coverage positioned Mark McGuire as the "pre-determined front runner" in the 1998 home run race against Sammy Sosa, never mentioning his white racial identity. Sosa, in contrast, was described in terms of his ethnic heritage as Dominican, and the media drew from racial stereotypes about men of color and immigrants, positioning him as a "sidekick" (236) and "intruder" (235) in the 1998 home run race.

White male athletes more readily occupy "heroic" status as a result of their whiteness (Butterworth 2007), and we speculate that similar cultural dynamics are at play for white female athletes. While the mythology of the "hero" has been linked historically with masculinity, we argue that white female athletes occupy a similar, albeit gendered feminine status as "cultural icons" (Heywood and Dworkin 2003) that are upheld as model citizens and role models. This is particularly illustrative in the ways in which Olympic female athletes like Missy Franklin become framed as "America's Sweetheart." Moreover, despite the hypersexualized imagery of Danica Patrick, Amanda Beard, and Maria Sharapova, these white female athletes achieve their status as "icons" by successfully balancing emphasized femininity and heteronormativity with whiteness and athleticism.

Summary and Conclusions

Gabby Douglas, alongside other girls of color who must negotiate consistent bodily surveillance, serves as a reminder of the persisting forms of inequality in girls' and women's sports, and the ways in which whiteness shapes and informs their participation. In this chapter we have demonstrated how controlling images marginalize women of color, and in particular Black female athletes. We discussed how discursive whiteness silences, erases, and excludes female athletes of color while maintaining white privilege in sport. Culturally, white female athletes are racially "unmarked" and discursively positioned as "normative." Unfortunately, the current scholarship on gender and the media too often ignores the ways in which representations of *all* female athletes, including white female athletes, are racialized. As Jamie Schultz (2005) argued, the blackness of the Williams sisters is constructed against whiteness. As such, scholars must centrally interrogate cultural imagery, representations, and meanings as constituted in and through whiteness, for both female athletes of color and white female athletes. Our goal was to examine racialized media representations of female athletes to illustrate the symbolic order and the way these types of images legitimize or potentially disrupt the racialized gender order and hegemonic representations of what girls are supposed to be.

We echo Michael Messner and Michela Musto's (2014) critique of the current scholarship on children/youth and sport, as well as their recommendations for future research. Our arguments and analysis are informed by the larger questions posed by Messner and Musto (2014, 112) including, "under what conditions does consumption of sports reinforce or even amplify actual participation in sports?" In this chapter we focused on racialized barriers to girls' sport participation as we drew attention to the young girls who do not play, given the disparities that currently exist in youth sport. So much attention has been given in the literature to the individual, interpersonal, and structural barriers girls encounter in sports contexts. And researchers have extensively examined cultural representations of female athletes. We explored how cultural representations of female athletes are racialized in ways that may contribute to and amplify disparities in girls' sport participation, and in particular the prevalence of controlling images in the media framings of Black female athletes.

Contemporary popular culture narratives regarding the types of empowerment girls and young women experience, as reflected in the sexualized imagery, and for our interests, the hypersexualized imagery of female athletes, may be a source of empowerment for young girls who occupy positions of privilege within the matrix of domination (Collins 2009) and may serve to enable their sport participation by creating spaces wherein female athleticism can exist alongside heteronormative femininity, rather than in opposition. We assert that a discussion of the potential empowerment contained in sexualized images of female athletes must be accompanied by considerations of how these images are gendered, raced, and classed as well as the broader power dynamics that shape the ways in which these images are produced, circulated, and consumed.

As such, here we return to Messner and Musto's (2014) argument that research conducted on kids who don't play sports should not focus solely on access and attrition. While this chapter has been concerned with cultural barriers to girls' sport participation, we do not endorse an uncritical embracing of sport participation. Indeed, our other research has illustrated the importance of not simply increasing participation rates, but ensuring girls have access to meaningful sporting opportunities that enhance and improve their lives (Cooky 2009; Rauscher and Cooky 2015; Rauscher, Kauer, and Wilson 2013).

Future research should examine the meanings of sport for the lives of girls of color, both as athletes and as producers and consumers of sport media. Researchers not only should ask girls why they do or do not participate, but also should explore the impact of cultural representations, images, and meanings. In what contexts do girls construct meanings and interpret media imagery, and how do those contexts shape their constructions? In what ways are girls and girl athletes creating their own cultural representations, for example, on social media (like YouTube, Twitter, Facebook), and do those representations reaffirm or challenge hegemonic cultural representations? For girls who participate in sport, how do they make sense of images of female athletes, particularly sexualized images, and how do these images shape their own identities as girl athletes?

While researchers are now asking girls how they make meanings of the images prevalent in sports media (see Krane et al. 2011) and also how girls make sense of their mediated identities and how that translates to physical education contexts (Fisette and Walton 2014), more studies are needed that explicitly utilize an intersectional approach and critical race/whiteness theories to girls' participation in sports (Cooky and McDonald 2005). Examining the ways in which cultural representations, discourses, and meanings enable or constrain girls' participation, and particularly the "have-nots" of sports (Sabo and Veliz 2008), will offer scholars and advocates a deeper understanding into the sporting lives of girls.

REFERENCES

Adams, Terry, and C. A. Tuggle. 2004. "ESPN's *SportsCenter* and Coverage of Women's Athletics: 'It's a Boys' Club.'" *Mass Communication and Society* 7: 237–248.

Adriaanse, Johanna A., and Janice J. Crosswhite. 2008. "David or Mia? The Influence of Gender on Adolescent Girls' Choice of Sport Role Models." *Women's Studies International Forum* 31: 383–389.

Azzarito, Laura. 2005. "A Reconceptualization of Physical Education: The Intersection of Gender/Race/Class." *Sport, Education, and Society* 10: 25–47.

Babey, Susan H., Theresa A. Hastert, and E. Richard Brown. 2007. "Teens Living in Disadvantaged Neighborhoods Lack Access to Parks and Get Less Physical Activity." Los Angeles: University of California, Los Angeles Health Policy Brief. UCLA Center for Health Policy Research.

Banet-Weiser, Sarah. 1999. "Hoop Dreams: Professional Basketball and the Politics of Race and Gender." *Journal of Sport and Social Issues* 23.4: 403–420.

Bishop, Ronald. 2003. "Missing in Action: Feature Coverage of Women's Sports in *Sports Illustrated*." *Journal of Sport and Social Issues* 27.2: 184–194.

Bissell, Kim, and Hal Hays. 2010. "Exploring the Influence of Mediated Beauty: Examining Individual and Social Factors in White and Black Adolescent Girls' Appearance Evaluations." *Howard Journal of Communication* 21: 385–411.

Branded. 2013. Directed by Heidi Ewing and Rachel Grady. Bristol, CT: ESPN Films. DVD.

Butterworth, Michael. 2007. "Race in 'The Race': Mark McGwire, Sammy Sosa, and Heroic Constructions of Whiteness." *Critical Studies in Media Communication* 24.3: 228–244.

Cahn, Susan. 1994. *Coming on Strong: Gender and Sexuality in Twentieth Century Women's Sport*. New York: Free Press.

Clarey, Christopher. 1999. "Bad Hair Day: Davenport Trounces Venus Williams." *New York Times*, January 27. http://www.nytimes.com/1999/01/27/sports/27iht-tennis.t_10.html.

Coakley, Jay J. 2008. *Sports in Society: Issues and Controversies*. 10th ed. New York: McGraw-Hill.

Collins, Patricia Hill. 1998. *Fighting Words: Black Women and the Search for Justice*. Minneapolis: University of Minnesota Press.

———. 2005. *Black Sexual Politics: African Americans, Gender, and the New Racism*. New York: Routledge.

———. 2009. *Black Feminist Thought*. New York: Routledge.

Cooky, Cheryl. 2009. "'Girls Just Aren't Interested': The Social Construction of Interest in Girls' Sport." *Sociological Perspectives* 52.2: 259–284.

———. 2010. "Do Girls Rule? Understanding Popular Culture Images of 'Girl Power!' and Sport." In *Learning Culture through Sports: Perspectives on Society and Organized Sports*, edited by Sandra Spickard Prettyman and Brian Lampman, 210–226. Lanham, MD: Rowman & Littlefield.

Cooky, Cheryl, Ranissa Dycus, and Shari L. Dworkin. 2013. "'What Makes a Woman a Woman?' vs. 'Our First Lady of Sport': A Comparative Analysis of Caster Semenya in U.S. and South African News Media." *Journal of Sport and Social Issues* 37.1: 31–56.

Cooky, Cheryl, and Mary G. McDonald. 2005. "If You Let Me Play: Young Girls 'Insider-Other' Narratives of Sport." *Sociology of Sport Journal* 22: 158–177.

Cooky, Cheryl, Michael A. Messner, and Robin H. Hextrum. 2013. "Women Play Sports, but Not on TV: A Longitudinal Study of Televised News." *Communication & Sport* 1: 203–231.

Cooky, Cheryl, Faye L. Wachs, Michael A. Messner, and Shari L. Dworkin. 2010. "It's Not about the Game: Don Imus, Race, Class, Gender, and Sexuality in Contemporary Media." *Sociology of Sport Journal* 27: 139–159.

Cosaro, William A. 2010. *The Sociology of Childhood*. Thousand Oaks, CA: Sage.

Crouse, Karen. 2014. "As (Very) Fast Friends, Two Young Americans Balance at Sport's Peak." *New York Times*, August 16. http://www.nytimes.com/2014/08/17/sports/missy-franklin-and-katie-ledecky-adjust-to-life-as-swimmings-royalty.html?_r=0.

Currie, Dawn H. 1999. *Girl Talk: Adolescent Magazines and Their Readers*. Toronto: University of Toronto Press.

Dagbovie-Mullins, Sika A. 2013. "Pigtails, Ponytails, and Getting Tail: Infantilization and Hyper-Sexualization of African American Females in Popular Culture." *Journal of Popular Culture* 46.4: 745–771.

Daniels, Elizabeth A. 2009. "Sex Objects, Athletes, and Sexy Athletes: How Media Representations of Women Athletes Can Impact Adolescent Girls and Young Women." *Journal of Adolescent Research* 24.4: 399–422.

Daniels, Elizabeth A., and Nicole M. LaVoi. 2012. "Athletics as Solution and Problem: Sports Participation for Girls and the Sexualization of Female Athletes." In *The Sexualization of Girls and Girlhood*, edited by Tomi-Ann Roberts and Eileen L. Zubriggen, 63–83. New York: Oxford University Press.

Douglas, Delia D. 2005. "Venus, Serena, and the Women's Tennis Association: When and Where Race Enters." *Sociology of Sport Journal* 22: 256–282.

———. 2012. "Venus, Serena, and the Inconspicuous Consumption of Blackness: A Commentary on Surveillance, Race Talk, and New Racism(s)." *Journal of Black Studies* 43.2: 127–145.

Driscoll, Catherine. 2002. *Girls: Feminine Adolescence in Popular Culture and Cultural Theory*. New York: Columbia University Press.

Eastman, Susan Tyler, and Andrew C. Billings. 2000. "Sports Casting and Sports Reporting: The Power of Gender Bias." *Journal of Sport and Social Issues* 24: 192–213.

Erkut, Sumru, Jacqueline P. Fields, Rachel Sing, and Fern Marx. 1996. "Diversity in Girls' Experiences: Feeling Good about Who You Are." In *Urban Adolescent Girls: Resisting Stereotypes*, edited by Bonnie J. Ross Leadbeater and Niobe Way, 53–64. New York: New York University Press.

ESPN Research. 2004. "Top 10 Williams Sisters Controversies." September 10. http://sports .espn.go.com/sports/tennis/usopen04/news/story?id=187688.

Fisette, Jennifer L., and Theresa A. Walton. 2014. "'If You Really Knew Me': I Am Empowered through Action." *Sport, Education, and Society* 19: 131–152.

Frankenberg, Ruth. 1993. *White Women, Race Matters: The Social Construction of Whiteness*. Minneapolis: University of Minnesota Press.

Gannon, Susan, Michele Byers, and Marnina Gonick. 2014. "Girls, Sexuality, and Popular Culture: 'Hey Pony! Come On.'" In *Becoming Girl: Collective Biography and the Production of Girlhood*, edited by Marnina Gonick and Susan Gannon, 115–136. Toronto: Women's Press.

Gill, Rosalind. 2012. "Media, Empowerment, and the 'Sexualization of Culture' Debates." *Sex Roles* 66: 736–745.

Grieser, Mira, Diane Neumark-Sztainer, Brit I. Saksvig, Jung-Sun Lee, Gwen M. Felton, and Martha Y. Kubik. 2008. "Black, Hispanic, and White Girls' Perceptions of Environmental and Social Support and Enjoyment of Physical Activity." *Journal of School Health* 78.6: 314–320.

Hanson, Sandra L. 2005. "Hidden Dragons: Asian American Women and Sport." *Journal of Sport and Social Issues* 29: 279–312.

Harrison, Kristen, and Barbara L. Frederickson. 2003. "Women's Sport Media, Self-Objectification, and Mental Health in Black and White Adolescent Females." *Journal of Communication* 53: 216–232.

Heywood, Leslie, and Shari L. Dworkin. 2003. *Built to Win: The Female Athlete as Cultural Icon*. Minneapolis: University of Minnesota Press.

Hunt, Darnell. 1997. "(Re)affirming Race: 'Reality,' Negotiation, and the 'Trial of the Century.'" *Sociological Quarterly* 38: 399–422.

Hunt, Darnell, and Angela James. 2008. "Making Sense of Kids Making Sense: Media Encounters and 'Multicultural' Methods." In *The Sage Handbook of Child Development, Multiculturalism, and Media*, edited by Joy Keiko Asamen, Mesha L. Ellis, and Gordon L. Berry, 365–378. Thousand Oaks, CA: Sage.

Jamieson, Katherine M., Kaori Araki, Yong Chul Chung, Sun Yung Kwon, Lisa Riggioni, and Victoria Acosta Musalem. 2005. "Mujeres (In)activas: An Exploratory Study of Physical Activity among Adolescent Latinas." *Women, Sport, and Physical Activity Journal* 14: 95–105.

Jordan-Zachary, Julia. 2013. "Now You See Me, Now You Don't: My Political Fight against the Invisibility/Erasure of Black Women in Intersectionality Research." *Politics, Groups, and Identities* 1.1: 101–109.

Kane, Mary Jo, and Ann M. Buysse. 2005. "Intercollegiate Media Guides as Contested Terrain: A Longitudinal Analysis." *Sociology of Sport Journal* 22: 214–238.

Kane, Mary Jo, Nicole M. LaVoi, and Janet S. Fink. 2013. "Exploring Elite Female Athletes' Interpretations of Sport Media Images: A Window into the Construction of Social Identity and 'Selling Sex' in Women's Sports." *Communication & Sport* 1: 269–298.

Kane, Mary Jo, and Heather D. Maxwell. 2011. "Expanding the Boundaries of Sport Media Research: Using Critical Theory to Explore Consumer Responses to Representations of Women's Sports." *Journal of Sport Management* 25: 202–216.

Kian, Edward M., John Vincent, and Michael Modello. 2008. "Masculine Hegemonic Hoops: An Analysis of Media Coverage of March Madness." *Sociology of Sport Journal* 25: 235–242.

Kim, Kayoung, Michael M. Sagas, and Nefertiti A. Walker. 2010. "Replacing Athleticism with Sexuality: Athlete Models in *Sports Illustrated* Swimsuit Issues." *International Journal of Sport Communication* 3: 148–162.

Kimm, Sue Y., Nancy W. Glynn, Andrea M. Kriska, Bruce A. Barton, Shari S. Kronsberg, Stephen R. Daniels, Patricia B. Crawford, Zak I. Sabry, and Kiang Liu. 2002. "Decline in Physical Activity in Black Girls and White Girls during Adolescence." *New England Journal of Medicine* 347.10: 709–715.

Krane, Vikki, Sally R. Ross, Montana Miller, Kristy Ganoe, Cathryn Lucas-Carr, and Katie Sullivan Barak. 2011. "'It's Cheesy When They Smile': What Girl Athletes Prefer in Images of Female Athletes." *Research Quarterly for Exercise and Sport* 82: 755–768.

Kusz, Kyle. 2007. *Revolt of the White Athlete: Race, Media, and the Emergence of Extreme Athletes in America*. New York: Peter Lang.

LaVoi, Nicole M. 2011. "Reducing Physical Inactivity and Promoting Active Living: From the Voices of East African Immigrant Adolescent Girls." *Qualitative Research in Sport, Exercise, and Health* 3: 211–237.

LaVoi, Nicole M., and Chelsey M. Thul. Forthcoming. "Sports-based Youth Development for Underserved Girls." Minneapolis: Tucker Center for Research on Girls & Women in Sport.

Levy, Ariel. 2006. *Female Chauvinist Pigs: Women and the Rise of Raunch Culture*. New York: Free Press.

Lumpkin, Angela. 2009. "Female Representation in Feature Articles Published by *Sports Illustrated* in the 1990s." *Women in Sport and Physical Activity Journal* 18: 38–51.

MacKay, Stephanie, and Christine Dalliere. 2009. "Campus Newspaper Coverage of Varsity Sports: Getting Closer to Equitable and Sports-Related Representations of Female Athletes?" *International Review of the Sociology of Sport* 44: 25–40.

Marques, Michelle. 2012. "Gabby Douglas' Hair: U.S. Olympic Gymnast Gets Heat via Twitter over Hairstyle." *Huffington Post*, August 1. http://www.huffingtonpost.com/2012/08/01/gabby-douglas-hair_n_1730355.html.

Massey, Douglas S., and Nancy A. Denton. 1998. *American Apartheid: Segregation and the Making of the Underclass*. Cambridge, MA: Harvard University Press.

McDonald, Mary G. 2000. "The Marketing of the Women's National Basketball Association and the Making of Postfeminism." *International Review for the Sociology of Sport* 35: 35–47.

———. 2009. "Dialogues on Whiteness, Leisure, and (Anti)racism." *Journal of Leisure Research* 41: 5–21.

McDonald, Mary G., and Cheryl Cooky. 2013. "Interrogating Discourses about the WNBA's 'Bad Girls': Intersectionality and the Politics of Representation." In *Fallen Heroes: Sport, Media, and Celebrity Culture*, edited by Lawrence A. Wenner, 193–207. New York: Peter Lang.

McIntosh, Peggy. 1988. "White Privilege: Unpacking the Invisible Knapsack." Working Paper 189. Wellesley, MA: Wellesley College Center for Research on Women.

McKay, James, and Helen Johnson. 2008. "Pornographic Eroticism and Sexual Grotesquerie in Representations of African-American Sportswomen." *Social Identities* 14.4: 491–504.

McRobbie, Angela. 1991. *Feminism and Youth Culture*. 2nd ed. London: Routledge.

Meân, Lindsey J. 2013. "On Track, Off Track, on Oprah: The Framing of Marion Jones as Golden Girl and American Fraud." In *Fallen Heroes: Sport, Media, and Celebrity Culture*, edited by Lawrence A. Wenner, 77–91. New York: Peter Lang.

Media Coverage & Female Athletes. 2013. TPT Co-Productions. St. Paul-Minneapolis: Twin Cities Public Television. DVD.

Messner, Michael A. 2002. *Taking the Field: Women, Men and Sports*. Minneapolis: University of Minnesota Press.

Messner, Michael A., and Michela Musto. 2014. "Where Are the Kids?" *Sociology of Sport Journal* 31: 102–122.

Milestone, Katie, and Anneke Meyer. 2011. *Gender & Popular Culture*. Cambridge: Polity.

National Federation of High School Associations. 2012–2013. "2012–2013 High School Athletics Participation Survey." http://www.nfhs.org/content.aspx?id=3282.

Poniatowski, Kelly, and Erin Whiteside. 2012. "'Isn't He a Good Guy?': Constructions of Whiteness in the 2006 Olympic Hockey Tournament." *Howard Journal of Communications* 23: 1–16.

Pratt, Judith, Kris Grappendorf, Amy Grundvig, and Ginger LeBlanc. 2008. "Gender Differences in Print Media Coverage of the 2004 Summer Olympics in Athens, Greece." *Women in Sport and Physical Activity Journal* 17: 34–41.

Pugh, Allison. 2009. *Longing and Belonging: Parents, Children and Consumer Culture.* Berkeley: University of California Press.

Rauscher, Lauren, and Cheryl Cooky. 2015. "Ready for Anything the World Gives Her? A Critical Look at Sports-Based Positive Youth Development for Girls." *Sex Roles.* doi:10.1007/s11199–014–0400-x.

Rauscher, Lauren, Kerrie Kauer, and Bianca Wilson. 2013. "The Healthy Body Paradox: Organizational and Interactional Influences on Preadolescent Girls' Body Image in Los Angeles." *Gender & Society* 27: 208–230.

Reis, Amy V., Joel Gittelsohn, Carolyn Voorhees, Kathleen M. Roche, Kelly J. Clifton, and Nan M. Astone. 2008. "The Environment and Urban Adolescents' Use of Recreational Facilities for Physical Activity: A Qualitative Study." *American Journal of Health Promotion* 23.1: 43–50.

Sabo, Don, and Philip Veliz. 2008. "Go Out and Play: Youth Sports in America." East Meadow, NY: Women's Sports Foundation.

———. 2011. "Progress without Equity: The Provision of High School Athletic Opportunity in the United States." East Meadow, NY: Women's Sports Foundation.

Schultz, Jamie. 2005. "Reading the Catsuit: Serena Williams and the Production of Blackness at the 2002 U.S. Open." *Journal of Sport and Social Issues* 29: 338–357.

Singh, Ishtla. 2013. "Weaves, Extensions, and Double-Binds: The Curious Case of Gabby Douglas' Hair." *Outwright: Journal for the Cambridge Society of Psychotherapy* 11: 25–31.

Staurowsky, Ellen J., Mary Jane DeSousa, Gaele Ducher, Noah Gentner, Kathleen E. Miller, Sohaila Shakib, Nancy Theberge, and Nancy I. Williams. 2009. "Her Life Depends on It II: Sport, Physical Activity, and the Health and Well-Being of Girls and Women." East Meadow, NY: Women's Sport Foundation.

Taylor, Wendell C., Antronette K. Yancey, Joanne Leslie, Nancy G. Murray, Sharon S. Cummings, Suzanne A. Sharkey, Christiane Wert, Jeanette James, Octavia Miles, and William J. McCarthy. 2000. "Physical Activity among African American and Latino Middle School Girls: Consistent Beliefs, Expectations, and Experiences across Two Sites." *Women & Health* 30: 67–82.

Thul, Chelsey M., and Nicole LaVoi. 2011. "Reducing Physical Activity and Promoting Active Living: From the Voices of East African Immigrant Adolescent Girls." *Qualitative Research in Sport, Exercise and Health* 3: 211–237.

Title IX of the Education Amendments of 1972 (discrimination based on sex), 20 USCA §§ 1681–1688 (West Supp. 2006).

Tucker Center for Research on Girls & Women in Sport. 2007. "Developing Physically Active Girls: An Evidenced-Based Multidisciplinary Approach." Minneapolis: University of Minnesota.

Wachs, Faye L., Cheryl Cooky, Michael A. Messner, and Shari L. Dworkin. 2012. "Media Frames and Displacement of Blame in the Don Imus Incident: Sincere Fictions and Frenetic Inactivity." *Critical Studies in Media Communication* 29.5: 421–438.

CHAPTER 4

Sport and the Childhood Obesity Epidemic

Toben F. Nelson

The proportion of children who are carrying excess body weight has substantially increased in the United States and elsewhere in the world over the past half century (Gortmaker et al. 1987; Ogden et al. 2002, 2012, 2014; Strauss and Pollack 2001; Wang and Lobstein 2006). Data from the US-based National Health and Nutrition Examination study, widely recognized as the most comprehensive study on the topic, show a large increase in children's and adolescents' weight (standardized for their height) over time (Ogden et al. 2002, 2010, 2012; 2014). Children aged six to eleven years old who meet criteria for obesity (Krebs et al. 2007) increased from 7 percent in 1980 to nearly 18 percent in 2012, and among adolescents aged twelve to nineteen years the increase was from 5 percent to more than 20 percent during the same period (Ogden et al. 2014). Most of this excess weight is stored in the body as fat.

Childhood obesity has serious health consequences. For example, children who were diagnosed with type 2 diabetes, a costly and difficult to manage chronic health condition, increased from 1.5 per 1000 in 2001 to 1.9 in 2009 (Dabelea et al. 2014). Similar increases in cardiovascular disease risk factors have been observed among adolescents (Weiss, Bremer, and Lustig 2013). These health threats, often resulting from a sedentary lifestyle and poor diet, have become the second leading actual cause of death in the United States (Biro and Wien 2010; Ford et al. 2012; Mokdad et al. 2004; US Department of Health and Human Services 2001).

Participation in youth sport is commonly championed as a potential remedy for the childhood obesity epidemic. For example, a report by the US Department of Education and the US Department of Health and Human Services identified increasing the number of opportunities for youth to be physically active, specifically through youth sport, as a critical national health priority (US Department of Health and Human Services and US Department of Education 2000). The report not only recommended that families encourage their children to participate in sport, but also encouraged communities to invest in quality youth sport programming to promote health. In addition, several national youth sport organizations (including the National Football League Play 60 initiative, US Youth Soccer, and USA Youth Hockey) promote participation in sports specifically to reduce or prevent obesity. However, at best, this position represents an uncritical and perhaps naïve view of the relationship between youth sport and obesity prevention (Nelson et al. 2011).

The childhood obesity epidemic and its consequences for public health stand in stark contrast to the youth sport participation data. Youth sport has never been more popular (Sabo and Veliz 2008). The National Council of Youth Sports (2008) estimates that 44 million boys and girls in the United States participated in sports annually in 2008 compared with 33 million in 1987. Many children and youth also participate on multiple teams across multiple sports (National Council of Youth Sports 2008). Similar changes have occurred at the high school level. In 1972, about 3.6 million boys and about 300,000 girls participated on an athletics team sponsored by their high school. By 2013, 4.5 million boys (about two in three of all boys) and 3.2 million girls (more than half of all girls), participated on school or community-based sport teams in the United States (National Federation of State High School Associations 2013; Sabo and Veliz 2008).[1] Yet the activity accrued through sport participation does not, by itself, appear to provide a protective effect for obesity on the population level. On the contrary, in this chapter, I argue that some aspects of youth sports, specifically the food and beverages that are routinely available in sport settings, may be undermining the potential health benefits of being physically active through sports.

I begin by grounding my argument in the field of social epidemiology, which argues that social and physical conditions shape human behaviors, and in turn influence health. A key part of my perspective is industrial epidemics, which explicitly identifies how commercial ventures shape social and physical environments. In my view, the marketing and sales of unhealthy food and beverages are significant factors that have influenced the childhood obesity epidemic more generally, and are evidenced in youth sport settings in subtle and not so subtle ways. Then I present and summarize the evidence on the relationship between youth sport participation and excess weight gain, arguing that the unhealthy food and beverage environment that pervades youth sport undermines the health benefits that participants derive from being physically active in sport. I conclude by identifying possible intervention strategies and providing recommendations for future research to improve our understanding of the role that youth sport can play in preventing obesity and its health consequences.

SOCIAL EPIDEMIOLOGY AND INDUSTRIAL EPIDEMICS

Epidemiology focuses on how health status is distributed within and across populations of people. In contrast to disciplines such as medicine, which is primarily concerned about the health (or more commonly sickness) of individuals, the focus of epidemiology is on groups. Epidemiology is a descriptive and numerical science, but it helps identify health determinants and possible interventions. Social epidemiology, a specialty within epidemiology, explores how social interactions and social conditions affect health (Link and Phelan 1995; Oakes and Kaufman 2006; Putnam and Galea 2008).[2] While the principles of epidemiology and social epidemiology have nonhuman applications, the primary focus is on human social interactions and health. Social epidemiology expressly considers factors that occur on the level of individuals (also called "proximal," "downstream," or "micro" determinants), including psychological, biological, physiological, and genetic processes. It is also concerned with factors on the population level (also called "distal," "upstream," or "macro" social determinants), such as interpersonal, social, economic, and political processes.

Importantly, macro social determinants are viewed within social epidemiology as fundamental causes of health status themselves, rather than simply ways in which micro determinants happen to be arranged (Link and Phelan 1995). Micro social determinants are of interest when appropriately placed within the larger social context. Powerful social forces create conditions that make some micro social determinants more likely to occur, but those larger social forces can work through several different pathways to influence health. A social epidemiology perspective, at its core, recognizes that social conditions created by humans, including public policy, are important and potentially effective tools for shaping population health.

Related to the social epidemiology perspective is the concept of "industrial epidemics." Within the field of epidemiology, the term "epidemic" takes on a specific meaning, referring to how diseases emerge or increase within a population during a specific time period. An *industrial* epidemic refers to the way that the production, consumption, sales, or marketing of commercial goods can increase diseases (Hastings 2012; Jahiel 2008; Majnoni d'Intignano 1998). By promoting a product that is an agent of disease, industrial epidemics are at least partially driven by corporate interests to achieve sales and profit. The most obvious product to generate an industrial epidemic is tobacco (Holden and Lee 2009), but the concept of industrial epidemics has also been extended to alcohol, illicit drugs, motor vehicles, and firearms (Jahiel and Babor 2007). Population targets for the health impacts of industrial epidemics can include employees (e.g., factory workers), residents of communities (e.g., neighbors of toxic waste sites), or consumers more broadly in a population where products are marketed and sold. Less attention, however, has focused on how sport-based food and beverages have contributed to the obesity epidemic.[3] I argue that some corporate entities specifically target young athletes, thus playing an important role in increasing youth obesity rates.

THE INFLUENCE OF YOUTH SPORT ON WEIGHT AND BEHAVIOR TARGETS FOR OBESITY PREVENTION

There is a general lack of research on the topic of obesity prevention and youth sport (Nelson et al. 2011). In a previous review of research, my colleagues and I found only a small number of studies that examined the relationship between sport participation and weight status. Similarly, few studies have explored the relationship of key behavioral targets for obesity prevention, such as physical activity and dietary behaviors, with sport. We identified a total of thirty-six studies that met our criteria (i.e., studies that compared participants and nonparticipants in sport or assessed the effects of sport participation using within-subject designs) and examined at least one of those outcomes. A considerably larger number of studies looked at only sport participants, but did not have a comparison group to estimate the effect of sport participation. In fact, the majority of this relatively small number of studies were primarily designed to address research questions on other topics. Many of the studies happened to include a single survey question, or a small number of items, to compare sport participants with nonparticipants on other variables. In other words, only a handful of studies were expressly designed to examine the effect of sport participation on preventing obesity or its behavioral determinants. Overall, the relative lack of studies in this area was notable for a topic on which there were already very specific recommendations promoting sport participation.

Our review found that there was not sufficient evidence to conclude that sport participation was protective for overweight or obesity (Nelson et al. 2011). Two studies published since our prior review found that sport participants were less likely to be overweight than nonparticipants (Basterfield et al. 2015; Drake et al. 2012). These studies had strong study designs and would appear to provide more conclusive evidence to address this question. However, a third study (Vella et al. 2013) continued a pattern we observed previously that large nationally representative studies employing objective measures do not seem to show that sport participation is advantageous for weight status. Interestingly, when looking across all of these studies, no clear differences emerge when considering only the higher quality studies, including those with large sample size, that were nationally representative, and that employed direct, objective measurement of weight status. The lack of differences in these strongly designed studies raises some doubt about whether the findings of lower or reduced weight observed in other types of studies are real or the result of study artifact. In particular, there may be some systematic bias in studies investigating the effect of sport on weight status. For example, it is possible that the differences observed in some studies may reflect that youth who are overweight are less likely to choose to be involved in sports (Nelson et al. 2011). More attention to these issues is needed in future research.

Furthermore, we found no published studies that specifically looked at longitudinal trends in overweight or obesity among sport participants. The Centers for Disease Control and Prevention collect trends data on youth obesity rates in their Youth Risk Behavior Surveillance System surveys, and the surveys also contain questions about sport participation. Table 4.1 shows previously unpublished data for the time period of 1999 to 2013.[4] The findings indicate that a significant increase has occurred in overweight and obesity for sport participants as well as nonparticipants over time among both boys and girls. There is no significant difference in the percentage of boys who were overweight or obese between those

TABLE 4.1

PERCENTAGE OF STUDENTS WHO ARE OVERWEIGHT OR OBESE,
BY SEX AND SPORTS TEAM PARTICIPATION, US HIGH SCHOOL
STUDENTS, YOUTH RISK BEHAVIOR SURVEY, 1999–2013

	Female		*Male*	
	PLAYED ON AT LEAST ONE SPORTS TEAM	DID NOT PLAY ON A SPORTS TEAM	PLAYED ON AT LEAST ONE SPORTS TEAM	DID NOT PLAY ON A SPORTS TEAM
	% (95% CI)	% (95% CI)	% (95% CI)	% (95% CI)
1999	17.2 (15.6–18.9)	24.4 (22.3–26.6)	28.1 (26.3–30.0)	29.6 (25.8–33.6)
2001	14.1 (12.5–15.8)	22.8 (20.6–25.2)	30.3 (28.0–32.6)	29.0 (27.4–30.7)
2003	17.4 (15.3–19.8)	27.2 (24.9–29.6)	28.4 (25.7–31.3)	33.8 (31.5–36.2)
2005	20.8 (18.7–23.1)	30.1 (27.8–32.4)	30.2 (28.2–32.4)	34.4 (31.7–37.3)
2007	18.8 (16.4–21.6)	29.6 (26.9–32.5)	31.7 (29.8–33.7)	34.4 (31.5–37.4)
2009	18.8 (17.2–20.5)	29.1 (27.1–31.1)	30.3 (27.4–33.4)	31.9 (29.0–35.0)
2011	21.3 (19.1–23.7)	29.1 (27.3–30.9)	29.6 (27.3–32.1)	32.9 (30.6–35.4)
2013	21.3 (19.2–23.6)	33.3 (30.0–36.8)	31.9 (28.8–35.2)	34.7 (32.0–37.4)

Source: Centers for Disease Control and Prevention, Youth Risk Behavior Survey (YRBS) data, 1999–2013, unpublished. Information about YRBS is available at www.cdc.gov/yrbs.

Note: Overweight is defined as ≥85th percentile but <95th percentile for body mass index, by age and sex, based on reference data. Obese is defined as ≥95th percentile for body mass index, by age and sex, based on reference data. Participation is defined as playing on at least one sports team sponsored by schools or community organizations.

involved in sport and those who were not. There was a significant difference observed in this same comparison for girls, with girls who are involved in sport less likely to report that they are overweight. These data illustrate that the rates of overweight and obesity are increasing for everyone, regardless of their participation in sports.

The recommendations that youth should participate in sport programs are based primarily on sport's role in promoting physical activity. An implicit assumption may be that because sports involve physical activity, they inherently prevent obesity. The evidence supporting higher levels of physical activity among youth involved in sport compared with those not involved in sport is strong and consistent: youth involved in sport are more physically active than those who are not. My colleagues and I found seventeen studies that all reported higher levels of physical activity among youth who participated in sports (Nelson et al. 2011). Studies published subsequent to our review had similar findings (Basterfield et al. 2015; Vella et al. 2013).

However, while the direction of the findings was consistent, the magnitude of the effect was relatively small. Two small but high-quality studies were particularly illuminating. Using accelerometers to objectively measure physical activity, these studies found that participation in sport contributed approximately thirty minutes of moderate and vigorous activity per day (Leek et al. 2011; Wickel and Eisenmann 2007). One of these studies indicated that only one in four youth participating in soccer, baseball, and softball met recommended levels of activity during their sport team practice (Leek et al. 2011). These are among the most popular participatory sports. Similar studies are needed looking at other sports, including individual and endurance sports such as swimming and cross-country running, because these specific sports may promote higher levels of activity. A study in Australia published after our review observed similar findings (Guagliano et al. 2014). Considering all the available evidence, it appears that sport provides a boost in physical activity but the effect is small and, on average, does not meet recommended guidelines for physical activity (US Department of Health and Human Services 2008). Together these findings suggest that the physical activity benefits of participating in at least some sports are relatively modest, and even when participating in sports on a regular basis, children are exercising for only a small amount of time.

An even smaller amount of research has examined the diet of youth sport participants compared with nonparticipants. A total of seven studies were identified that met our criteria. While these studies did not consistently assess components of diet and the small number of studies overall makes it difficult to draw firm conclusions, these studies suggest that youth involved in sport are more likely to consume fruits, vegetables, and milk, which may be considered healthy (Nelson et al. 2011). On the other hand, sport participants were more likely than nonsport participants to eat fast food, drink sugary beverages, and consume more calories overall (Bauer et al. 2009; Croll et al. 2006). These behaviors are directly linked to greater risk of obesity and complications for health (Field et al. 2014; Gortmaker, Long, and Wang 2009; Hu and Malik 2010; Rosenheck 2008). Sugar-sweetened beverages include drinks such as soda pop, as well as sport drinks, which contain a comparable amount of added sugar (Story and Klein 2012). The American Academy of Pediatrics reports that sports drinks "can substantially increase the risk for overweight or obesity in children and adolescents" and discourages their consumption (Schneider and Benjamin 2011).

An emerging group of studies suggests that these kinds of food and beverages are common in youth sport settings. Youth sport participants are likely to be exposed to excess calories in sport settings in the form of snacks, convenience and fast foods, and sugar-sweetened beverages (Kelly et al. 2008; Thomas et al. 2012). Parents reported that these foods and beverages offerings were unhealthy (Irby, Drury-Brown, and Skelton 2014; Kelly et al. 2008; Thomas et al. 2012). Typical foods observed in these settings included chocolate, candy, ice cream, salty snacks (e.g., chips), sugary beverages (including sports drinks), and entrees such as hot dogs and pizza, with few healthier alternatives. In particular, sports drinks are frequently consumed by youth sport participants before, during, and after sports events. Originally developed to aid in hydration during vigorous activity performed in extreme weather conditions, sports drinks are marketed as a healthy alternative to other sugar-sweetened beverages, but many contain added sugars and other ingredients (Schneider and Benjamin 2011; Story and Klein 2012). In addition, parents routinely provided unhealthy foods and beverages to children in sport settings. Organized postgame "snacks" or "treats" that parents describe as "unhealthy" are common, and parents regularly pick up fast food because sport schedules often conflicted with meal times (Thomas et al. 2012). Although parents expressed some unease about these choices, they felt their children's sporting activities offset the poor diet choices (Thomas et al. 2012).

Energy Balance and Youth Sport

The benefits of sport participation for obesity prevention depend, in part, upon maintaining energy balance as well as the nutritional content of the types of food consumed (Prentice and Jebb 2004; Wang et al. 2006). Studies among elite athletes suggest that overall energy intake increases as activity levels and expenditure increase (Garcia-Roves et al. 2000; Rico-Sanz et al. 1998), however little formal research beyond this has been done with sport participants. As I noted previously, the additional energy youth expend through physical activity in sport is a relatively small amount. Less clear are the amount of energy intake and the type of food associated with sport participation. A school-based physical activity intervention study found that increases in moderate activity levels resulted in energy surplus because subjects overcompensated for their physical activity by eating more (Sonneville and Gortmaker 2008). If this commonly occurs in youth sport, then promoting sport participation may be counterproductive for obesity prevention.

The modest amount of energy expended during sport may not compensate for this amount of energy intake. The best available estimates of energy expenditure for youth are based on the energy costs for various sports and effort levels derived from the Compendium of Energy Expenditures for Youth (Ridley, Ainsworth, and Olds 2008). Using the compendium, I calculated individual energy expenditure by multiplying the metabolic equivalent of task (MET) value for the individual sport by the resting metabolic rate, weight, and number of minutes of activity performed (Ridley, Ainsworth, and Olds 2008). This calculation assumes continuous activity and intensity for the entire duration of the game or practice, but energy expenditure during youth sport activities is likely to be intermittent (Guagliano et al. 2014; Leek et al. 2011). Figure 4.1 compares the estimated energy expenditure for sixty minutes of physical activity at light, moderate, and vigorous participation intensities, respectively, with estimated energy intake from

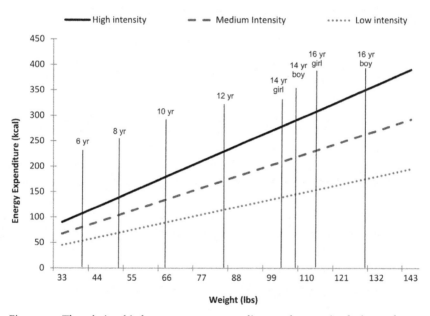

Figure 4.1. The relationship between energy expenditure and energy intake in youth sport by weight. Source: The Compendium of Energy Expenditures for Youth (Ridley, Ainsworth, and Olds 2008).

Note: Vertical lines represent the median weight (in kg) for a typical child for each age. Energy expenditure is estimated for exercise at high (METS = 8), moderate (METS = 6), and low (METS = 4) intensity. Median weights for boys and girls are nearly identical through twelve years of age.

snacks and beverages associated with youth sports. Vertical lines demarcate the weight of a child at the fiftieth percentile for every two years of age from six to twelve years. By age fourteen, differences between boys and girls begin to emerge and are displayed on the graph. According to these estimates, a ten-year-old boy who weighs 35 kilograms (77 pounds) expends approximately 300 calories during sixty minutes of activity at moderate intensity, assuming continuous activity. A postgame snack can easily total 450 calories, approximately 150 calories more than what was expended. Over time, this surplus may contribute to weight gain.

Food Availability and Marketing

Food and beverage marketing is a multibillion-dollar industry, and youth are a primary target market (Botha et al. 2008; Nestle 2006; Story and French 2004). In 2013 more than $127 million was spent by the industry to advertise and promote sports drinks alone (Harris et al. 2014), and strong evidence exists that advertising influences food and beverage preferences, purchase requests, and consumption among children aged two through eleven (Committee on Food Marketing and the Diets of Children and Youth et al. 2006). The specific content of food and beverage advertising to children is largely unregulated in the United States (Wilde 2009), but companies, restaurants, and the media have been encouraged to promote a healthy lifestyle to children and youth (Committee on Food Marketing and the Diets of Children and Youth et al. 2006). The Council of the Better Business Bureau formed the Children's Food and Beverage Advertising Initiative (CFBAI) to encourage food and beverage companies to advertise healthier food and beverages to children under age twelve, and several large companies have voluntarily joined this effort (Committee on Food Marketing and the Diets of Children and Youth et al. 2006). CFBAI recommends that participating companies devote at least 50 percent of their advertising to children under twelve to promote healthy dietary choices and lifestyles (Council of the Better Business Bureau 2010). To meet this requirement, advertisements either can promote products that meet minimum dietary standards or can include messages that encourage physical activity or good eating habits consistent with government standards (Council of the Better Business Bureau 2010). Very few of the actively marketed products meet minimum dietary standards, and many companies are choosing to promote physical activity and emphasize youth sport instead of improving their offerings.

Although youth sport marketing associates products with health and fitness, many products targeting youth tend to be low in nutrients and high in calories, sugar, or fat (Powell et al. 2007). For example, Powerade—the official sports drink of Little League Baseball and Softball—indicated their product was "the perfect partner for boys and girls looking to drink healthy and be healthy" (Little League Communications Division 2008). Gatorade also focuses its promotions on sport

(PepsiCo 2007). Kellogg's promotes its sugar-sweetened breakfast cereal line Frosted Flakes through sport, portraying its mascot Tony the Tiger as a "coach and mentor who helped kids train for sporting events" (Facenda 2008). Youth may come to expect, demand, and consume sports drinks or food in sport settings as a result of the heavy marketing of these products (Story and French 2004; Story and Klein 2012). Furthermore, this marketing effort appears to generate positive opinions of the companies among parents and youth, which may make them less likely to support possible restrictions on availability and promotion of sports drinks or other unhealthy foods and beverages (Kelly et al. 2011, 2013).

Summary of What We Know about Obesity Prevention and Youth Sport

Organized sports programs clearly have the potential to help youth be more physically active. This outcome is very consistent with public health goals, and it is on the basis of this outcome that sports are recommended to promote health and prevent obesity, a major public health problem. However, it appears that the magnitude of the contribution of sports to physical activity is, on average, small. Most youth involved in sports are probably not achieving daily physical activity standards. In addition, it remains unclear whether involvement in sports helps prevent youth from becoming overweight. Some studies have shown that youth involved in sports are less likely to be overweight. However, this pattern is not consistent across studies, and some of the largest and highest quality studies have shown no differences. More research needs to be conducted in this area.

Very few studies have explored the dietary habits of youth sport participants, and more research is needed. It appears from the limited amount of work that has been done that youth involved in sport have some better, and some worse, dietary habits than their peers who are not involved in sports. In particular, youth in sports appear to consume more fast food, more sugary drinks, and more calories overall (Bauer et al. 2009; Croll et al. 2006). Similarly, a few studies have begun to explore the food environment in youth sport settings. The initial results are concerning from a public health perspective. The foods and beverages offered in youth sport settings are generally unhealthy and have few healthy options. Even more alarming is that some youth may be in energy surplus following participation in sports. Overall, these studies indicate that current practices in youth sport may undermine sport's potential to promote health and public health goals more broadly.

How Did We Get to a Point Where Sport
May Be Compromising the Health of Youth?

Youth sport programs appear to be increasing in intensity. Now, there is increased emphasis on sport specialization, out-of-season participation, out-of-town and out-of-state travel, and use of professional coaching for skill development (DiFiori et al. 2014; Hyman 2012; National Council of Youth Sports 2008; Sabo and Veliz 2008). At least two troubling trends may be associated with these shifts. Youth sports are becoming increasingly costly for participants and their families. Vulnerable youth, including youth of lower socioeconomic position, minority racial/ethnic groups, and those who live in poor areas, appear to have declining access to organized sport programs (Basterfield et al. 2015). The childhood obesity epidemic has occurred at disproportionately greater rates among some minority groups and families of lower socioeconomic position (Ogden et al. 2012; Wang 2011). The role that inequalities in access to sport programs play in overweight and obesity disparities is not known, but they at least partially explain group differences in activity, weight status, and health (Basterfield et al. 2015; Kanters et al. 2013; Khan et al. 2012).

Furthermore, in order to support increased costs associated with sport participation, and in an attempt to keep sports accessible to vulnerable youth and families, youth sport organizations increasingly turn to commercial sponsorships and fund-raising (Hyman 2012). These funds are used to pay for expenses such as uniforms, coaching, facilities for practices and events, and travel. Often these sponsorships are for food and beverage products that are unhealthy for children and their families (Olstad and Raine 2013). Promotion through sport has important benefits for the companies that produce and market foods and beverages, including promoting a sense of community established through sport as their products become associated with sport (Danylchuk and MacIntosh 2009; Harris et al. 2009; Nestle 2006). They may also benefit from a "halo" effect, which associates their products with fitness and health and other positive imagery linked with sports. The halo effect is particularly useful for companies that market and sell products that are not healthy. For example, McDonald's commonly employs sports-related marketing, including Olympic sponsorship and marketing that highlights youth sport.[5] Food and beverage companies are viewed as appropriate sponsors of sporting events (Danylchuk and MacIntosh 2009), and the primary constituencies and stakeholders in youth sport organizations, including those with fewer existing resources, are likely to seek more sponsorship relationships with local restaurants and distributors.

Opportunities for Promoting Energy Balance in Youth Sport

There are opportunities to facilitate energy expenditure and limit energy intake from sources of low nutritional value in youth sport settings. Existing research and experience in other settings such as schools and after-school programs can help guide recommendations and interventions. Youth, parents, and coaches may not recognize how calories are contained in snacks and beverages commonly offered in youth sport settings, understand how many calories children expend during sport, or be aware of health-promoting levels of physical activity. Youth sport coaches and league administrators are often volunteers with little formal training in physical education, coaching, or nutrition. Training and education materials that help youth coaches organize and structure practices and events, together with an explicit focus on increasing physical activity, limiting sedentary time and promoting healthy eating during youth sport could encourage energy balance in youth sport. Targeted education efforts may increase the awareness of parents and key decision makers in youth sport leagues about energy balance and obesity prevention. The Institute of Medicine recognized the potential for food and beverage sales in youth sport to contribute to the childhood obesity epidemic and recommended that programs encourage the sale of healthier options in youth sport venues, but no system or guidelines are currently in place (Koplan, Liverman, and Kraak 2005). Simple interventions for youth sport leagues include the development of guidelines for fund-raising and for parents who organize postgame snacks to include health-promoting products. Regulation of advertising and sponsorship in youth sport could be implemented by either governmental or youth sport governing bodies. However, limiting sources of private funding could seriously restrict opportunities to participate in youth sport. These important trade-offs need to be more carefully examined.

Interventions, including policies, to improve the food and beverage environment for youth are common in school and some out-of-school settings, and some have demonstrated success at improving youth diets (Caballero et al. 2003; Chen and Wang 2013; Gortmaker et al. 1999; Kubik et al. 2013; Mozaffarian et al. 2010; Nanney et al. 2010; Story, Nanney, and Schwartz 2009; Wiecha et al. 2004, 2012). However, even when implemented, it can remain difficult to systematically improve the food and beverages at youth sport and recreational facilities (Olstad, Raine, and McCargar 2012). Although the provincial government in Alberta offers voluntary nutrition guidelines to improve access to healthy food and beverage choices for children, they are generally not followed in recreational facilities (Olstad, Raine, and McCargar 2012). Even in the few settings where the guidelines were adopted, the food environment was not necessarily healthier (Olstad, Raine, and McCargar 2013). Facility managers, moreover, indicated that profits guide their choices about what is offered; they believed more healthful foods and beverages would result in lower profits. They also indicated that facilities would be unlikely to take efforts to improve the healthfulness of their offerings without government standards or accountability to those standards. Dana L. Olstad and colleagues argued for a stronger government role, including standards and regulations about what can be sold in recreational facilities, in order to improve access to more healthful foods and beverages in youth sport environments (Olstad 2014; Olstad et al. 2015; Olstad and Raine 2013). The findings are consistent with those of a study in Australia (Kelly et al. 2008), which found that parents supported government intervention to improve the healthfulness of food and beverage offerings at community sports facilities.

WHAT TYPE OF RESEARCH IS NEEDED?

The topic of obesity prevention in youth sport settings is an emerging subfield. Research in this area should be encouraged and supported because childhood obesity is a significant public health challenge. Sport is a powerful social force that garners wide participation and has the potential to help reduce youth obesity. We know little about how current conditions in sport that influence or prevent obesity, or what, if anything, about sport can be modified to improve current youth sport offerings. We need to generate knowledge about the role of youth sport in excess weight. The negative health consequences associated with youth sport and potential solutions in sport settings for slowing and reversing the childhood obesity epidemic should also be explored.

Potential areas to pursue include the assessment of potential sources of variation within sport (e.g., type of sport, playing time, intensity level, skill level, practice effectiveness, coach expertise, availability of appropriate programs, equipment, and facilities, availability of food) that may impact weight status, physical activity, and diet. This effort would require the development of appropriate measures to provide a more detailed assessment of sport participation. Research is needed to compare energy expenditure with energy intake in youth sport settings. It may be the case that standard measures of overweight or obesity in epidemiologic studies, including weight for height measures that do not directly assess body composition (i.e., distinguish between body fat and lean body mass) such as body mass index, are not good indicators of overall health for sport participants if they tend to have more lean body mass than nonparticipants (Menke et al. 2007; Nelson et al. 2011). Appropriate measures of body composition for sport participants, perhaps including waist circumference and percentage body fat, should be identified, utilized, and compared in youth sport settings.

Most of the existing research on weight status, physical activity, and diet in youth sport uses observational and other nonexperimental study designs. It is currently unclear how selection bias might shape the relationship among sport participation, weight status, physical activity, and diet. Population-based longitudinal studies assessing the association of sport participation with weight status, physical activity, and diet are needed. These designs can help examine the effects of sport dropout on physical activity and diet. They may also illuminate the weight status outcomes among those who discontinue sport participation. We also need to conduct more small intervention studies to assess the effects of changes in sport programs on weight status, physical activity, and diet.

Improved and expanded studies could explore the potential mechanisms by which youth sport places youth at risk for development of excess weight. Preliminary evidence suggests that youth are uniquely exposed to foods and drinks that are unhealthy. More research is needed to assess the contribution of drinks and snacks consumed in sport settings to total daily caloric intake and whether youth compensate for that consumption through additional activity or reduced caloric intake at other meals.

Conclusions

Youth sport is a promising setting for obesity prevention. Sufficient evidence exists to raise concern about the potential negative influence of sport participation on weight status and diet. Devoting increased attention to sport settings has broad potential to influence obesity levels among youth. Participants, parents, coaches, league administrators, and physicians are important target audiences for awareness and intervention. More discussion, research, and intervention efforts are needed before the promise of obesity prevention in youth sport can be realized.

ACKNOWLEDGMENTS

This chapter was made possible with the support of several grant awards, including a Career Development Award through the Transdisciplinary Research on Energetics and Cancer Grant U54CA116849 funded by the National Cancer Institute at the University of Minnesota, and pilot grant awards from the Minnesota Obesity Center (http://www.mnoc .umn.edu/) and the Obesity Prevention Center at the University of Minnesota (http://www .opc.umn.edu/). I want to thank Megan Thomas, RD, MPH, for her contributions to this line of research. Megan's effort was supported, in part, by a Ruth Steif Fellowship in Public Health Nutrition.

NOTES

1. The increase in sport participation has been particularly dramatic among girls as a result of Title IX legislation, which increased sport opportunities for girls.

2. Both social epidemiology and sociology focus on social factors beyond the level of the individual. Social epidemiology differs from sociology in its focus primarily on health, disease prevention, and understanding the interplay between the micro and macro levels of health.

3. Other sport-related products that may contribute to the childhood obesity epidemic include sport-themed video games that promote inactivity. Indeed, reducing time spent in front of a video screen (e.g., television, nonacademic computer time, video games) is a

behavior target for addressing childhood obesity, along with improving diet and promoting physical activity (Pearson and Biddle 2011).

4. Data presented are from the Youth Risk Behavior Surveillance System, obtained with the assistance of Dr. Nancy Brener, Division of Adolescent and School Health, Centers for Disease Control and Prevention. The data are based on a nationally representative sample of high school students in the United States.

5. For an example of this type of marketing, see the McDonald's "Victory" television advertisement that aired during the 2008 Summer Olympics (http://youtu.be/QLyh32axLoo).

REFERENCES

Basterfield, Laura, Jessica K. Reilly, Mark S. Pearce, Kathryn N. Parkinson, Ashley J. Adamson, John J. Reilly, and Stewart A. Vella. 2015. "Longitudinal Associations between Sports Participation, Body Composition, and Physical Activity from Childhood to Adolescence." *Journal of Science and Medicine in Sport* 18.2: 178–182.

Bauer, Katherine W., Nicole I. Larson, Melissa C. Nelson, Mary Story, and Dianne Neumark-Sztainer. 2009. "Socio-Environmental, Personal, and Behavioural Predictors of Fast-Food Intake among Adolescents." *Public Health Nutrition* 12.10: 1767–1774.

Biro, Frank M., and Michelle Wien. 2010. "Childhood Obesity and Adult Morbidities." *American Journal of Clinical Nutrition* 91.5: 1499S–1505S.

Botha, Scott, Keith Fentonmiller, Carol Jennings, Mary Johnson, Kial Young, Heather Hippsley, and Mary Engle. 2008. *Marketing Food to Children and Adolescents: A Review of Industry Expenditures, Activities and Self-Regulation*. Washington, DC: Federal Trade Commission.

Caballero, Benjamin, Threresa Clay, Sally M. Davis, Becky Ethelbah, Bonnie H. Rock, Timothy Lohman, James Norman, Mary Story, Elaine J. Stone, Larry Stephenson, and June Stevens. 2003. "Pathways: A School-Based, Randomized Controlled Trial for the Prevention of Obesity in American Indian Schoolchildren." *American Journal of Clinical Nutrition* 78.5: 1030–1038.

Chen, Hsin-Jen, and Youfa Wang. 2013. "Influence of School Beverage Environment on the Association of Beverage Consumption with Physical Education Participation among U.S. Adolescents." *American Journal of Public Health* 103.11: E63–E70.

Committee on Food Marketing and the Diets of Children and Youth, J. Michael McGinnis, Jennifer A. Gootman, and Vivica I. Kraak. 2006. *Food Marketing to Children and Youth: Threat or Opportunity?* Washington, DC: Institute of Medicine.

Council of the Better Business Bureau. 2010. "Children's Food and Beverage Advertising Initiative." http://www.bbb.org/us/about-children-food-beverage-advertising-initiative/. Accessed March 24, 2010.

Croll, Jillian K., Dianne Neumark-Sztainer, Mary Story, Melanie Wall, Cheryl Perry, and Lisa Harnack. 2006. "Adolescents Involved in Weight-Related and Power Team Sports Have Better Eating Patterns and Nutrient Intakes Than Non-sport-involved Adolescents." *Journal of the American Dietetics Association* 106.5: 709–717.

Dabelea, Dana, Elizabeth J. Mayer-Davis, Sharon Saydah, Giuseppina Imperatore, Barbara Linder, Jasmin Divers, Ronny Bell, Angela Badaru, Jennifer W. Talton, Tessa Crume, Angela D. Liese, Anwar T. Merchant, Jean M. Lawrence, Kristi Reynolds, Lawrence Dolan, Lenna L. Liu, and Richard F. Hamman. 2014. "Prevalence of Type 1 and Type 2 Diabetes among Children and Adolescents from 2001 to 2009." *Journal of the American Medical Association* 311.17: 1778–1786.

Danylchuk, Karen E., and Eric MacIntosh. 2009. "Food and Non-alcoholic Beverage Sponsorship of Sporting Events: The Link to the Obesity Issue." *Sport Marketing Quarterly* 18: 69–80.

DiFiori, John P., Holly J. Benjamin, Joel S. Brenner, Andrew Gregory, Neeru Jayanthi, Greg L. Landry, and Anthony Luke. 2014. "Overuse Injuries and Burnout in Youth Sports: A

Position Statement from the American Medical Society for Sports Medicine." *British Journal of Sports Medicine* 48.4: 287–288.

Drake, Keith M., Michael L. Beach, Meghan R. Longacre, Todd Mackenzie, Linda J. Titus, Andrew G. Rundle, and Madome A. Dalton. 2012. "Influence of Sports, Physical Education, and Active Commuting to School on Adolescent Weight Status." *Pediatrics* 130.2: e296–e304.

Facenda, Vanessa L. 2008. "Kellogg Energizes Frosted Flakes." *Adweek*, February 4.

Field, Alison E., Kendrin R. Sonneville, Jennifer Falbe, Alan Flint, Jess Haines, Bernard Rosner, and Carlos A. Camargo Jr. 2014. "Association of Sports Drinks with Weight Gain among Adolescents and Young Adults." *Obesity* 22.10: 2238–2243.

Ford, Earl S., Manuela M. Bergmann, Heiner Boeing, Chaoyang Li, and Simon Capewell. 2012. "Healthy Lifestyle Behaviors and All-Cause Mortality among Adults in the United States." *Preventive Medicine* 55.1: 23–27.

Garcia-Roves, Pablo M., Sereafina Fernandez, Manuel Rodriguez, Javier Perez-Landaluce, and Angeles M. Patterson. 2000. "Eating Pattern and Nutritional Status of International Elite Flatwater Paddlers." *International Journal of Sport Nutrition and Exercise Metabolism* 10.2: 182–198.

Gortmaker, Steven L., Lilian W. Cheung, Karen E. Peterson, Ginny Chomitz, Jay H. Cradle, Hank Dart, Mary K. Fox, Reba B. Bullock, Arthur M. Sobol, Graham Colditz, Alison E. Field, and Nan Laird. 1999. "Impact of a School-Based Interdisciplinary Intervention on Diet and Physical Activity among Urban Primary School Children: Eat Well and Keep Moving." *Archives of Pediatric & Adolescent Medicine* 153.9: 975–983.

Gortmaker, Steven L., William H. Dietz Jr., Arthur M. Sobol, and Cheryl A. Wehler. 1987. "Increasing Pediatric Obesity in the United States." *American Journal of Diseases of Children* 141.5: 535–540.

Gortmaker, Steven L., Michael Long, and Y. Claire Wang. 2009. "The Negative Impact of Sugar-Sweetened Beverages on Children's Health: A Research Synthesis." Healthy Eating Research. Princeton, NJ: Robert Wood Johnson Foundation. http://www.rwjf.org/content/dam/farm/reports/reports/2009/rwjf50143. Accessed September 21, 2015.

Guagliano, Justin M., Chris Lonsdale, Gregory S. Kolt, and Richard R. Rosenkranz. 2014. "Increasing Girls' Physical Activity during an Organised Youth Sport Basketball Program: A Randomised Controlled Trial Protocol." *BMC Public Health* 14: 383.

Harris, Jennifer L., Jennifer L. Pomeranz, Tim Lobstein, and Kelly D. Brownell. 2009. "A Crisis in the Marketplace: How Food Marketing Contributes to Childhood Obesity and What Can Be Done." *Annual Review of Public Health* 30: 211–225.

Harris, Jennifer L., Marlene B. Schwartz, Megan LoDulce, Christina Munsell, Frances Fleming-Milici, James Elsey, Sai Liu, Maia Hyary, Renee Gross, Carol Hazen, and Cathryn Dembeck. 2014. "Sugary Drink FACTS 2014." Hartford, CT: Rudd Center for Food Policy and Obesity.

Hastings, Gerald. 2012. "Why Corporate Power Is a Public Health Priority." *BMJ Clinical Research* 345: e5124.

Holden, Chris, and Kelley Lee. 2009. "Corporate Power and Social Policy: The Political Economy of the Transnational Tobacco Companies." *Global Social Policy* 9.3: 328–354.

Hu, Frank B., and Vasanti S. Malik. 2010. "Sugar-Sweetened Beverages and Risk of Obesity and Type 2 Diabetes: Epidemiologic Evidence." *Physiology and Behavior* 100.1: 47–54.

Hyman, Mark. 2012. *The Most Expensive Game in Town: The Rising Cost of Youth Sports and the Toll on Today's Families.* Boston: Beacon.

Irby, Megan B., Marcie Drury-Brown, and Joseph A. Skelton. 2014. "The Food Environment of Youth Baseball." *Childhood Obesity* 10.3: 260–265.

Jahiel, Rene I. 2008. "Corporation-Induced Diseases, Upstream Epidemiologic Surveillance, and Urban Health." *Journal of Urban Health* 85.4: 517–531.

Jahiel, Rene I., and Thomas F. Babor. 2007. "Industrial Epidemics, Public Health Advocacy, and the Alcohol Industry: Lessons from Other Fields." *Addiction* 102.9: 1335–1339.

Kanters, Michael A., Jason N. Bocarro, Michael B. Edwards, Jonathan M. Casper, and Myron F. Floyd. 2013. "School Sport Participation under Two School Sport Policies: Comparisons by Race/Ethnicity, Gender, and Socioeconomic Status." *Annals of Behavior Medicine* 45.1: S113–S121.

Kelly, Bridget, Louise A. Baur, Adrian E. Bauman, Lesley King, Kathy Chapman, and Ben J. Smith. 2013. "Views of Children and Parents on Limiting Unhealthy Food, Drink, and Alcohol Sponsorship of Elite and Children's Sports." *Public Health Nutrition* 16.1: 130–135.

Kelly, Bridget, Kelly Chapman, Louise A. Baur, Adrain E. Bauman, Lesley King, and Ben J. Smith. 2011. *Building Solutions to Protect Children from Unhealthy Food and Drink Sport Sponsorship.* Sydney: Cancer Council New South Wales and Prevention Research Council.

Kelly, Bridget, Kathy Chapman, Lesley King, Louise Hardy, and Louise Farrell. 2008. "Double Standards for Community Sports: Promoting Active Lifestyles but Unhealthy Diets." *Health Promotion Journal of Australia* 19.3: 226–228.

Khan, Karim M., Angela M. Thompson, Steven N. Blair, James F. Sallis, Kenneth E. Powell, Fiona C. Bull, and Adrain E. Bauman. 2012. "Sport and Exercise as Contributors to the Health of Nations." *Lancet* 380.9836: 59–64.

Koplan, Jeffery P., Catharyn T. Liverman, and Vivica A. Kraak. 2005. *Preventing Childhood Obesity: Health in the Balance.* Washington, DC: Institutes of Medicine of the National Academies.

Krebs, Nancy F., John H. Himes, Dawn Jacobson, Theresa A. Nicklas, Patricia Guilday, and Dennis Styne. 2007. "Assessment of Child and Adolescent Overweight and Obesity." *Pediatrics* 120.4: S193–S228.

Kubik, Matha Y., Cynthia Davey, Marilyn S. Nanney, Richard F. MacLehose, Toben F. Nelson, and Brandon Coombes. 2013. "Vending and School Store Snack and Beverage Trends: Minnesota Secondary Schools, 2002–2010." *American Journal of Preventive Medicine* 44.6: 583–588.

Leek, Desiree, Jordan A. Carlson, Kelli L. Cain, Sara Henrichon, Dori Rosenberg, Kevin Patrick, and James F. Sallis. 2011. "Physical Activity during Youth Sports Practices." *Archives of Pediatric Adolescent Medicine* 165.4: 294–299.

Link, Bruce G., and Jo Phelan. 1995. "Social Conditions as Fundamental Causes of Disease." *Journal of Health and Social Behavior* 35: 80–94.

Little League Communications Division. 2008. "POWERade Teams Up with Little League." http://www.littleleague.org/media/newsarchive/2008stories/POWERade_Teams_Up_With _Little_League.htm. Accessed March 24, 2010.

Majnoni d'Intignano, Beatrice. 1998. "Industrial Epidemics." In *Governments and Health Systems: Implications of Differing Involvements*, edited by David Chinitz and Joshua Cohen, 585–595. West Sussex, UK: John Wiley.

Menke, Andy, Paul Muntner, Rachel P. Wildman, Kristi Reynolds, and Jiang He. 2007. "Measures of Adiposity and Cardiovascular Disease Risk Factors." *Obesity* 15.3: 785–795.

Mokdad, Ali H., James S. Marks, Donna F. Stroup, and Julie L. Gerberding. 2004. "Actual Causes of Death in the United States, 2000." *Journal of the American Medical Association* 291.10: 1238–1245.

Mozaffarian, Rebecca S., Jean L. Wiecha, Barbara A. Roth, Toben F. Nelson, Rebekka M. Lee, and Steven L. Gortmaker. 2010. "Impact of an Organizational Intervention Designed to Improve Snack and Beverage Quality in YMCA After-School Programs." *American Journal of Public Health* 100.5: 925–932.

Nanney, Marilyn S., Toben F. Nelson, Melanie Wall, Tarek Haddad, Martha Kubik, Melissa N. Laska, and Mary Story. 2010. "State School Nutrition and Physical Activity Policy Environments and Youth Obesity." *American Journal of Preventive Medicine* 38.1: 9–16.

National Council of Youth Sports. 2008. "Report on Trends and Participation in Organized Youth Sport." Stuart, FL: National Council of Youth Sports.

National Federation of State High School Associations. 2013. "Annual Report." http://www .nfhs.org/media/885658/2013-nfhs-annual-report.pdf. Accessed January 5, 2015.

Nelson, Toben F., Steven D. Stovitz, Megan Thomas, Nicole M. LaVoi, Katherine W. Bauer, and Dianne Neumark-Sztainer. 2011. "Do Youth Sports Prevent Pediatric Obesity? A Systematic Review and Commentary." *Current Sports Medicine Reports* 10.6: 360–370.

Nestle, Marion. 2006. "Food Marketing and Childhood Obesity—A Matter of Policy." *New England Journal of Medicine* 354.24: 2527–2529.

Oakes, J. Michael, and Jay S. Kaufman. 2006. "Advancing Methods in Social Epidemiology." In *Methods in Social Epidemiology*, edited by J. M. Oakes and J. S. Kaufman, 3–20. San Francisco: John Wiley.

Ogden, Cynthia L., Margaret D. Carroll, Lester R. Curtin, Molly M. Lamb, and Katherine M. Flegal. 2010. "Prevalence of High Body Mass Index in US Children and Adolescents, 2007–2008." *Journal of the American Medical Association* 303.3: 242–249.

Ogden, Cynthia L., Margaret D. Carroll, Brian K. Kit, and Katherine M. Flegal. 2012. "Prevalence of Obesity and Trends in Body Mass Index among US Children and Adolescents, 1999–2010." *Journal of the American Medical Association* 307.5: 483–490.

———. 2014. "Prevalence of Childhood and Adult Obesity in the United States, 2011–2012." *Journal of the American Medical Association* 311.8: 806–814.

Ogden, Cynthia L., Katherine M. Flegal, Margaret D. Carroll, and Clifford L. Johnson. 2002. "Prevalence and Trends in Overweight among US Children and Adolescents, 1999–2000." *Journal of the American Medical Association* 288.14: 1728–1732.

Olstad, Dana L. 2014. "Assessing and Catalyzing Adoption and Implementation of the Alberta Nutrition Guidelines for Children and Youth in Recreational Sports Settings." *Applied Physiology, Nutrition, and Metabolism* 39.7: 842.

Olstad, Dana L., Kelly Poirier, Patti J. Naylor, Cindy Shearer, and Sara F. Kirk. 2015. "Policy Outcomes of Applying Different Nutrient Profiling Systems in Recreational Sports Settings: The Case for National Harmonization in Canada." *Public Health Nutrition* 18: 2251–2262.

Olstad, Dana L., and Kim D. Raine. 2013. "Profit versus Public Health: The Need to Improve the Food Environment in Recreational Facilities." *Canadian Journal of Public Health* 104.2: E167–E169.

Olstad, Dana L., Kim D. Raine, and Linda J. McCargar. 2012. "Adopting and Implementing Nutrition Guidelines in Recreational Facilities: Public and Private Sector Roles. A Multiple Case Study." *BMC Public Health* 12: 376.

———. 2013. "Adopting and Implementing Nutrition Guidelines in Recreational Facilities: Tensions between Public Health and Corporate Profitability." *Public Health Nutrition* 16.5: 815–823.

Pearson, Natalie, and Stuart J. Biddle. 2011. "Sedentary Behavior and Dietary Intake in Children, Adolescents, and Adults: A Systematic Review." *American Journal of Preventive Medicine* 41.2: 178–188.

PepsiCo. 2007. "PepsiCo Strengthens Marketing Practices to Children." *PR Newswire*, July 18. http://www.prnewswire.com/news-releases/pepsico-strengthens-marketing-practices-to-children-52747837.html. Accessed June 21, 2009.

Powell, Lisa M., Glen Szczypka, Frank J. Chaloupka, and Carol L. Braunschweig. 2007. "Nutritional Content of Television Food Advertisements Seen by Children and Adolescents in the United States." *Pediatrics* 120.3: 576–583.

Prentice, Andrew, and Susan Jebb. 2004. "Energy Intake/Physical Activity Interactions in the Homeostasis of Body Weight Regulation." *Nutrition Reviews* 62.7(pt. 2): S98–S104.

Putnam, Sara, and Sandro Galea. 2008. "Epidemiology and the Macrosocial Determinants of Health." *Journal of Public Health Policy* 29.3: 275–289.

Rico-Sanz, Jesus, Walter R. Frontera, Paul A. Mole, Miguel A. Rivera, Anita Rivera-Brown, and Carol N. Meredith. 1998. "Dietary and Performance Assessment of Elite Soccer Players during a Period of Intense Training." *International Journal of Sport Nutrition* 8.3: 230–240.

Ridley, Kate, Barbara E. Ainsworth, and Tim S. Olds. 2008. "Development of a Compendium of Energy Expenditures for Youth." *International Journal of Behavioral Nutrition and Physical Activity* 5: 45.

Rosenheck, Rachel. 2008. "Fast Food Consumption and Increased Caloric Intake: A Systematic Review of a Trajectory towards Weight Gain and Obesity Risk." *Obesity Reviews* 9.6: 535–547.

Sabo, Don, and Philip Veliz. 2008. "Go Out and Play: Youth Sport in America." East Meadow, NY: Women's Sports Foundation.

Schneider, Marcie B., and Holly J. Benjamin. 2011. "Sports Drinks and Energy Drinks for Children and Adolescents: Are They Appropriate?" *Pediatrics* 127.6: 1182–1189.

Sonneville, Kendrin R., and Steven L. Gortmaker. 2008. "Total Energy Intake, Adolescent Discretionary Behaviors, and the Energy Gap." *International Journal of Obesity* 32.6: S19–S27.

Story, Mary, and Simone French. 2004. "Food Advertising and Marketing Directed at Children and Adolescents in the U.S." *International Journal of Behavioral and Nutrition Physical Activity* 1.1: 3.

Story, Mary, and Laura Klein. 2012. *Consumption of Sports Drinks by Children and Adolescents: A Research Review*. Princeton, NJ: University of Minnesota School of Public Health.

Story, Mary, Marilyn S. Nanney, and Marlene B. Schwartz. 2009. "Schools and Obesity Prevention: Creating School Environments and Policies to Promote Healthy Eating and Physical Activity." *Milbank Quarterly* 87.1: 71–100.

Strauss, Richard S., and Harold A. Pollack. 2001. "Epidemic Increase in Childhood Overweight, 1986–1998." *Journal of the American Medical Association* 286.22: 2845–2848.

Thomas, Megan, Toben F. Nelson, Eileen Harwood, and Dianne Neumark-Sztainer. 2012. "Exploring Parent Perceptions of the Food Environment in Youth Sport." *Journal of Nutrition Education and Behavior* 44.4: 365–371.

US Department of Health and Human Services. 2001. "The Surgeon General's Call to Action to Prevent and Decrease Overweight and Obesity." Rockville, MD: GPO.

———. 2008. "2008 Physical Activity Guidelines for Americans." Washington, DC: US Department of Health and Human Services.

US Department of Health and Human Services and US Department of Education. 2000. "Promoting Better Health for Young People through Physical Activity and Sports: A Report to the President from the Secretary of Health and Human Services and the Secretary of Education." Silver Spring, MD.

Vella, Stewart A., Dylan P. Cliff, Anthony D. Okely, Maree L. Scully, and Belinda C. Morley. 2013. "Associations between Sports Participation, Adiposity, and Obesity-Related Health Behaviors in Australian Adolescents." *International Journal of Behavioral Nutrition and Physical Activity* 10: 113.

Wang, Y. Claire, Steven L. Gortmaker, Aathur M. Sobol, and Karen M. Kuntz. 2006. "Estimating the Energy Gap among US Children: A Counterfactual Approach." *Pediatrics* 118.6: e1721–e1733.

Wang, Youfa. 2011. "Disparities in Pediatric Obesity in the United States." *Advances in Nutrition* 2.1 (2011): 23–31.

Wang, Youfa, and Tim Lobstein. 2006. "Worldwide Trends in Childhood Overweight and Obesity." *International Journal of Pediatric Obesity* 1.1: 11–25.

Weiss, Ram, Andrew A. Bremer, and Robert H. Lustig. 2013. "What Is Metabolic Syndrome, and Why Are Children Getting It?" *Annals of the New York Academy of Sciences* 1281: 123–140.

Wickel, Ertic E., and Joey C. Eisenmann. 2007. "Contribution of Youth Sport to Total Daily Physical Activity among 6- to 12-Yr-Old Boys." *Medicine and Science in Sports and Exercise* 39.9: 1493–1500.

Wiecha, Jean L., Alison M. El Ayadi, Bernard F. Fuemmeler, Jill E. Carter, Shirley Handler, Stacy Johnson, Nancy Strunk, Debra Korzec-Ramirez, and Steven L. Gortmaker. 2004.

"Diffusion of an Integrated Health Education Program in an Urban School System: Planet Health." *Journal of Pediatric Psychology* 29.6: 467–474.

Wiecha, Jean L., Georgia Hall, Ellen Gannett, and Barbara Roth. 2012. "Healthy Eating in Out-of-School Time: The Promise and the Challenge." Wellesley, MA: National Institute on Out-of-School Time, Wellesley Centers for Women, Wellesley College.

Wilde, Parke. 2009. "Self-Regulation and the Response to Concerns about Food and Beverage Marketing to Children in the United States." *Nutrition Reviews* 67.3: 155–166.

CHAPTER 5

The Children Are Our Future

THE NFL, CORPORATE SOCIAL RESPONSIBILITY, AND THE PRODUCTION OF "AVID FANS"

Jeffrey Montez de Oca, Jeffrey Scholes, and Brandon Meyer

What we tried to do was not just expect that kids would come to the NFL and the game would be handed down to them, but that they could find the NFL in all the places where they're already spending time.
—Peter O'Reilly, NFL VP/Fan Strategy & Marketing (cited in "Child's Play" 2010)

Imagine "Andrew," a third-grader at a public school in Jacksonville, Florida, goes to his morning math class and listens to his teacher ask a question to the class: "If the Denver Broncos score two touchdowns plus extra points, three field goals and a safety, and the Jacksonville Jaguars score three touchdowns plus extra points and two field goals, which team won the game?" At lunch in the cafeteria, Andrew notices several of his friends are wearing "Fuel Up to Play 60" T-shirts and standing around a brand-new, oversized refrigerator filled with bottles of milk. Next to a life-size cardboard cutout of one of his favorite Jaguars players is the actual player in the same promotional T-shirt. After lunch, Andrew walks into the gym for PE to find it festooned with the Play 60 logo all over the walls. Jaxson, the mascot of the Jaguars, is dancing with the National Dairy Council's own mascot, an upright cow. Andrew is handed his own Play 60 T-shirt, he listens to several Jaguars players speak on proper training and safety, and then lastly he joins his schoolmates in an hour of calisthenics with the players. While it is hard to imagine such crass marketing taking place in schools, in fact scenes like the one described here take place in schools all over the United States and are eagerly captured by the cameras of the National Football League (NFL) (e.g., "PLAY 60 Jaguars Story" 2014).

What exactly is the NFL doing, and how could it have such unrestrained access to youth in schools? Connecting to youth is a strategic imperative and a top priority for the NFL. According to Jon Show (2009), 55 percent of *avid* NFL fans, those that buy more game tickets and merchandise as well as watch more games than casual fans, engaged with football in elementary school or earlier. And 75 percent of avid fans and 62 percent of casual fans participated in football at some level as children (Show 2009). Furthermore, the NFL Players Union estimates that 60 to 70 percent of all NFL players begin their careers in Pop Warner football (Fainaru and Fainaru-Wada 2013). Yet as Peter O'Reilly indicates, the traditional ways of attracting kids to the NFL by "natural" means have been abandoned in favor of a more "artificial" and ubiquitous product placements.

This proactive, rather than reactive, recruitment strategy is a calculated response to a variety of current social forces, including (1) an expansion of entertainment options such as competing sports (e.g., basketball, soccer, mixed martial arts, alternative sports, etc.) and new media technologies (e.g., video games, social media, portable devices, etc.) and (2) growing anxieties about the health risks of football, especially among middle-class parents (Strudler 2013). Given these pressing concerns, the NFL has chosen not to bombard youth and parents with traditional media messages that can easily be discounted. Instead, the NFL is deploying corporate social responsibility (CSR) marketing campaigns to address a real social problem, youth health, and to construct an image of a healthy lifestyle that weaves NFL marketing messages into "all the places where they're already spending time."[1]

CSR straddles a fundamental tension between attempts to create social goods and to further business interests by gaining a return on investment (Babiak 2010; Carroll 1999). On the side of social good, the NFL provides resources and expertise for fostering the health of youth on two fronts: decrease the rate of childhood obesity and reduce the rate of injuries in youth football. In terms of return on investment, the NFL attempts to achieve two interrelated goals: counter the growing impression that football is unhealthy and create avid fans from children who are increasingly drawn away from football by other leisure options. To do so, the NFL's CSR initiatives attempt to develop corporate-led grassroots marketing campaigns, otherwise known as AstroTurfing (Anderson 1996). These campaigns mobilize state and nonstate resources to engage children in spaces such as schools and parks. For example, through NFL PLAY 60, the NFL offers schools competitive grants to build health infrastructure, expert knowledge, and visits by NFL stars. To win the grants and visits, however, schools must agree to remove competing brand images and grant access to NFL experts (who understandably crowd out other authorities at the school) who will teach children healthy lifestyle choices and provide them with activities through which youth can produce themselves as certain kinds of subjects. Because these types of CSR initiatives are not regulated by the FTC (Federal Trade Commission) or FCC (Federal Communications Commission), the NFL gains a significant advantage over its past use of traditional marketing messages on television or the Internet. Whereas television and the Internet are regulated by the Children's Television Act of 1990 and the Children's Online Privacy Protection Act of 1998 and competition for the attention of viewers is more intense (Montgomery and Chester 2009; Moore and Rideout 2007), the NFL is able to create unregulated, "brand-pure" spaces that are both pedagogical and performative.

People certainly do benefit from a healthy diet and regular exercise. Indeed, social reformers in the early twentieth-century's playground movement argued that health and spaces to play were fundamental rights (see Clarke 1993, 251; see also Azzarito, Munro, and Solmon 2004; Frost 1978; Marsden 1961; McArthur 1975; Spencer-Wood 1994). While there is debate in the United States as to whether access to proper nutrition and playful exercise in an affluent society should be considered aspects of "social citizenship" (see Marshall 1964), there is little debate that these concerns have traditionally fallen under the category of "public health." However, when the management of access to healthy alternatives for the citizenry moves from a public jurisdiction and into a corporatized private realm, then "consumer citizenship" begins to replace social citizenship. By "consumer citizenship," we mean the idea that subjects perform a national subjecthood by attending to self-management and "correct" rather than pathological consumption patterns. And, as imagined, it is corporations that, through marketing techniques, "educate" the public on what and how much to consume. In short, consumer citizenship requires citizens to productively engage society through responsible, ethical consumption of commodities (Banet-Weiser 2007, 9; see also Banet-Weiser and Lapsansky 2008; Johnston 2008; Miller 2007; Özkan and Foster 2005; Scammell 2003).

In this chapter, we draw upon trade journal articles as well as NFL publicity material and documents to demonstrate how the NFL uses its youth CSR to participate in the governance of society and to produce future fans by moving youth into the category of consumer citizens. The two primary discourses that the NFL's CSR utilizes to govern and then mobilize kids to become brand loyal are those involving the "epidemic" of childhood obesity and concerns over the safety of football at all levels. Both issues tap into legitimate societal worries and permit the NFL to step in and govern the lives of children and their parents for the purpose of solving these problems. The means by which the NFL is allowed to intervene in this way and create new consumer citizens is through a hybrid governmental formation that emerges from a complex web of strategic alliances between private- and public-sector actors and organizations—the hallmark of neoliberal governmentality. This chapter exposes the inherent tension between the word and deed of both the NFL and broader neoliberal ideologies. What will become clear is, on one hand, the shrewdness of the NFL in its use of CSR through which it intends to maintain its unquestioned supremacy in US sports and, on the other hand, some flaws in the neoliberal agenda that encourages private corporations to act in the governance of society.

Neoliberal Governmentality and
Corporate Social Responsibility

CSR emerged with neoliberal transformations in capital during the late twentieth century. We use the term "neoliberalism" to describe the emergence of a form of capitalism in the United States and around the world following the collapse of postwar Fordism and the Keynesian state in the early 1970s (Antonio and Bonanno 2000; Gilmore 1998/1999; Harvey 1990, 2010). David Harvey argues that capital is not a thing but a dynamic "process in which money is perpetually sent in search of more money" (Harvey 2010, 40), and neoliberalism denotes a political-economic philosophy and set of policies that attempt to constantly speed up the flow of capital through a fully globalized economy. Therefore, neoliberalism, at least in the Global North, is characterized by deregulation that releases constraints upon capital; the utilization of new technologies (communication, transportation, production, and management) to maximize efficiencies and flexibility within a globalized production, distribution, and consumption environment; and the ascendance of an ideology of personal responsibility that states that individuals alone are the bearers of their own destinies (Antonio and Bonanno 2000; Best and Kellner 1997; Bourdieu 1998; Castells 1996; Gilmore 1998/1999; Kochhar, Fry, and Taylor 2011; Martinez and Garcia 1996; Miller 2007). The effect since the 1970s has been to magnify relations of inequality as the state and corporations divest from the public in favor of voluntary participation of private organizations and citizens. As the cost of living rises and the funding of social welfare (including schools) declines, people profoundly feel transformations in the economic environment because labor is forced to take up costs previously paid by the state and the capitalist class. As economic inequality intensifies with a shrinking of the public, neoliberal capitalism expands the private and supports greater governance of society by corporations, hence the creation and legitimacy of corporate citizenship.

As the state withdraws from the public, corporations like the NFL step into the lurch by providing public goods and funding for services, such as education and health initiatives, which were previously provided by the state. Archie B. Carroll (1999) argues that these modern CSR practices emerged in the 1950s, expanded during the 1960s, and have become more prevalent since the 1970s. Carroll (1979) initially outlined three primary aspects to a corporation's social responsibility. First, since businesses are the fundamental economic institutions in a capitalist society; they have a primary social responsibility to make a profit by producing goods and providing services. Second, corporations are responsible to society to make a profit legally since the rule of law governs society. Third, social responsibility includes a voluntary dimension that is composed of the societal expectations of businesses beyond what is required by law (Carroll 1979, 504). Carroll later added that corporations should engage in philanthropic activities, or corporate citizenship (Carroll 1991, 43). From his perspective, *making a profit is a public good* and is not something a firm does only for itself (Carroll 1999, 284). However, as Kathy Babiak (2010) argues, this overlooks an inherent contradiction in the goals of CSR by linking social good (value rationality) with profitability (instrumental rationality). But can the public good truly be realized through private interest as Adam Smith's famous invisible hand quote suggests? Or will the striving for the public good as *the* end always work at cross-purposes with activities that seek private gain as its sole end? Indeed, we argue that this is a fundamental contradiction that NFL CSR attempts to flatten but cannot remove.

It is no coincidence that the expansion of CSR in the United States coincides with the ascendance of neoliberalism. Scholars note the many advantages CSR offers businesses: a healthy free society is good for capitalism; brand differentiation; favorable publicity that creates a cushion from negative publicity; increased brand loyalty; and the gain of support for tax breaks and other government subsidies by building the public trust (see Babiak 2010; Babiak and Wolfe 2006; Carroll 1979, 1991, 1999; Pharr and Lough 2012). These CSR activities not only create publicity opportunities for corporations, but also allow corporations to take on a governmental role by funding and structuring services that formerly were provided by the state (McMurria 2008). Furthermore, when corporations take on a governmental role of this nature, they gain marketing access to children (considered in trade and communications policy a vulnerable population) in unregulated spaces. Indeed, and perhaps ironically, policies that allow ruling capitalist class fractions to divest from the public have created a public context of need, such as the defunding of school-based athletic programs, which justifies corporations' voluntary intervention into governance via voluntary CSR marketing activities.

The focus on health and fitness provides a powerful form of governmentality that applies funding and expert knowledge to the problem of individuals producing themselves according to an idealized model of subjecthood. Michel Foucault defines governmentality as "the conduct of conduct" and thus as a term which ranges from "governing the self" to "governing others" (Foucault 1991). Thomas Lemke (2001) adds that this includes solving "problems of self-control, guidance for the family and for children, management of the household, directing the soul, etc." (Lemke 2001, 191). And we see this in NFL CSR: children are given knowledge and techniques of self-care for themselves and their families in public spaces that lack competing marketing messages ("NFL Announces" 2011; "NFL Play 60 Super School Contest" 2013). In this way, the social problem of childhood obesity and the cost of ameliorating it become a private problem and a matter of citizens' self-care (Dworkin and Wachs 2009) that is funded by the NFL and guided by the expert knowledge of professional athletes. And this makes NFL CSR a neoliberal rather than liberal form of governmentality.

As far as the NFL is concerned, the production of the subject as citizen and future worker becomes tied to his or her future as a football fan. As Peter O'Reilly, NFL VP/Fan Strategy & Marketing, states in regard to investing in school athletics, "We have a strategic imperative of getting kids connected to the game at a young age. We know the correlation of kids playing the game and then becoming fans of the game. When you start to cut into the access to play sports and to play football, the prospect of that impacts our fan base over the long haul" (cited in King 2010). In other words, school-based athletics have historically produced football fans by training youth to love football, and as school-based athletics is defunded, the NFL is permitted to step into this lacunae and market itself as "true football" in the process. So while NFL Films and popular history books may tell heroic stories about football players that teach youth the excitement and lore of the game, the NFL's CSR marketing grabs hold of their bodies and reaches into their souls with reduced barriers from the state. In what follows, we outline how the NFL actually does this.

Play 60: Improved Diet and Exercise to End the "Epidemic" of Childhood Obesity

To get the future Packer Cheeseheads or the future Redskin Hogettes studies show that kids have to be interested in the NFL early. Is it working? In the season opener there was a 30% jump in viewership among kids 12-and-under.
                    —Journalist Lee Cowan (cited in "Child's Play" 2010)

The NFL's youth health CSR is housed under the rubric of Play 60 that has two components: NFL PLAY 60 and Fuel Up to Play 60. NFL PLAY 60 attempts to "tackle childhood obesity by getting kids active through in-school, after-school and team-based programs, online child-targeted outreach on NFLRUSH.com, and many partnerships with like-minded organizations" ("NFL PLAY 60" 2009). Fuel Up to Play 60 is "an in-school nutrition and physical activity campaign launched by the National Dairy Council (NDC), the nutrition research and education arm of the dairy checkoff and the National Football League" ("Dairy Checkoff" 2010).[2] The basic message behind PLAY 60 is children should eat less and exercise more in order to realize the ambitious goal to *end childhood obesity in a generation* ("Ending Childhood Obesity" 2010). To that end, NFL PLAY 60 encourages children to burn more calories by getting "at least sixty minutes of physical activity a day" ("Why and How" 2014) and Fuel Up to Play 60 fosters the taking in of fewer calories by improving school-based nutrition programs and spreading knowledge of a healthful diet (Kalb 2010). Given the contemporary cultural linkage among health, thinness, and personal responsibility, Play 60's message seems inoffensive as it articulates dominant cultural imperatives (Markula and Pringle 2006).

Health researchers generally agree that since the 1980s childhood obesity has become a growing social problem. But many are critical of labeling it an "epidemic," arguing that obesity rates have been greatly overstated, the epidemic label medicalizes a social problem, and it narrows ways of understanding or ameliorating obesity (Boero 2007; Evans 2006; Gard 2011; Guthman 2009, 2013a, 2013b; Lee 2013; Saguy and Riley 2005; Wright 2009). Nevertheless, the epidemic label, embraced by the NFL and sympathetic journalists, provides a powerful, fear-inducing frame that legitimates immediate and significant policy interventions to protect children and thereby the future. For instance, sports consultant Andy Dolich stokes this fear by proclaiming, "The threat of childhood obesity to the health of America's children has never been greater. For the first time in our history, the United States is raising a generation of children whose health and wellness is in jeopardy" (Dolich 2010).[3]

We understand the epidemic label through the concept of healthism, or how health promotions, including marketing, construct ideas in popular culture about normality, well-being, and morality (Crawford 1980). Healthism constructs moral hierarchies by labeling some bodies "healthy" and others "unhealthy" or pathological. As a mother quoted in a NFL-*Newsweek* publication said of her four-hundred-pound son, "I'm just hoping that Malik can be normal and do some of the things that regular-size kids can do" (Cornblatt 2010, 21). Shari Dworkin and Faye Wachs (2009) argue that healthism produces a neoliberal discourse that turns social problems, such as obesity, into personal problems by making the body a marker of a good, moral, and appropriate lifestyle. Similarly, "bad health" is pathological and a signifier for an individual's moral lack as translated as the lack of discipline to resist unhealthy temptations or the lack of motivation to work off the day's sins in the gym (Dworkin and Wachs 2009, 11–13). Fundamentally, healthism relies on the idiom of personal responsibility at a moment when public support has been stripped away. Hines Ward of the Pittsburgh Steelers reflects this view: "And now with the economy taking away school programs that educate students on how to eat healthy, it's really up to the kids to get outside and apply their knowledge on how to eat well on their own instead of sitting on their couch playing Xbox all day" (cited in Rodriguez 2010, 27).

The "eat less, exercise more" slogan recapitulates the biblical prohibitions against sloth and gluttony in contemporary language (Sifferlin 2014) while shifting the cost of social problems onto individuals. Through the lens of moral failings, the obese can "be seen as posing a risk to society in general, demonstrated in policy and media reporting through frequent reference to the amount obesity costs in health care and lost time from work" (Evans 2006, 262). The epidemic label transforms a symptom of social problems into a disease, a medical condition in need of direct and swift intervention. And the "eat less, exercise more" slogan transfers the burden of structural explanations, such as poverty and barriers to education, for weight gain onto individuals through a discourse of personal responsibility and subsequent moral failing (Brownell et al. 2010). Ultimately, healthism depoliticizes health by individualizing it and severely downplaying the structural forces that contribute to health outcomes. It, thus, necessitates profitable medical interventions to fight the supposed epidemic while increasing the power of private institutions to dictate the terms of the epidemic and thereby wielding incredible control over (children's) bodies (Crawford 1980).

There is tremendous irony in the NFL using professional football players in a campaign to end obesity since one study found 56 percent of active NFL players are obese in comparison to 31 percent of all US men and women (Harp 2005). Of greater irony is the fact that the NFL dismissed the study by claiming BMI does not accurately measure obesity ("NFL: Study Finds" 2005) but uses BMI as unquestioned evidence of an "epidemic of childhood obesity." While this raises questions about the NFL's commitment to health and the healthfulness of football, the NFL has made a significant investment in youth health(ism). Currently, the NFL donates about $115 million annually to charity, with $20 to $25 million distributed through the NFL Foundation,[4] about $8 million directed to NFL Charities, and another $100 million to Play 60 (Kaplan 2009).[5] The NFL believes these investments will generate return on investment, as O'Reilly states that their research "affirms a lot of what we hypothesized in terms of the importance of marketing to youth. . . . Not everyone that's a fan is going to play the game, so we've really built out what we think is a good portfolio of ways to connect with kids in the six to thirteen range" (cited in Show 2009).

NFL CSR attempts to create governmental formations dedicated to teaching healthy lifestyles where youth are trained in personal responsibility and proper consumption of commodities. For instance, the NFL PLAY 60 Super School program offers thirty-four schools (thirty-two of which are located in a NFL market) grants of ten thousand dollars for health and wellness programming or equipment ("NFL Announces" 2011). The "winning schools will have the opportunity to host a visit from their favorite NFL team and an NFL player and participate in the Ultimate NFL Physical Education Class" ("NFL Announces" 2011). To enter the contest, a school representative must (1) explain how the school will brand itself an NFL school, (2) outline its program and needs, and (3) explain how the school's programming supports the Play 60 mission. As DallasCowboys.com explains, "participants have to write three essays about how their school is celebrating the return of football, the condition of their school's PE environment and how their school is teaching the importance of health and wellness" (Helman 2013). The NFL provides school representatives with suggestions for branding their school: "Are you incorporating football words into spelling lessons? Using touchdowns and field goals in math problems? Designing/coloring your own jerseys in art class?" ("NFL Play 60 Super School Contest" 2013).

To extend their reach and defer costs, the NFL engages in multiple strategic alliances in its CSR. Tom Vilsack, the secretary of agriculture, describes Fuel Up to Play 60 as an "unprecedented partnership" among the NFL, the National Dairy Council (NDC), and the USDA that "will help educate our youth about steps they can and should take to lead healthy lives" (cited in "NDC, USDA and NFL" 2010). Through the "Breakfast Blitz" campaign the NDC offers quarter-million-dollar grants to schools in order to improve their food infrastructure and hires NFL stars to promote dairy consumption. Victor Cruz of the New York Giants succinctly states the importance of milk to living a well-ordered, moral life: "Living a healthy lifestyle was important when I was growing up, and I credit it with helping me get to where I am today. . . . It's something I'm teaching my daughter now, even though she's very young. We make sure every morning includes milk. The Breakfast Blitz program helps fund healthy breakfasts in schools. Nothing else sets you up for a great day like a morning meal with milk" ("got milk?" 2013; "NFL's Victor Cruz" 2013). Through funding and education, Fuel Up to Play 60 is a governmental formation organized by the economic geography of thirty-two regional NFL markets in conjunction with local dairy councils and schools ("NDC, USDA and NFL" 2010). Because obesity is thought of as an individualized, personal problem, corporations like the NFL and the dairy industry are thus able to market their brand as the solution for these social problems.

The pamphlet *How to Build a Healthy Kid: Back-to-School Guidebook* (Rosenberg 2010) deserves special attention since it was produced by *Newsweek* magazine in partnership with Fuel Up to Play 60 and is centrally about public-private sector alignments in the governance of citizens' bodies. The first article in the pamphlet, marked "Advertisement" to differentiate it from other articles (all of the articles marked as advertising were paid for by Fuel Up to Play 60), begins with the fear-invoking claim of epidemic that is tied to budget cuts, a testing culture, and the reduction of physical education: "OUR KIDS ARE BECOMING UNHEALTHY AND SEDENTARY, yet budget cuts and the pressure to boost test results mean physical education and school teams have been reduced or slashed altogether" (Rosenberg 2010, 1). The article then presents Fuel Up to Play 60 as a solution to the crisis since the USDA, all thirty-two NFL teams, and local dairy councils with the support of numerous health and nutrition organizations encourage "students to collaborate with teachers and other school staff on healthy eating and exercise strategies" (Rosenberg 2010, 1).

A similar crisis-solution narrative familiar to advertising structures the other articles in the guidebook as well. In the next article, Tom Vilsack claims that today's children may not live as long as their parents but through collaborative efforts like Fuel Up to Play 60 the trends can be reversed (Vilsack 2010). David Satcher, former US surgeon general, argues that the conditions of modern life produce "couch potatoes" susceptible to ailments like diabetes and heart disease. He then declares that schools are the key institution to intervene in the social body since they, in collaboration with Fuel Up to Play 60, can normalize healthy lifestyles for large groups of people (Satcher 2010). Food and health writer Claudia Kalb describes the terrible conditions in most schools' lunch rooms and argues that "revolutionizing school lunch is no easy task" (Kalb 2010, 9). She then provides instruction on institutional transformation of school lunch service to create healthier environments. An "advertisement" titled "Reading, Writing and . . . Eating" uses parents' fears of losing control over their children in middle school to legitimate state and corporate interventions into middle schools to teach children proper consumption patterns (e.g., eating vegetables). The advertisement features a photograph of Roberto Garcia, Chicago Bears, and a photo of an African American boy carrying a tray loaded with dairy products while wearing a Fuel Up to Play 60 hoodie (Rosenberg 2010, 14–15). The advertisement goes on to explain that correcting the lifestyles of children also exerts a governing effect on families. A teen in a Fuel Up to Play 60 program in Huntington, West Virginia, which is the poorest area in the state (McComas 2014) and was identified by the Centers for Disease Control and Prevention as one of the least healthy places in the United States, stated, "My eating habits have definitely changed at home, too. . . . My family has listened, too. I told them about good nutrition and now they are eating better" (Rosenberg 2010, 17). The message suggests that even in the most depressed, backward, unhealthy food environments, NFL CSR can teach healthy lifestyles and children can become the parents of a healthier tomorrow. However, that healthier tomorrow is predicated on corporate governance of society and consumer citizenship.

Protecting the Future through Proper Tackling and Improved Safety Equipment

Football will remain the hard-hitting, physical sport that you love. And we will continue to be vigilant in seeking ways to make the game even better and safer. The future of football is brighter, bigger, better, and more exciting than ever.
—Roger Goodell (2013)

Throughout its history, football in the United States has struggled with a central conundrum: fans are attracted to and exhilarated by the spectacular violence on the field, but many people, fan and nonfan alike, are horrified by the physical, mental, and emotional damage caused by that violence. The current health panic centers on neurological damage caused by violent blows to the head and concussions. And while media mostly focus on NFL players, Little League, high school, and collegiate players numerically are at far greater risk physically, mentally, and financially (Easterbrook 2014). High school football players sustain an estimated 43,200 to 67,200 concussions per year, though the actual number may be higher due to underreporting (Broglio et al. 2009). As a result, middle-class parents are increasingly hesitant to sign up their children for tackle football (Strudler 2013). President Barack Obama famously declared in early 2014, "I would not let my son play pro football" (Remnick 2014), and Hall of Fame quarterbacks Terry Bradshaw and Troy Aikman have agreed with that sentiment (McIntyre 2012). Pop Warner football witnessed a 9.5 percent drop in participation between 2010 and 2012 mostly attributed to concerns about the dangers of concussions (Fainaru and Fainaru-Wada 2013). However, it is crucial for the long-term success of the NFL that children watch and play football at a young age. If parents route their children into other activities and away from football, then the NFL risks losing a crucial node in the process of producing both labor (players) and consumers (avid fans). What this means is that the spectacular violence at the center of football that is both the motor and limit of its growth must be managed.

Violence cannot be removed from the game since it defines football. As a result, the NFL is attempting to manage the violence by branding the game as safe and healthful. We have already seen how the NFL brands itself as healthful. The NFL engages in youth football CSR by sponsoring USA Football (a national governing body for youth football) and Heads Up Football (a football training and certification program) that together attempt to reduce young football players' risk of injury by teaching proper tackling technique and supporting improved football safety technology ("More Than 900 Youth Leagues" 2013).

USA Football composes the center of the NFL's youth football CSR. "USA Football engages with parents and players through Heads Up Football®, Protection Tour events, USA Football's website and other opportunities, making them part of the education process" (USA Football 2014, 12). And as youth football's national governing body, it "leads the game's development, inspires participation, and ensures a positive experience for all youth, high school, and other amateur players" (usafootball.com). Guided by a "train-the-trainer" strategy, USA Football organizes football clinics, camps, and other events through which it attempts to produce a cadre of leaders at the local level who will disseminate USA Football–generated knowledge (USA Football 2014, 8). USA Football organizes regional player development camps that "feature two days of competition, including individual drills, one-on-one training and seven-on-seven situations" (usafootball.com/trials-registration). Similarly, the organization sponsors a "Protection Tour" that "is a free, one-day event held at NFL and college football training facilities for youth football players and parents to learn the Heads Up Football[SM] curriculum" (usafootball.com/protection-tour). Ultimately, USA Football mobilizes local leaders to spread the NFL word and mobilize thousands of parents and youth to produce themselves as NFL subjects.

The central message—that football is safe for children—is communicated primarily through teaching techniques, as Melissa Stark reported on *NFL Total Access*: "Heads Up Football is all about teaching coaches the safest way to tackle and the safest way to fit equipment" ("NFL Makes Unprecedented Commitment" 2013).

USA Football also invested a million and a half dollars in research and development (USA Football 2014, 23) that supports its central message: "research commissioned by USA Football unearthed exciting insights and gained national attention
on how *youth football will continue to be made safer*" (USA Football 2014, 5, emphasis added). USA Football also has a Medical Advisory Committee and a Tackle
Advisory Committee staffed by experts in their relative fields to help develop the
Heads Up curriculum and other safety information (usafootball.com/).

Perhaps USA Football's most powerful rhetorical tool in branding football as
safe is the image of a concerned yet supportive parent. Stephon Blackwell, Youth
Football commissioner, stated, "Parents love their kids, and they want the safest
possible environment for their kids to participate in" (USA Football 2014, 6).
Even more powerful than the generic parent is the image of a good mother
whose fears are set aside by Heads Up Football. Charlotte Jones Anderson, NFL
Foundation chairman, speaks simultaneously as an NFL executive and a mother
when talking to *NFL Total Access*: "Clearly as moms we think about things a lot
differently. And we really want our kids to be safe. A lot of this is education.
A lot of moms don't know the rules; they don't know a thing about their
coaches; they don't know how to help their kids. So this gives us a platform
to educate them so they can in turn help their kids and put them in the right
position" ("NFL Makes Unprecedented Commitment" 2013). The good mother
image in NFL discourse works to create a sense of comfort and health while
demonstrating the NFL's concern for kids and community. A Heads Up Football
PSA featuring an African American boy and his attractive, light-skinned mother
visually constructs the message of comfort and health. The PSA begins with the
son walking toward the camera in a bucolic park; the mother's arm is around
him. The shot is well lit and upbeat; non-diegetic music softly plays as a gentle
voice-over narration states,

> Together we make the game safer from the ground up.
> By making sure the fit of the equipment is every bit as good as the equipment.
> By making proper tackling the goal from the very first snap.
> And by making certification more important than any win-loss record.
> We make it safer because to us it is so much more than a game.
> Make sure your coach is Heads Up certified today, go to usafootball.com.

As the narrator speaks, the viewer sees images of adults carefully fitting children
with protective gear and training them in a variety of settings. The video ends
as the mother and son, presumably after the game, walk away from the camera
holding hands and we hear the final words of the narration, "Because Together
We Make Football." In effect, a Black mother brings her child to a football game
and turns him over to a multiracial group of NFL-trained men who take on the
fatherly role of training, conditioning, and socializing the boy before returning
him safe and sound back to the mother. With the aid of the NFL and through

football as a technology of self, the commercial suggests, the family and community are made healthful and whole.

Mothers in NFL CSR are cleverly enlisted in the use of pedagogy over the concern with violence. They become willing students of the NFL that is instructing them on the efforts made to keep their kids safe. In addition, mothers, in turn, become grateful recipients of this knowledge, thus legitimizing the NFL as a kind of surrogate father. Moreover, mothers are constructed as a progressive force supporting reforms to make football safe that men tend to resist. Shane Bregar, Pride of Iowa Youth Football commissioner, stated about Heads Up Football, "There are a lot of coaches hesitant to change and who maybe don't agree or understand what is safest for the players. . . . But I have had a lot of the mothers thanking me. They think it is great that we are trying to make it safer for their children" (USA Football 2014, 15). By valorizing mothers, the NFL likely hopes to neutralize the greatest potential opponents to boys playing football and potentially draw them into a broader community of football fans.

The NFL walks a racial tightrope in its youth health CSR marketing messages. This PSA as well as the *How to Build a Healthy Kid* pamphlet indicate that the NFL is aware that the United States is increasingly becoming a multiracial society with growing affluence in some communities of color. As a result, we see a kind of liberal multiculturalism where racial difference is visible but unacknowledged. At the same time, the NFL must also be aware that its core fan base remains white, middle-class baby boomers who tend to view football as a vehicle of social mobility for poor white and minority kids (Eitzen 1999; Montez de Oca 2012, 2013a, 2013b). NFL publicity follows a postracial strategy of demonstrating inclusivity and diversity divested of politics, conflict, or structural transformation (Banet-Weiser 2007). Relying upon a familiar trope of social uplift through individual effort and personal responsibility, NFL publicity mobilizes existing stereotypes of racial minorities (e.g., cannot self-govern, high rates of single-mother-headed households, mothers cannot socialize children alone, etc.) to construct its image of public good and in doing so reifies white supremacist ideologies.

Corporate Citizens and Consumer Citizenship

The art of government essentially appears in this literature as having to answer the question of how to introduce economy—that is to say, the proper way of managing individuals, goods, and wealth, like the management of a family by a father who knows how to direct his wife, his children, and his servants.

—Michel Foucault (1991, 92)

It should surprise no one that the NFL makes a lot of money. Reportedly, the NFL saw $9.5 billion in revenue in 2012 (Isidore 2013), and NFL executives boldly proclaim their intention to generate $25 billion a year by 2027 (Schrotenboer 2014). In addition to its revenue streams, the NFL also enjoys tremendous public subsidies and tax breaks that keep operating costs down (Easterbrook 2013). So while $115 million is a significant amount of money to give to charity, it is but 1.2 percent of their annual revenues and should more accurately be considered a part of their marketing budget rather than an altruistic gesture. These are not, however, traditional marketing campaigns that scream for viewers' attention. Instead they harken to the individual in far more subtle ways through systems of governance that intervene in people's everyday lives and instantiate a particular form of subjectivity. Through healthism, NFL CSR constructs the subject as the sole bearer of his or her own fate and divorces social responsibility from large-scale health patterns. So obesity is understood within a moral hierarchy of individual choices and discipline. Similarly, injuries in football are defined as resulting from improper (individual) techniques, improper use of equipment, and bad decisions rather than being endemic to the game itself. Ameliorating negative health patterns is reduced to educational programs that work more effectively to brand the NFL.

The NFL's CSR marketing highlights Foucault's point that any institution, both state and nonstate, can become instruments of government (Foucault 1991, 99) by intervening in people's lives and directing regimes of thought and ways of life (Lemke 2001, 191). Engaging in corporate citizenship allows the NFL to produce an image of a corporation generating public goods in terms of youth health broadly construed. More accurately it cynically accrues a greater good for the corporation by gaining marketing access to children and their parents in unregulated spaces. Once present in those spaces, it is able to enlist its celebrity athletes to deliver education on consumer citizenship framed by the language of epidemic. Through pedagogy on consumer citizenship the NFL is able to equate football with a healthy lifestyle and membership in the nation. More insidiously, the NFL is enlisting parents as deputized teachers of its efforts to make football as safe as possible. As the Foucault quote implies, the creation and sustenance of children as proper consumer citizens may begin with NFL directives, but is a dead letter without the direct management that only parents can convey in the home.

All the while, the NFL is not shy about stating its overriding goal: build a base of avid fans in the future so that it can continue to enjoy growing market share and revenue streams. It should also be noted that since the early twentieth century football has been equated with an essential American ethos and spirit (Montez de Oca 2013a, 2013b). By teaching youth healthful ways of life based on proper consumption of commodities in schools and parks as well as mollifying the justified fears of parents, the league boosts its image as a good corporate citizen that is looking out for you. Our research does not allow us to see how youth respond to or negotiate the ideological terrain constructed by NFL CSR.

Still, it is reasonable to assume that while there are varying degrees of buy-in among youth, they also appropriate the imagery and commodities for their own purposes that may or may not support NFL directives.

Still it is a testament to the overwhelming success of neoliberal ideology in the United States that, in the name of freedom, a private corporation can so seamlessly assume the role of the state in matters of the body politic. As researchers, we should be very skeptical of the NFL's commitment to the health of anything other than its own bottom line. Given the many exciting, less expensive athletic alternatives to tackle football, the health negatives clearly outweigh the health benefits of the game, as can be seen in the long-term injuries that football players sustain and their elevated obesity rates. From Richie Incognito to Ray Rice, the NFL and its franchises have been demonstrably insensitive to the health of their players and the players' families. Indeed, the NFL is notoriously cynical and unhealthful in its attitudes toward women. For instance, Mark Walker, NFL chief marketing officer, stated, "So 'the female' of the species—or as I like to call them, 'women'—are important to the NFL because they produce babies who could grow up to play football, watch football, and consume football-related items" (cited in Hess 2014). And, when the NFL partners with the dairy industry, Domino's, and McDonald's to promote youth health, we must question if it is public goods or private profits that these campaigns generate. Fundamentally, we need to ask if neoliberal political and economic policies that privatize governance actually serve the public's interest or primarily corporations that profit off of the public.

NOTES

1. We use "CSR" in this chapter as a term to describe a whole set of initiatives, policies, and practices that corporations engage in. We do so because this is standard nomenclature in the literature on CSR.

2. The national dairy checkoff is a dairy-promotion program that dairy farmers can contribute to through Dairy Management Inc. (2014).

3. Muscle gap critics made virtually identical and equally hyperbolic claims in the 1950s, which is ironic given that fifties youth are often envisioned as a model for youth today. See Montez de Oca (2005).

4. The NFL Foundation was previously known as the Youth Football Fund. Its mission is to improve "the health and safety of sports, youth football and the communities in which we live." See "Mission" (2014).

5. Since there is overlap in their contributions, the NFL estimates that $115 million is the approximate amount it gives.

REFERENCES

Anderson, Walter Truett. 1996. "Astroturf: The Big Business of Fake Grassroots Politics." New America Media http://news.newamericamedia.org/news/view_article.html?article_id= 18742ff01ca47064f33f58a05e73ce0e. Accessed June 19, 2014.

Antonio, Robert J., and Alessandro Bonanno. 2000. "A New Global Capitalism? From 'Americanism and Fordism' to 'Americanization-Globalization.'" *American Studies* 41.2/3: 33–77.

Azzarito, Laura, Petra Munro, and Melinda Solmon. 2004. "Unsettling the Body: The Institutionalization of Physical Activity at the Turn of the 20th Century." *Quest* 56.4: 377–396.

Babiak, Kathy. 2010. "The Role and Relevance of Corporate Social Responsibility in Sport: A View from the Top." *Journal of Management & Organization* 16.4: 528–549.

Babiak, Kathy, and Richard Wolfe. 2006. "More Than Just a Game? Corporate Social Responsibility and Super Bowl XL." *Sport Marketing Quarterly* 15.4: 214–222.

Banet-Weiser, Sarah. 2007. *Kids Rule! Nickelodeon and Consumer Citizenship*. Durham, NC: Duke University Press.

Banet-Weiser, Sarah, and Charlotte Lapsansky. 2008. "RED Is the New Black: Brand Culture, Consumer Citizenship, and Political Possibility." *International Journal of Communication* 2: 1248–1268.

Best, Steven, and Douglas Kellner. 1997. *The Postmodern Turn*. New York: Guilford.

Boero, Natalie. 2007. "All the News That's Fat to Print: The American 'Obesity Epidemic' and the Media." *Qualitative Sociology* 30: 41–60.

Bourdieu, Pierre. 1998. "The Essence of Neoliberalism: Utopia of Endless Exploitation." http://mondediplo.com/1998/12/08bourdieu. Accessed March 6, 2007.

Broglio, Steven P., Jacob J. Sosnoff, SungHoon Shin, Xuming He, Christopher Alcaraz, and Jerrad Zimmerman. 2009. "Head Impacts during High School Football: A Biomechanical Assessment." *Journal of Athletic Training* 44.4: 342–349.

Brownell, Kelly D., Rogan Kersh, David S. Ludwig, Robert C. Post, Rebecca M. Puhl, Marlene B. Schwartz, and Walter C. Willett. 2010. "Personal Responsibility and Obesity: A Constructive Approach to a Controversial Issue." *Health Affair* 29.3: 378–386.

Carroll, Archie B. 1979. "A Three-Dimensional Conceptual Model of Corporate Performance." *Academy of Management Review* 4.4: 497–505.

———. 1991. "The Pyramid of Corporate Social Responsibility: Toward the Moral Management of Organizational Stakeholders." *Business Horizons* 34.4: 39–48.

———. 1999. "Corporate Social Responsibility: Evolution of a Definitional Construct." *Business Society* 38.3: 268–295.

Castells, Manuel. 1996. *The Rise of the Network Society: The Information Age: Economy, Society and Culture*. Vol. 1. Malden, MA: Blackwell.

"Child's Play: NFL Targeting Kids, Young Fans with New Initiatives." 2010. http://www .sportsbusinessdaily.com/Daily/Issues/2010/09/Issue-11/Leagues-Governing-Bodies/Childs -Play-NFL-Targeting-Kids-Young-Fans-With-New-Initiatives.aspx. Accessed November 19, 2013.

Clarke, Alan. 1993. "Civic Ideology in the Public Domain: Victorian Ideology in the 'Lifestyle Crisis' of the 1990s." In *Sport in Social Development: Traditions, Transitions, and Transformations*, edited by A. G. Ingham and J. W. Loy, 245–65. Champaign, IL: Human Kinetics.

Cornblatt, Johannah. 2010. "A Fitness Revolution: Obesity Killed Her Brother. Now Pamela Green-Jackson Is Helping Schools Close the Phys-Ed Gap." In Rosenberg, *How to Build a Healthy Kid*, 20–21.

Crawford, Robert. 1980. "Healthism and the Medicalization of Everyday Life." *International Journal of Health Services* 10.3: 365–388.

"Dairy Checkoff Kicks Off Second Year of Fuel Up to Play 60 Program." 2010. *Dairy Foods* 111.10: 15.

Dairy Management Inc. 2014. http://www.dairy.org. Accessed May 27, 2014.

Dolich, Andy. 2010. "A Perfect Fit for Sports Philanthropy." http://www.sportsbusinessdaily .com/Journal/Issues/2010/11/20101108/Opinion/Aperfect-Fit-For-Sports-Philanthropy .aspx. Accessed November 30, 2013.

Dworkin, Shari, and Faye Wachs. 2009. *Body Panic: Gender, Health, and the Selling of Fitness*. New York: New York University Press.

Easterbrook, Gregg. 2013. "How the NFL Fleeces Taxpayers." http://www.theatlantic.com/magazine/archive/2013/10/how-the-nfl-fleeces-taxpayers/309448/.

———. 2014. *Reminder: Most People Endangered by Football Don't Play in the NFL.* http://www.theatlantic.com/entertainment/print/2014/01/reminder-most-people-endangered-by-football-dont-play-in-the-nfl/283464/. Accessed January 30, 2014.

Eitzen, D Stanley. 1999. *Fair and Foul: Beyond the Myths and Paradoxes of Sport.* Lanham, MD: Rowman & Littlefield.

"Ending Childhood Obesity within a Generation." 2010. In Rosenberg, *How to Build a Healthy Kid*, 30.

Evans, Bethan. 2006. "'Gluttony or Sloth': Critical Geographies of Bodies and Morality in (Anti)Obesity Policy." *Area* 38.3: 259–267.

Fainaru, Steve, and Mark Fainaru-Wada. 2013. "Youth Football Participation Drops." http://espn.go.com/espn/print?id=9970532&type=story. Accessed November 14, 2013.

Foucault, Michel. 1991. "Governmentality." In *The Foucault Effect: Studies in Governmentality with Two Lectures by and an Interview with Michel Foucault*, edited by G. Burchell, C. Gordon, and P. Miller, 87–104. Chicago: University of Chicago Press.

Frost, Joe L. 1978. "The American Playground Movement." *Childhood Education* 54.4: 176–182.

Gard, Michael. 2011. "Truth, Belief and the Cultural Politics of Obesity Scholarship and Public Health Policy." *Critical Public Health* 21.1: 37–48.

Gilmore, Ruth. 1998/1999. "Globalization and US Prison Growth: From Military Keynesian to Post-Keynesian Militarism." *Race & Class* 40.2/3: 171–188.

Goodell, Roger. 2013. "A Message from the NFL Commissioner." October 4.

"'got milk?®' and Fuel Up to Play 60 Kick Off 'Breakfast Blitz' to Fuel America's Mornings with Milk." 2013. http://www.prnewswire.com/news-releases/got-milk-and-fuel-up-to-play-60-kick-off-breakfast-blitz-to-fuel-americas-mornings-with-milk-186003572.html. Accessed November 19, 2013.

Guthman, Julie. 2009. "Teaching the Politics of Obesity: Insights into Neoliberal Embodiment and Contemporary Biopolitics." *Antipode* 41.5: 1110–1133.

———. 2013a. "Beyond Counting Calories: Take the Obesity Fight to Environmental Toxins, Stress, and Capitalism." *Breakthrough*. http://thebreakthrough.org/index.php/journal/debates/the-making-of-the-obesity-epidemic-a-breakthrough-debate/disrupting-the-narrow-obesity-debate/.

———. 2013b. "Fatuous Measures: The Artificatual Construction of the Obesity Epidemic." *Critical Public Health* 23.3: 263–273.

Harp, Joyce B. 2005. "Obesity in the National Football League." *JAMA* 293: 1061–1062.

Harvey, David. 1990. *The Condition of Postmodernity: An Enquiry into the Origins of Cultural Change.* Cambridge, MA: Blackwell.

———. 2010. *The Enigma of Capital: and the Crises of Capitalism.* New York: Oxford University Press.

Helman, David. 2013. "NFL Play 60 Super School Contest Gives Chance at Grant, Team Visit." DallasCowboys.com.

Hess, Amanda. 2014. "The NFL Opines on 'the Role of the Female.'" http://www.slate.com/blogs/xx_factor/2014/09/18/nfl_on_women_football_marketer_explains_the_role_of_the_female.html. Accessed September 18, 2014.

Isidore, Chris. 2013. "Why Football Is Still a Money Machine." CNN, February 1. http://money.cnn.com/2013/02/01/news/companies/nfl-money-super-bowl/. Accessed July 10, 2014.

Johnston, Josée. 2008. "The Citizen-Consumer Hybrid: Ideological Tensions and the Case of Whole Foods Market." *Theory and Society* 37.3: 229–270.

Kalb, Claudia. 2010. "Lunchroom Makeover: How Schools Can Plant the Seeds for Healthy Eating." In Rosenberg, *How to Build a Healthy Kid*, 8–11.

Kaplan, Daniel. 2009. "NFL Goes Deep with Youth Health and Fitness." September 14. http://www.sportsbusinessdaily.com/Journal/Issues/2009/09/20090914/SBJ-In-Depth/NFL-Goes-Deep-With-Youth-Health-And-Fitness.aspx. Accessed November 20, 2013.

King, Bill. 2010. "High School Sports Running on Empty." http://www.sportsbusinessdaily
.com/Journal/Issues/2010/08/20100802/SBJ-In-Depth/High-School-Sports-Running-On
-Empty.aspx. Accessed November 20, 2013.

Kochhar, Rakesh, Richard Fry, and Paul Taylor. 2011. "Twenty-to-One: Wealth Gaps Rise
to Record Highs between Whites, Blacks, and Hispanics." In *Secondary Twenty-to-One:
Wealth Gaps Rise to Record Highs between Whites, Blacks and Hispanics*, edited by Paul
Taylor, 1–32. Washington, DC: Pew Research Center.

Lee, Helen. 2013. "The Making of the Obesity Epidemic: How Food Activism Led Public
Health Astray." *Breakthrough*. http://thebreakthrough.org/index.php/journal/past-issues/
issue-3/the-making-of-the-obesity-epidemic.

Lemke, Thomas. 2001. "'The Birth of Bio-Politics': Michel Foucault's Lecture at the Collège
de France on Neo-Liberal Governmentality." *Economy and Society* 30.2: 190–207.

Markula, Pirkko, and Richard Pringle. 2006. *Foucault, Sport, and Exercise: Power, Knowledge,
and Transforming the Self*. London: Routledge.

Marsden, Gerald. 1961. "Philanthropy and the Boston Playground Movement, 1885–1907."
Social Service Review 35.1: 48–58.

Marshall, T. H. 1964. "Citizenship and Social Class." In *Class, Citizenship, and Social Development: Essays by T. H. Marshall*, edited by S. M. Lipset, 65–122. Chicago: University of
Chicago Press.

Martinez, Elizabeth, and Arnoldo Garcia. 1996. "What Is Neoliberalism? A Brief Definition
for Activists." http://www.corpwatch.org/article.php?id=376. Accessed August 21, 2005.

McArthur, Benjamin. 1975. "The Chicago Playground Movement: A Neglected Feature of
Social Justice." *Social Service Review* 49.3: 376–395.

McComas, Josh. 2014. "Huntington Area Most Poverty Stricken in West Virginia." WSAZ
NewsChannel 3. http://www.wsaz.com/home/headlines/REPORT-Huntington-Area
-Most-Poverty-Stircken-in-West-Virginia-170573566.html. Accessed August 14, 2014.

McIntyre, Brian. 2012. "Terry Bradshaw Wouldn't Let Son Play Football Now." NFL.com,
June 14, 2012. http://www.nfl.com/news/story/09000d5d829d33b9/article/terry-bradshaw
-wouldnt-let-son-play-football-now. Accessed July 7, 2014.

McMurria, John. 2008. "Desperate Citizens and Good Samaritans: Neoliberalism and Makeover Reality TV." *Television & New Media* 9.4: 305–332.

Miller, Toby. 2007. *Cultural Citizenship: Cosmopolitanism, Consumerism, and Television in a
Neoliberal Age*. Philadelphia Temple University Press.

"Mission." 2014. http://www.nflfoundation.org/#mission.

Montez de Oca, Jeffrey. 2005. "'As Our Muscles Get Softer, Our Missile Race Becomes
Harder': Cultural Citizenship and the 'Muscle Gap.'" *Journal of Historical Sociology* 18.3:
145–171.

———. 2012. "White Domestic Goddess on a Postmodern Plantation: Charity and Com-
modity Racism in *The Blind Side*." *Sociology of Sport Journal* 29.2: 131–150.

———. 2013a. *Discipline and Indulgence: College Football, Media, and the American Way of
Life during the Cold War*. New Brunswick, NJ: Rutgers University Press.

———. 2013b. "Sport as Social Institution: Football Films and the American Dream." In
Cinematic Sociology: Social Life in Film, edited by J.-A. Sutherland and K. Feltey, 320–333.
Thousand Oaks, CA: Pine Forge Press.

Montgomery, Kathryn C., and Jeff Chester. 2009. "Interactive Food and Beverage Marketing: Targeting Adolescents in the Digital Age." *Journal of Adolescent Health* 45.3:
S18–S29.

Moore, Elizabeth S., and Victoria J. Rideout. 2007. "The Online Marketing of Food to Children: Is It Just Fun and Games?" *Journal of Public Policy & Marketing* 26.2: 202–220.

"More Than 900 Youth Leagues Commit to Safer Football Through USA Football's Heads Up
Football Program." 2013. http://usafootball.com/health-safety/more-900-youth-leagues
-commit-safer-football-through-heads-football-program. Accessed March 24, 2013.

"NDC, USDA and NFL Join Forces for School Wellness." 2010. *Dairy Foods*, February, 10.

"NFL Announces 34 Play 60 Super School." 2011. National Football League, October 31. http://nflcommunications.com/2011/10/31/nfl-announces-34-play-60-super-schools/. Accessed November 25, 2013.

"NFL Makes Unprecedented Commitment to USA Football." 2013. *NFL Total Access*. video.

"NFL PLAY 60: The NFL Movement for an Active Generation." 2012. National Football League, July 26. http://www.nfl.com/news/story/09000d5d80b4a489/article/nfl-play-60 -the-nfl-movement-for-an-active-generation. Accessed May 23, 2014.

"NFL Play 60 Super School Contest." [web site] [cited September 24, 2013]. Available from http://nflsuperschool.teamdigital.com/official-rules.php. Accessed September 24, 2013.

"NFL: Study Finds 56 Percent of Players Obese." 2005. *New York Times*, March 3.

"NFL's Victor Cruz Teams with Breakfast Blitz; $250k to Be Awarded to FUTP 60 Schools." 2013. Innovation Center for U.S. Dairy. http://dairygood.org/nfls-victor-cruz-teams-with -breakfast-blitz-250k-to-be-awarded-to-futp-60-schools/. Accessed November 20, 2013.

Özkan, Derya, and Robert J. Foster. 2005. "Consumer Citizenship, Nationalism, and Neoliberal Globalization in Turkey: The Advertising Launch of Cola Turka." *Advertising & Society Review* 6.3. http://www.volkskunde.uni-muenchen.de/vkee_download/derya/colaturka _ozk.pdf.

Pharr, Jennifer R., and Nancy L. Lough. 2012. "Differentiation of Social Marketing and Cause-Related Marketing in US Professional Sport." *Sport Marketing Quarterly* 21.2: 91–103.

"PLAY 60 Jaguars Story." 2014. *NFL Rush*. video.

Remnick, David. 2014. "Annals of the Presidency: Going the Distance." *New Yorker*, January 27. http://www.newyorker.com/reporting/2014/01/27/140127fa_fact_remnick?currentPage= all. Accessed July 7, 2014.

Rodriguez, Nayeli. 2010. "Throw Away the Junk Food: Two NFL Superstars Share Their Secrets about Exercise and Healthy Eating." In Rosenberg, *How to Build a Healthy Kid*, 26–28.

Rosenberg, Debra, ed. 2010. *How to Build a Healthy Kid: Back-to-School Guidebook*. New York: Newsweek.

Saguy, Abigail C., and Kevin W. Riley. 2005. "Weighing Both Sides: Morality, Mortality, and Framing Contests over Obesity." *Journal of Health Politics, Policy and Law* 30.5: 869–923.

Satcher, David. 2010. "A Call to Action: An Epidemic of Obesity Threatens Our Children's Future. What We Can Do About It." In Rosenberg, *How to Build a Healthy Kid*, 4–7.

Scammell, Margaret. 2003. "Citizen Consumers: Towards a New Marketing of Politics?" In *Media and the Restyling of Politics: Consumerism, Celebrity, and Cynicism*, edited by J. Corner and D. Pels, 117–137. London: Sage.

Schrotenboer, Brent. 2014. "NFL Takes Aim at $25 Billion, But at What Price?" *USA Today*, February 5. http://www.usatoday.com/story/sports/nfl/super/2014/01/30/super-bowl-nfl -revenue-denver-broncos-seattle-seahawks/5061197/. Accessed July 10, 2014.

Show, Jon. 2009. "Leagues Aim to Build Next Generation of Fans." *Sports Business Daily*, August 17. http://www.sportsbusinessdaily.com/Journal/Issues/2009/08/20090817/SBJ-In -Depth/Leagues-Aim-To-Build-Next-Generation-Of-Fans.aspx. Accessed November 20, 2013.

Sifferlin, Alexandra. 2014. "'Eat Less, Exercise More' Isn't the Answer for Weight Loss." *Time*. http://news360.com/article/241865423. Accessed June 4, 2014.

Spencer-Wood, Suzanne M. 1994. "Turn of the Century Women's Organizations, Urban Design, and the Origin of the American Playground Movement." *Landscape Journal* 13.2: 124–137.

Strudler, Keith. 2013. "Youth Football Takes Hard Hit: One-Third of Americans Less Likely to Allow Son to Play Football Because of Head Injury Risk." HBO Real Sports/Marist Poll. Poughkeepsie, NY: Marist College Institute for Public Opinion.

USA Football Annual Report. 2014. Indianapolis, IN: USA Football. http://usafootball.com/ sites/default/files/uploads/2013_usafb_annual_report.pdf.

Vilsack, Tom. 2010. "Call for Collaboration: An Open Letter to America's Educators." In Rosenberg, *How to Build a Healthy Kid*, 3.

"Why and How to Play 60." 2014. National Football League, May 27. https://school .fueluptoplay60.com/welcome/why-and-how-to-play60.php. Accessed March 27, 2014.

Wright, Jan. 2009. "Biopower, Biopedagogies, and the Obesity Epidemic." In *Biopolitics and the "Obesity Epidemic": Governing Bodies*, edited by J. Wright and V. Harwood, 1–14. New York: Routledge.

PART II

Fields of Play

KIDS NAVIGATING SPORT WORLDS

CHAPTER 6

Athletes in the Pool, Girls and Boys on Deck

THE CONTEXTUAL CONSTRUCTION OF GENDER IN COED YOUTH SWIMMING

Michela Musto

Although it is only eight o'clock in the morning, the swimming pool at the Sun Valley Aquatics Center is bustling with activity.[1] It is a warm, sunny day in Southern California, and three hundred kids are participating in a Sun Valley Swim Team (SVST) meet. Girls and boys as young as five years old rummage through their swim bags, grabbing goggles and swim caps as they walk toward the starting blocks. Between races, swimmers slather their arms with waterproof sunblock, laugh with their friends, and offer each other bites of half-eaten bagels. To my right, three eleven-year-old boys, Alex, Kevin, and Andrew, are sitting in a semicircle, scrutinizing a "heat sheet" that lists the names of other boys and girls they are racing against in their upcoming events.[2] Alex notices he is the only boy in his race, sparking the following conversation:

> ALEX: They're all girls! That's sad.
> KEVIN: That must suck.
> ANDREW: I know her [points to a name on the paper]. You're the only male! Have fun! You have the second-fastest time—she's first, you're second.
> ALEX: What's her time?
> ANDREW: [Sophia's] really fast. She was in Sharks.

Andrew flips the page, and the boys continue looking at their other events. Throughout their conversation, Alex, Kevin, and Andrew draw upon multiple and contradictory meanings of gender. Although they agree that it "sucks" to be the "only male" in an "all girls" event, the boys then discuss Sophia's athleticism in a relatively unremarkable manner. Instead of teasing Alex for being slower

125

than a girl, Andrew nonchalantly informs Alex that Sophia is "really fast," something neither Alex nor Kevin contests. How was it possible for gender to simultaneously be of minimal and significant interest to the swimmers?

Because gender is a social structure that is embedded within individual, interactional, and institutional relations, social change toward gender equality is uneven across the gender order (Connell 1987, 2009; Lorber 1994; Martin 2004; Risman 2004). The salience of gender varies across contexts, allowing some contexts to support more equitable patterns of gender relations than others (Britton 2000; Connell 1987; Deutsch 2007; Schippers 2002; Thorne 1993). Within a context, both structural mechanisms and hegemonic beliefs play an important role in determining whether individuals draw on and affirm group boundaries between the genders—what Barrie Thorne (1993) calls "borderwork" (Messner 2000; Morgan and Martin 2006; Ridgeway 2009; Ridgeway and Correll 2004). Although scholars have theorized that alternative patterns of gender relations may shape social relations when gender is less salient (Britton 2000; Connell 1987; Deutsch 2007; Ridgeway 2009; Schippers 2007), few empirical studies have followed a group of individuals across different contexts to understand how gender relations and meanings may change. As the dialogue among the boys on the swim team suggests, because individuals negotiate different systems of accountability as they move from one setting to the next, gender can take on multiple meanings as a result of contextually specific, group-based interactions.

In this chapter, I analyze nine months of participant observation research and fifteen semistructured interviews conducted with eight- to ten-year-old swimmers at SVST. I build upon scholarship that examines the contextual salience of gender (Britton 2000; Deutsch 2007; Messner 2000; Morgan and Martin 2006; Ridgeway 2009; Ridgeway and Correll 2004; Thorne 1993), arguing that the variable salience of gender played an important role in shaping the meanings swimmers associated with gender within and across different contexts at the pool. To do so, I outline the "gender geography," or the divisions of space and activity between girls and boys (Thorne 1993) within two contexts at the pool: focused situations when swimmers followed their coach's instructions, and unfocused free time when swimmers had fun with their friends. Within the most focused aspects of practice, gender was less salient and structural mechanisms encouraged the swimmers to interact in ways that undermined hegemonic patterns of gender relations. When the swimmers hung out with their friends before and after practices, however, gender was highly salient and the swimmers engaged in borderwork. In this context, similarities between the genders were obscured and the swimmers affirmed categorical and essentialist—but nonhierarchical—meanings of gender. Because the swimmers associated nonhierarchical meanings with gender across both contexts, I conclude by considering whether more equitable gender meanings and relations can potentially "spill over" from one context to another.

THE VARIABLE SALIENCE OF GENDER ACROSS CONTEXTS

Existing scholarship has identified specific structural mechanisms, such as formal and informal policies and practices, within an array of institutions that help explain how gender becomes a salient organizing principle in interactions (Messner 2000; Thorne 1993). In schools, the formal age separation and large number of students encourage boys and girls to engage in borderwork (Thorne 1993). At the same time, teachers can implement rules and seating charts that allow children to interact in "relaxed and non-gender-marked ways" (Moore 2001; Thorne 1993, 64). Similarly, bureaucratic policies reduce the amount of discrimination women experience within office workplaces (Morgan and Martin 2006; Ridgeway and Correll 2004). Yet the organization of many out-of-office business settings—such as having different tees for men and women on golf courses—continues to hold women professionals accountable to normative conceptualizations of gender (Morgan and Martin 2006).

In addition to structural mechanisms, hegemonic cultural beliefs also impact the salience of gender within interactions (Ridgeway 2009, 2011; Ridgeway and Correll 2000, 2004). Although the "default expectation" (Ridgeway and Correll 2004, 513) may be to treat individuals in accordance with hegemonic beliefs, these beliefs can be less salient within interactions depending on a context's gender composition, gender-typing, and institutional frame (Ridgeway 2009, 2011; Ridgeway and Correll 2000,; 2004). However, even when structural mechanisms allow for less oppressive gender relations within some contexts, individuals often "implicitly fall back on cultural beliefs about gender" in new and unscripted settings (Ridgeway 2009, 156), thus reinscribing hegemonic patterns of gender relations.

Although individuals are often framed by hegemonic patterns of gender relations within interactions, interactions can also be framed by less oppressive patterns of gender relations and meanings (Deutsch 2007; Hollander 2013; Ridgeway 2009; Ridgeway and Correll 2000, 2004; Schippers 2007). However, the processes that allow individuals to enact alternative patterns of gender relations remain undertheorized within existing scholarship (Finley 2010; Hollander 2013; Schippers 2002; Wilkins 2008). As sociologists have argued, there is not always a direct relationship between the cultural order and the meanings individuals associate with cultural representations (Connell 1987; Eliasoph and Lichterman 2003; Fine 1979; Swidler 1986). Instead, hegemonic meanings are negotiated and contested within group-based interactions (Eliasoph and Lichterman 2003). When applied to gender theory, the meanings people associate with gender may vary, perhaps dramatically, across contexts depending on whether gender is a salient organizing principle within group-based relations. Furthermore, if a context allows for nonhegemonic patterns of gender relations, perhaps aspects of the more egalitarian patterns of social relations can transfer across contexts (Hollander 2013).

Competitive youth swimming is an ideal setting to examine how gender boundaries and meanings are constructed and negotiated within everyday life (McGuffey and Rich 1999; Messner 2000). Within the United States, sport has historically played a visible role in naturalizing hierarchical, categorical, and essentialist differences between the genders (Kimmel 1996; Lorber 1994; Messner 2002, 2011). Because the institutional "center" of sport often affirms hegemonic masculinity (Messner 2002), girls' and boys' interactions within athletic contexts often help strengthen hierarchical and categorical group boundaries between the genders, thus maintaining the power, prestige, and resources boys have over girls (McGuffey and Rich 1999; Messner 2000; Thorne 1993). Yet at the same time, research finds that girls' and women's athleticism is becoming normalized (Ezzell 2009; Heywood and Dworkin 2003; Messner 2011), potentially calling into question hegemonic gender meanings pertaining to athleticism (Kane 1995; Messner 2002). Since it may be easier for individuals to enact alternative patterns of gender relations within contexts that are considered feminine (Finley 2010), the enactment of alternative patterns of gender relations may be especially apparent within competitive youth swimming, a sport that has historically been considered acceptable for white, middle-class girls to participate in (Bier 2011; Cahn 1994).

In this chapter, I follow a group of eight- to ten-year-old swimmers across different contexts at swim practices, asking: Do the meanings swimmers associate with gender vary as a result of their contextually specific, group-based interactions? If so, what are the conditions that allow swimmers to associate alternative cultural meanings with gender? To answer these questions, I outline the "gender geography" of swimmers' gender relations within two main contexts, arguing that when gender was less salient and children could "see" athletic similarity between the genders, children interacted in ways that undermined hegemonic beliefs about gender. Yet when the salience of gender was high and structural mechanisms encouraged kids to engage in borderwork, swimmers affirmed beliefs in essentialist and categorical—but nonhierarchical—differences between the genders. By paying attention to structural mechanisms and the variable salience of gender, we can thus see whether and how children associate different meanings with gender across contexts. Furthermore, because the swimmers enacted nonhierarchical gender relations in both contexts, I introduce the concept of "spillover," theorizing that aspects of less oppressive gender relations may transfer across contexts.

METHOD

From November 2011 to August 2012, I conducted participant observation research with the Sun Valley Swim Team (SVST), a competitive youth swim team in the Los Angeles metropolitan area. Among girls and boys under the age of ten, athletes were separated into three groups based on ability: Dolphins, Piranhas, and Sharks. Given the close link between athleticism and boys' social status, boys who excel in sports often have much at stake in preserving hegemonic patterns of gender relations (Adler and Adler 1998; McGuffey and Rich 1999; Thorne 1993). Consequently, I chose to study the Sharks group—composed of the fastest "ten and under" swimmers on the team—in order to witness the ways that kids construct and negotiate gender boundaries.

About twice a month, Sharks swimmers attended weekend swim meets, and SVST placed in the top five at several regional and statewide swim meets during the 2011–2012 swimming season.[3] Throughout the nine months I spent at the pool, the Sharks group was composed of sixteen girls and six boys. Seven of the girls were white, six were Asian, one was Latina, and two were multiracial (identifying as Asian and white). Three of the boys were white, one was Latino, and two were multiracial (identifying as Asian and white). With the exception of one eight-year-old girl, all the athletes in the Sharks group were nine or ten years old. The swimmers were from predominately middle- and upper-middle-class backgrounds, and Elizabeth—a white, middle-class former Olympic swimmer in her mid-thirties—coached the group.

At the pool, I spent my time before and after practices hanging out with swimmers, approaching fieldwork from the assumption that children actively negotiate and challenge adult-generated knowledge and values within their peer groups (Corsaro 2003; Prout and James 1990; Thorne 1993). To gain access to the kids' peer groups, I distanced myself from adult authority figures, like the swimmers' coaches, during research. I helped establish rapport by talking with the swimmers about my own experiences in competitive youth swimming and collegiate athletics. As the swimmers became more comfortable with my presence, many of the athletes began to break team rules and discuss "taboo" topics around me. Once, for example, several of the Sharks boys told me about watching a "puberty video" in school. While observing events that transpired before, during, and after swim practices, I made mental and brief written notes, which I developed into field notes after returning home from the pool (Emerson, Fretz, and Shaw 1995).

Between May and July 2012, I conducted fifteen semistructured interviews with Sharks swimmers, six boys and nine girls. Three of the boys I interviewed were white, one was Latino, and two were multiracial (identifying as Asian and white). Five of the girls I interviewed were white, three were Asian, and one was multiracial (identifying as Asian and white). I interviewed all but one of the swimmers at the pool before or after swim practices, and swimmers chose between completing the interview alone or with a friend. Cody, Jon, and Elijah completed the interview together, as did two girls, Molly and Zoe. Brady's interview became a group interview when his best friend Nick—who had previously been interviewed—started talking with Brady. Because Brady became more animated with Nick, Nick participated in the remainder of Brady's interview. During interviews, I asked swimmers the same general questions about various aspects of swim practice, their involvement in other extracurricular activities, and what they enjoyed the most and the least about swimming. Because of the athletes' age, the interviews were brief, ranging from twenty-five to sixty minutes. Fourteen of the interviews were recorded and transcribed.[4]

Field notes and interview transcripts were read numerous times and coded according to key themes that inductively emerged during fieldwork (Emerson, Fretz, and Shaw 1995; Glaser and Strauss 1967). There is reason to believe, however, that my social location as a white middle-class woman influenced the themes that developed throughout this project. As I outline in the findings section, the swimmers at SVST drew on and reinforced gender boundaries much more frequently than racial or class boundaries. Because of my own childhood experiences in middle-class extracurricular activities like youth sports (Lareau 2011), I may have been desensitized to some of the class-based aspects of the swimmers' day-to-day experiences and the color blindness present within their racial ideologies (Bonilla-Silva 2006; Perry 2002; Wilkins 2008). It is also possible that the Asian and Latina/o swimmers may not have felt comfortable openly discussing racial issues with a white researcher.

Although I remained cognizant of the ways that my class and race privilege may have influenced my research, I used my socioeconomic status and whiteness to my advantage when conducting fieldwork. The fact that I shared a class background with the swimmers and previously participated in competitive swimming helped minimize age-related power dynamics between the young swimmers and me. Additionally, because my speech patterns and presentation of self closely aligned with the metacommunicative routines at the pool— which were implicitly based on white, middle-class styles, values, and demeanor (Cooky and McDonald 2005)—I was able to minimize the scrutiny I faced from gatekeepers, such as parents and coaches, which allowed me to study the team in a relatively unobtrusive manner.

The "Gender Geography" of Sun Valley Swim Team

On my first day of research with SVST, Coach Elizabeth started Sharks swim practice with a team meeting. The day before, she explained, she had to "excuse" the athletes from practice early for misbehaving—something she had not done to a group of swimmers in more than three years. While solemnly addressing the swimmers, Elizabeth reminded the athletes that they were the fastest swimmers in their age category; she thus expected more from them than if they were in the Dolphins or Piranhas groups. Elizabeth told the swimmers that while they were at swim practices, "There are a time to listen and a time for fun." When it was "time to listen," Elizabeth stressed that the swimmers should pay attention, remain focused, and follow her instructions. By doing so, they would achieve their goals of becoming faster swimmers.

As Elizabeth's speech suggests, there were two main contexts that organized swimmers' relations at the pool: focused athletic contexts in which swimmers were expected to follow their coach's instructions, and unfocused free time in which swimmers had fun with their friends. As summarized in table 6.1, the variable salience of gender at the pool played an important role in shaping the different meanings swimmers associated with gender within and across these contexts. As a result of the structural mechanisms instituted by Coach Elizabeth during focused aspects of practice, gender was less salient in this context, and the swimmers interacted in non-antagonistic ways. While doing so, the swimmers regularly witnessed athletic parity between the genders and associated alternative, nonhegemonic meanings pertaining to athleticism. Because the gender meanings changed across contexts at the pool, however, gender was highly salient during the swimmers' free time. Structural mechanisms instead encouraged the kids to engage in borderwork in this context. Because swimmers tended to interact in antagonistic ways in their free time, similarities between the genders were less visible, ultimately encouraging the swimmers to associate gender with categoricalism and essentialism.

TABLE 6.1

THE GENDER GEOGRAPHY OF SUN VALLEY SWIM TEAM

	Focused aspects of practice	Unfocused free time
Context	Athletes are expected to listen and follow their coach's instructions	Kids have fun with their friends
Gender relations	Girls and boys are formally together; gender is less salient	Girls and boys are informally apart; gender is highly salient
Structural mechanisms	Coaches instruct boys and girls to share lanes, race one another, and compare times	Lack of adult supervision and rules; risk of heterosexual teasing; swimmers enter and exit pool deck through gender-segregated locker rooms
Gender meanings	Girls and boys undermine opposite and antagonistic group-based gender boundaries	Boys and girls affirm opposite and antagonistic group-based gender boundaries

Racing "for Times": Focused Aspects of Practice

The most focused aspects of Sharks swim practices occurred when athletes raced "for times." While racing for times, athletes swam a distance, such as fifty or one hundred yards, as fast as they could—like they did during formal competitions. Afterward, the athletes calculated how fast they swam the interval and reported their times to Coach Elizabeth. In interviews, athletes described racing for times as having "to sprint and go as fast as you can" while trying "to get the same time [as] in the [swim] meet." Zoe, a nine-year-old Asian girl, told me that during these workouts, she compares herself to Olympians like Michael Phelps and Natalie Coughlin, reminding herself, "If you were one of them, you wouldn't be able to stop, so just try to push through it and work hard and think of something else besides how hard it is." As Zoe's strategy suggests, racing for times was not a time to goof around. Instead, in this context, swimmers were expected to work hard, swim fast, and push themselves when tired.

During these workouts, Elizabeth often organized swimmers into groups according to their athletic ability. While assigning the swimmers to lanes, Elizabeth either instructed the fastest athletes to share a lane or assigned several fast swimmers to each lane. To motivate the athletes, Elizabeth often encouraged the swimmers to race the swimmers next to them, catch the swimmers in front of them, and compare times with other swimmers in their lanes. Because the girls and boys had relatively equal athletic abilities, racing for times was a context where swimmers of both genders regularly trained and raced together. The following example is representative of the swimmers' interactions while racing for times:

> The kids are swimming two-hundred-yard individual medleys [IMs] for times. Sophia (ten, multiracial), Jon (ten, multiracial), and Nick (nine, multiracial) are each leading their respective lanes. The swimmers finish in the following order: Sophia, Nick, Jon, Allison (nine, white), Lesley (ten, white), Cody (nine, white), and Joanna (nine, Latina). After asking each of the athletes for their times, Elizabeth says, "Lesley, come over here and go second." She points to the lane that Jon and Cody are in, indicating that Lesley will go after Jon and before Cody. On the next two-hundred-yard IM, as the athletes push off the wall, Elizabeth reminds them to try to catch the person swimming in front of them and to race the people swimming in the lanes next to them. Halfway through the two hundred, Sophia looks to the side, gauging where she is in relation to Nick and Jon. Sophia swims the two-hundred-yard IM in 2 minutes and 36 seconds [2:36], Nick swims a 2:43, and Jon a 2:45. Elizabeth calls out their times as they touch the wall. Before starting the next two hundred, Elizabeth tells Nick and Jon, "Boys, faster on the first hundred. Don't let Sophia get so far in front of you." Nick looks up at Elizabeth and nods.

As evidenced by this example, during focused aspects of practice, Coach Elizabeth organized lanes based on athletes' fastest times, not gender. While following Elizabeth's instructions to race other swimmers, Nick and Jon compared themselves to Sophia—a girl. After hearing Lesley's time on the first two-hundred-yard individual medley, Elizabeth instructed Lesley to swim with faster swimmers—both were boys. Instances where the girls and boys compared times and raced each other occurred regularly in this context.

As previous scholarship has argued, gender is often highly salient when kids engage in mixed-gender competitions—especially within athletic contexts (McGuffey and Rich 1999; Messner 2000; Moore 2001; Thorne 1993). While racing for times, Sophia could have teased Nick and Jon for losing to "a girl," or Jon could have told Lesley that "girls suck" at swimming. However, when coaches or athletes directly compared girls' and boys' performances during SVST practices, I never heard athletes use these comparisons as an opportunity to evoke antagonistic interactions. Instead, similar to how teachers can encourage boys and girls to interact in relaxed, non-antagonistic ways by dividing students by reading abilities instead of gender (Thorne 1993), the informal policies instituted by Coach Elizabeth minimized the salience of gender within this context. The swimmers were instructed to complete tasks with specific goals (Moore 2001; Ridgeway 2011), allowing the girls and boys to interact in ways that did not affirm group boundaries between the genders.

"It's Just, Like, the Same Thing": Alternative Meanings of Gender

Because gender was less salient during focused aspects of Sharks swim practices, the swimmers interacted in ways that allowed them to associate alternative meanings with gender. This became clear when the athletes discussed instances they raced against swimmers of the other gender. Without nervously giggling or averting his eyes, Jon talked about getting "killed" by Sophia when they swam breaststroke. Cody leaned back and shrugged as he told me, "It doesn't matter . . . it's just, like, the same thing" if he loses to a girl or a boy. When asked who he races during practices, Nick spontaneously compared his times to Sophia's: "When Brady [eleven, white] was in the group I always raced against him. Now that he's gone the only one left is Sophia. Which, two hundred IMs, no question, she's gonna win because my breaststroke sucks. Butterfly . . . I'll usually [win]—well, most of the time. Backstroke, it's a fifty-fifty game, and freestyle, fifty-fifty. Breaststroke, no doubt she's in front."

Without a hint of defensiveness about losing to a girl, Nick made detailed comparisons between himself and Sophia. Even in butterfly, his fastest stroke, Nick recognized that he wins only "most of the time." Although boys often have much at stake in maintaining hierarchical and categorical differences between the genders (McGuffey and Rich 1999; Thorne 1993), at SVST the boys instead associated alternative meanings with gender while talking about racing for times, where athleticism was not associated with hierarchy or difference.

The girls also talked about racing for times in ways that suggested they were not inferior or fundamentally different athletes because of their gender. Chelsea, a ten-year-old Asian girl, told me that boys are "not always faster [in swimming], sometimes they can be slower." Similarly, Anna, a ten-year-old white girl, discussed a race she lost to Elijah, a ten-year-old white boy. Instead of justifying defeat by saying that boys are always faster than girls, Anna identified a specific reason why she lost. She explained that when she dove into the water, "I [dove] to the side. It was not a good dive." Even Wendy, a nine-year-old white girl—one of the slowest athletes in the group—told me that because Sophia is as fast as Nick, there was "not really" a difference between the girls' and boys' swimming abilities.

There are two reasons Sharks swim practices were an ideal context for swimmers to enact nonhegemonic patterns of gender relations pertaining to athleticism. First, the Sharks swimmers were the fastest group of "ten and under" swimmers on the team, and highly committed to athletics. Many of the Sharks swimmers told me they attended practice to "get better times" or to "get better" at swimming. Several of the boys and girls expressed a desire to swim in the Olympics one day, and Grace, a ten-year-old white girl, even chose to attend swim practice instead of her best friend's birthday party. Because of the athletes' commitment, the majority of swimmers willingly followed Elizabeth's instructions—even if it meant sharing lanes with swimmers of the other gender. Swimmers in the other "ten and under" groups on the team, however, did not always follow their coaches' instructions as readily. I occasionally noticed girls and boys in the Dolphins and Piranhas group make faces and shriek when instructed to share lanes with swimmers of the other gender—something Sharks swimmers never did while racing for times. As a result of the Sharks swimmers' commitment to athleticism, acting in accordance with the structural mechanisms instituted by Elizabeth likely mattered more than it did to other "ten and under" athletes.

Additionally, while following Elizabeth's instructions to share lanes and race one another, the swimmers compared times, a relatively transparent measure of ability. If the athletes were playing a team sport like basketball or soccer, where athleticism is assessed through less quantifiable skills, such as dribbling or blocking ability, it may have been easier for the boys to marginalize or masculinize the girls' abilities (McGuffey and Rich 1999; Thorne 1993). Indeed, during interviews, several of the girls and boys discussed instances during recess and physical education classes when boys invoked hierarchical and categorical notions of gender while playing team sports, such as when they refused to play with girls or became upset after losing to girls. During Sharks swim practices, however, the swimmers were frequently provided with specific, quantifiable instances of girls beating boys and boys beating girls. Through these time-based comparisons, it became clear that the girls' and boys' abilities overlapped (Kane 1995). As a result, within a context where swimmers willingly interacted in ways that illuminated similarities between the genders, girls and boys associated nonhegemonic meanings with gender.

Having Fun with Friends: Unsupervised Free Time

The least focused aspects of swimming occurred during the swimmers' free time. Sharks swimmers were never completely unsupervised on the pool deck, but there were times—such as before swim practices or between races at swim meets—when SVST coaches were busy coaching other swimmers. As opposed to focused aspects of practice, which were "hard" and "tiring," unsupervised free time was a chance for the kids to have fun with their friends. David, a ten-year-old Latino boy, explained that before and after swim practice, he and his friends had "lots of fun together." Grace told me, "It's always fun to come here and see [my friends]," and Chelsea similarly said that she had "fun" while "hanging out" with her friends before practices.

The unsupervised aspect of the swimmers' free time played an important role in shaping kids' social interactions with their friends. At the pool, I did not observe patterns of age and racial separation that other scholars have observed among children in schools and summer camps (Lewis 2003; Moore 2001; Perry 2002). In interviews, furthermore, most of the swimmers had a difficult time naming their closest friends on the team, explaining that they were close friends with "everyone" and had "a lot of good friends [on the team]." Despite the ostensive unity among the swimmers, none of the swimmers reported being friends with kids of the other gender. For example, Nick, a multiracial nine-year-old, named every male swimmer and male coach he could think of when describing his "good friends":

MM: Who are some of your good friends on the team?
NICK: Let's see, we have . . . Brady [eleven, white]! It's gonna be a very long, very, very, long list. So beware. Let's see, we have Coach Tom [mid-twenties, white]!

MM: He's one of your friends?
NICK: Yeah, we often chat a lot. I have Coach Brad [mid-thirties, white], Jayden . . . um . . . Jon [ten, multiracial], Andrew [eleven, Latino], David [ten, Latino], Cody [nine, white], Justin [eleven, white], Derrick [ten, white], Dominick [ten, white] . . . well, he used to be on the swim team. Let's see, we have . . . Samantha—my sister [eight, multiracial], although she can be very annoying at some times. . . . Let's see . . . um . . . one of the

people who works in the café, he gives me a lot of free samples. And he once let me get a discount, so that's pretty good. Zach [eleven, white] . . . did I say Caleb [eleven, white]?

Nick's "good friends" range from boys in the Sharks group to one of the men who worked at the pool's café. Like other swimmers in the Sharks group, moreover, Nick developed friendships across racial and age categories. Although the requirements for being Nick's friend are not particularly stringent—you simply needed to "chat a lot" or give him a discount on food—the only girl he mentions is his sister, who can be "very annoying." This is striking because Nick's parents were good friends with the parents of Chelsea, a girl in the Sharks group. On several different occasions, Nick talked about going fishing with Chelsea's family and having her family over for barbecues. Once, he even told me he dreamed about raiding her family's food pantry. Based on Nick's criteria, Chelsea should count as a friend. However, when I asked Nick if he ever "hangs out" with Chelsea, he simply responded, "No." When asked to elaborate, he explained, "I don't hang out with girls."

As Nick's comments suggest, gender was a highly salient category that structured kids' friendships during their free time. Among swimmers in the Sharks group, this gender separation was marked with extensive physical separation. After changing into their swimsuits in sex-segregated locker rooms, the girls would set their swim bags near the right end of the bleachers that lined the length of the pool. The boys would walk past the girls, often without even glancing in their direction, to the far end of the benches, placing their bags almost fifty meters from the girls' space.

There were three reasons why gender became a highly salient organizing principle within the kids' group-based relations during unsupervised free time. First, as opposed to when Coach Elizabeth instructed the girls and boys to share lanes and compare times, in unsupervised aspects of practices, no policies encouraged the boys and girls to interact. Because the swimmers' unsupervised free time was not formally scripted, the kids relied on gender as a highly salient criterion when developing friendships (Ridgeway 2011). Furthermore, similar to how formal gender segregation on soccer teams and golf courses can increase the salience of gender within interactions (Messner 2000; Morgan and Martin 2006), the policy of physically separating the swimmers into gender-segregated locker rooms before and after practice formally marked the boys and girls as different when they entered and exited the pool deck. And finally, the crowded nature of the pool deck may have contributed to the salience of gender in this context (Thorne 1993). Because there were often between fifty and one hundred kids on the pool deck during SVST practices, there were plenty of witnesses who could tease kids for having "crushes" on kids of the other gender, making it risky for the girls and boys to socialize with each other. Thus, in the swimmers' free time, rather than developing friendships based on similar interests or athletic ability, the lack of rules, the threat of heterosexual teasing, and gender-segregated locker rooms helped create a context where gender was highly salient.

"Boys Are Always Wild" and "Girls Are Very Nice and Sweet": Hegemonic Meanings of Gender

Given the high salience of gender boundaries during swimmers' unsupervised free time, the girls' and boys' interactions often strengthened gender-based group boundaries during unsupervised aspects of practice (McGuffey and Rich 1999; Messner 2000; Thorne 1993). Once, before practice, Nick shouted his last name while jumping toward Katie. While mimicking his motion, Katie shouted, "Weirdo!" back at him. Several times, I watched Nick, Brady, and Sophia dump cold water on one another's heads after practice. After a swimming fund-raiser, Katie, Jon, and Cody spent ten minutes hitting and splashing one another with foam swimming "noodles" in the pool. Toward the end of a swim meet, several boys filled their swim caps with water and tried splashing Lesley and Grace. After wrestling the swim caps out of the boys' hands, Grace came over to me and told me that Elijah gave her "cooties."

Although the swimmers tended to interact in antagonistic ways during their free time, borderwork at the pool did not seem to be based on beliefs in male supremacy. Unlike existing research has suggested (McGuffey and Rich 1999; Messner 2000; Thorne 1993), boys did not provoke antagonistic relations more frequently than girls, nor did the boys control more space on the pool deck. Furthermore, the girls never tried to avoid confrontations with the boys, and instead seemed confident in their ability to interact as equals. Once, for example, I was talking with Katie when Amy, an eleven-year-old Asian girl, walked over to us. Elijah and Jon were standing several feet away, wearing swimming flippers on their hands. Katie warned Amy that the boys would "smack you with that fin" if Amy got too close. Amy, however, rolled her eyes and told Katie, "I'm not scared." She then punched Katie's arm a couple of times, demonstrating how she would fight if provoked.

If the swimmers had believed that boys on the pool deck were stronger than the girls, Amy may have been more cautious about fighting Jon and Elijah. Instead, she confidently proclaimed that she was "not scared" and demonstrated how she would punch them. Other girls in the Sharks group also seemed confident in their ability to engage in borderwork as equals with the boys. Once, much to the girls' excitement, Katie "pantsed" Elijah at a swim meet.[5] Another time, after Nick dumped what he described as "ice cold" water on Sophia's head, she got "revenge" by pouring red Gatorade on him. If Katie or Sophia had believed the boys were stronger or more powerful than the girls, they may have been afraid to instigate such interactions. Fear of the boys' reactions, however, did not stop Katie from "pantsing" Elijah, or Sophia from dumping a red, sticky drink on Nick's head. Although hegemonic cultural beliefs about gender often become activated when gender is a salient aspect of social interactions (Ridgeway 2011), the swimmers' antagonistic interactions in this context did not appear to be based upon a sense of male supremacy. Instead, they were transformative in the sense that they allowed the girls to occupy space and express agency when interacting as equals with the boys. However, because these interactions continued to affirm categorical and essentialist differences between the genders, they simultaneously undermined and reproduced aspects of hegemonic gender relations.

Furthermore, all the swimmers talked about sharing close physical space with kids of the other gender in ways that were markedly different from how they talked about racing one another. When talking about racing for times, the swimmers willingly recognized and discussed the overlap between girls' and boys' abilities. However, on a social level, the meanings kids associated with gender were firmly grounded in categorical differences. Perhaps because of the risk of heterosexual teasing (Thorne 1993), boys and girls told me that spending time with athletes of the other gender was "not fun," "awkward," "annoying," "awful," "super uncomfortable," "gross," "kinda weird," and "really bad and really messed up." Many of the kids also articulated essentialist understandings of gender within these narratives, explaining that "boys are always wild," "girls are very nice and sweet," "girls are more limber," and "boys are more competitive." Notably, however, the swimmers did not include assumptions about male supremacy within these explanations. Instead, as suggested by their patterns of borderwork, the swimmers associated categorical and essentialist—but nonhierarchical— meanings with gender.

As an observer who spent an equal amount of time with the girls and boys, it was puzzling to hear girls and boys make categorical and essentialist distinctions between the genders. If girls were always "more limber" than boys, then how could the swimmers account for the boy from the Sharks group who frequently did the splits before swim practice? If "girls are very nice and sweet," then how could they explain the times when the girls screamed at and hit one another? Although it was easy for me to think of exceptions to the kids' generalizations, whenever I asked kids about these exceptions, my questions were met with shrugs and surprise. Despite being quite knowledgeable about one another's swimming abilities, the girls and boys were relatively unaware of the other group's social experiences. Because the swimmers tended to provoke antagonistic interactions with one another, similarities between the genders were obscured. Unlike focused aspects of practice, structural mechanisms did not illuminate the similarities between the girls and boys (Kane 1995). In this less scripted context, the kids instead drew upon and enacted aspects of hegemonic patterns of gender relations (Morgan and Martin 2006; Ridgeway 2009, 2011). The swimmers, however, did not default to enacting all aspects of hegemonic gender relations. The swimmers' group-based interactions led the swimmers to associate gender with categorical and essentialist meanings, but the assumption that boys are superior to girls was notably absent from swimmers' interactions during unsupervised free time.

CONCLUSION

Gender is a social structure embedded within individual, interactional, and institutional relations (Connell 1987, 2009; Lorber 1994; Martin 2004; Messner 2000; Risman 2004). At the institutional level, femininities and masculinities are ranked in societal-wide, historically based hierarchies that are created and re-created through laws, policies, practices, collective representations, symbols, and hegemonic meanings of gender (Connell 1987; Lorber 1994), but the impact of structural mechanisms and hegemonic cultural beliefs within interactions varies based on the context (Britton 2000; Connell 1987; Deutsch 2007; Messner 2000; Morgan and Martin 2006; Ridgeway 2009, 2011; Ridgeway and Correll 2004; Thorne 1993).

My research contributes to existing literature by exploring how gender meanings and relations change across contexts. By following the same group of individuals across different contexts, I found that the meanings kids associated with a social category such as "gender" did not always align with hegemonic beliefs. Instead, the swimmers' understandings of gender were filtered through group-based interactions and thus varied dramatically depending on the context (Eliasoph and Lichterman 2003; Fine 1979; Swidler 1986). During focused aspects of practice, when swimmers followed their coach's instructions to compare times and race one another, gender was less salient and athletes interacted in non-antagonistic ways. As a result of their group-based interactions in this context, swimmers regularly witnessed athletic parity between the genders, making it difficult to sustain beliefs in categorical gender difference and male superiority (Kane 1995). Because structural mechanisms enabled a different pattern of group-based relations during the swimmers' unsupervised free time, the meanings associated with gender changed across contexts at SVST. During the swimmers' unsupervised free time, gender was highly salient and swimmers interacted in antagonistic ways. As a result, their interactions obscured the similarities between the genders, encouraging the swimmers to associate gender with categorical and essentialist—yet nonhierarchical—meanings.

The fact that swimmers' understandings of gender did not uniformly align with hegemonic cultural beliefs has broader theoretical implications for gender theory. When the salience of gender is low and structural mechanisms allow individuals to interact in ways that illuminate similarities between the genders, it is possible for individuals to associate gender with nonhegemonic beliefs. This study thus provides a glimpse into the types of practices that can potentially enable interactional gender expectations to become less oppressive (Connell 1987; Martin 2004; Ridgeway 2009; Risman 2004). Furthermore, unlike existing research (McGuffey and Rich 1999; Messner 2000; Morgan and Martin 2006; Ridgeway 2009; Ridgeway and Correll 2000; Thorne 1993), the swimmers did not default to enacting all aspects of hegemonic gender relations when interacting within a relatively unscripted setting. Beliefs in male supremacy were notably missing from both contexts, highlighting the need to explain the lack of gender hierarchy at the pool.

If individuals enact more equitable gender relations in one context, aspects of these gender relations may "spill over" into other settings within daily life. At SVST, structural mechanisms illuminated the similarities between the genders during focused aspects of practice. While sharing lanes and racing one another, time-based comparisons made it clear that girls and boys were equally strong and talented swimmers. Perhaps the embodied strength and confidence girls developed while racing for times allowed them to be more expansive in their appropriation of space and more confident in their antagonisms with the boys (Hollander 2013; Messner 2011; Travers 2008). The boys' in-pool experiences of losing to the girls may have helped create a baseline of respect for the girls outside of the pool (Anderson 2008; Messner 2011), making the boys less inclined to invade the girls' space and provoke antagonistic relations. As a result, although structural mechanisms encouraged the swimmers to deploy categorical and essentialist meanings of gender in their unsupervised free time, the nonhierarchical aspects of the swimmers' gender relations may have transferred across contexts. The spillover effect likely weakened as the swimmers entered situations further removed from SVST (Ridgeway and Correll 2000), but the swimmers' in-pool experiences appeared to reduce the overall degree of gender inequality at the pool.

The fact that the swimmers compared times—a relatively quantifiable measure of ability—probably facilitated the enactment of alternative gender relations during focused aspects of practice and the potential spillover of these relations into other contexts. In other institutions, such as workplaces and schools, measures of performance may be less transparent than in a timed sprint, perhaps making it more difficult to enact alternative patterns of gender relations. Additionally, the spillover effect I observed occurred within youth swimming. When compared to sports like basketball, swimming has historically been considered a more gender-"appropriate" sport for girls (Bier 2011; Cahn 1994). Activities that are considered to be feminine likely create more space for the development of egalitarian attitudes and patterns of gender relations when compared to activities that are considered more masculine (Finley 2010; Prokos and Padavic 2002; Ridgeway 2009; Schippers 2002; Wilkins 2008).

Race and class also may operate as hidden resources within contexts where kids enact alternative patterns of gender relations. At SVST, most of the Sharks swimmers were from upper-middle-class families, and drew upon class-based resources while regularly attending swim practices with high-quality coaches, equipment, and facilities. However, not all children have equal access to sport (Sabo and Veliz 2008), nor do all parents have the resources to foster their children's talent and interest in extracurricular activities (Lareau 2011). The overlap between girls' and boys' athletic abilities may not be illuminated as easily among kids who lack the resources to become committed and talented athletes. Furthermore, the kids might have enacted alternative patterns of gender relations primarily because they conformed to other aspects of white, middle-class social relations. In order to be successful athletes, the Sharks swimmers participated in activities that reinforced neoliberal individualism and white, middle-class values, such as deferring to authority figures, valuing hard work, and believing in meritocracy (Bettie 2003; Cooky and McDonald 2005; DeLuca 2013; Perry 2002). The fact that Sharks swimmers reinforced key aspects of white, upper-middle-class values might have afforded them some leeway for enacting nonhegemonic patterns of gender relations (Wilkins 2008). At least within competitive youth sports, the enactment of alternative patterns of gender relations may create tensions within hegemonic gender relations, while simultaneously leaving existing class- and race-based systems of inequality in place (Bettie 2003; Cooky and McDonald 2005), ultimately prefiguring the public world the kids may enter as professional-class adults (Friedman 2013; Messner 2009). It remains to be seen by future research whether spillover can occur in contexts that undermine not only hegemonic gender relations, but also hegemonic patterns of race and class relations.

NOTES

1. The swim team name and names of all participants are pseudonyms.

2. SVST coaches occasionally organized intrasquad swim meets, where boys and girls of all ages race against one another in heats arranged from slowest to fastest.

3. Practices were offered six days a week throughout the year, but most swimmers attended four practices weekly.

4. Katie did not want to be audio-recorded, so I took handwritten notes during her interview.

5. Because the kids often wore pants and T-shirts over their swimsuits during their free time, swimmers occasionally tried to pull down other swimmers' pants, revealing their swimsuits in the process.

REFERENCES

Adler, Patricia A., and Peter Adler. 1998. *Peer Power: Preadolescent Culture and Identity.* New Brunswick, NJ: Rutgers University Press.

Anderson, Eric. 2008. "'I Used to Think Women Were Weak': Orthodox Masculinity, Gender Segregation, and Sport." *Sociological Forum* 23: 257–280.

Bettie, Julie. 2003. *Women without Class: Girls, Race, and Identity.* Berkeley: University of California Press.

Bier, Lisa. 2011. *Fighting the Current: The Rise of American Women's Swimming, 1870–1926*. Jefferson, NC: McFarland.

Bonilla-Silva, Eduardo. 2006. *Racism without Racists: Color-Blind Racism and the Persistence of Racial Inequality in America*. Lanham, MD: Rowman & Littlefield.

Britton, Dana M. 2000. "The Epistemology of the Gendered Organization." *Gender & Society* 14.3: 418–434.

Cahn, Susan K. 1994. *Coming on Strong: Gender and Sexuality in Twentieth-Century Women's Sport*. Cambridge, MA: Harvard University Press.

Connell, Raewyn. 1987. *Gender and Power: Society, the Person, and Sexual Politics*. Stanford, CA: Stanford University Press.

———. 2009. *Short Introductions: Gender*. Malden, MA: Polity.

Cooky, Cheryl, and Mary G. McDonald. 2005. "'If You Let Me Play': Young Girls' Insider-Other Narratives of Sport." *Sociology of Sport Journal* 22.2: 158–177.

Corsaro, William A. 2003. *We're Friends, Right? Inside Kids' Culture*. Washington, DC: Joseph Henry Press.

DeLuca, Jaime R. 2013. "Submersed in Social Segregation: The (Re)production of Social Capital through Swim Club Membership." *Journal of Sport and Social Issues* 37.4: 340–363.

Deutsch, Francine M. 2007. "Undoing Gender." *Gender & Society* 21.1: 106–127.

Eliasoph, Nina, and Paul Lichterman. 2003. "Culture in Interaction." *American Journal of Sociology* 108.4: 735–794.

Emerson, Robert M., Rachel I. Fretz, and Linda L. Shaw. 1995. *Writing Ethnographic Fieldnotes*. Chicago: University of Chicago Press.

Ezzell, Matthew B. 2009. "'Barbie Dolls' on the Pitch: Identity Work, Defensive Othering, and Inequality in Women's Rugby." *Social Problems* 56.1: 111–131.

Fine, Gary Alan. 1979. "Small Groups and Culture Creation: The Idioculture of Little League Baseball Teams." *American Sociological Review* 44.5: 733–745.

Finley, Nancy J. 2010. "Skating Femininity: Gender Maneuvering in Women's Roller Derby." *Journal of Contemporary Ethnography* 39.4: 359–387.

Friedman, Hilary Levey. 2013. *Playing to Win: Raising Children in a Competitive Culture*. Berkeley: University of California Press.

Glaser, Barney G., and Anselm L. Strauss. 1967. *The Discovery of Grounded Theory: Strategies for Qualitative Research*. New Brunswick, NJ: Aldine Transaction.

Heywood, Leslie, and Shari L. Dworkin. 2003. *Built to Win: The Female Athlete as Cultural Icon*. Minneapolis: University of Minnesota Press.

Hollander, Jocelyn A. 2013. "'I Demand More of People': Accountability, Interaction, and Gender Change." *Gender & Society* 27.1: 5–29.

Kane, Mary Jo. 1995. "Resistance/Transformation of the Oppositional Binary: Exposing Sport as a Continuum." *Journal of Sport and Social Issues* 19.2: 191–218.

Kimmel, Michael. 1996. *Manhood in America*. New York: Free Press.

Lareau, Annette. 2011. *Unequal Childhoods: Class, Race, and Family Life*. Berkeley: University of California Press.

Lewis, Amanda. 2003. *Race in the Schoolyard: Negotiating the Color Line in Classrooms and Communities*. New Brunswick, NJ: Rutgers University Press.

Lorber, Judith. 1994. *Paradoxes of Gender*. New Haven, CT: Yale University Press.

Martin, Patricia Yancey. 2004. "Gender as Social Institution." *Social Forces* 82.4: 1249–1273.

McGuffey, C. Shawn, and B. Lindsay Rich. 1999. "Playing in the Gender Transgression Zone: Race, Class, and Hegemonic Masculinity in Middle Childhood." *Gender & Society* 13.5: 608–627.

Messner, Michael A. 2000. "Barbie Girls versus Sea Monsters: Children Constructing Gender." *Gender & Society* 14.6: 765–784.

———. 2002. *Taking the Field: Men, Women, and Sports*. Minneapolis: University of Minnesota Press.

———. 2009. *It's All for the Kids: Gender, Families, and Youth Sports.* Berkeley: University of California Press.

———. 2011. "Gender Ideologies, Youth Sports, and the Production of Soft Essentialism." *Sociology of Sport Journal* 28.2: 151–170.

Moore, Valerie Ann. 2001. "'Doing' Racialized and Gendered Age to Organize Peer Relations: Observing Kids in Summer Camp." *Gender & Society* 15.6: 835–858.

Morgan, Laurie A., and Karin A. Martin. 2006. "Taking Women Professionals Out of the Office: The Case of Women in Sales." *Gender & Society* 20.1: 108–128.

Perry, Pamela. 2002. *Shades of White: White Kids and Racial Identities in High School.* Durham, NC: Duke University Press.

Prokos, Anastasia, and Irene Padavic. 2002. "'There Oughtta Be a Law against Bitches': Masculinity Lessons in Police Academy Training." *Gender, Work & Organization* 9.4: 439–459.

Prout, Alan, and Allison James. 1990. "A New Paradigm for the Sociology of Childhood? Provenance, Promise, and Problems." In *Constructing and Reconstructing Childhood: Contemporary Issues in the Sociological Study of Childhood,* edited by Allison James and Alan Prout, 7–34. London: Falmer Press.

Ridgeway, Cecilia L. 2009. "Framed before We Know It: How Gender Shapes Social Relations." *Gender & Society* 23.2: 145–160.

———. 2011. *Framed by Gender: How Gender Inequality Persists in the Modern World.* New York: Oxford University Press.

Ridgeway, Cecilia L., and Shelley J. Correll. 2000. "Limiting Inequality through Interaction: The End(s) of Gender." *Contemporary Sociology* 29.1: 110–120.

———. 2004. "Unpacking the Gender System: A Theoretical Perspective on Gender Beliefs and Social Relations." *Gender & Society* 18.4: 510–531.

Risman, Barbara J. 2004. "Gender as a Social Structure: Theory Wrestling with Activism." *Gender & Society* 18.4: 429–450.

Sabo, Don, and Philip Veliz. 2008. "Go Out and Play: Youth Sports in America." East Meadow, NY: Women's Sport Foundation.

Schippers, Mimi. 2002. *Rockin' Out of the Box: Gender Maneuvering in Alternative Hard Rock.* New Brunswick, NJ: Rutgers University Press.

———. 2007. "Recovering the Feminine Other: Masculinity, Femininity, and Gender Hegemony." *Theory and Society* 36.1: 85–102.

Swidler, Ann. 1986. "Culture in Action: Symbols and Strategies." *American Sociological Review* 51.2: 273–286.

Thorne, Barrie. 1993. *Gender Play: Girls and Boys in School.* New Brunswick, NJ: Rutgers University Press.

Travers, Ann. 2008. "The Sport Nexus and Gender Injustice." *Studies in Social Justice* 2.1: 79–101.

Wilkins, Amy C. 2008. *Wannabes, Goths, and Christians: The Boundaries of Sex, Style, and Status.* Chicago: University of Chicago Press.

CHAPTER 7

The Voices of Boys on Sport, Health, and Physical Activity

THE BEGINNING OF LIFE THROUGH A GENDERED LENS

Murray J. N. Drummond

My daughter recently had her sixteenth birthday and my son is twelve. Our family is very active; their lives are heavily laced with physical activity, sport, and competition. As former national- and international-level athletes, my wife and I have encouraged our children to engage in sport to the utmost of their ability. As academics in the sport and health field, my wife and I strongly understand the importance of exposing children to a range of sports and activities. Doing so enhances broad participation and develops motor skills, potentially providing children with the opportunity to take part in sports and activities they feel comfortable with and enjoy.

Our children are intimately involved in track and field and surf lifesaving. My wife and I used to have a high level of involvement in track and multisport events, and continue now at the master's level. It is not unusual that our children "naturally" gravitated to the activities that my wife and I were involved in. Indeed, for most families, children's choice of sport is often shaped by those their parents played, and potentially still play (Yang, Telama, and Laakso 1996). Involvement in sport and physical activity in our family is a very shared experience. Not only do we take our children to their own training, but the four of us often swim in the ocean, run through the hills and sand dunes, and paddle board together. Some days we will catch waves on surf lifesaving "Malibu" boards for fun. It has become a way of life as much as it is about the sport itself.

Sport has been a major part of my life (see Drummond 2010). I have trained, played, and competed in a variety of sports and at the social, club, and elite levels. My passion for sport was such that I studied it to become a physical education teacher and then went on to study a master's in health and physical education.

With my enthusiasm further enhanced, I was fortunate enough to be awarded a scholarship to undertake doctoral research that investigated the social construction of masculinity in elite level sports. As a researcher of the social aspects of sport, and now as a parent of a daughter and a son, I have been a keen observer of gender issues among children. Over the years I have noticed certain differences in meanings attached to sports by girls and boys as well as "others" such as parents. Like much of the literature has suggested (Biddle et al. 2005; Knowles, Niven, and Fawkner 2011), I have noticed many of my daughter's teammates appear to be less engaged from around the age of fourteen years. As a result of this attrition, in some of the girls' events in athletics, particularly around fifteen to sixteen years, there are no heats. Instead, the girls in these age groups participate in what is deemed to be a "straight final," irrespective of "talent" and ability. For the boys, however, there is rarely a lack of participants across the majority of age groups. This is consistent with the literature around girls' disengagement from sport and physical activity, more so than boys, at the age of around fifteen years (Biddle et al. 2005; Knowles, Niven, and Fawkner 2011). Indeed Cheryl Cooky (2009) has argued that there are certain forms of constraining factors in thwarting girls' engagement and continued participation in a variety of sports and activities. It appears there are myriad reasons to try to explain this disengagement ranging from body image to increased socializing beyond sports to factors such as sweating and fear of being labeled as not feminine (Slater and Tiggemann 2010). As Amy Slater and Marika Tiggemann have aptly identified, sometimes sport for girls is simply seen as being "not cool" (2010).

As a competitor in elite-level running and triathlon in the late 1980s through to the mid-1990s, I would always recognize the difference in participant numbers across genders. With respect to watching my children's involvement in sports, it seems little has changed in this regard. Indeed in the latest Australian Bureau of Statistics (2011–2012) data on sport and physical activity rates identified that boys maintain a 15 percent greater participation rate than girls in the fifteen to seventeen age group. This is the most significant gap across all age groups. It is noteworthy that twenty years later, while my own research as an academic has diversified and taken courses that have led to a range of interesting intellectual places, I keep coming back to masculinity and sports. It seems we never move too far away from our real passions. Having a son has certainly brought me back to the research area. However, having a daughter has provided important context and meaning, which in turn have enabled me to understand the issues of masculinity in sports for boys in a more meaningful way.

STUDYING BOYS, SPORT, AND HEALTH

While not unique, listening to voices of children in qualitative health research has been limited. Drummond, Drummond, and Birbeck (2009) claimed that although there is a wealth of literature on children and health, the voices of the children themselves are absent from the literature. Indeed, the majority of studies in this area are *about* children and *on* children, but seldom *include* children's voices.

Six years ago, I began a longitudinal study of thirty-three then five- and six-year-old boys. Today, they are around eleven to twelve. Annually for the past six years, I have gathered the boys into focus groups and asked them to reflect on the meaning of sport, health, and physical activity within the context of their lives. Each year, the boys have different ways of articulating the meaning of sport, health, and physical activity in their lives. Mostly, the boys talk about their enjoyment of sport and physical activity and its contribution to health. At other times, they discuss the stereotypical nature of men's sports, including those that are known to them as "blood sports." However, I have been most struck with the *way* the boys, from a very early age, consistently compared and contrasted the sports and physical activities that boys and men do, with those of girls of women. They also reflect on muscular differences in bodies as well what they believe men's and women's bodies *can do* and *cannot do*. Now in their preteen years, the boys are also considering the meaning of being gay within the context of their discussions on sport, health, and physical activity. It is clear that as the boys become older, the types of issues they discuss transcend the original topic of sport, health, and physical activity. This chapter allows us to understand some of the emerging issues for boys as they begin to negotiate a life that is filled with gendered expectations. From an early age, these boys claim that sport, health, and physical activity are areas in which gendered expectation is assumed.

The Study

The thirty-three boys involved in my six-year longitudinal study are from a middle-class primary school in metropolitan Adelaide. I received institutional ethics approval as well as consent from the boys' parents for the duration of the six-year project. Starting when they were five to six years old, I interviewed the boys in focus groups of about four to six members. The thirty-three boys were from three different classes. As often happens within the context of early childhood education, the children do not often venture out of their class structure even within the playground. Therefore most of the boys did not know the names of the boys outside their own class. As a consequence it was imperative to interview the boys within the context of their own class and with boys with whom they felt most comfortable. This was the first time they had ever been interviewed in such a manner, and if this was going to be an ongoing longitudinal study I needed to make it as fun and exciting as I could within the constraints of a "research project." Andrea Fontana and James Frey (2000) assert that a focus group interview is a technique for gathering rich, descriptive qualitative data in a systematic manner. Michael Q. Patton (2002) adds that the objective of the focus group is to use a social context where people consider their own views and those of others in order to gain high-quality data. In this study, the interviewing techniques adopted enabled broad discussion around specific aspects of sport, health, and physical activity across the age groups from early childhood through to middle primary school.

I developed an interview guide, drawing on my own extensive experience and previous research in the field as well as from contemporary scholarly literature on boys, sport, and health (Hickey and Fitzclarence 1999; Patton 2002). This was a theoretically sound and pragmatic approach given that as the boys aged there was a need to modify and change the types of questions and approach to interviewing in accordance to their developmental age. I then recorded the interviews—which lasted between twenty and thirty minutes—with a digital voice recorder. I took a phenomenological approach, taking the boys' responses as a basis for further enquiry and exploration. Patton (2002) identifies this as being an ideal way to capture as much rich, descriptive data as possible. The interview guide then allowed me to refocus the line of enquiry to ensure that all topics were covered and the same set of core issues were covered within each focus group.

While the boys have been interviewed each year since early childhood, the first and second rounds of interviews in reception (called kindergarten in the United States) and year 1 involved a methodology based around drawing pictures. Being an early childhood cohort, this group of boys required a slightly more structured approach with respect to an interview schedule. Inviting the boys to draw pictures elicited rich descriptive responses directly related to the pictures. In the first round of interviews, the boys were specifically asked to draw pictures associated with health, sport, physical activity, and fitness, and they were asked to draw a picture of a man. I then asked them questions about the more prominent physical features of the man they had drawn such as musculature, size, and shape.

During the second round of interviews (year 1) the boys were asked to draw a picture of a healthy alien. The reason an alien was chosen came about inadvertently. Given that the boys had previously drawn pictures of "health" or people in the act of "doing health" the year before, some of the boys badgered me to draw "something else." One of the boys asked if he could draw an alien, to which I replied, "Yes, you can, but only if it's a healthy alien." This was not a preconceived methodological ploy. It came about as a result of keeping the boys interested and responsive. It also came about through the experience of being a reflexive researcher. Regarding research reflexivity, Kristi Malterud (2001, 484–484) claims, "A researcher's background and position will affect what they choose to investigate, the angle of investigation, the methods judged most adequate for this purpose, the findings considered most appropriate, and the framing and communication of conclusions." Being reflexive and responsive is important as a researcher. It is arguably more so with a challenging cohort of boys in early child-hood who often struggle to maintain concentration on the topic during a focus group interview. Therefore, taking the lead from Christensen and Prout (2002), I needed to explore ways in which to meaningfully engage this group of boys with the research. This approach clearly resonated with these young boys as they all chose to take up the option of drawing an alien figure. In turn, this provided the opportunity to discuss elements of health, with respect to this alien, in depth. We then discussed how the aliens might reflect aspects of their own, or others,' lives similar to the pictures they had drawn the year prior when they used human participants "doing health."

I interviewed the boys in a range of settings within the school environment. Institutional research ethics protocol meant that each interview had to be within close proximity to classroom. However, to eliminate the boys' potential fear of retribution about speaking openly and candidly, interviews were not conducted in "ear shot" of the teachers. This also reduced the teachers' "positional power" and further enhanced the opportunity for the boys to speak freely. Enabling the boys the opportunity to provide rich, descriptive, qualitative data is important to understand the issues that confront boys from a range of perspectives associ-ated with their health and well-being. As Allison Pugh (2014) has aptly argued, children are not passive and therefore have the capacity to provide an enormous amount of insight by asking, questioning, and querying aspects of their lives.

The interviews were transcribed verbatim and then open coded (Strauss and Corbin 1998) and analyzed using inductive analysis. Patton (2002) claims that inductive analysis enables categories to emerge from open-ended observations while the researcher gains an understanding of the patterns that exist. Further-more, Patton states that inductive analysis involves recognizing categories, pat-terns, and themes in data through constant interaction with the data. Differences and similarities were documented based on the author's personal understand-ing, the author's professional knowledge, and the literature (Strauss and Corbin 1998). When conducting a longitudinal research project such as this, it is impera-tive that the process is conducted well. That is, every interview needed to be conducted in a similar manner and each year the types of questions and lines of enquiry built on those from the last, given the boys are not only chronologically aging, but also emotionally and intellectually aging. I have certainly noticed a big step up in terms of the types of responses I have received in recent years as the boys "play around" with swear words as well as start to explore sexist and homo-phobic language. As a researcher I have had to adapt during the focus groups to explore these comments and discourse and appear not to be confronted by their conversation, or seem judgmental. As a researcher I have had to utilize my reflex-ive research skills in order to attain high-quality data from a diverse and evolving participant cohort.

Boys, Sport, and Health

While I hoped to focus the research on masculinities, sport, health, and physical activity, boys' somewhat random musings frequently raised issues that stretch beyond the scope of this chapter. Here, I present the data emerging around what boys perceive to be the key aspects of sport within the context of their lives. Having said that, it is clear that each year there are notable differences among the cohort with respect to the type of discussion in which they engage and the topics they raise independently of the questions that are asked. Similarly the boys' demeanor and the type of language they use have changed somewhat over time, as one would expect, particularly in more recent years as they approach adolescence. For instance, as I alluded to earlier, most recently the boys have been experimenting with common swear words as well as derogatory connotations such as "homo" and "gay." This language is heavily influenced by traditional masculine ideologies that include disparaging remarks not only concerning sexualities but also toward girls. It is noteworthy that these types of remarks within all-male group settings have been identified by scholars as having the capacity to enhance group solidarity through masculinized discourse and misogynist banter (Messner and Montez de Oca 2005; Pascoe 2007).

When I deployed inductive thematic analysis of the data, a number of strong themes emerged, several of which are age-specific. Over time, some themes have diminished in salience, while new ones materialized. For instance one of the early themes revolved around the boys' idealistic notions of holistic health in which lifelong health is simplistically associated with eating healthy and exercising. As the boys have moved out of early childhood and beyond middle school, they now perceive health to be linked to the way a body appears. Therefore aesthetics have taken precedence in determining their perception of health. While themes within specific age contexts tell us much about children and their developmental periods, for the purposes of this chapter I focus on three themes that have transcended the developmental periods of early childhood, boyhood and emerging adolescence: (1) men and masculinized sports, often discussed as "tough sports–blood sports"; (2) boys are superior to girls (beating girls in sport); and (3) muscles, men, and masculinity.

Men and Masculinized Sports: "Tough Sports–Blood Sports"

Over the six years, the boys have repeatedly talked about sports they call "blood sports." In their younger years, boys more often called it by this name. For example when I asked the boys in the early years to explain the types of the sports they most enjoyed, many were unanimous in concurring with a boy who stated, "It's got to be the blood sports. You know, sports like footy and rugby. They're the real sports." As they aged, the boys continued to reinforce the importance and significance of males' involvement in aggressive and violent sports. Indeed, one of the boys recounted the central role blood sports have played in the numerous conversations he has had with both peers and adults about the sports he plays. This boy is heavily involved in swimming, athletics, and surf lifesaving, and has won numerous state titles across a range of events. He stated, "When people ask me what sport I do I tell them swimming, athletics, and surf lifesaving. Then they say, 'No, what sports do you really do? You know, football or basketball.' They think that I have to play sports that bash and crash like all the other boys."

When I explored this comment further with this incredibly talented young athlete, he identified to me that this perception was attributed not solely to his peers, but also to some adults whom he has met. Seemingly this notion of "blood sports" or sports that are seen to be highly masculinized, and with a degree of "bash and crash," are those that have been historically and culturally embedded as men's sports. The interesting and somewhat perplexing thing from an Australian cultural perspective is that some of the nation's most revered sportsmen have hailed from the sports in which he engages. However, at the top of the hierarchy there is a list of heroes who are revered for their involvement and achievements in the so-called blood sports.

It can be argued that much of this notion surrounding the "tough sports–blood sports" ideology has been socially constructed through the media. In particular, of significance is the way in which the commentators of Australian football and rugby, who are often former players, laud and applaud perceived masculinized acts including "taking the hits," playing with visible injury and bandages, and even being concussed. These types of public vindication for traditional ideological masculinized "performances" influence the way young males come to view the expendable nature of males involved in sports and the sacrificial acts in which they are expected to engage (Messner, Dunbar, and Hunt 2000; McKay 1991).

In the following discussion with the six- to seven-year-old boys, the excitement and enthusiasm with which they expressed the meanings associated with toughness were palpable. It was clear that when talking about hitting, crashing, and bumping within the context of the more violent sports, the boys were visibly excited en masse within the focus groups.

A1:   Strength means toughness.

Q: What do you mean by toughness?

A2:   Rugby is tough. They actually hold the ball and they crash out the other teams, like a bomber. Like a big bomb. They go like this, "pow" [slamming his fist into his palm].

Q: Do they hurt each other?

A2:   Yeahhhh [excitedly moving forward on his seat]. Because you can hit into each other. And they might bleed.

A1:   No, the toughest thing in the world is wrestling.

Q: Really, why's that?

A3: Because you punch and jump on people.

A2: Yeah and there's sometimes blood.

In the ensuing dialogue that is presented I urge you, the reader, to invest yourself into the ways that the comments made by several of these six- to seven-year-old boys illuminate the socially constructed nature of the ways boys are "supposed to act" during their early childhood. As a lecturer not only in the area of sociology of sport, but also in men's and boys' health, I argue to my university students that the type of ideology that is espoused within the following discussion is representative of many fathers in particular. Such an ideology can ultimately be harmful to the way in which a young male views himself, his body, and his own health.

Q: So what is a tough sport?

A1: Football.

Q: Why would that be a tough sport?

A1: Because you have to kick hard balls.

A2: And you've got to watch out so you don't knock any people out (sounding excited).

Q: Would rugby be a tough sport?

A2: That's a really tough sport [looking serious].

Q: Why is that really tough?

A2: Because sometimes you get knocked over and stuff so it's really tough.

A1: I know, and sometimes they bleed [smiling].

A3: And sometimes that doesn't hurt.

Q: Sometimes it doesn't hurt? What about if it does hurt?

Q: Are you allowed to cry if it hurts?

A1: No [looking dejected].

Note: At this point the four boys within the focus group became silent. Indeed it was apparent that the silence was unnerving for some as they quickly focused their eyes down on the paper in front of them and aimlessly colored in the pictures they had previously drawn.

Q: Why not?

A1: Because then you'll feel like a baby.

Q: You'll feel like a baby?

A1: And that could mean that you're a little kid or something [displaying sadness].

Q: Really? But what about if you guys get hurt do you cry?
A2: Nuh.
A1: Sometimes I don't, like when I fall down and then my head hurts. Sometimes I don't even cry [appearing proud].

Q: Why don't you cry?
A1: Maybe 'cause I'm growing up.
A2: Because maybe it doesn't hurt.

Q: Tell me about this you're saying that you shouldn't cry?
A1: Because they treat you like a baby [looking despondent].

Q: They treat you like a baby if you cry?
A1: Yeah.

Q: Okay. Has anyone taught you not to cry?
A1: Yeah.

Q: Who?
A1: Daddy told me not to cry [in a matter-of-fact manner].
A3: I just learned it myself.

Q: So your daddy told you not to cry, what does he say?
A1: He sent me up to my bedroom, that's what he's done.

Q: If you start crying he'll send you up to your bedroom, really?
A1: If I do something, when I cried daddy said he'd put me in my bedroom [sounding as if he had done something wrong].

Q: Why does he do that?
A1: 'Cause he's cross, he doesn't like me crying [all the boys are quiet].

These comments by the boys cut to the heart of issues surrounding how we, as a Western society, treat boys. Boys are seen as less than masculine (i.e., feminine) in the event of an injury or when displaying pain or visible blood; this is an issue that requires attention (Pollack 1999; Sabo 1986). In a study involving Australian footballers as well as gay athletes from a range of sports (Filiault, Drummond, and Agnew 2012), it was noted by the Australian footballers that to display pain and not continue playing was to be labeled as being "soft." Filiault, Drummond, and Agnew claim,

To be labeled as "soft" implies something less than a man and indeed, a female (Bordo 1999). This notion of soft as being undesirable is underscored by the participant's laughter after stating that he doesn't want to be viewed as soft. The laughter either denotes a soft man as being a joke, or that not wanting to be soft as so self-evident as being humorous. In either case, the interpretation is clear: Ultimately, in an aggressive and physical team sport such as AFL, "soft" also means not being a "team man," given that one is not prepared to "take a hit for the good of the team." (8–9)

Boys need to be nurtured and taught that to display emotions is crucial to ongoing personal physical and mental health (Drummond 2012). Boys also need to be aware that upon entering sports, and in particular highly masculinized sports, there are significant influential factors at play that can impact the way they are "supposed" to act.

Boys Are Superior to Girls (Beating Girls)

One of the consistent themes to run across all of the age groups has been that of "boys are superior to girls," where sports and physical activities are concerned, particularly in more masculinized sports or those that require speed and endurance. The boys view aesthetic sports and activities such as gymnastics and dance as a feminized domain of girls. The boys were not concerned with girls being perceived as skilled and talented in these areas. In fact, a juxtaposition between masculinized blood sports and the aesthetic nature of gymnastics and dance provided a visible point of difference between boys and girls. For example, the boys in year 1 stated,

A1: Hey Tyler, your picture looks like a ballerina [all boys laugh].
A2: Nah, ballet's not my stash.

Q: What's wrong with ballet?
A2: Ballet's for girls [contorts face].
A3: Yeah, it's a dumb sport.
A1: I like laser tag because you get to run around and shoot people, not like ballet.

In a similar vein, some of the boys in year 2 claimed,

A1: Girls are not really good at sport [laughing].
A2: But I know a girl that's good at running.
A3: Girls are not really good at football.

Q: Yeah but are they as good as you at other sports?
A1: No, no, no, no, no.

Q: Why not.
A1: Sometimes, running.

Q: What about ball sports and some of rough games you talk about?
A1: Nah.

Q: Why not?
A1:   Too delicate.

Q: No, so oh that's an interesting comment. What do you mean by that?
A1:   Fragile.

Q: Fragile. Do you think so?
A1:   Because they're not used to getting bruises and scratches.

Q: Bruises and scratches, okay.
A1:   Yeah, they're not used to it.

The boys were also keen to highlight that in sports and activities that they perceived as being gender-neutral, it was the boys who were more accomplished. For example, on many occasions, the boys argued that while some girls were good runners, the boys were even better. They also noted that in any given running race, whether it be a sprint event on track or and endurance event, boys will be superior, simply by virtue of being boys. This is consistent with the work of Michela Musto (2014), who identified that some boys do struggle with the notion of girls being faster (better), specifically in swimming. Not until boys start attaining higher levels of muscularity upon reaching puberty, several years later, do they begin to swim faster than girls. However, according to the boys in the current longitudinal research, swimming is a little different from running because boys have the capacity to attain speed and endurance every day at school given that they regularly play running games, enhancing their ability. They highlighted that simply their status as boys and the activities in which they engaged at school lunch breaks enabled them to be faster and fitter than girls. The boys in year 3 stated,

A1:   Boys run faster because they are fitter than girls.
A2:   Yeah, girls just sit around at lunchtime and talk and stuff. Boys are always out doing things like playing chasey and stuff.

Q: Do you think that makes a difference?
A1:   Yeah [all agree].
A2:   For sure. We do more running so we can run faster.
A3:   Yeah, girls can't even run 5ks [5 kilometers].

Q: Why do you think that is?
A1:   Because they're just not as fit as us.
A2:   Because they sit around and talk all the time.

Noteworthy with each of these sets of quotations is the underlying notion of boys being better and more dominant at sports simply by virtue of the fact that they are male. Accordingly the boys suggest they are better because their very inborn nature provides them with the opportunity to be dominant. It is their belief that boys are both genetically superior (i.e., not fragile) and socially constructed (i.e., always playing chasey and not sitting around) to be dominant in sporting endeavors. This is despite all of the evidence to indicate the significant numbers of women involved in all manner of elite-level sports throughout the world. The difference, however, is that men occupy the majority of rough sports and so-called blood sports that dominate the media attention. Given men's clear physiological advantage at the elite level in these types of sports, the boys make a simple assumption that this domination translates across the majority of sports.

MUSCLES, MEN, AND MASCULINITY

In discussions and assessments of being a man, it is evident from the boys of all ages within this research that there is a significant importance placed on size, and specifically muscular size. Regardless of age, the majority of boys had a comprehensive understanding that they are not capable, at present, of attaining a highly muscular physique, as some boys stated, "like my dad." Therefore the interviews did not reveal any disappointment or anguish over any perceived bodily inadequacies. Indeed, most boys anticipated becoming muscular as they moved through adolescence and toward adulthood; there was even a sense of inevitability in the boys' beliefs that they would become big and muscular simply by becoming men. In the following quotations, the reception-age boys (five to six years) discuss their perceptions of muscularity and express when they think their musculature will occur:

Q: What are some things you can tell me about men.
A1: Men have strong muscles.
A2: Men are strongest.

Q: Why?
A1: Because they get fit exercising.
A2: Because they eat healthy food. Not junk food.

Q: But can women get muscles too if they eat healthy food?
A1: No.
A2: No.

Q: Why not?
A1: Because they don't have any muscles. Because they're not boys.

Q: So only boys can have muscles, is that right?
A1: Yes.
A2: Yeah. Strong boys.

Q: What do they have?
A2:   Muscles.

Q: And what does it mean? What does it mean if you've got muscles?
A3:   Because they get healthy food, and they buy heaps of healthy things because they want to get really strong.
A1:   So they can get in the Olympics.
A2:   Yeah, because they want to win.

Q: Do you think you'll ever have muscles one day?
A1:   Yeah.
A3:   I could beat Jason up.
A2:   Me too.
A4:   I won't get muscles until I'm older.

During their discussions on muscularity the boys also identified the importance of strength as a seemingly foreseeable consequence of musculature and argued that being strong was an indicator of being a man. For many of these boys, the only point of reference to "test" their strength was to compare and contrast theirs with that of girls and women (see Drummond 2012). Regardless of the boys' current size and strength, there appeared to be a sense of inevitability that simply as a consequence of becoming a man both musculature and power would follow. This provided the boys with a source of calm that positioned them well in terms of being superior to girls and possibly other males in the future, if they were seen to be currently less "physical." However, in the following conversation, the boys reveal their conception of the meaning of muscles and the size of those muscles. They explain that for those boys with larger muscles they may have what Filiault and Drummond (2007) have termed a "hegemonic aesthetic" that places those with visibly larger muscles at a distinct masculine advantage that they might feel empowered to use to disempower others. In the following dialogue some of the boys in year 1 attempt to explain their understanding of the way in which some males can display power through visible musculature and use this power to humiliate others with less developed muscles.

A1:   Strong men have big boobies [pectoral muscles].
A2:   It's mean to show people your muscles to other people because if they have smaller muscles and someone has bigger muscles and then they'll go "Ha, ha you have small muscles," it will be mean to them.

Q: Do you think so? Have you ever seen anyone do that before?
A1:   Yep.
A2:   I have.

Q: What do they do?
A2:   I saw them going like this [flexes bicep].

Q: He was flexing his muscles.

A2: Yeah, but then it got smaller. It was big then it got smaller then they went "Ha, ha you've got small muscles; you've got small muscles."

Q: Was that a boy at school or was it outside?

A2: Outside.

A1: If you are strong, you have muscles.

Q: What does a strong person look like?

A2: Muscle man.

Q: Is being muscley important?

A2: Yes, because you can win.

This discussion provides evidence that the boys have the capacity to interpret the notion of muscularity in a number of different ways. They also have the ability to change these interpretations in a relatively short period of time. However, there is a common thread around the meanings of muscularity that runs across the majority of interviews. It is based on a somewhat fundamental equation that muscles equal strength equals power and dominance. Throughout the interviews

Figure 7.1. Thomas, age five. "This is a picture of a man. You can see he is a man because he has lots of muscles."

Figure 7.2. Christopher, age five. "I drew a picture of a man. He has a lot of muscles on his arms."

over the past six years the boys have not been able to identify which aspect in this equation is likely to come first. That is, if a male is strong he is likely to have muscles and display power and dominance (i.e., strength equals muscles equals power). Similarly if a male displays power and dominance he is likely to have strength and musculature (i.e., power equals strength equals muscles). The following conversation with the year 1 boys underlines the manner in which they have the ability to articulate a variety of issues relating to musculature and strength in the process of reflecting on the drawings they were completing as a part of the research process.

Q: Can you draw me a picture of a man.
A1: A strong man with muscles on the legs?

Q: What does a strong man look like?
A1: He has a four-pack.

Q: Does he? What's a four-pack?
A2: No, eight. I've got one.

Q: What, you've got a four-pack?
A2: Yeah I'm going to get one.

Figure 7.3. Jack, age five. "This is a picture of a man who likes to go to the gym. My dad goes to the gym a lot to make him strong."

Q: Yeah?
A1:   Yeah, here we go, a strong man.
A3:   Look at my guy.

Q: Well, look at that.
A3:   Look at him.

Figure 7.4. Max, age five. "The man I drew is really happy. He has really good muscles on his arms and he is strong."

Q: What are they? Are they muscles?
A3: Yeah muscles.

Q: Wow, and what are they? Are they muscles on his arms, are they?
A3: Yep.

Q: Jake, what are you drawing?
A4: Those are his arms and they're steel because they're very strong.

Q: Okay.
Q: Are they like weights are they, Jake?
A4: Yeah, weights but except they are attached to him.

Q: That's great.
A2: Look at mine!

Q: What's that? Are they muscles as well?
A2: Yeah.

Q: Wow he's got lots of muscles.
A2: And he's really strong.

Q: Oh, is he?
A2: Yeah.
A1: My guy doesn't have a T-shirt on.
A2: Look, he has heaps of muscles on his arms and body. He's a muscle man
     [sounding very excited].
A4: This is a one hundred weight, those are one hundred weights.
A: Who's that?
A4: Strong man.

As this conversation highlights, the boys were firm in their conviction that men are strong and display muscles. What was also conspicuous was the conversation around the "six-pack." The regular use of such language provides an insight into a part of the male body that has rarely been reflected on among boys, and certainly early childhood and prepubescent boys previously in research (see Drummond and Drummond 2015 for a comprehensive discussion on this). It is also reflective of the boys' immersion in contemporary culture, which is placing the aesthetic gaze upon males and their bodies unprecedentedly.

Where To from Here?

Convention suggests that book chapters should end with a conclusion. However, I have attempted to make this a chapter in which the reader has engaged with the boys' voices in order to develop a sense of meaning these boys place on "being a boy." I have utilized the boys' discussion surrounding the body and sport as exemplars of what they perceive to be some of the most important aspects of growing up. It is clear that what the body looks like, how it performs (particularly with reference against girls), and what it performs (in terms of perceived masculinized activities and sports) are crucial to the ways in which boys would like to be acknowledged. Therefore the primary aim of this chapter was to engage the reader within the boys' words and allow the voices to provide a context in which we can begin to challenge some of the ideologies surrounding boys and traditional masculinities. It should be recognized that these data are from just several years of a study that is now in its seventh year of an eight-year project. Therefore the boys have so much more to say, and their views and perspectives are somewhat fluid as they gradually head toward adolescence. While some things do change, such as goals and perspectives, others, such as their relationship with girls, have stayed the same. It seems in this cohort of boys being compared, and definitively contrasted, to girls is a critical definer of masculinity.

From an academic perspective and watching these boys grow up as I interview them each year, it is clear that there is a need to engage young males in early awareness initiatives that reflect a range of masculinities. Problematically, the information they receive in classrooms is often different from the reality they face beyond the controlled class environment. The construction of contemporary Western society through historical ideologies plays a significant role in how the boys are raised. It influences the way they act and behave, the sports they play, and the perceived expectations upon them, among many other aspects of life. With the advent of social media, we have an additional element that has the capacity to socially construct boys in traditional ideological ways. However, it also has the capacity to challenge these ideologies. One of the significant elements of social media is that both boys and girls can engage in conversations and provide important perspective, thereby influencing social norms. While most of these boys are not yet at the stage of engaging heavily in social media conversations, they soon will be. I am looking forward to meeting up with the boys again this year and next to discuss how they are working with and exploring the world of social media. Most of the boys will not be on Facebook or Instagram during this study. However, they are beginning to email and utilize a free web-based messaging system. I am keen to see how this moves forward and how it might play a role in their development as young males. Importantly, interviewing these boys over the next few years, as they move into adolescence, will provide vital information in terms of how they are navigating themselves, or being navigated, toward a happy and healthy manhood.

REFERENCES

Australian Bureau of Statistics. 2011–2012. "Participation in Sport and Physical Recreation, Australia." http://www.abs.gov.au/ausstats/abs@.nsf/Products/4177.0~2011–12~Main+Features~Characteristics+of+persons+who+participated?OpenDocument.

Biddle, Stuart J. H., Sarah H. Whitehead, Toni M. O'Donovan, and Mary E. Nevill. 2005. "Correlates of Participation in Physical Activity for Adolescent Girls: A Systematic Review of Recent Literature." *Journal of Physical Activity and Health* 2: 423–434.

Bordo, Susan. 1999. *The Male Body: A New Look at Men in Public and Private.* New York: Farrar, Straus and Giroux.

Christensen, Pia, and Allison Prout. 2002. "Working with Ethical Symmetry in Social Research with Children." *Childhood* 9.4: 477–497.

Cooky, Cheryl. 2009. "'Girls Just Aren't Interested': The Social Construction of Interest in Girls' Sport." *Sociological Perspectives* 52.2: 259–283.

Drummond, Murray J. 2010. "The Natural: An Autoethnography of a Masculinised Body in Sport." *Men and Masculinities* 12.3: 374–389.

———. 2012. "Boys' Bodies in Early Childhood." *Australasian Journal of Early Childhood* 37.4: 107–114.

Drummond, Murray J., and Claire Drummond. 2015. "It's All about the Six-Pack: Boys' Bodies in Contemporary Western Culture." *Journal of Child Health Care* 19.3: 293–303. doi:10.1177/1367493514538128.

Drummond, Murray J., Claire Drummond, and David Birbeck. 2009. "Listening to Children's Voices in Qualitative Health Research." *Journal of Student Wellbeing* 3.1: 1–13.

Filiault, Shaun M., and Murray J. Drummond. 2007. "The Hegemonic Aesthetic." *Gay and Lesbian Issues and Psychology Review* 3.3: 175–184.

Filiault, Shaun M., Murray J. Drummond, and Deborah Agnew. 2012. "Gender, Pain, and Male Athletes: A Qualitative Analysis." *Gay and Lesbian Issues and Psychology Review* 8.1: 3–14.

Fontana, A., and J. Frey. 2000. "The Interview: From Structured Questions to Negotiated Text." In *The Sage Handbook of Qualitative Research*, edited by Norman K. Denzin and Yvonna S. Lincoln, 645–672. Thousand Oaks, CA: Sage.

Hickey, Christopher, and Lindsay Fitzclarence. 1999. "Educating Boys in Sport and Physical Education: Using Narrative Methods to Develop Pedagogies of Responsibility." *Sport, Education, and Society* 4.1: 51–62.

Knowles, Ann-Marie, Ailsa Niven, and Samantha Fawkner. 2011. "A Qualitative Examination of Factors Related to the Decrease in Physical Activity Behaviour in Adolescent Girls during the Transition from Primary to Secondary School." *Journal of Physical Activity and Health* 8.8: 1084.

Malterud, Kristi. 2001. "Qualitative Research: Standards, Challenges, and Guidelines." *Lancet* 358: 483–488.

McKay, Jim. 1991. *No Pain, No Gain? Sport and Australian Culture*. Sydney: Prentice Hall.

Messner, Michael A., Michele Dunbar, and Darnell Hunt. 2000. "The Televised Sports Manhood Formula." *Sport and Social Issues* 24.4: 380–394.

Messner, Michael A., and Jeffrey Montez de Oca. 2005. "The Male Consumer as Loser: Beer and Liquor Ads in Mega Sports Media Events." *Journal of Women in Culture and Society* 30.3: 1879–1909.

Musto, Michela. 2014. "Athletes in the Pool, Girls and Boys on Deck: The Contextual Construction of Gender in Coed Youth Swimming." *Gender & Society* 28.3: 359–380.

Pascoe, C. J. 2007. *Dude, You're a Fag: Masculinity and Sexuality in High School*. Berkeley: University of California Press.

Patton, Michael Q. 2002. *Qualitative Research and Evaluation Methods*. Thousand Oaks, CA: Sage.

Pollack, William. 1999. *Real Boys: Rescuing Our Sons from the Myths of Boyhood*. New York: Henry Holt.

Pugh, Allison. 2014. "The Theoretical Costs of Ignoring Childhood: Rethinking Independence, Insecurity, and Inequality." *Theory and Society* 43: 71–89.

Sabo, Donald. 1986. "Pigskin, Patriarchy, and Pain." *Changing Men: Issues in Gender, Sex and Politics* 16: 24–25.

Slater, Amy, and Marika Tiggemann. 2010. "'Uncool to Do Sport': A Focus Group Study of Adolescent Girls' Reasons for Withdrawing from Physical Activity." *Psychology of Sport and Exercise* 11: 619–626.

Strauss, Anselm, and Juliet Corbin. 1998. *Basics of Qualitative Research.* Newbury Park, CA: Sage.

Yang, Xiao Lin, Risto Telama, and Lauri Laakso. 1996. "Parents' Physical Activity, Socioeconomic Status, and Education as Predictors of Physical Activity and Sport among Children and Youths—A 12-Year Follow-Up Study." *International Review for the Sociology of Sport September* 31.3: 273–291.

CHAPTER 8

"A Right to the Gym"

PHYSICAL ACTIVITY EXPERIENCES OF
EAST AFRICAN IMMIGRANT GIRLS

Chelsey M. Thul, Nicole M. LaVoi, Torrie F. Hazelwood,
and Fatimah Hussein

It's six o'clock, and a typical Wednesday evening inside the gym. The sparkling white walls of the newly repainted gym without windows stand in stark contrast to the blue bleachers which frame the left side of a basketball court. All four doors leading into the gym are closed and all but one is locked to deter and prevent boys from entering this community space—a space typically reserved for the activities of males. Thirty animated and energetic, East African teenage girls, who believe they too have "a right to the gym," file into the space through the one unlocked door. Most of the girls are wearing head scarves and colorful, loose-fitting, floor-length dresses or skirts and long sleeves. All are excited to take advantage of their limited gym time designated for girls-only physical activity.

Our research journey together examining the physical activity experiences of immigrant girls began shortly after of the release of the 2007 Tucker Center for Research on Girls & Women in Sport research report, "Developing Physically Active Girls," which synthesized the current trends and evidence-based approaches to girls' physical activity participation. Three key themes emerged from that report: (1) girls were participating in organized sports in record numbers, (2) despite increased participation, however, boys outnumbered girls in sport and were more active than girls, and (3) diverse populations of girls were the least active of all youth. What became clear to us was that lower levels of physical activity helped explain disparate health and developmental outcomes between underserved girls and girls from more privileged race and class backgrounds.

After the release of the report, East African girls became increasingly visible as an underserved group in need of physical activity programming in our own community. Minnesota, and particularly the Twin Cities metro area (Minneapolis and St. Paul), is home to the largest Somali diaspora in the United States. Somalis, one subgroup of East Africans, are a growing immigrant population in the United States and are the fourth largest immigrant group in Minnesota (Minnesota Compass 2014). Few existing studies have examined East African girls' experiences with physical activity or have drawn upon East African girls' own perspectives on sport and physical activity. We found this gap in evidence troubling because we felt girls' voices should be included to help develop successful physical activity programs (Felton et al. 2005).

Subsequently, Thul and LaVoi began exploring the physical activity experiences of a group prominent in our own community—East African first- and second-generation immigrant girls, a majority of whom identify as Muslim. Our work contributes to the rich and growing field of interdisciplinary and sociological children and youth studies and adds to Michael Messner and Michela Musto's (2014, 116–117) call for "deep research engagements in the worlds of children and sports, especially from qualitative and interpretive sociologists who are best positioned to investigate kids as active, meaning-making agents." Over the past eight years, we have cultivated a community participatory action research partnership with a group of East African immigrant girls, their adult female leaders, and community partners. In this chapter we summarize what is known about the physical activity of Muslim immigrant girls and share results from our ongoing work to illuminate how East African Muslim immigrant girls in a large Midwest urban area interpret, experience, and negotiate physical activity.

PHYSICAL ACTIVITY AND IMMIGRANT GIRLS

Messner and Musto's (2014, 113) observation that "we just don't know that much about the ways that kids experience and make gender meanings in youth sports" is especially true for immigrant Muslim girls in the United States. Immigrant youth and children of immigrants in the United States are rarely the focus of physical activity research, with some exceptions (Rothe et al. 2010; Sabo and Veliz 2008; Thul and LaVoi 2011). Don Sabo and Philip Veliz (2008) reported a significant gender participation gap in which US immigrant boys (75 percent) are more likely to participate in sport than their female counterparts (43 percent). One explanation for this gap stems from the fact that immigrant parents' beliefs and values about their daughters' interest in sports, compared to values related to their sons, can result in less support for physical activity participation for girls. Parent- and community-related concerns pertaining to adherence to religious and cultural practices may inhibit immigrant Muslim girls' participation in physical activity, such as preventing contact with the opposite sex and protection from the male gaze (Kahan 2013; Rothe et al. 2010; Thul 2012; Thul and LaVoi 2011), maintaining female-only physical activity spaces to maintain modesty (Benn and Dagkas 2006; Dagkas and Benn 2006; De Knop et al. 1996; Kay 2006;

Pfister 2000; Strandbu 2005; Thul 2012; Thul and LaVoi 2011), providing loose and modest sport clothing options to cover skin (Bashire-Ali and Elnour 2003; Dagkas, Benn, and Jawad 2011; Pfister 2000; Strandbu 2005; Thul 2012; Thul and LaVoi 2011), and performing family duties (Rothe et al. 2010; Thul 2012; Thul and LaVoi 2011). While gender-segregated physical activity space is not a universally held requirement for all Muslims, it is a common concern for parents and for girls (Palmer 2008; Rothe et al. 2010; Thul 2012; Thul and LaVoi 2011; Walseth and Strandbu 2014) and gender-segregated physical activity increased parent- and community-approved participation among immigrant Muslim girls (Rothe et al. 2010). Therefore, understanding the impact of social norms, attitudes, beliefs, and behavior controls on Muslim girls, their families, and community participation in physical activity, whether in the United States or elsewhere, is a key component in mediating potential constraints (Kahan 2013; Kay 2006; Rothe et al. 2010; Thul and LaVoi 2011).

In addition to examining barriers to participation, scholars outside the United States examine participation of immigrant youth as a means for social integration. A social integration approach includes the desire for receiving communities to develop multicultural understandings in and through sport, with the goal that sport involvement by immigrant youth leads to integration in society (Walseth 2006a; Walseth and Fasting 2004). While many European scholars have criticized the "sport for integration" model and its implementation, scholars such as Kristin Walseth, Kari Fasting, Åse Strandbu, and Mette Andersson, among others, have applied a gendered lens to the integration model and recorded lived experiences of immigrant girls or daughters of immigrant parents to inform their research (Andersson 2002; Dagkas, Benn, and Jawad 2011; Pfister 2000; Walseth 2006b, 2013; Walseth and Fasting 2004; Walseth and Strandbu 2014). Two concepts emerge from this body of research: (1) the consistency of the need for gender-segregated physical activity spaces and (2) the variation in needs among immigrant Muslim girls. This latter finding, that immigrant experiences vary by religious affiliation, economic status, race, citizenship, ethnicity, place of residence, and age, makes scholars cautious about the dangers of generalizing research across and within immigrant populations (Bashire-Ali and Elnour 2003; Oliver, Hamzeh, and McCaughtry 2009).

For example, while Muslims share the same religious beliefs and many practices, there are distinct cultural differences based on ethnic beliefs and economic status, among others, that influence lifestyle and worldviews—including variations of abiding by Islamic principles, which in turn influence beliefs about how females should dress and participate in physical activity. A majority of existing scholarship pertains to Muslim girls and women living in the United States and in Western Europe, yet it is important to recognize that differences exist among and between females in different cultural groups that practice Islam (Bashire-Ali and Elnour 2003). Just as with any group, Muslim women are not monolithic, and to assume so is irresponsible and inaccurate. For example, Manal Hamzeh and Kimberly L. Oliver (2012) illuminate diverse interpretations parents hold with regard to wearing the hijab, which results in variations and flexibility with how, or if, the hijab is worn. Therefore, one Islamic practice—wearing a hijab—is fluid, negotiable, and variant based on girls' agency, parents' religious beliefs, culture, and community influence (Hamzeh and Oliver 2012; Walseth and Strandbu 2014). Finally, immigrant girls are active subjects who create their own social worlds (Messner and Musto 2014).

If we are to create successful sports programs for Muslim immigrant girls, it is essential to listen to the voices of Muslim immigrant girls (Kahan 2013). Empowering girls as experts on their own needs and their preferences toward and experiences within physical activity is critical to broadening the field of physical activity and immigrant youth (Dagkas, Benn, and Jawad 2011; Thul and LaVoi 2011). Next we share our own research, which illuminates the voices of East African immigrant girls and their unique perspectives, needs, values, and beliefs in the negotiation of physical activity participation. While we present our work here in three phases for the sake of comprehension, we want to emphasize that this work is not linear. Each phase emerged out of the prior phase in an organic, iterative, and collaborative nature.

Listening to the Voices of Immigrant Girls

In the initial phase of our research, we interviewed East African adolescent girls to understand their experiences with and beliefs about physical activity, including their suggestions for creating and promoting physical activity programming (Thul and LaVoi 2011). Participants included nineteen East African (twelve Somali and seven Ethiopian) adolescent girls twelve to eighteen years old. All were physically active and practicing Muslims. Fewer than half (eight) were first-generation and eleven were second-generation immigrants to the United States. An exploratory qualitative approach was used to understand their lived experience with physical activity. In focus groups, we asked girls about their definition of and preferences for physical activity, barriers to and facilitators of physical activity, and their suggestions for culturally relevant physical activity programming.

Our findings revealed that East African girls perceived a wide range of physical activities as culturally relevant and desirable—including swimming, fitness activities (e.g., running, jumping rope, aerobics), dance (e.g., traditional East African dances, hip-hop), and team sports (e.g., basketball, soccer). While some girls wanted to participate in competitive, organized sport, the majority of girls were more interested in less organized, recreational sport opportunities. Swimming in a female-only space was the primary activity of choice because it was seen, in the words of one of the girl, as "freeing and just so fun" (Thul and LaVoi 2011, 221).

The girls easily identified and discussed an array of barriers that impeded their physical activity participation (Thul and LaVoi 2011). For example, they discussed a lack of time for physical activity due to upholding family roles and school responsibilities. One girl described, "Mostly all of us, like girls in our religion can't, like, really we can't, like, have fun time. We have to stay at home to cook, clean. Basically technically we don't have time. We're basically like mothers because our parents work. In our culture we barely have time for it. And we have to help the children do their homework and do all that kind of stuff." Another barrier was persistent and common male peer gender stereotypes, as one girl said: "We want to play but boys say, like, we girls are kind of weak, so they play hard and think we can't play hard, you know. The boys are saying that and it's our culture, you know. The boys have to play on their side and the girls have to play on their side."

As mentioned in previous research, parental perceptions also impacted girls' physical activity participation: "Most parents they would say 'no' [to their girls being active] because they just don't feel comfortable with their girls being outside or staying after school. . . . They're worried about our safety, and they believe girls are supposed to be home to take care of the family. . . . They think the girls might do something bad." Girls also described how a lack of committed, culturally competent coaches acted as a barrier to their activity:

> We need good coaches that are here every single day that actually want to coach us and that also understand our culture. Coaches are either scared of us or they don't care. Like, there are some coaches that come in and they're, like, here for two weeks and then they're gone and it's like we have other coaches from the boys' teams come over here and coach us and they don't even want to coach us. . . . Sometimes the coaches, you know, they get tired of us because of our culture, because of the way we play, because we can't take our hijab off, so they're like, "This is so stupid you're not even trying," and then they start yelling, and the next thing you know they're like, "We don't want to coach these stupid kids," "They annoy us." And then they say something about us and they don't care. And then the next day we leave and then we have a new coach. Not anyone who really wants to be there.

Girls also expressed several access barriers—access to resources, access to opportunities, and access to spaces—to their physical activity participation, primarily because resources were dedicated to the boys: "I would like to go outside and play tennis and volleyball and everything, but then in our community they have soccer and basketball and basically it's all for boys, you know. There's not something for girls." The most commonly discussed barrier was the clothing the girls wore to stay covered (especially in the presence of males) so they could uphold cultural and religious values of privacy and modesty: "I mean, we all want to do these sports, but then there's another situation. There's boys right there and we can't really play as good as we want to play. Because when we're around boys our religion says that we can't take off your clothes. Like right now, like we're wearing our hijabs. Sometimes all you want to do is take them off because it's hot, but you can't. All the boys are right there and you have to wear them."

Many of the barriers described by the girls we collaborate with are similar to constraints faced by nonimmigrant and non-Muslim girls whose physical activity is limited or who opt out of sports. However, clothing is a specific barrier to Muslim populations. Given their candid explanation of constraints, it was not surprising they also offered a variety of strategies to combat the multiple and complex barriers to physical activity. Their suggestions included offering programming at various times (not just after school), providing activities based on what girls actually want, not what researchers/programmers think they want (highlighting the importance of asking girls about their interests), and providing instruction via a committed female coach who is both athletically and culturally competent. Above all in this initial phase of our research, the girls expressed the desire and need for private, female-only physical activity spaces and programming that promoted health, was inclusive, and encouraged positive development.

THE G.I.R.L.S. PROGRAM

After listening to the girls and sharing our findings with the community, the second phase of our community collaboration emerged. In 2008, Fatimah Hussein—a Somali American Muslim woman—created the Girls' Initiative in Recreation and Leisurely Sports (G.I.R.L.S.) Program. G.I.R.L.S. is a female-only community-based physical activity program that provides strength-focused, youth-engaged, holistic, and positive youth development opportunities that are tailored to the specific interests and needs of East African girls. A majority of G.I.R.L.S. programming takes place in the gymnasium described in the opening of this chapter.

Over the last six years for two to three hours every Wednesday evening and Sunday afternoon, G.I.R.L.S. has averaged about thirty participants per session—the majority of whom are Somali and practicing Muslims, ranging in age from ten to twenty-two years old. In addition to Thul, who has been a volunteer researcher and programmer since the inception of G.I.R.L.S., other program partners include the program founder, coaches and volunteers, the girls who participate, and members from several community organizations.

While spending time in the G.I.R.L.S. program and the Cedar Riverside Neighborhood, Thul noticed the community center gymnasium and other physical activity spaces in the neighborhood appeared to be contested spaces wherein "real and symbolic boundaries have been drawn to limit access" (Cooky 2009, 260). Specifically, Thul observed that gender, race, ethnicity, class, religion, and culture intersected to limit girls' access to several physical activity spaces.

One of the girls summed up the intersectional and spatial tension best, when she explained,

> Like women don't do much physical activity because of our religion. We don't have the area to go to and play because there's always going to be boys who will be watching us. . . . The boys, they like to take all of the place, you know. Like, they say, "We are the boys, we like doing this," you know, and just take it. I don't know, they just like taking all of the place, especially in our community . . . the whole place. And we have, like, a big field, you know, and they play on the whole thing. They have the big boys and the small boys, they have groups to take over the whole place.

We continued to believe that giving voice to the girls was imperative for understanding their experiences with, and perceptions of, physical activity spaces. Understanding the contested nature of space and how it could be negotiated to increase physical activity for girls became the impetus for the third phase—Thul's dissertation research (Thul 2012)—and built upon and extended our previous research as a collaborative team.

Understanding Girls' Physical Activity Spatial Experiences and Needs

The purpose of the third phase was twofold: (1) to explore Somali adolescent girls' experiences with, and perceptions of, the intersection of gender, race, ethnicity, class, religion, and culture in physical activity spaces, and (2) to understand the implications for locating and implementing future culturally relevant physical activity programming. Using a mixed-methods approach, Thul conducted a participatory mapping activity and focus groups with Somali adolescent girls. She employed aspects of a feminist participatory action research (FPAR) design that included the G.I.R.L.S. leaders at the time (Fatimah Hussein and Salma Hussein) and the adolescent girls who were directly involved in most stages of the research project (e.g., research development, data collection, interpretation, and action). Specifically, the girls participated in a "Take Action" meeting at the culmination of the third phase where they strategized plans to create change (e.g., created a girls running club so girls could run together on nearby trails). Participants included thirty Somali adolescent girls fourteen to twenty-two years old. All girls were physically active and practicing Muslims. Over half (seventeen) were first-generation and thirteen were second-generation immigrants to the United States. All participants in the third phase had attended the G.I.R.L.S. program at least once.

At the beginning of the focus group sessions, participants were asked their definition of physical activity, as well as what activities they considered "physical activities." They described a wide range of physical activity definitions—from being "motivated," to "doing something that is beneficial for your health," to "having fun and doing stuff that you like to do, and getting active while you're doing it," to "something where your legs are physically moving and that you're moving around and your body is getting worked up and you're sweating somewhere, like you're actually like working." The girls also discussed a continuum of more to less active physical activities, including sports (recreational and competitive sports such as soccer, volleyball, hockey, football), fitness activities (e.g., walking, jogging, running, aerobics, weight training, etc.), dance, domestic activities requiring movement (e.g., gardening, cooking, cleaning), and praying, as culturally relevant.

The girls noted several trends in the participatory mapping activity. First, they selected the gymnasium where the G.I.R.L.S. program takes place (located in the community center in the heart of the Cedar Riverside Neighborhood) as the space where they were most active, of which their parents and community were most supportive, and as the most culturally and religiously appropriate as it can be locked to keep out males and has no windows so males cannot gaze upon them. The girls wanted the majority of future programming in the gymnasium, but also wanted to venture to other spaces for experiential variety. The girls preferred indoor over outdoor physical activity spaces, though they wanted to experience participating in the latter "every now and then." In general, the girls perceived low availability of both indoor and outdoor physical activity spaces in their neighborhood. Specifically, they perceived males to occupy and have access to more physical activity spaces than females in the neighborhood.

The girls discussed the contested nature of spaces identified in the mapping activity in more depth during focus groups. They detailed how community gender ideologies that females "need protection" and "should uphold traditional gender roles" impacted their access to physical activity spaces. For example, one girl said, "There's less supervision on the boys than the girls. Because within our culture, the girls, our parents focus on a lot, because they have a lot of fears for the girls. Like, if you're out at a certain time, they fear, you know, you're gonna get hurt, you're gonna raped, you know, you're gonna get picked on just because you're a girl . . . which limits when and where you can be active." Another girl discussed, "We [girls] have less freedom and opportunities to be active, and like play sports or do fitness, because like we're supposed to do what society says or what the culture says—that we're supposed to stay home and clean."

The girls named male peers and female elders as the two most influential social agents impacting the girls' experiences with and perceptions of space and resulting negotiation of physical activity. Illustrating the ways that boys constrain girls' participation, one girl said, "They [the boys] take over everything. They put in their heads that this is their gym, their park, like their space, and it shouldn't be for girls, and we should have a specific time that we tell them we're going to come play. We can't just come on a daily basis and go play even though, like, the space is supposed to be just as much for us as them. It's not fair at all, you know, 'cause we have just as much a right to be there as they do even though they don't think so." Another girl elaborated, "The gym is meant to be boys and girls a lot of time, but then they had to make [a] girls' gym because there was no place for girls to play, the boys would hog the ball. If you dropped the ball they'd take it from you and never give it back to you, so you have no point of even being in there, so you leave or walk out or watch them play if you're not going to get anything out of it. If you're just going to watch 'cause you can't get a ball, so what's the point?" Several girls in a focus group discussion reinforced each other's view that power and privilege played a role in their spatial tension with boys:

SPEAKER 1: The boys get really mad whenever we have girls' gym because it's a privilege that they're losing, you know. It's like, their privilege to play anywhere they want, and then you make them, you tell them, "You're losing this privilege. There is this group [of girls] that needs to play there," you know. And it's like, "Oh," you know, like, "Damn-it, why am I losing my privilege that I had?"

SPEAKER 2: That's why they used to bang on the doors angry, and sometimes still try to come in. They still aren't okay we took days.

SPEAKER 3: Well, we're not taking away from anyone. We're just, you know, asking for something that you have the right for. We're not taking, we're not stealing anything, like you, have a right to the gym just as much as they do.

SPEAKER 2: Yeah, but they don't see it that way. Like that's why they get mad and try to keep us girls out even more. Like they have little tournaments and stuff like that in their little circles and then don't let us play.

SPEAKER 1: 'Cause like, they say, "You have your two days, stay out."

The girls also perceived female elders to impact the lived space and resulting negotiation of physical activity. For instance, one girl said, "I don't know why they [elderly ladies] watch over us and judge us in [our community]. I feel like it's wrong, because it stops me and a lot of people from being active, especially outside and [in the community], because like that's where they really only go and can watch us.... It's sad, because it makes us uncomfortable and worry and keeps us from like actually doing something, 'cause some people, like me, do care about other people's image, like how other people see them as and stuff." Another girl elaborated, noting, "I think some girls don't go in the gym 'cause they're scared of people judging them, and they don't want to bring shame to their families. A lot of times when I used to go in there elderly ladies would be like, 'Oh why are you guys playing with the boys, play with the girls, go do something else.' And I would just never get it, and I would go to my parents and my parents would be like, 'Stay away from the boys, other people are watching. Just leave it alone.'"

Based on data collected in all three phases, it is clear that inequalities for these girls are being actively created and at times contested (Messner and Musto 2014).

The girls' primary suggestion to combat spatial inequalities was to provide more physical activity opportunities (e.g., more days per week and times, a wider variety of activities) in private, female-only spaces mostly within but occasionally outside of the community. Together we continue to collaborate with the girls, G.I.R.L.S. program leaders and partners, as well as a variety of academic and community partners to provide physical activity opportunities that meet the needs of the girls. For example, the girls created and led a running club, and together we have set up tennis outings and swimming lessons, among other physical activity opportunities. Because most girls voiced their physical activity clothing is restrictive, uncomfortable, and prohibitive, the fourth phase of our work together is under way. The goal of our collaborative work—with Dr. Elizabeth Bye and students from the College of Design at the University of Minnesota and G.I.R.L.S. participants themselves—is to codesign and make culturally sensitive physical activity clothing for the girls, of which they will sew with female community elders, wear in their own physical activity, and hopefully sell to the community to help sustain and grow G.I.R.L.S.

KEY LESSONS FROM OUR RESEARCH

In all phases of our research and community collaboration, we asked and listened to immigrant girls as they illuminated their perceptions of, experiences with, and strategies for increasing culturally relevant physical activity spaces and programming. Providing a platform for the girls' voices was important so they were longer "mute helpless spectators" (Hardman 1973, as cited in Messner and Musto 2014); rather they are actively constructing their own lives by informing what sorts of programs we, G.I.R.L.S. partners and leaders, and the community are building with them. A great example of this is the running club they set up on their own.

In our work we have specifically talked with girls who identified as East African, specifically Somali and Ethiopian. Hearing from this particular population of immigrant underserved girls was important, given that surveys at the state and national levels often do not ask about ethnicity, nationality, or immigrant status. Thus, East African youth are typically grouped with Black youth from other African countries and US-born African Americans into either a "Black" or "African American" category, masking the potentially unique intersectionality of subgroups (Minnesota Department of Health 2012). In order to embrace the complexity of youth and meet their needs, learning from immigrant subgroups is needed so that programming will become closer to being truly culturally tailored and sensitive.

Throughout the studies, the girls provided a broad definition of, and desire for a variety of, physical activities that stretched beyond Western-defined physical activity—sport and American fitness activities (e.g., going to the gym, aerobics, swimming)—to encompass everyday movement activities (e.g., gardening, praying, housework, babysitting) and forms of traditional East African dance. Their wide-ranging perspectives suggest that girls' physical activity advocates need to recognize an inclusive definition and more culturally comprehensive contexts including physical activity and rituals that are a daily part of some Eastern cultures (Leinberger-Jabari et al. 2005). For example, the World Health Organization (2014) "defines physical activity as any bodily movement produced by skeletal muscles that requires energy expenditure—including activities undertaken while working, playing, carrying out household chores, traveling, and engaging in recreational pursuits." Adhering to this culturally inclusive definition broadens the scope of understanding to Eastern populations, avoids minimizing the physical activity that is occurring, and helps diminish the development of ineffective and colonial programming.

Furthermore, the exemplar quotes from the girls highlight the complexity of immigrant girls' physical activity perceptions and experiences, within their unique intersectional social locations. Across both studies, multiple identity constructs (e.g., gender, religion, culture, race, ethnicity, class), agents (e.g., personal, social—parents, male peers, female peers, adults), and structures (e.g., environmental and spatial disparities, ideologies, expectations, norms) are evidenced in the girls' words.

Not only did we listen to the girls' voices regarding barriers, but we also asked for their strategies for change. The girls energetically shared their ideas, and were excited to help make them a reality. In all phases, hearing that the girls wanted and needed female-only programming was not enough; rather working with the girls and the community to make such programming become reality was essential. Working "with" rather than working "on" or "for" immigrant youth in this way and striving to conduct research for positive change allow us to move beyond doing research for research's sake (e.g., just finding out what the barriers are and not doing anything about them) and minimize exploitation.

Throughout our work we acknowledge our positionality, power, and privilege (the three Ps) as white, middle-class, non-Muslim, female, and feminist and physical activity advocates and academics (Thul, LaVoi, and Hazelwood) and a Somali American, middle-class, highly educated, Muslim, female, and community advocate (Hussein). Andrew C. Sparkes and Brett Smith (2009) suggest it is important to acknowledge the authors' positionality in any study, since it shapes all aspects of research (e.g., the questions asked, the method(s) chosen, etc.). We were, and are, aware of the three Ps and consciously work to uphold a power balance by truly listening to the girls and providing the space for them to drive the research agenda as much as possible, explaining the complexities of the girls throughout the studies and representing their voices as directly as possible. Likewise, we listen to, and deeply value, the voices of all our many partners and community liaisons who work together with us. We also conducted both studies in community settings and worked to build trust and rapport by being present in the community (e.g., at the G.I.R.L.S. program, attending other community events, engaging in regular conversations with the girls, G.I.R.L.S. leaders, and partner community liaisons) to manage biases and assumptions throughout the studies. Indeed, acknowledging and actively negotiating the three Ps are imperative in working with immigrant youth regardless of the context. While it was not a goal of our research, the standpoint of marginalized groups can supply researchers with an invaluable critical understanding of the workings of power, privilege, and subordination (Collins 1986), and our work is no exception.

Limitations and Future Research

While our line of inquiry expands understanding of East African immigrant girls, it has several limitations and uncovers additional gaps that remain. There is variation within all cultural groups, and our research serves only as a starting point into understanding the complexity and unique perspectives of East African girls. In our work, our collaborators were limited to adolescent girls, but a better understanding of younger immigrant children's—both girls' and boys'— physical activity experiences is also needed. Following youth longitudinally from childhood to adulthood is also an understudied area in sport sociology. The girls in our studies identified as physically active to various degrees, but the voices of inactive and sedentary youth form an additional and important gap to fill (Messner and Musto 2014).

Conclusion

In summary, listening to and taking seriously the voices of Muslim immigrant girls, and other populations of immigrants, are essential to inform programming aimed at initiating and sustaining physical activity. Our ongoing collaborative community research in which we strive to hear untold stories and empower girls as experts on their own uniquely positioned needs and their preferences regarding and experiences within physical activity is critical to broadening the growing field of interdisciplinary and sociological children and youth studies as well as effective and sustainable culturally relevant physical activity programming. We agree the girls have "a right to the gym," and we are committed to working with them to achieve and sustain that belief.

ACKNOWLEDGMENTS

The following people compose our community partner team—Fatimah Hussein (G.I.R.L.S. founder, GirlsWin), Salma Hussein (Multicultural Center for Academic Excellence, University of Minnesota), the G.I.R.L.S. Participants, Jennifer Weber (G.I.R.L.S. coach, Cedar-Riverside Community School), Muna Mohamed (G.I.R.L.S. coach, Augsburg

College student), Zahra Hassan and Hiba Sharif (University of Minnesota Medical Center–Fairview), and Chelsey M. Thul, Nicole M. LaVoi, and Torrie F. Hazelwood (Tucker Center for Research on Girls & Women in Sport, School of Kinesiology, University of Minnesota).

REFERENCES

Andersson, Mette. 2002. "Identity Work in Sports: Ethnic Minority Youth, Norwegian Macro-Debates, and the Role Model Aspect." *Journal of International Migration and Integration* 3.1: 83–106.

Bashire-Ali, Khadar, and Awatif Elnour. 2003. "Teaching Muslim Girls in American Schools." *Social Education* 67.1: 62–65.

Benn, Tansin, and Symeon Dagkas. 2006. "Incompatible? Compulsory Mixed-Sex Physical Education Initial Teacher Training (PEITT) and the Inclusion of Muslim Women: A Case-Study on Seeking Solutions." *European Physical Education Review* 12.2: 181–200.

Collins, Patricia Hill. 1986. "Learning from the Outsider Within: The Sociological Significance of Black Feminist Thought." *Social Problems* 33.6: S14–S32.

Cooky, Cheryl. 2009. "'Girls Just Aren't Interested': The Social Construction of Interest in Girls' Sport." *Sociological Perspectives* 52.2: 259–283.

Dagkas, Symeon, and Tansin Benn. 2006. "Young Muslim Women's Experiences of Islam and Physical Education in Greece and Britain: A Comparative Study." *Sport, Education, and Society* 11.1: 21–38.

Dagkas, Symeon, Tansin Benn, and Haifaa Jawad. 2011. "Muslim Voices: Improving Participation of Muslim Girls in Physical Education and School Sport." *Sport, Education, and Society* 16.2: 223–239.

De Knop, Paul, Marc Theeboom, Helena Wittock, and Kristine De Martelaer. 1996. "Implications of Islam on Muslim Girls' Sport Participation in Western Europe: Literature Review and Policy Recommendations for Sport Promotion." *Sport, Education, and Society* 1.2: 147–164.

Felton, Gwen A., Ruth P. Saunders, Dianne S. Ward, Rod K. Dishman, Marsha Dowda, and Russell R. Pate. 2005. "Promoting Physical Activity in Girls: A Case Study of One School's Success." *Journal of School Health* 75.2: 57–62.

Hamzeh, Manal, and Kimberly L. Oliver. 2012. "Because I Am Muslim, I Cannot Wear a Swimsuit: Muslim Girls Negotiate Participation Opportunities for Physical Activity." *Research Quarterly for Exercise and Sport* 83.2: 330–339.

Hardman, Charlotte. 1973. "Can There Be an Anthropology of Children?" *Journal of the Anthropological Society of Oxford* 4.2: 85–99.

Kahan, David. 2013. "Islam and Physical Activity: Implications for American Sport and Physical Educators." *Journal of Physical Education, Recreation, and Dance* 74.3: 28–54.

Kay, Tess. 2006. "Daughters of Islam: Family Influences on Muslim Youth Women's Participation in Sport." *International Review for the Sociology of Sport* 41.3: 357–373.

Leinberger-Jabari, Andrea, Diana Dubois, Sirad Abdirahman, Saeed Fahia, Qamar Ibrahim, Khadija Sheikh, and Z. Mohammed. 2005. "Diet and Physical Activity in the Somali Community: Somali Health Care Initiative Focus Group Findings." Minneapolis, MN: WellShare International (Formerly Minnesota International Health Volunteers). http://www.wellshareinternational.org/sites/default/files/Diet%20and%20PA%20PDF.pdf.

Messner, Michael A., and Michela Musto. 2014. "Where Are the Kids?" *Sociology of Sport Journal* 31: 102–122.

Minnesota Compass. 2014. "Overview: Quickly Accessing Information about Minnesota's Diverse and Burgeoning Immigrant Population." http://www.mncompass.org/immigration/overview.

Minnesota Department of Health. 2012. *The Health and Well-Being of Minnesota's Adolescents of Color and American Indians: A Data Book.* St. Paul, MN: Center for Health Statistics.

Oliver, Kimberly L., Manal Hamzeh, and Nate McCaughtry. 2009. "Girly Girls Can Play Games/Las Niñas Pueden Jugar Tambien: Co-creating a Curriculum of Possibilities with Fifth-Grade Girls." *Journal of Teaching in Physical Education* 28: 90–110.

Palmer, Catherine. 2008. "Soccer and the Politics of Identity for Young Muslim Refugee Women in South Australia." *Soccer and Society* 10.1: 27–38.

Pfister, Gertrude. 2000. "Doing Sport in a Headscarf? German Sport and Turkish Females." *Journal of Sport History* 27.3: 497–524.

Rothe, Elizabeth, Christina Holt, Celine Kuhn, Timothy McAteer, Isabella Askari, Mary O'Meara, Abdimajid Sharif, and William Dexter. 2010. "Barriers to Outdoor Physical Activity in Wintertime among Somali Youth." *Journal of Immigrant Minority Health* 12: 726–736.

Sabo, Donald, and Philip Veliz. 2008. "Go Out and Play: Youth Sports in America Executive Summary." East Meadow, NY: Women's Sports Foundation.

Sparkes, Andrew C., and Brett Smith. 2009. "Judging the Quality of Qualitative Inquiry: Criteriology and Relativism in Action." *Psychology of Sport and Exercise* 10: 491–497.

Strandbu, Åse. 2005. "Identity, Embodied Culture, and Physical Exercise: Stories from Muslim Girls in Oslo with Immigrant Backgrounds." *Young: Nordic Journal of Youth Research* 13.1: 27–45.

Thul, Chelsey M. 2012. "Exploring Intersectionality in Physical Activity Spaces among Somali Adolescent Girls: Implications for Programming." PhD dissertation, University of Minnesota.

Thul, Chelsey M., and Nicole M. LaVoi. 2011."Reducing Physical Inactivity and Promoting Active Living: From the Voices of East African Immigrant Adolescent Girls." *Qualitative Research in Sport, Exercise, and Health* 3.2: 211–237.

Walseth, Kristin. 2006a. "Sport and Belonging." *International Review for the Sociology of Sport* 41.3: 447–464.

———. 2006b. "Young Muslim Women and Sport: The Impact of Identity Work." *Leisure Studies* 25.1: 75–94.

———. 2013. "Muslim Girls' Experiences in Physical Education in Norway: What Roles Does Religiosity Play?" *Sport, Education, and Society* 18.2: 1–19.

Walseth, Kristin, and Kari Fasting. 2004. "Sport as a Means of Integrating Minority Women." *Sport in Society* 7.1: 109–129.

Walseth, Kristin, and Åse Strandbu. 2014. "Young Norwegian-Pakistani Women and Sport: How Does Culture and Religiosity Matter?" *European Physical Education Review* 20.4: 489–507.

World Health Organization. 2014. "Physical Activity." http://www.who.int/topics/physical _activity/en/.

CHAPTER 9

Transgender and Gender-Nonconforming Kids and the Binary Requirements of Sport Participation in North America

Ann Travers

Ray-Ray took off one time in a race—this was probably about grade five or six—and there was a guy standing on the edge of the field to tell the kids when they can cut in. He's one of the officials. He takes off running across the field yelling at the top of his lungs with the megaphone, "There's a girl on the track." And I was out there and I jogged beside him and I said, "That's a boy. He's my son. His name is Ray-Ray and he'll probably win." And I walked away. . . . That's how bad it was and he just went, he just persisted. But other kids I know who are gender-nonconforming would be horrified.

—Ray-Ray's mother

Since the 1950s, transgender and gender-nonconforming individuals have emerged as polemic and sensationalized figures in North American media accounts. Some of the controversy has centered on their participation in sex-divided sporting spaces—from Rene Richards's groundbreaking appearance on the Women's Tennis Association tour in 1977 (Birrell and Cole 1990) to more recent cases in amateur and professional sport. An increasing body of literature documents transgender and transsexual inclusion in sport (Birrell and McDonald 2000; Caudwell 2014; Karkazis et al. 2012; Martin and Martin 1995; Messner 1988; Pilgrim, Martin, and Binder 2002; Spencer 2000; Tagg 2012; Travers 2006; Travers and Deri 2010). Literature in this field focuses almost exclusively on adult populations, however. This chapter illuminates how transgender and gender-nonconforming kids and their parents/guardians navigate social environments when attempting to access physical activity. I argue that sex-segregated facilities/

locker rooms and sex-segregated or sex-differentiated sporting and physical recreation activities operate as points of crisis for transgender and gender-nonconforming kids. The barriers to participation they face are often catalysts to kids' binary and medical transition.

Trans Kids and Sport

Transgender and gender-nonconforming children are often invisible due to their tremendous efforts to avoid teasing, persecution, and scorn from peers, teachers, and family. Although limited, data currently shows that kids who "fail" to conform to or deliberately defy gender norms are disproportionately victims of "gendered harassment" (E. Meyer 2010) and bullying (Brill and Pepper 2008; Ehrensaft 2011; Hellen 2009; Kennedy 2008; E. Meyer 2008; Whittle et al. 2007) and experience "minority stress" (I. H. Meyer 2003). The intense social policing of gender identity among children makes it appear as if gender-nonconforming children are a rather tiny minority. However, the gender-censoring environment of most family, peer, school, sports, and religious settings reflects the circular reasoning of the Thomas Theorem: "Situations that are defined as real become real in their consequences" (Macionis and Gerber 2011, 332). The overwhelming practice of sorting children into boy and girl categories and teaching them to adhere to a racialized heteronormative gender order makes it appear as if these are natural lines of demarcation.

Transgender athletes present a challenge to sporting institutions and programs. By virtue of sex-segregated sporting spaces and grossly unequal cultural and economic spaces, sport in North America and much of the world is organized in terms of taken-for-granted racialized assumptions of binary and hierarchical sex difference. The underlying assumption of sex-segregated sporting spaces is that someone who is born male naturally has an "unfair advantage" when competing against women in sport (Sykes 2006). A number of scholars have refuted this assumption of athletic superiority (Cavanagh and Sykes 2006; Fausto-Sterling 2000; Kane 1995; McDonagh and Pappano 2008; Ring 2008; Sykes 2006) and is something I address substantially in several articles (Travers 2006, 2008, 2011, 2013; Travers and Deri 2010). More broadly, sport also normalizes the European diaspora morality of whiteness, heterosexual masculinity, and class privilege (Hall 2002; Lemert 2002; Lenskyj 2003; Love and Kelly 2011; McDonagh and Pappano 2008; Travers 2008, 2013). Assumptions of unfair advantage, for example, lean heavily on a Western trope of white, middle-class female frailty to justify a long-reviled and scientifically unfounded practice of sex-verification testing. This practice performs a cultural role in maintaining the naturalness of the two-sex system and assumptions, social structures, and practices that normalize and perpetuate racialized gender difference (Love 2014; Sullivan 2011).

The pressure and constraint that kids feel to act in "gender appropriate" ways, depending on their racial and class location (Kumashiro 2002; Pascoe 2007), occur because gender is structured into institutions like families, sport, and school (Lorber 2005; Messner 2011). Nowhere is this more evident than the dilemmas experienced by transgender and gender-nonconforming kids in sport and physical recreation. As Elizabeth Meyer (2010, 9) observes, "Most traditional extracurricular activities have subtexts that subtly and overtly teach that certain forms of masculinity and femininity are valued over others. The clearest example of such an activity is that of elite amateur and professional athletic teams and the cheerleaders and dance squads that accompany them."

The study I present in this chapter critically examines key policies for transsexual and transgender inclusion in sport and focuses very specifically on the experiences—as related mostly by their parents—of a sample of transgender and gender-nonconforming kids ages four to seventeen. My research is situated within the tradition of "reading sport critically" (McDonald and Birrell 1999), whereby cultural events relating to sport are read as texts that reveal relations of power and resistance. I apply this method to existing policy documents and high-profile reports relating to transsexual and transgender inclusion; the transcripts of "active" interviews (Holstein and Gubrium 1997) with parents of transgender and gender-nonconforming kids, with youth who speak for themselves; and the transcripts of interviews with three advocates for this population.

Sport Policy and Transgender People

Key policy documents and reports have recommended transgender participation in international and North American amateur sport. In 2004, the International Olympic Committee (IOC) developed the Stockholm Consensus to govern the participation of transsexual athletes. The Stockholm Consensus allows transsexual athletes who have obtained new medical-legal identities via full hormonal and surgical transition for at least two years and legal recognition of their new sex by their home governments to compete in elite amateur athletics. This policy has been roundly criticized by critical sport scholars (Cavanagh and Sykes 2006; Love 2014; Sykes 2006) as well as the Canadian Centre for Ethics in Sport (2012) for requiring genital surgeries that have no bearing on athletic performance. As Adam Love (2014, 379) argues, "While policies modeled on the one adopted by the IOC may provide a certain level of inclusion for some individuals, they do so in a way that is gender conforming rather than gender transforming."

Although many national and international sporting federations follow IOC protocol, youth and high school sports often adopt different standards. For example, Pat Griffin (Women's Sports Foundation) and Helen Carroll (National Council Lesbian Rights) deemed the Stockholm Consensus inappropriate for high school athletes altogether. In their influential 2010 report relating to the US context, "On the Team: Equal Opportunity for Transgender Student Athletes," they recommend that no hormonal or surgical treatment should be required for high school athletes. At least for this age group, they refute the discourse of unfair male advantage by acknowledging the considerable overlap in athletic ability across sex categories (Kane 1995). Instead, they place a higher priority on the benefits of participation. This report thus recommends the maintenance of binary sex categories for high school students but allows for mobility between them without medical intervention. Although "On the Team" has been the most influential report in shaping intercollegiate policies in the United States and Canada, other reports have also developed measures for transgender inclusion in North American youth sport. The US Transgender Law and Policy Institute's "Guidelines for Creating Policies for Transgender Children in Recreational Sports" (2009) emphasizes the importance of students participating in sport based on their affirmed gender. Disputing assumptions of male athletic advantage among preadolescent children, the report argues that no "hormonally-based advantage or disadvantage between girls and boys exist" prior to adolescence, that "gender segregation in children's sports is purely social," and that "individual variation with respect to athletic ability *within* each gender is much more significant than any group differences between boys and girls" (2–3).

Similarly, in "Sport in Transition: Making Sport in Canada More Responsible for Gender Inclusivity," the Canadian Centre for Ethics in Sport (2012) speaks out against sex verification testing, acknowledging that the science of sex difference is flawed and therefore not a basis for organizing sport: "Where feasible, transitioning sport will aim for the widest and easiest possible inclusion by supporting integrated sport activities" (29). Finally, two additional Canadian reports—"Supporting Transgender and Transsexual Students in K–12 Schools: A Guide for Educators" (Canadian Teachers Federation 2012) and "Questions and Answers: Gender Identity in Schools" (Public Health Agency of Canada 2010)— also recommend allowing gender-variant youth to participate in sports teams on the basis of their self-identified gender, without requiring they undergo medical treatment. Notably, "Supporting Transgender and Transsexual Students in K–12 Schools" also explicitly mandates that transgender students have access to locker rooms, changing rooms, and bathrooms of their choice. Private facilities should be made available to *any* student who requires them for *any* reason.

Human rights discourse has effectively changed policies in a handful of school districts that stipulate that binary-based transgender kids be treated according to their affirmed gender.[1] However, recommendations for transgender inclusion in high school at the national level in either the United States or Canada have yet to be adopted, and it is too soon to tell how recently introduced policies will work in practice. The interview data I collected clearly show how the binary organization of sport negatively impacts transgender and gender-nonconforming kids and that the desire to participate in sport plays a significant role in decisions relating to medicalized transition.

Gender Inclusion on the Ground

I interviewed thirteen parents of transgender or gender-nonconforming kids and two youth between July 2012 and September 2014. I found participants through word of mouth and snowball sampling and via two national US conferences for transgender kids and their families.[2] Participants' demographic information is presented in table 9.1. Pseudonyms are used for all kids except a seventeen-year-old trans guy, Cory Oskam, who is a very public trans activist.

Barrie Thorne (1993) cautions against relying on parents' understandings of young people's experiences, and I acknowledge this limitation. Obtaining clearance to interview transgender or gender-nonconforming persons under the age of sixteen—as they are considered to be a vulnerable population by my university's research ethics board—would have prevented me from documenting immediate issues on the ground. The perspectives of parents, while not synonymous with those of their children, make important contributions because it is parents—especially mothers—who enroll and advocate for their children (Manning, forthcoming). The challenges they report thus shed light on institutionalized obstacles to participation in sport and physical recreation settings.

The sample I obtained has shortcomings in terms of diversity or representativeness. Knowledge about this population's lived experience necessarily must come from the minority of transgender and gender-nonconforming kids whose parental support enables their visibility and agency (Ajeto 2009; Ehrensaft 2011). Intersecting axes of social privilege (Collins 2005; Crenshaw 1998; Spade 2011) make visibility more likely for privileged kids. Of the twelve children whose parent spoke with me, two are African American Canadian, one is Aboriginal Canadian, one is Asian American, and one is Asian Canadian. Only two of these children, however, have parents of color. Both of the youth I interviewed are white, as am I. My participants are distributed throughout North America. To the best of my knowledge, with the exception of one working-class family, my sample is uniformly middle-class. Indeed, six of the parents I interviewed are university professors and hold critical perspectives on gender—no accident in predicting their children's ability to affirm a nontraditional gender. One of the kids whose parent spoke with me is French Canadian, an identity that is important within the Canadian context where French-language rights and the preservation of French Canadian culture are key points of contention. Three of the kids are from single-parent (not lone-parent) families, and two have same-sex parents (one with two moms; one with two dads). At least three of the children have a visibly gender-nonconforming parent. I interviewed eleven mothers and two fathers. All of the parents I interviewed, to varying but significant degrees,

TABLE 9.1

LIST OF INTERVIEW PARTICIPANTS

Pseudonym	Gender identity	Age/interview year	Regional location
Cody	Gender nonconforming male; likes both superheroes and pretty things	5/2012	Oregon, USA
Dave	Male	17/2012	Manitoba, Canada
Bailey	Gender nonconforming, masculine identified	9/2012	Vermont, USA
Sydney	75% girl/25% boy	10/2012	Québec, Canada
Sean	Gender nonconforming girl	9/2013	British Columbia, Canada
River	Gender nonconforming boy	7/2013	Ontario, Canada
Wren	"I was born a boy but I like being a girl"	9/2014	British Columbia, Canada
Cory Oskam (real name)	Genderqueer/ gender fluid/trans guy/"all of the above"	17/2014	Vancouver, Canada
Silver	"Just Silver"	9/2013	British Columbia, Canada
Ben	Boy	6/2014	British Columbia, Canada
Emily	Girl	4/2014	Newfoundland, Canada
Everest	Male	15/2012	New Jersey, USA
Ray-Ray	Genderqueer	15/2014	British Columbia, Canada
Shane	Masculine-identified, butch lesbian	11/2014	British Columbia, Canada
Madelaine	Girl	9/2013	British Columbia, Canada

have deliberately created space from the outset for their children to defy gender stereotypes and assert nontraditional gender identities.

There are three different types of barriers transgender and gender-nonconforming kids encounter when attempting to participate in sport/physical recreation: issues of access resulting from the sex-segregated structure of many sports, programs, and facilities; sex-differentiated activities within gender integrated sports/activities; and the climate of actual environments. As a result of barriers transgender and gender-nonconforming kids face to participation, I argue that the desire to participate in sport is often a catalyst to kids' binary and medical transition.

Issues of Access (Sex-Segregated Sports, Programs, and Facilities)

Sex-segregated sporting facilities and programs are predicated on the assumption of fundamental differences between only two sexes and a corresponding belief in male athletic advantage. This creates a crisis situation for transgender and gender-nonconforming kids. All but one of the people I interviewed cited sex segregation and differentiation as the major obstacle to sport participation.

Dave (seventeen, male, white, Manitoba) participated in many sports when he was still presenting as a girl. Speaking on his own behalf, Dave said, "I pretty much stopped playing sports when I transitioned to male." As a boy, he described himself as too small to succeed in hockey, and he feels the competition in table tennis is much stiffer. His participation is limited by the binary organization of sport. Shane's (eleven, masculine-identified, butch lesbian Asian Canadian, British Columbia) mom expressed similar concerns about the athletic superiority of boys of the same age: "His skill level cannot compete; it is getting to that point when all the boys start, you know, into puberty, right? So now their strength level [is much greater]."

Institutions, social policy, and everyday cultural interactions actively maintain a gender binary, resulting in both institutional and informational erasure of transgender people, but also, I fear, normalizing and facilitating binary-based transitions only. Neither side of the binary is right for some kids, and this produces a sense of crisis because mixed spaces for sport are rare. The difficulties faced by kids who want to identify outside the binary are extraordinary. According to her mom, Bailey (nine, gender-nonconforming, masculine-identified, potentially transgender boy, Asian American, Vermont) "will play sports with me in the yard but . . . she's not interested in joining a team." As an example, Bailey's mom explains that

> there was this "girls on the run" after-school program that got promoted at the school last year when she was in third grade and it was all about redefining girlhood . . . and looking at the messages that come to you from the culture

and . . . being able to choose to do sports and be athletic or . . . it was all about helping girls to think outside the box. So I thought "Wow, this would be, this would be, so this could be such a great thing for her! Right?" Then I started talking to her about that she just looked at me sort of incredulous and said, "Are boys allowed to do it?" And I went "No, it's for girls. It's 'girls on the run.' Yeah, it would be great, wouldn't it, if it was a program for everybody but it is a program for girls," and she said, "Then I don't want to do it."

The sports teams in Bailey's school and wider community "are divided by sex. The soccer team is either a girls' soccer team or a boys' soccer team." Bailey's mom wonders, "Is it that she really doesn't want to play sports or is it that she wouldn't be able to play on the team that she would think of herself as wanting to be on?" Similarly, although she tried to sign River (seven, gender-nonconforming boy, white, Ontario) up for a dance program at their local community center, River's mom found it impossible to do so without specifying sex.

Shane has recently come out as a boy at school and asked for a name change and to be referred to using male pronouns. His mother reports that he does not want to take hormone blockers. He likes the way his body is changing through puberty and recently told his mother he sees himself more as a butch lesbian than a male. Last summer, Shane was always outside: playing with his friends and riding his bike around the neighborhood. Since he came out, the boys who were his friends have dropped him completely. But several of the girls in his class became staunch allies! Still, nobody comes to his house to play, and he rarely goes outside, playing video games alone in his bedroom. Once Shane's body started to develop he informed his mother that he no longer wanted to take swimming lessons because he felt uncomfortable in a bathing suit. He used to play floor hockey but now feels he doesn't belong on the girls' team because of his gender identity and he doesn't belong on the boys' team because of his body. His mother believes that the separation of girls' and boys' teams has made it impossible for her son to participate. He would like to participate in recreational activities and has looked online for summer camp options but experiences dismay when trying to imagine how he could fit in/navigate these normatively gendered spaces. And yet, his mother tells me, he is happy; after several years of being treated for a mood disorder, his family's support of his gender expression and his new name and pronoun at school have made the difference: "So now he's so happy these days. No play dates, and he's by himself, but still happy. I am so amazed that he's just happy. And a big smile like." Shane's mother admires his strength of character, that he would "rather have no friend" and be himself.

Sydney's (ten, 75 percent girl, 25 percent boy, French Canadian white, Québec) mom explains that swimming used to be a central family activity but is no longer an option, in part because of his gender nonconformity:[3] "I did enroll Sydney in September and I spoke to my husband I said, 'What the hell did I do?'

And I cancelled actually because I told that, put him in a predicament of feeling uncomfortable because Sydney doesn't want to go swimming without girls' stuff anymore. So for Sydney it's important to have the girl swimming costume. Now in a swimming pool in a swimming lesson I can't enroll him in a girl's class with the girl's swimming costume without having any problems, you know what I mean? Because you see everything. It's difficult to hide the penis." Skiing continues to be a positive activity for Sydney and his family. As Sydney's mom explained, "He's really happy" to ski, in part because "nobody knows . . . what he's got in between his legs." Gender essentialism is clearly "harder" (Messner 2011) in some sports than others, as a result of the way certain sports are organized. Tight and revealing uniforms—such as swimsuits—likely present more of a challenge to trans and gender-nonconforming youth than the bulkier uniforms athletes wear in other sports. However, Sydney's family is able to draw upon their class privilege to continue to allow him to participate in skiing, a sport many other trans and gender-nonconforming youth may not have access to.

Madelaine (girl, African Canadian, British Columbia) played soccer in a mixed league until the age of six, when she and her parents were surprised to discover the league was being divided along traditional gender lines. Although she identifies as a girl, Madelaine sees herself, according to her dad, as "one of the guys," and she is treated by them as "one of their people." Madelaine and another girl were permitted to stick with the boys they had been playing with but will have to play on a girls' team when they turn ten. Madelaine's dad foresees positive and negative effects: being one of the best on the girls' team could boost her confidence; he is concerned, however, because "it's really an interruption of what we've been building. Because what we've been building has been, you know, she's got a five-year connection with the coach, she's got a team that she's been on for five years, you know, acceleration of skills and all those other components. . . . Those points that are really important to her, that peer connection and all that would be really ripped out." Segregating children's sports by gender makes difficult for children's cross-sex friendship/peer networks.

The "bathroom problem" (Halberstam 1998) is a clear and pervasive theme in queer and trans literature. The difficulties many of the kids in my study experience when they need to use a bathroom are gut-wrenching. These issues are central to the general well-being of the population and are of obvious relevance to participation in sport and physical recreation, where sex-segregated locker/changing rooms are the norm. They also highlight the ways in which some children and adults commit gender-policing microaggressions against gender-nonconforming people.

For example, Silver's (nine, white and aboriginal, British Columbia) mom relayed the problems her gender-nonconforming child had accessing bathrooms. While Silver's mom uses a female pronoun to refer to her child, she resists all gender labels anyone might impose, insisting that Silver is "just Silver." Her mom explains that Silver is consistently read by people who don't know her as a boy and that Silver is comfortable with this—except when she needs to use a public bathroom. When Silver was enrolled at a public school in a major city in British Columbia, she also encountered difficulties related to using the bathroom. Her mom reports that

> about halfway through grade one . . . Silver told me, "this kid came in and she pointed at me in the bathroom and she said, 'You boy, out'" and Silver said, "No I'm a girl" and the kid repeated, "You boy, out" so what I think is that the kid was actually scared there was a big boy in the girls' bathroom. . . . So Silver left the bathroom and she went to the boys' bathroom and then a teacher found her so she still hasn't gone pee by this time and she's probably six years old in grade one. . . . So the teacher sent her to the principal's office because she was in the boys' bathroom which isn't allowed . . . and so she peed her pants. So Silver no longer had anywhere to pee at the school. . . . So in grade one she started on a daily basis peeing her pants and [for] two weeks . . . she peed her pants every day. She started bringing an extra shirt so she could tie it around her waist to cover up the pee so . . . I started . . . leaving work taking my lunch; I'm driving across town at lunch time and taking her pee and then leaving work so I could be there at quarter to three. . . . Obviously it wasn't sustainable . . . [but] she was scared to go into the bathroom even with me.

After trying and failing to get the school principal to allow Silver to use a single-stall bathroom for staff, Silver's mom switched her to a different school where she was immediately accommodated. Silver now feels safe to use the bathroom at school. But she—like Wren (nine, "I was born a boy but like being a girl," African American Canadian, British Columbia)—does not feel safe going into public bathrooms without an adult accompanying her. According to Bailey's mom, Bailey regularly experiences a dilemma about choosing which bathroom to use:

> She chooses right now to use the girls' room and she wants to have and does have a peer from her class always with her because she experiences people who don't know her thinking she's a boy and that she's in the wrong bathroom and that is very upsetting to her. But she's not ready to/she only uses the boys' rooms when she can go in there with her dad and she uses girls' rooms in public when she can go with me and when it's a gender-neutral bathroom it's just not an issue. . . . They had to make hopes wishes and dreams for fourth grade and her hope for fourth grade is that her school would create a bathroom for both boys and girls. . . . But then she decided not to reveal that.

Bailey's mom thinks that her child would actually feel more comfortable in a boys' bathroom but is not willing to endure the process of coming out to her peers that this would entail.

Difficulties involved in using the bathroom or the changing room were referenced by all but one of my participants at some point, either in the past or in the present. According to her mom, when Wren was five "she said, 'Mommy, the bathrooms at church make me sad.' She didn't know which one to use but knew loss would accompany whichever one she picked." Cassandra (five, transgender girl, white, British Columbia) said to her mom upon seeing a sign with symbols indicating it was for people with disabilities/men/women, "I wish all bathrooms had that sign . . . then anybody could use any bathroom." Participating in sport and physical recreation often requires the use of a sex-segregated changing room and the "bathroom problem" becomes the "changing room problem." This is a significant barrier to physical recreation participation for transgender and gender-nonconforming kids.

Sex Differentiation within Sport/Physical Activity

Although many sports are formally sex-segregated, some parents were able to enroll their gender-nonconforming and trans kids in sex-integrated activities. While the formal sex segregation of sport has received much attention, sex-integrated activities remained problematic for children and youth in this study, albeit in more insidious ways. Within integrated sports, formal and informal rules differentiate different activities and uniforms for boys and girls. These rules pose problems for trans kids. In ballet or gymnastics, for example, boys and girls wear different uniforms and are required to train their bodies to perform in different ways that reflect and reassert widespread cultural beliefs in gender essentialism and male athletic superiority (Kane 1995). Consequently, sports that are ostensibly integrated continue to perpetuate binary gender differences.

The sex differentiation of activities within particular sports or forms of physical recreation often constrains children. Sean (girl, white, British Columbia) is enrolled in gymnastics but prevented from doing the rings because they are designated as a "boys only" apparatus. As her dad explained, sex-differentiated programs in gymnastics have caused her both disappointment and disadvantage: "When she went in gymnastics she . . . had her heart set on doing the rings but the rings are not allowed to her . . . but she started gymnastics with a Brazilian coach who came and asked the girls . . . 'Can anybody do a chin-up?' But nobody could and then Sean came and just ripped off nine chin-ups and he was so excited he took her to all the other coaches but she came back to me and said, 'I dunno what to do because I can't do the rings.'" Sean's dad observes that this has the effect of reinforcing assumptions about gendered strength. He said, "The thing too that strikes me is that you get to see these kids . . . the boys that are struggling, they're not as strong as her but they're doing it every day and . . . in a few years hence they will become proficient, strong at this and if . . . Sean does not end up doing those exact muscle-building things she will not so then it will become this . . . self-perpetuating . . . dynamic that's going on." Mary Jo Kane (1995) notes the ways in which the "gender continuum" of overlapping sport performance is rendered invisible via such gendered rules and practices, with the result that the natural basis of sex segregation and male "unfair advantage" goes unquestioned.

According to his mom, separate programs in gymnastics drove Sydney out of a sport he had loved participating in within a gender-integrated setting in another country:

> He did many, many gymnastics courses, was happy to do them. . . . He liked the gymnastics because you could wear leotard and stuff like that and so he really liked it. When we got to Canada we enrolled again in gymnastics and suddenly we found him liking it less because here it's gender-distinctive: Boys do program and girls do program. And I said, "Ah, c'mon, don't you have gender-neutral gymnastic classes?" And they said, "No, because at nine years . . . they develop differently, and they need to develop muscle, different muscle." And so . . . they put Sydney into the boys' class and obviously Sydney don't [makes noise showing distaste] so he stopped playing gymnastics.

Even in integrated community center dance classes, it is often impossible to register children without sharing information about their sex, something that made River's mom really mad. Such information is used to organize their participation in gender-appropriate ways. Both Ben (six, gender-nonconforming boy, white, British Columbia) and Wren signed up for ballet when they were four but experienced difficulties with dance teachers who reinforced gendered roles. Wren's mom describes the difficulties she encountered in attempting to find a dance class for her (at the time) gender-nonconforming son (Wren subsequently affirmed a female identity):

> When Wren was four and still identifying as a boy he took a ballet course through the community center and because he wanted the leotard and the tutu that the girls had—there were no other boys in the class—I got them for him and he basically blended in until my use of the male pronoun in a conversation with his teacher outed him as a boy. I asked the teacher to keep letting him dance as a girl and it seemed to be going fine. Until the little performance at the end of the class. He was dancing in his pink leotard and tutu in the special performance in front of all the parents and friends of the dancers. When it ended, the teacher called out to him in front of everyone and instructed him to bow, not curtsy, that boys should bow, not curtsy. Everyone there looked very puzzled and Wren was mortified.

Like many parents when they encounter that first moment of overt discrimination against their child, Wren's mother marshaled her resources: "I was angry about it and did not sign him up there again. Instead I went through a long and arduous process to find a dance class where my son could dance as a girl without censure. I was surprised at how difficult it was. I did find one of the really serious programs that was fine with him doing it. But when I chatted with other parents before, during, and after the dance class I avoided using any pronouns to refer to Wren because I did not want to provoke any negative reactions or interfere with Wren's ability to fit in with the other kids. This felt really, really weird." Similar to Wren, Ben found it painful to have to be a bat when the girls in his ballet class got to be bumblebees.

Wren, Ben, and Cody (five, gender-nonconforming boy, white, Oregon) routinely get "mistaken" for girls. According to Cody's mom, he has long hair and a "mixed" wardrobe, and he likes superheroes, rough-and-tumble play, pretty things, and ballet. In his current ballet class they "dress the boys and girls in different clothes."

> He is supposed to wear a uniform. He's supposed to . . . wear black leggings and a white shirt and the girls are supposed to wear I think a black leotard and they can wear pink tights and they have pink ballet shoes. And he has black ballet shoes and I was so worried that he was going to flip his shit because he did not get to wear the pink ones [laughs] and the pink tights. It turned out not to be a problem and he's willing to go along with it. I mean it does visually distinguish him as like clearly he is one of the boys in the dance class with his really long blond hair that several weeks ago he wanted me to put up in a bun.

Issues of Climate/Informal Inequality

Ray-Ray (fifteen, genderqueer, white, British Columbia) has experienced regular gender policing for his failure to present convincingly "as a boy" from an early age. Ray-Ray has been competing in track since he was in third grade, and his mother reports that he is regularly marshaled away from the boys' competition and toward the girls.' "His name is Raymond Marvolo," his mother explains, but "they would move his name to the girls' marshaling list when they saw his long hair and then the guy marshaling the girls would stand there yelling his name until one of the kids who knew who he was from racing against him would say, 'He's not a girl, he's a boy.' And the guy still wouldn't get it. And I would often have to go to the marshaling tent. In fact, I almost always went to the marshaling tent to get him sorted and racing as a boy."

Ray-Ray's mother shares this and other examples to emphasize how crucial it has been for her to run interference at every track-and-field event he attends. Ray-Ray's mother regularly has to say, "This is my son, he is a boy." Ray-Ray has tremendous resilience in the face of this gender policing: his mother reports that he laughs it off. The importance of parental advocacy to facilitate their children's participation, a task that most often falls to mothers (Manning, forthcoming; Messner 2009) and that speaks to cultural capital and economic resources, is a key theme that emerges from the data. Kids who are marginalized require a great deal of parental support and advocacy work if they are to achieve some measure of social inclusion and self-esteem; the experiences of almost all of the kids in my study speak to this.

Ray-Ray's gender nonconformity marks him as "other" on all-boy teams, and the treatment he is accorded as a result hurts. Ray-Ray tried soccer a year ago but quit because the other boys never treated him as a team member and this was intolerable. His experience on his high school's mixed-sex Ultimate Frisbee team has been positive, however. Ultimate Frisbee requires that a certain number of girls/women be on the field at all times. Even though he now stands six foot two inches, Ray-Ray is often read by opponents as a girl. This is actually an advantage for his team because they are often short of girl players. His coach asked Ray-Ray if he would be okay to continue "playing as a girl," and he happily agreed. His mom says he actually finds it kind of funny and fun! Even though sex differentiation is built into the game, Ultimate Frisbee provides a more welcoming place for Ray-Ray.

In group discussions or news interviews, it is not unusual to hear parents of trans kids talk about the importance of their child being able to bond with their teams in the locker room. Cory talked about the importance of team bonding and how necessary it was to use the same locker room as everyone else. When he was first transitioning, the school suggested he use a gender-neutral space, but he purposefully positioned himself as fundamentally male (rather than more authentically genderqueer) to enable himself to dress with the team. Despite being an important place for team bonding, male locker rooms are notorious for misogyny and homophobia (Curry 1991; Sabo 1999). Cory described his discomfort in a boys' hockey dressing room a few years ago, as one of his teammates make homophobic remarks to the group. He waited until they were alone to ask him, "Dude, why do you say those things?" It takes courage to stand up to boys/men who are performing orthodox masculinity. On a number of occasions, Cory has heard "faggot" and "pussy" used as pejoratives in the locker room, bringing to mind C. J. Pascoe's (2007) observation that "fag" is used as an abject category in the construction of adolescent masculinity. Dave, however, drew on the homophobic climate of the locker room to deflect attention away from his post-top-surgery chest. A boy asked him, "Why do your nipples look so weird?" Dave responded, "Dude, why are you looking at my nipples?" In contrast, Cory explained that the guys in his locker room used these terms to "really put down women," which he experienced as "really offensive because I do identify as like someone who was female at one point. And I do identify like as female once in a while. So it was not pleasant to hear." Cory responded to this by asking for help from his coach. He told his coach that "they're, you know, saying these words that make me feel uncomfortable and he's like, 'yeah those are words that shouldn't be said in the dressing room.' And then they were addressed in, um, just a very anonymous fashion by coach saying like 'I've heard that there's bad language in the dressing rooms and that needs to go away.' And it really did stop."

Informal Recreational Spaces

Interviews with several parents reminded me to broaden the focus of discussion around sport/physical recreation to include issues relating to unorganized recreational activity in playgrounds and parks. My conversations with these parents drew my attention to a limitation I carried into this research—I had been focusing on adult-supervised activities, not the informal spaces of play that constitute a good part of children's worlds (Thorne 1993). As Annette Lareau's (2011) work suggests, the frequency with which children play without supervision is classed in important ways. Adult-organized and supervised activities take up a good portion of middle-class kids' time, whereas working-class kids have much more time for informal play.

These informal spaces are not the responsibility of stipulated adults and may or may not be in view of parents/guardians. This clearly played a significant role in the examples of bathroom and changing room problems discussed earlier, but gender policing is also an issue on playgrounds and other spaces where children engage in informal play. For example, Ben has been physically assaulted by children at local playgrounds because of his long hair. His mother told me he has been pushed and spat on. Often the children who are bullying Ben are inadequately supervised or are at the park alone. Ben's mother intervenes to protect him, but sometimes she has to leave the park because the behavior of other children continues and her child is unsafe: "They've gotten physical with him . . . pushed him around. . . . We were at a playground here actually and there was kids that I knew that he wanted to play with them. They didn't want to play with him. And then they sort of lured him over to the other side of the playground—so I was with [my younger child] on one side—they lured him over to the other side—he was littler at this point—and then spat in his hair." Although informal recreational spaces like playgrounds could provide an alternative to formal sport settings, they continue to be problematic, in part because of the way kids police gender when adults are not supervising their play, or often even when adult supervisors are complicit in gender policing.

Coping Strategies: Resistance/Survival/Acquiescence

Transgender and gender-nonconforming kids and their parents in my study applied four strategies to negotiate these barriers preventing full participation: continuing to play, going stealth, undergoing medical treatment, and quitting altogether.

Continuing to participate is easier in some sports than others, such as how Sydney had an easier time continuing to ski versus swim. However, this strategy relies on parental support and advocacy. As previously mentioned, without his mother's advocacy at track meets, things would have been much harder for Ray-Ray. She regularly has to intervene when organizers call him out as not being a boy in very public ways. As a result, the strategy of continuing to play requires significant amounts of class and race privilege. For example, Wren's mom's account of finding a dance class where her son could wear the pink outfit and dance "as a girl" exemplifies how parents must draw upon these privileges when negotiating physical recreation spaces. If Wren's mom had not been able to devote the time and energy, lacked the know-how to navigate these spaces, or had been unable to put aside cost in favor of comfort, Wren would have had to quit dancing, dance as a boy/wear the boys' outfit, or endure the occasional shaming and censure from the teacher if he continued to dance as a girl.

Children and adults who defy cisgender binary categorization tend to experience frequent gender policing from children and adults alike in the form of *the* most common question: "Are you a boy or girl?"[4] As a result, some trans kids who want to play sport go "stealth," meaning they present themselves as their affirmed rather than their birth sex. Going "stealth" works better for trans kids who embrace a binary identity and who are able to pass, either because they are younger or because they undergo medical treatment like Dave and Cory did. Wren's mother wonders how much her daughter's decision to pass as a girl two years ago had to do with wanting to dance and dress the way she likes to without having to constantly explain herself to others—children and adults. Wren now participates in dance, baseball, and various summer camps as a girl: "I was throwing ground balls to Wren—a baseball-related activity—in the front yard and he made a fabulous diving grab of a ball. I pretended to be the play-by-play announcer on TV and said 'And he makes a fabulous diving stop.' Wren got up, looked right at me, pointed at her chest, and said 'she' emphatically. I said 'All right, then!' Now that she has solidified her identity as female, it has become really easy to enroll her in physical recreation programs." Wren's mother reports that her participation in a swim and skate day camp program two years ago was the impetus for her transition from gender-nonconforming boy to a girl. She says that

> Wren got really clear about wanting to change her pronouns when . . . we put
> her in summer camp. . . . [My partner] asked her when we were in the sign-up

process, "Do you want to go to camp as a boy or a girl?" Which I thought was really, like, neat that she asked her, in spite of how annoyed I was that she had to tick one of two boxes on the intake form. Wren said, "A girl." And so [my partner] signed her up as a girl. She showed her how to change privately in the change room and Wren was totally successful and I think it gave her a lot of confidence. Two years later she's still doing it and she totally passes. We have grave concerns about the future, however, as she enters puberty.

Wren's mother wonders how this will play out as her daughter encounters bodily changes associated with puberty. Wren's mothers are certainly prepared to provide their daughter with access to hormone blockers to delay the puberty that will make it more difficult to pass as female if necessary, but they do not want their daughter's choices to be limited to one of two binary-based choices. They are taking great care to follow their daughter's lead as much as possible. "It's a tricky balancing act," according to Wren's mother.

The sex-segregated structure of sport may be a deciding factor in driving kids who would otherwise not transition to undergo medical treatment. According to Diane Ehrensaft, author of *Gender Born, Gender Made: Raising Healthy Gender-Nonconforming Children* and a psychologist with a clinical practice in the Bay Area specializing in children, youth, and gender (personal interview), the desire to participate in sport is a major factor driving kids who are more gender liminal to undergo binary transition. For example, one of the youth who participated in my study, Cory, wanted to be able to undergo hormone therapy *and* continue to play on the girls' team. In girls' hockey, he was an elite goalie with good prospects for college scholarships, but on the boys' team, he found himself unexceptional. Taking testosterone—considered a performance-enhancing drug in mainstream sport circles (Sykes 2006)—was really important for Cory because he did not want to develop breasts or have a period. He thus had to balance his desire to participate in girls' hockey with his need to shape his body in a manner consistent with his gender identity. Although Cory's former name was Annika and they had a very public gender-nonconforming identity of "just Annika" from age eight to thirteen, he decided to medically transition. Cory explained that his desire to take testosterone and still be able to play hockey ultimately was the difference maker in his decision to medically transition to a male identity. "Just Annika" just wasn't working anymore.

Finally, several kids in my study stopped participating in particular sports or stopped playing sports altogether when they transitioned. While this represents a loss for some kids, others are happy to quit. According to his mother, when Everest (fifteen, male, white, New Jersey) was given the option of dropping out of physical education, he jumped at it. He experienced his school's reluctance to allow him to participate fully as a boy as a blessing. His mom explained that "Everest hated PE and when the principal gave him the option of quitting [a course that was normally compulsory], he was thrilled." At the time of the interview (2011), Everest was happily participating in his school's marching band, where gender has not been an issue for him.

Conclusion: Sex-Segregated Sport as an Obstacle to or Catalyst for Binary Transition

This study has two major findings. First, sex-segregated facilities/locker rooms and sex-segregated or sex-differentiated sporting and physical recreation activities operate as points of crisis for transgender and gender-nonconforming kids. This is a major barrier to participation. And second, because of this, the desire to participate in sport is often a catalyst to kids' binary and medical transition.

Transgender children are likely to become marked as trans during puberty, thereby becoming incredibly vulnerable to violence or institutionally coerced medicalization. Although transgender children are not forced to take hormones against their will, the social context they find themselves in is so normatively gendered that hormone blockers and hormones are essential for their very survival. This is highly significant for at least two reasons. First, sex-segregated and sex-differentiated structures and programs in sport and physical recreation are often a catalyst for medical transition. And, second, the option of medical transition is a privilege disproportionately associated with whiteness and wealth. The solution is not to deny privileged kids hormone blockers and hormone therapy but to expand access to all kids who need such medical care. We also must take aim at oppressive gender systems and other vectors of vulnerability and security that disproportionately link transgender and gender-nonconforming kids with vulnerability and risk. I conjecture that most trans kids who lack access to parental support or appropriate health care either adapt to peer pressure or have their gender diversity driven underground, strategies that place kids disproportionately at risk of self-harm and suicide.

Advocacy and activism should target the organization of children by sex/gender and the structural inequalities that children encounter and are shaped by. According to trans activist and critical theorist Dean Spade (2011, 29), "We need to shift our focus from the individual rights framing of discrimination and 'hate violence' and think more broadly about how gender categories are enforced on all people in ways that cause particularly dangerous outcomes for trans people." Targeting gender systems and their intersections with other systems of oppression is the most effective way to improve the quality of life and life chances of transgender and gender-nonconforming kids and has the required effect of opening space for gender self-determination for all kids. This places a target for correction squarely on the sport and physical recreation programs and spaces designed for kids that normalize the gender binary and female inferiority in conjunction with systems of privilege based on race and class.

If it were not for the totalizing pressure of gender categorization that children are subjected to (Berkowitz and Ryan 2011; Hellen 2009), if instead there was greater cultural flexibility concerning sex and gender identities, more kids would likely exhibit gender nonconformity. Currently, children from families with less cultural capital are disproportionately likely to remain invisible or "closeted," not because their families have less progressive views regarding gender, but because they lack the resources for successful child advocacy. Children who lack this kind of parental support are extremely difficult to access; for any insights we must rely on older youth or young adults whose reports are inevitably retrospective and potentially out of touch with current realities. This strongly indicates that inclusion strategies, therefore, must be fundamentally intersectional by addressing the overlapping regimes of gender, sexuality, racialization, and class and focus on shaping environments in general as well as responding to the needs of a particular visible child or youth.

It is my hope that my findings will be useful in changing how sport and recreation institutions treat transgender and gender-nonconforming kids. We must reduce how all kids are subjected to gender norms and gender policing. Because we know that most transgender and gender-nonconforming kids are invisible, sport programs must avoid passive solutions, such as "waiting for a transgender kid to show up" before adopting measures for inclusion (Travers 2014). We should certainly advocate for the kids who are able to be visible, but there is a need for a broader emphasis on undoing the structures of gender that, in tandem with racist and classist regimes, shape and regulate these institutions and spaces. If we leave it to transgender kids and their parents to be assertive in their self-advocacy, then we put the onus for justice on these individuals. We also close off avenues for gender self-determination to kids from poor and working-class backgrounds, whose parents are less likely to have the social and educational capital, not to mention the time, to advocate for their kids in the same ways that parents in this study have been able to.

And yet how do we increase transgender inclusion without completely eliminating spaces for girls and young women to develop confidence? In a previous work (Travers 2008), I argued that we need to eliminate male-only sport and physical recreation teams and spaces while maintaining optional segregated spaces for girls and women, so long as the latter have transinclusive boundaries, as an interim measure. This is an issue that needs a lot of thought and attention, lest we undo much of the progress that has been made in increasing the participation of girls and women in sport. There may be resistance to some short-term changes, but developing nonbinary sports institutions for kids with transgender inclusive policies are worthy rallying points for social activism and advocacy, not only on behalf of transgender and gender-nonconforming kids, but for all young people.

ACKNOWLEDGMENTS

Funds in support of this research were provided by the Social Sciences and Humanities Research Council of Canada and the Faculty of Arts and Social Sciences, Simon Fraser University. I wish to thank three allies/advocates for these populations who allowed me to interview them—in 2013, Diane Ehrensaft, author of *Gender Born, Gender Made*, and in 2012, Asaf Orr, attorney with the National Council for Lesbian Rights (NCLR), and Helen Carroll, author of *An Equal Place on the Team*, also employed by the NCLR as director of their Sport Initiative. These interviews informed my understanding of relevant legal and policy issues.

The editors of this book, Michael Messner and Michela Musto, believed in my work from the outset and helped me to present it effectively. They were such a pleasure to work with, and I thank them for their hard work. Jennifer Thomas and Meagan Simon were both highly capable research assistants who helped with a variety of tasks that were essential to the completion of this project. A final thank-you to my kids—Langston, Kendry, and Hanna—and my precious partner and coparent—Gwen Bird—for making it all matter so much and not minding too much my occasional need to disappear for a weekend into my office.

NOTES

1. For example, transgender eleven-year-old Tracey Wilson's parents launched a human rights complaint on her behalf against the Vancouver-area Catholic diocese and achieved the desired policy change to recognize transgender girls and boys as their affirmed sex (Canadian Press 2014). Similarly, Maine's highest court ruled in 2014 that a transgender student's rights were violated when her school forced her to use a staff bathroom rather than the girls' bathroom (Byrne 2014). The recent passage into law of AB 1266 in California, signed by the governor on August 12, 2013, allows children "to participate in sex-segregated programs, activities, and facilities" based on their affirmed gender rather than their birth sex. The law allows students to use bathrooms and locker rooms that correspond to their affirmed rather than assigned gender. Also see San Francisco Unified School District (2004); Toronto District School Board (2011); Edmonton Public Schools (2011); Vancouver School Board (Canadian Press 2014).

2. Gender Spectrum, Berkeley, CA, 2012; Gender Odyssey, Seattle, WA, August 2012.

3. Shortly after the interview Sydney switched pronouns from the masculine to the feminine. When she read a draft of this chapter, Sydney's mom found it very strange to see the use of the male pronoun for Sydney but agreed to leave it as is because it represented where things were at that point in Sydney's journey.

4. "Cisgender" refers to the sex/gender identity of people whose gender identity correlates with the reproductive organs that marked them as their birth sex (Aultman 2014).

REFERENCES

Ajeto, Denise. 2009. *A Soul Has No Gender: Love and Acceptance through the Eyes of a Mother of Sexual and Gender Minority Children*. Rotterdam: Sense.

Aultman, B. 2014. "Cisgender." *Transgender Studies Quarterly* 1.1–2: 61–62.

Berkowitz, Dana, and Maura Ryan. 2011. "Bathrooms, Baseball, and Bra Shopping: Lesbian and Gay Parents Talk about Engendering Their Children." *Sociological Perspectives* 54.3: 329–350.

Birrell, Susan, and C. L. Cole. 1990. "Double-Fault: Renee Richards and the Construction and Naturalization of Difference." *Sociology of Sport Journal* 7: 1–21.

Birrell, Susan, and Mary G. McDonald. 2000. "Reading Sport, Articulating Power Lines." In *Reading Sport: Critical Essays on Power and Representation*, edited by Susan Birrell and Mary G. McDonald, 3–13. Boston: Northeastern University Press.

Brill, Stephanie, and Rachel Pepper. 2008. *The Transgender Child*. San Francisco: Cleis Press.

Byrne, Matt. 2014. "Maine's Highest Court: Transgender Student's Rights Were Violated." *Press Herald*, January 30. http://www.pressherald.com/2014/01/30/maine_supreme_court __transgender_student_s_rights_were_violated/. Accessed August 29, 2014.

Canadian Centre for Ethics in Sport. 2012. "Sport in Transition: Making Sport in Canada More Responsible for Gender Inclusivity." Ottawa: Canadian Centre for Ethics in Sport.

Canadian Press. 2014. "Human Rights Complaint Prompts New Gender Policy in Vancouver Catholic Schools." CBC, July 14. http://www.cbc.ca/news/canada/british-columbia/ human-rights-complaint-prompts-new-gender-policy-in-vancouver-catholic-schools-1 .2709429. Accessed August 29, 2014.

Canadian Teachers Federation. 2012. "Supporting Transgender and Transsexual Students in K–12 Schools: A Guide for Educators." Ottawa: Canadian Teachers Federation.

Caudwell, Jane. 2014. "[Transgender] Young Men: Gendered Subjectivities and the Physically Active Body." *Sport, Education, and Society* 19.4: 398–414.

Cavanagh, Sheila, and Heather Sykes. 2006. "Transsexual Bodies at the Olympics: the International Olympic Committee's Policy on Transsexual Athletes at the 2004 Athens Summer Games." *Body and Society* 12: 75–102.

Collins, Patricia Hill. 2005. *Black Sexual Politics: African Americans, Gender, and the New Racism*. New York: Routledge.

Crenshaw, Kimberle. 1998. *Fighting the Post–Affirmative Action War*. New York: Essence Communications.

Curry, Timothy 1991. "Fraternal Bonding in the Locker Room: A Profeminist Analysis of Talk about Competition and Women." *Sociology of Sport Journal* 8: 119–135.

Edmonton Public Schools. 2011. "Sexual Orientation and Gender Identity Policy." http:// www.epsb.ca/ourdistrict/policy/h/hfa-bp/.

Ehrensaft, Diane. 2011. *Gender Born, Gender Made: Raising Healthy Gender-Nonconforming Children*. New York: The Experiment.

Fausto-Sterling, Ann. 2000. *Sexing the Body: Gender Politics and the Construction of Sexuality*. New York: Basic Books.

Griffin, Pat, and Helen Carroll. 2010. "On the Team: Equal Opportunity for Transgender Student Athletes." Washington, DC: NCLR, Women's Sports Foundation, and It Takes a Team.

Grossman, Arnold, and Anthony R. D'Augelli. 2007. "Transgender Youth and Life-Threatening Behaviours." *Suicide and Life-Threatening Behaviors* 37.5: 527–537.

Halberstam, Judtih. 1998. *Female Masculinity*. Durham, NC: Duke University Press.

Hall, M. Ann. 2002. *The Girl and the Game*. Toronto: Broadview Press.

Hellen, Mark. 2009. "Transgender Children in Schools." *Liminalis* 3: 81–99.

Holstein, James A., and Jaber F. Gubrium. 1997. "Active Interviewing." In *Qualitative Research: Theory, Method, and Practice*, edited by David Silverman, 113–129. London: Sage.

Kane, Mary Jo. 1995. "Resistance/Transformation of the Oppositional Binary: Exposing Sport as a Continuum." *Journal of Sport and Social Issues* 19: 191–218.

Karkazis, Katrina, Rebecca Jordan-Young, Georgiann Davis, and Silvia Camporesi. 2012. "Out of Bounds? A Critique of the New Policies on Hyperandrogenism in Elite Female Athletes." *American Journal of Bioethics* 12.7: 3–16.

Kennedy, Natacha. 2008. "Transgendered Children in Schools: A Critical Review of Homophobic Bullying: Safe to Learn—Embedding Anti-Bullying Work in Schools." *Forum* 50.3: 383–396.

Klomek, Anat Brunstein, Frank Marrocco, Marjorie Kleinman, Irvin Sam Schonfeld, and Madelyn S. Gould. 2008. "Peer Victimization, Depression, and Suicidality in Adolescents." *Suicide and Life-Threatening Behavior* 38.2: 166–180.

Kumashiro, Kevin. 2002. *Troubling Education: Queer Activism and Anti-oppressive Pedagogy*. New York: Routledge.

Lareau, Annette. 2011. *Unequal Childhoods: Class, Race, and Family Life*. Berkeley: University of California Press.

Lemert, Charles. 2002. *Dark Thoughts: Race and the Eclipse of Society*. New York: Routledge.

Lenskyj, Helen. 2003. *Out on the Field*. Toronto: Women's Press.

Lorber, Judith. 2005. *Breaking the Bowls: Degendering and Feminist Change*. New York: Norton.

Love, Adam. 2014. "Transgender Exclusion and Inclusion in Sport." In *Routledge Handbook of Sport, Gender, and Sexuality*, edited by Jennifer Hargreaves and Eric Anderson, 376–383. New York: Routledge.

Love, Adam, and Kimberly Kelly. 2011. "Equity or Essentialism? US Courts and the Legitimation of Girls' Teams in High School Sport." *Gender & Society* 25.2: 227–249.

Macionis, John, and Linda Gerber. 2011. *Sociology*. Toronto: Pearson.

Manning, Kimberley. Forthcoming. *Attachment Politics and the Rights of the Trans Child*.

Martin, Beth A., and James H. Martin. 1995. "Compared Perceived Sex Role Orientations of the Ideal Male and Female Athlete to the Ideal Male and Female Person." *Journal of Sport Behavior* 18.4: 286–302.

McDonagh, Eileen, and Laura Pappano. 2008. *Playing with the Boys*. New York: Oxford University Press.

McDonald, Mary, and Susan Birrell. 1999. "Reading Sport Critically: A Methodology for Interrogating Power." *Sociology of Sport Journal* 16: 283–300.

Messner, Michael A. 1988. "Sports and Male Domination: The Female Athlete as Contested Ideological Terrain." *Sociology of Sport Journal* 5.3: 197–211.

———. 2009. *It's All for the Kids: Gender, Families, and Youth Sports*. Berkeley: University of California Press.

———. 2011. "Gender Ideologies, Youth Sports, and the Production of Soft Essentialism." *Sociology of Sport Journal* 28: 151–170.

Meyer, Elizabeth. J. 2008. "Gendered Harassment in Secondary Schools: Understanding Teacher's (Non)interventions." *Gender and Education* 20.6: 555–572.

———. 2010. *Gender and Sexual Diversity in Schools*. New York: Springer.

Meyer, Ian H. 2003. "Prejudice, Social Stress, and Mental Health in Lesbian, Gay, and Bisexual Populations: Conceptual Issues and Research Evidence." *Psychological Bulletin* 129.5: 674.

Pascoe, C. J. 2007. *Dude, You're a Fag: Masculinity and Sexuality in High School*. Berkeley: University of California Press.

Pilgrim, Jill, David Martin, and Will Binder. 2002. "Far from the Finish Line: Transsexualism and Athletic Competition." *Fordham Intellectual Property, Media, and Entertainment Law Journal* 13.2: 495–549.

Public Health Agency of Canada. 2010. "Questions and Answers: Gender Identity in Schools." Ottawa: Public Health Agency of Canada.

Ring, Jennifer. 2008. *Stolen Bases: Why American Girls Don't Play Baseball*. Chicago: University of Illinois Press.

Sabo, Don. 1999. "The Myth of the Sexual Athlete." In *Reconstructing Gender: A Multicultural Anthology*, edited by Estelle Disch, 274–278. London: Mayfield.

San Francisco Unified School District Policy. 2004.

Spade, Dean. 2011. *Normal Life: Administrative Violence, Critical Trans Politics, and the Limits of Law*. Brooklyn, NY: South End Press.

Spencer, Nancy E. 2000. "Reading between the Lines: A Discursive Analysis of the Billie Jean King vs. Bobby Riggs 'Battle of the Sexes.'" *Sociology of Sport Journal* 17.4: 386–402.

Sullivan, Claire F. 2011. "Gender Verification and Gender Policies in Elite Sport: Eligibility and 'Fair Play.'" *Journal of Sport and Social Issues* 35: 400–419.

Sykes, Heather. 2006. "Transsexual and Transgender Policies in Sport." *Women in Sport and Physical Activity Journal* 15.1: 3–13.

Tagg, Brendon. 2012. "Transgender Netballers: Ethical Issues and Lived Realities." *Sociology of Sport Journal* 29.2: 151–167.

Thorne, Barrie. 1993. *Gender Play: Girls and Boys in School*. New Brunswick, NJ: Rutgers University Press.

Toronto District School Board. 2011. "Toronto District School Board Guidelines for the Accommodation of Transgender and Gender Independent/Non-conforming Students and Staff." http://www.tdsb.on.ca/AboutUs/Innovation/GenderBasedViolencePrevention/AccommodationofTransgenderStudentsandStaff.aspx. Accessed August 29, 2014.

Travers, Ann. 2006. "Queering Sport: Lesbian Softball Leagues and the Transgender Challenge." *International Review for the Sociology of Sport* 41.3–4: 431–446.

———. 2008. "The Sport Nexus and Gender Injustice." *Studies in Social Justice Journal* 2.1: 79–101.

———. 2011. "Women's Ski Jumping, the 2010 Olympic Games, and the Deafening Silence of Sex Segregation, Whiteness, and Wealth." *Journal of Sport and Social Issues* 35.2: 126–145.

———. 2013. "Thinking the Unthinkable: Imagining an 'Un-American,' Girl Friendly, Women- and Trans-inclusive Alternative for Baseball." *Journal of Sport and Social Issues* 37.1: 78–96.

———. 2014. "Transformative Gender Justice as a Framework for Normalizing Gender Variance." In *Supporting Transgender and Gender Creative Youth: Schools, Families, and Communities in Action*, edited by E. Meyer and A. Pullen Sansfacom, 54–68. New York: Peter Lang.

Travers, Ann, and Jillian Deri. 2010. "Transgender Inclusion and the Changing Face of Lesbian Softball Leagues." *International Review for the Sociology of Sport* 46.4: 488–507.

US Transgender Law and Policy Institute. 2009. "Guidelines for Creating Policies for Transgender Children in Recreational Sports." US Transgender Law and Policy Institute.

Whittle, Stephen, Lewis Turner, Maryam Al-Alami, Em Rundall, and Ben Thom. 2007. *Engendered Penalties: Transgender and Transsexual People's Experiences of Inequality and Discrimination*. Wetherby: Communities and Local Government Publications.

CHAPTER 10

Examining Boys, Bodies, and PE Locker Room Spaces

"I DON'T EVER SET FOOT IN THAT LOCKER ROOM"

Michael Kehler

For many boys, time spent in high school gym, or what is formally known as "physical education" (PE), is a fond and distant memory. The fondness does not, however, imply it was enjoyable for all. Rather, it conveys happiness that PE is over and done with, a memory that some would rather forget. Secondary school PE in particular is often characterized by a competitive model that promotes and encourages one-upmanship among boys. Striving to out run, pump more iron, or do more push-ups than your classmate, while not always intended, is nonetheless part of the culture in many boys' PE classes. Proving to your peers that you are stronger, faster, and more able-bodied is often accepted and encouraged in PE classes. Boys need to be tough; competition in sport is what makes them men! Reaffirming to some, this masculine culture oppresses and silences other boys. However, it is prevalent in many schools and regularly considered normal, "boys being boys." Sports, masculinity, and schooling have long been associated with a problematic culture that has been more about "measuring up" and performing or expressing a hypermasculinity and less about promoting healthy life practices. There is an accepted and unquestioned practice in PE that *all* boys adhere to a shared set of normative practices that make them boys (Paechter 2003).

Today there is a noticeable reconfiguration of the visual landscape of billboard and magazine advertising. Once dominated by women, it is now increasingly shared with scantily clad muscled bodies of men. Rosalind Gill, Karen Henwood, and Carl McLean (2005, 39) argue that "the male body has become an object of the gaze rather than simply the bearer of the look." The impact of this shift on how boys define themselves through the body is significant and at the heart of this chapter. For some adolescent boys, high school PE is a time

characterized by fear, anxieties, and outward alienation. The constant bodily surveillance and harassment some boys experience leave many feeling anxious and
ashamed of their bodies and, moreover, less likely to continue in PE (Atkinson
and Kehler 2012).

High school experiences, and specifically "sport" for adolescent boys in mandatory PE class, is not a new area of scholarly inquiry. What is, however, gaining
increasing significance is the social-cultural context in which adolescent boys
navigate masculinities in school PE (Hauge and Haavind 2011). Research examining the increase in media images and commercialization of men's bodies and
men's products has found "men are increasingly falling into the same appearance-
orientated cultural trap that women have experienced for years" (Ricciardelli,
Clow, and White 2010, 66). We have witnessed a significant shift in which "men's
bodies, *as bodies*, have gone from near invisibility to hypervisibility in the course
of a decade" (Gill, Henwood, and McLean 2005, 39). Under this intense public
and private scrutiny of male bodies, it is not surprising that adolescent boys are
experiencing troublesome and troubling issues related to adolescent masculinity, body image, and the broader cultural definitions of masculinity captured by
media images (Atkinson and Kehler 2012; Frost 2003; Kehler and Atkinson 2013;
Krayer, Ingledew, and Iphofen 2008; Norman 2011; Shilling 2010).

In this chapter I examine the conceptual and practical challenges adolescent boys face as they manage both their bodily practices in school PE classes
and the broader ideological accounts of masculinity that inform these everyday
practices. I argue that with the expansion of a visual landscape that has increasingly commodified male bodies, adolescent boys are under increased public as
well as private scrutiny in what Liz Frost (2003, 54) describes as an "intensified
engagement with the visual self-production" of youth. In other words, I draw a
connection between the growing awareness boys have of their physical bodies
and the possibilities to speak to and from their bodies in relation to prevail-
ing masculine ideologies. I extend understandings of youth identities, and more
specifically adolescent masculinities, that are routinely negotiated among and
between boys in high school locker rooms. By exploring the ways boys explain,
describe, and interpret bodily practices, I examine the masculinized practices
displayed and exercised among boys. Observing these youth interactions helps
us to better understand the ways boys come to name themselves through the
body. Moreover, I argue throughout this chapter that there is a growing need in
education to broaden our repertoire of ways for identifying and acknowledging
adolescent masculinities through bodily practices and the performative subjectivities that emerge in the interactions among boys in an unsupervised space
such as secondary school PE locker rooms.

NAVIGATING THE BODILY PRACTICES OF BOYS

At a time when we are increasingly told to look, feel, and be certain ways, it is particularly salient to consider how youth make sense of these messages, especially in light of a dominant discourse intersecting health, body image, and masculinities. Youth and a growing number of adolescent boys in particular are confronted with a barrage of images depicting buff boys with ripped abs (Gill, Henwood, and McLean 2005; Krayer, Ingledew, and Iphofen 2008; Shilling 2010). They are told directly that tight bodies and well-defined muscles make a man. And if muscles alone don't make them a man, boys are lead to believe that muscles do allow them to show others who is the man. There are few other sex-segregated places like high school locker rooms that provide a more poignant and troubling context for observing the interplay between masculinities and health education. Michael Messner and Michela Musto (2014) remind us that significant research remains to be done in the areas of intersecting inequalities, namely sex segregation, gender, and class. And in relation to schooling and physical health education, Ian Wellard (2007, 85) argues that "sport not only provides a site for learning social codes relating to gender but can be considered a prime site in which hegemonic masculinities are made and remade." Adolescent boys' relationship to sport is often traced to the sex-segregated experiences they have in school PE. It is during this significant and formative time in early adolescence that young men are increasingly engaged in the competing and sometimes conflicting ways of being boys among boys, particularly in masculinized spaces such as school locker rooms and PE sex-segregated classes where participation and attendance are compulsory.

This study builds on previous theorizing and research that locate the bodily practices of youth as a significant means through which to better understand, name, and know how boys interpret masculinities through gender performativity. Raewyn Connell (1995, 45) argues that "true masculinity is almost always thought to proceed from men's bodies—to be inherent in a male body or to express something about a male body." She argues that our bodies are more than the physical; they are the emblematic representation of specific versions of masculinity. The masculine body is imbued with all that it means to be a man. Strength, dominance, and aggression contrast with the more vulnerable, weaker, and less able-bodied boys we often recount from childhood days. The outward expression of bodily practices that capture and affirm narrow, heteronormative masculinities while excluding, marginalizing, and oppressing others emerges as significant and troubling findings in the study that follows.

In recent studies, Frost (2003, 53), for example, speaks of "appearance-based identity construction" and offers a cautionary note about positioning boys as the new victim in a "help the boys" climate concerned with underachievement levels in school (for a critique of this discourse and the repositioning of boys, see also Kehler 2010, 2012). She argues that current issues of representation, body image, identity politics, and having the right bodies and clothes are limited by debates that further entrench a binary divide between masculinities and femininities. Her research brings to light the struggles intersecting consumer capitalism and the taken-for-granted "shopping for subjectivities" (Frost 2003, 55) that are evident among youth. Frost (2003, 67) accounts for the ways boys shop for good looks and adorn themselves with the accoutrements that make for good bodies. The anxieties experienced by boys and girls are similar in their desire for group membership and the difficulty youth experience in "being unable or unwilling to produce the necessary style, shape, and size. Their bodies—how they adjust and adorn them—may leave them subjected to humiliation and isolation, as well as identification and inclusion." Similar to Frost (2003), Ann Phoenix et al. (2013, 417) examined the ways in which "young people construct their identities through consumption." Their analysis affirms the ways boys and girls "do" gender by involving specific codes and familiar tropes of heteronormative masculinity and femininity. Their research illuminates the gender positioning that occurs among boys and girls within various contexts. In their study of 140 males aged fifteen through thirty-five in the United Kingdom, Gill, Henwood, and McLean (2005, 41) provide a close analysis of the ways men talk about their bodies. Linking broader social issues including consumerism and the commodification of the male body, Gill and coauthors "explore the idea that the surface of the body has come to constitute a 'project' and key source of identity for young men." In the next section I consider some of the challenges men face when they are increasingly looking toward their own bodies while confronting the scrutiny and surveillance that monitor how the male body is (re)presented publicly.

The performativity of gendered identities, particularly in sex-segregated situations such as high school locker rooms, allows young men to reproduce hegemonic masculinities and reaffirm heteronormative masculinity among their peers. Sex-segregated contexts provide a domain within which expectations and terms of engagement, such as gender-normative behaviors, attitudes, and expressions, are routinely operationalized and moreover manifest themselves without interrogation or critical scrutiny. These spaces within schools allow stereotypical attitudes and behaviors to go unchecked and in some cases actually promote and encourage sexism, misogyny, and heterosexism to be legitimated and valorized. As Chris Shilling (2004, 482) argues, "dominant conceptions of masculinity encourage boys to participate in body-building activities that increase their strength, self-confidence, and capacity to occupy space." In his research, Moss Norman (2011, 441, 442) explains that even when there are "multiple and contradictory performances of masculinity, there were nonetheless contextually regulated limits to this multiplicity where gendered subjectivities were policed through discourses of gender and heterosexuality." His research illustrates how boys "deploy dominant discourses of masculinity that position the feminine as appearance-oriented and masculinity as performance-oriented, thereby laying out, reproducing, and naturalizing the 'proper' way for young men to relate to their gendered bodies." Locker rooms and change areas are perhaps one of the most troubling sex-segregated school spaces where the conduct, behaviors, and attitudes of youth remain out of the purview of adults and thus are problematic because they are not well monitored for inappropriate, threatening, and aggressive conduct among students.

Whose Body Is It Anyway? When the Body Is Named

I begin this section by raising a series of questions that guide this section and invite the reader to consider when and how the male body is named. It is worth asking for example: Under what conditions do boys and men have license to see or look upon other males' bodies? How in/visible is the male body? To what extent has the hypervisibility of the masculine body contributed to the naming and defining of male bodies? How does the increased visibility contribute to men's/boy's bodies as textual representations of raced, classed, and sexualized masculinities? To what extent has the growing consumption and availability of masculine bodies in the public mainstream allowed for or inhibited reconfigurations of masculine identities through the body? The sociology of the body in schools not surprisingly raises more questions than answers. Nonetheless researchers, teachers, and school administrators are left with troubling signs that, for example, while body building per se is not taught as part of the formal curriculum, there is an increased awareness among adolescent boys for whom, according to Carrie Paechter (2003, 56), "the look of the body is pre-eminent, designed for visual consumption, and the body is explicitly 'pumped up' into artificial poses that show the musculature to best advantage." Gill, Henwood, and McLean (2005, 51) have found that men do indeed care about how they look. "The skill for men seems to be in negotiating the boundaries between appropriate concern and vanity." The implications of this study and others that aim at opening up conversations of bodily practices and sex-segregated spaces such as locker rooms and PE classes are significant for school policies, curriculum development, and promoting healthier, safer school climates (Martin and Govender 2011; O'Donovan and Kirk 2007).

Contextually located and bounded by the practices promoted and supported in PE, the adolescent male body is emerging as a wider representational tool of masculinities in both the public consumer culture as well as the private spaces of school locker rooms/changing rooms. Shilling (2010, 165) argues that "much research remains to be undertaken in relation to the precise articulation of bodily norms and the methods by which these are re-contextualized within schools" and moreover argues its relevance in relation to "the specific issue of how the means, experiences and outcomes of school-based body pedagogies shape young people's engagements with society in general." The body is increasingly monitored, surveyed, and accounted for in schools, especially within the current climate of "panic," mobilizing an obesity discourse that, according to Emma Rich (2010, 806), has led to a damaging set of conditions and predispositions imbedded in policies and practices aimed at "children as subjects particularly in terms of a developing sense of embodiment."

Drawing on Judith Butler's (2004) theory of gender performativity, I argue that boys routinely navigate gender spaces in very regulated and normatively sanctioned ways. In short, boys in particular draw on a set of codes of masculinities that often inform and form what they deem appropriate masculine behavior. Rather than a bio-determinist model that argues boys are aggressive, rational, and naturally inclined to a set of predetermined masculine behaviors and attitudes, I contend that boys purposefully navigate and negotiate a set of masculine beliefs and ideologies. Gender and the expression of masculinities is an outward display and expression of valued and often valorized forms of masculinities intentionally produced and reproduced to ensure membership and acceptance within and across peers (Smolak 2004). "Students' gendered bodies and behaviors are both scrutinized and disciplined by their peer group, with public and negative labeling for those unwilling or unable to conform to group norms" (Paechter 2003, 49). In other words, with regard to changing gender relations and power dynamics among boys, the climate in schools in particular has witnessed a shift to not only an acknowledgment of the body as present but moreover an acknowledgment of the body as imminent, dominant, active, and visually ever present in the constant surveillance of schooled bodies (Frost 2003; Paechter 2011; Rich 2010).

Media images and targeted campaigns that manufacture unrealistic and airbrushed images of idealized masculine bodies are familiar marketing strategies that lead to body dissatisfaction. Adolescent masculinities are regularly and routinely constituted through the body. We must examine further how the rise in the commodification of male body images in the media has allowed for or tailored the ways in which boys understand their bodies. Bodies of other boys are powerful reference points. Schools are ubiquitous sites in which competing discourses of masculinity, particularly within PE, invoke skills-based, strength-based, and performance-based models that promote boys "doing" bodies in particularly narrow and restrictive ways. And while admittedly the physicality, muscularity, and general awareness of the masculine body are not new, what is increasingly under investigation of importance in schools is how and when adolescent men engage in body projects and what conditions allow men to operate within and beyond such boundaries imposed by, for example, a health, obesity, or fat phobia discourse (see, for example, Evans, Davies, and Rich 2008; Norman 2011; Sykes and McPhail 2008) that operates in tandem with various discourses of masculinity.

In the following section, I take up adolescent male bodies to better understand how diversely situated adolescent boys shift within and about their bodies through daily social practices in school PE classes. I argue the body is incomplete and is transformed in PE locker rooms and PE classes. Bodies as such remain unfinished work. Adolescent boys are routinely problematically positioned as marginalized, valorized, and minimized bodies all with varying levels and locations of privilege not strictly named through the body, but largely understood silently around the body.

PE and PE locker rooms are unsettling places because of the ways in which they promote and even perpetuate bodily practices that revolve around a culture of privilege, power, and popularity among boys. Many adolescent bodies, I argue, have remained a relative source of power, dominance, and oppression, while others have not. Our understandings of the strains and tensions that inhere in processes of embodiment among adolescent males have been limited, curtailed, and silenced, as I argue elsewhere (Kehler and Atkinson, forthcoming), because of the gatekeeping that occurs in schools to prevent the body from being seen and heard (see also Paechter 2011; Shilling 2010). My research makes visible these processes of embodiment.

THE STUDY

Conducted over a three-year period (2008–2011), this qualitative study examined the reasons some adolescent boys are reluctant to participate in required secondary school PE classes in three major cities across Canada. Funded by the Social Science and Humanities Research Council of Canada, this collaborative project was conducted with two other researchers who shared in data collection and analysis. The goal was to more closely examine the issues adolescent boys identified as factors negatively influencing their experience of health education in ninth grade PE, the introductory secondary level class. A primary goal was to uncover the subtleties of the daily experiences in PE. Ethics approval was received at the University of Western Ontario, and the project was later granted ethics approval from three different school boards. The data presented in this chapter are a partial representation but reflect a consistent and recurring set of themes and analysis that emerged across the larger study. Our aim was not to make generalizations beyond this study but rather to look across different geographical contexts in similar school spaces, namely high school locker rooms. Our approach provided opportunities for the boys to distill some of their perspectives from the daily routines of school PE interactions. We saw these young men as active subjects intentionally and purposefully managing their social worlds. The findings are presented with the understanding that such "truths" and "voices" have not previously been heard let alone verified.

Data were collected using participant observation and semistructured interviews. Our team recruited seventy-seven boys, between the ages of fourteen and fifteen, using a variety of techniques. The author, also the principal investigator for this project, presented information-style talks at schools that expressed a willingness to participate in this study. Letters of permission and information along with posters were distributed in schools and at a YMCA, and the project was advertised through a local newspaper. Snowballing was also used, as some participants spoke to their peers and recruited them to the study. A nominal gift card to a local shopping mall was provided to students who donated their time to be interviewed and participated in the follow-up blogging that ensued. Semistructured interviews lasting between forty-five minutes and one and a half hours were conducted at times and places chosen by the participants, including guidance counselor offices, empty classrooms, coffee shops, restaurants, and libraries. In line with a more collaborative research approach and to promote a participatory and respectful dialogue with the participants, boys chose their own pseudonyms, thus allowing the young men more control over how they are named in this study. Interviews were audio-taped and transcribed. Interview data were shared across researchers, and emerging themes were identified through consistent and recurrent patterns. Participant observations during structured PE class time were conducted as a way to contrast students' narratives with their daily experiences in PE. Students were observed during class time over a period of two to three days depending on schedules, teacher permissions, and interruptions at individual schools.

Locker Rooms and the Private Spaces That Hide Us

Boys actively make sense of their bodies in relation to the self-identities they negotiate in high school locker rooms, and these male self-identities are often calibrated against the sorts of masculinities that are routinely constructed within specific sporting contexts (Pringle and Hickey 2010). Drawing on the school context, I identify two relatively distinct spaces within locker rooms in which boys are regularly positioned among other boys. I refer to these spaces as identifiably separate on the basis of the amount or level of privacy and protection they allow boys within locker rooms. Either normative or nonnormative, these spaces allow for boys to adhere to or transgress bodily practices dictated and predicated upon heteronormative codes of masculinity. I draw attention to these spaces as powerful and troubling contexts within which adolescent boys routinely become hyperconscious of the meanings of their own and other boys' bodies. The bodily practices of boys in PE locker rooms have a significant bearing on the long-term healthy life practices among adolescent boys.

PROTECTED SPACES AND AVOIDANCE STRATEGIES

For some boys, going to the locker room was anxiety-inducing, and they dreaded PE because of the interactions they had with their peers in the space. As a result, many of the boys expounded strategies they used to avoid locker rooms. I argue that there remains a private discomfort and set of anxieties in which adolescent young men are very body conscious and fearful and (a)shamed in many cases by how their body is viewed. The impact this has in relation to their PE experience is noteworthy (O'Donovan and Kirk 2007). As we examine these experiences and hear the voices of young men we must acknowledge "the habitual nature of changing room interactions," but most important we must consider "what strategies could be used to upset the established environment and challenge the reasons for the development of such a culture" (O'Donovan and Kirk 2007, 406). What I describe as *nonnormative spaces* are areas of the locker room that are not easily viewed by others outside of those boys who already have membership in this confined space. Nonnormative spaces also allow boys a different level of personal security and safety not found in normative spaces. Membership in this case is based on a common or shared access—namely, these boys were ninth grade PE students. Other students were not allowed in the locker room at this time, so access was restricted to this population of students. These spaces are distinct because they do not require normative conduct, behavior, or attitudes to be openly expressed while using them. These are relatively private spaces and include stalls, or areas of the locker room that are sheltered or shielded, including corners. These spaces provide a sense of protection, real or imagined, from the more open, easily peer-scrutinized spaces. There is also less chance of any form of taunting or physical aggression occurring in these spaces. Boys purposefully use these spaces in locker rooms because of the level of protection and safety they provide.

The privacy and the ability to skirt or avoid peer surveillance were important in locker room maneuvers among the young men in this study. In a conversation, Connor made a distinction identifying specific safe spaces, including the washroom stall, where some boys change "so that other people don't watch them." During our research, the boys consistently referred to zones or spaces in school locker rooms that had an impact on how they managed and conducted themselves. Different groups of boys regularly took up space and used separate parts of the locker room. Just as classrooms often have seating plans, the locker room too was organized by different groups of boys in different areas.

Many of the boys identified groups within PE class based on "athleticity" and level of caring or investing in the class. Chewi describes one group of boys by saying, "They really just don't do anything because they don't try and they don't care and maybe some of the people in the low athletic group might eventually switch over there because they don't like being made fun of and they'll just stop trying." According to many of the boys the "jocks" and the "popular" boys were regularly found in the center of the locker rooms. The less athletic boys often changed at lockers or in spaces just beyond the central area. Many of the boys depicted their locker rooms with references to the size and composition of the spaces. Locker rooms were described similarly across the research sites. Most of the students referred to the room's size and physical geography. "You walk in and it's a ten-by-ten-meter room" and "the main area with all the benches" or "you walk in and there's a wall and then the showers are past the benches." I refer to the washroom within locker rooms as *a nonnormative space*. As such boys are more easily able to escape the surveillance of their peers and avoid harassment and belittling comments made by the "popular boys" who control the central change area or what I refer to as the *normative space*. The *normative spaces* are more public and open to peer scrutiny, verbal harassment, and physical banter among boys. The boys purposefully use washrooms and changing room stalls to remove themselves from the larger population of their classmates. They avoid changing with their peers, conversing, and participating as regular class members. In the following conversation James explains he does not go into the locker room, but he nonetheless has a strong opinion and developed a strategy to avoid using the locker room. John similarly had managed to avoid changing in the locker room. He had been shamed and ridiculed in the past and had since developed a routine for avoiding this harassment. Such a strategy reflects significantly on the anxieties the boys have about using or entering the locker room:

> See these clothes I'm wearing? These are my gym clothes. I wear these clothes to school. I wear gym shoes to school. I don't ever set foot in that locker room just because I don't want to be in there and I don't want to be half naked in there. (James)

> Okay, therein lies where it's really gone wrong for me because I have not brought my gym uniform, my gym clothes to school on so many occasions that if I don't pass the exam I'm not going to get the credit for gym and that was a conscious choice on my part because I did not want to participate because I brought it [my gym uniform] a few times but I would wear it underneath my other clothes and I would just take those off in the change room and have my gym uniform on because I was uncomfortable with my body and I was afraid of what other kids would say to me because in grade eight I know in the change room I got made fun of a lot. When I would take my shirt off to change into my other shirt other people would scream and look away and stuff just to make fun of me. So I had enough of that and I decided that I was either not going to bring my uniform or just not participate at all. (John)

John continues to explain his discomfort with other people seeing him and a history of weight-based teasing in school locker rooms: "When I was in the change room and I'd forgotten to wear my gym clothes underneath my other clothes and so I would actually take my shirt off just by the sleeves and then I put my other shirt on and then I would kind of pull my other shirt off at the same time. So I'm not comfortable with people seeing me because I'm not comfortable with myself and that's because I have been made fun of before." James made a clear and firm decision to never "set foot in that locker room," just as John decided he had "had enough of that" and would either "bring my uniform or just not participate at all." The culture of the changing room, including its characteristics, rules, and features, both physically and socially impacts the ways students engage or disengage from PE class. John expresses both his fears of the peer surveillance that occurs in the changing room and his anxieties about his own body. Both James and John developed ways to respond to a threatening and unwelcoming climate. Each strategy was intentional and purposeful to protect themselves from teasing and peer scrutiny of their bodies. John's eighth grade experience in changing rooms was damaging and unchecked by teachers. As none of the boys in our study referred to any adult supervision in the changing rooms, they were left alone to change and prepare themselves for class.

The *normative spaces* in school locker rooms are delineated and maintained through routine and frequent social coercion and verbal taunts. Largely open spaces, these areas are purposefully and aggressively maintained on the basis of rules and codes of normative masculinity. The boys themselves carefully monitor outward physical and verbal exchanges or interactions among boys in these spaces. Anything that appears less than masculine or contravenes acceptably masculine conduct becomes easy fodder for public humiliation. Conversations in these areas typically focus on sport performance or athletic prowess. Chewi, for example, describes that after class "it would just be like walking into the change room and then they all start saying, 'oh you just fell' and 'that was terrible' kind of stuff and that always happens after gym." Similarly Joey commented that in class "I usually drop balls if they're thrown to me and that kind of gets people mad that are on my team. They always tell me when we're changing." The more popular boys, often those with considerable physical prowess, regularly exchanged barbs with the less athletic students. Both skill-based and appearance-based teasing among boys was similarly found by Linda Smolak (2004).

Relative comparisons are made among boys as a means to maintain a hierarchical structure. Athletic ability and physical attributes are often cited as points of comparison and contribute to growing body dissatisfaction among more adolescent boys than previously thought (Krayer, Ingledew, and Iphofen 2008). In the following excerpt Dave describes the intimidation some boys experience in the locker room: "I know in some schools, some of the skinny, small guys . . . all the big guys kind of pick on them for not being as good and they don't like going in the locker room because they might get bullied or stuffed in a locker." This accepted culture of locker rooms is often dismissed as "normal" boy culture.

Stereotypes of boys jockeying for position, flexing muscles, and demonstrating prowess at the expense of other, often weaker boys has been a regular part the boys' characterizations of their locker room and class experiences across the schools in our study. The comments and experiences of the young men in this study are reason for further investigation into school locker room climates and the taken-for-granted exchanges among boys. In the next instance, Chewi describes his strategy for getting to the changing room ahead of his classmates to avoid the awkwardness of changing with his peers: "I was always on time and I always got changed and in the gym by the time they all already came in but still, it was awkward, yeah." This strategic and careful planning to avoid being with his peers while changing reveals unexplained anxieties some boys have in these masculinized spaces. This awkwardness was also evident with regard to showering after PE class. Chewi remarks, "I actually never ever once stepped in there, never showered once in the change room. Thankfully I had last period gym so I'd just come home after." And while Chewi was able to avoid using the showers, this was nonetheless an issue the PE teacher directly addressed with the students: "Like our teacher even said, you can use the showers if you want. If you feel uncomfortable, bring a swimsuit, but no one still did. No one used the showers and I don't know why. I guess just the whole security thing. . . . Like the way they're feeling, their security." However, the discomfort Chewi expresses is not often openly discussed among boys. The PE teacher's allowing of swimsuits demonstrates his understanding that boys might be uncomfortable about their bodies in a public space, but he did not actually respond to "the whole security thing," which remained unresolved throughout the semester.

The level of anxiety and uncertainty about nudity as well as personal safety is striking. In fact, Jarred Martin and Kaymarlin Govender (2011, 235–236) found that the intersections between concerns for perceived body ideals, muscularity, and traditional masculine beliefs "are constricting and damaging as they enforce and perpetuate a culture of secrecy and silence over talking about one's vulnerabilities and anxieties as a male." In Chewi's case the teacher was aware of the discomfort among his students and offered a coping strategy but failed to actually address the insecurities. There is a deeply held belief that boys can navigate, participate, and enter highly masculinized places such as boys' and men's locker rooms because of an assumed acceptance of and comfort with normative masculine ideology.

In an interview Bob similarly expresses a discomfort in boy's locker rooms: "Maybe the guys like seeing each other but I don't think so. I don't know why they have open showers for guys but you get used to it and actually I don't [shower] anymore." Bob explains that while he eventually accepted the lack of privacy he opts not to shower and thus avoids his peers' surveillance. Interestingly, Bob also comments on the possible pleasure in seeing each other in the showers, but quickly dismisses it. His discomfort is related to "open showers for guys." He does not make any explicit comparison to the showers provided for girls, which at that school were closed and separated by curtains. Bob realized the physical differences in locker rooms when his class was rescheduled to meet at the girls' changing room because their room was unavailable. In the following conversation, Rod describes the showers as a space where "you're kind of away from the teacher" and where boys are able to do "things to harass you." "I don't shower anymore. I just shower when I get home and again, the guy who bugged me, he's like, 'Why don't you take a shower.' So I said, 'Because I don't feel like it.' . . . It's like when you're kind of away from the teacher, they want to pick on you more like in the showers or the stalls, they would pick on you more and you would feel uncomfortable just being in there with a group of naked boys just playing around, doing things to harass you." But as Andrew explains, although the "big kids" avoid the locker room so as not to be seen changing, the privileged-bodied boys understand and notice the strategy:

> He won't go in the change room. He will change in the bathroom upstairs. He'll come down and he will smell because he doesn't . . . they don't shower after gym. They don't put on deodorant. They'll just go in the change room but wear their gym clothes under their normal clothes and they'll just take them off. So they don't have to go in and take off their shirt or they don't have to take off their pants and put on their shorts. They'll do it in the bathroom. They'll go into a stall or stuff like that so they don't have to be seen without their shirt. They shouldn't have to do that because he will . . . and everyone notices, like what's the point of doing that when everyone knows that you're doing it because of that. Like everyone will be like, "Oh where is he?" Like they'll notice that he's not there. "Where's the big kid?" Oh he must . . . you wonder where he is and then he just pops out and he's all changed. So they realize that the overweight kids, they don't go in the change room.

The exchange Bob had with his peer reflects one example of surveillance in segregated locker room spaces. Rod describes a sense of bodily discomfort "just being in there with a group of naked boys" but also a sense of fear of the harassment that occurs "away from the teacher." Across the boys in this study, many like Chewi, Bob, and Rod developed strategies of avoidance and withdrawal. The discomfort, anxieties, and concerns these young men expressed about their bodies and the locker room harassment in particular are troubling. Harrison Pope, Katharine Phillips, and Roberto Olivardia (2000, 60) explain, "Because men aren't supposed to worry or complain about their looks, few would ever admit that they'd secretly like to have a steroid-sized body or that they fret about their inadequacies when examining their bodies in the mirror. Fewer still would acknowledge that their obsessions about body appearance have anything to do with threatened masculinity." If left unaltered, unsupervised spaces like school locker rooms will continue to foster and perpetuate normative codes of masculinity that threaten to alienate and marginalize boys, particularly those who do not agree with the rules and codes of behavior generally accepted in these spaces.

Richard Pringle and Christopher Hickey (2010) describe a set of tensions, moral and ethical, that young men negotiate within sport cultures. Not dissimilar to the tensions his participants navigated, the adolescent boys I interviewed also had to navigate hypermasculine performances of adolescent masculinity often unregulated in school changing rooms. They demonstrated a certain level of reflection on how boys constructed the self in relation to other boys. The participants in our study developed a set of "specific techniques of self that struggle against hypermasculine forms of subjection" (Pringle and Hickey 2010, 134). I am not suggesting these young men were critically engaged in the self-reflection or techniques that allowed them to dislocate themselves from a dominant and oppressive set of codes of heteronormative masculinity. I am arguing, however, that these boys navigated various power arrangements among boys that emerge from the masculine body in particular. Their ability to develop self-protective strategies provides a foundation from which to begin interrogating and better understanding the culture of masculinity that prevails in many locker rooms.

In the following conversation James demonstrates a keen awareness of the kind of cultural capital masculine athletic and able bodies were granted in this PE culture. James describes a community of adolescent bodies where he is located and subjugated. "I guess other people are like, 'Hey, look at me flex.' You know, like Harley: 'Why don't you flex? . . . Look at that. That's epic. I have an entire straight line.' I guess that's how I became aware that I was weak but again I don't care. I guess I became aware I was weak when I couldn't run for more than a bit without getting out of breath. I couldn't throw the ball when everyone else could. Seeing their abilities compared to mine made me realize that I'm not very good at gym and then I realized I don't really want to be." The ripped body of Harley with "an entire straight line" extending down his abdomen was an invitation for James to gaze upon his body and moreover to critically assess his own body and abilities in sport. Harley's invitation suggests that adolescent boys are increasingly defining themselves through their bodies. Being big, strong, and ripped and being able to show it to classmates matter. Boys are "subject to a set of evaluative standards relating to their physicality, about which they frequently have little control and may, even with hours in the gym or training for sports, be able to do little about" (Frost 2003, 67).

TEASING IN THE BOY'S ROOM

Teasing, especially weight-based teasing, is a powerful and damaging form of peer control exerted among adolescent boys in locker rooms. Appearance-related teasing, weight-related comments, and degrading other boys for having what are referred to as "man boobs" occur regularly as a form of social control within boy peer groups (see Krayer, Ingledew, and Iphofen 2008; Smolak 2004; Taylor 2011). In her study of gender- and weight-based teasing in secondary schools, Nicole Taylor (2011, 191) describes teasing's enduring damage that not only is common but has become part of "the verbally and physically abusive culture of the boys' locker room." There is growing evidence that boys regularly deploy both verbal and physical intimidation in school locker rooms and succumb to various forms of hazing, which tends to be underreported (Taylor 2011). During our interview, Spikeshade describes the kind of teasing he experienced while contrasting it between elementary school and secondary school: "One of the reasons for my poor self-image would probably be people making fun of me in elementary school and even a little bit here too. I had some kids. . . . I'm not going to name any names but some kids in my gym class would make fun of me for my weight." He continues, "It was more accepting [in elementary school] like in gym class they wouldn't make fun of you because you couldn't run or anything like that but here [in secondary school] I would get made fun of for my weight or when I run because you know, I'm overweight and people. . . . I've received a lot of comments that I care not to repeat really but they've basically been about my weight and how when I run it's just like, my fat bounces. So it's just . . . I didn't get that so much in elementary school really because people were just there to have fun and we were kids."

Spikeshade further explains the impact appearance-based teasing has on him in PE class: "I know that the experiences that stand out for me are probably when somebody would make a rude comment to me about my weight and I just wouldn't retaliate because there's just no point. I'm not sinking to their level. They can say whatever they want. It doesn't really affect me but well, evidently it does because years of it has led to my poor body image but at the moment it doesn't affect me and there have been a few times where I'm just going to come right out and say this, where I've been like people have smacked my fat and laughed at it because it jiggled and I've been smacked right across, well, my man boobs." Spikeshade contrasts this weight-based teasing to the privilege associated with being thin: "Well, they're thin, that's the thing. They're not necessarily buff or really muscular but they're all thinner than I am, most of them, like 99 percent of them and so they really have no problems with it. I mean I'm pretty sure in the summer if they got hot and sweaty, they'd just take their shirt off and walk around shirtless. . . . Usually me and the other big guys are usually the ones that would get made fun of and not the thin guys." Spikeshade is clear about the ridicule and teasing directed at him, that being thin is more desirable and less likely to be a source of teasing. He also demonstrates the gradual shift in locker room climate between the elementary and secondary levels. At elementary PE Spikeshade and classmates "were kids and just there to have fun"; in secondary school he endures the teasing but reluctantly acknowledges the long-term impact: "They can say whatever they want. It doesn't really affect me but well, evidently it does because years of it has led to my poor body image but at the moment it doesn't affect me."

Like many of the boys subject to weight-based teasing, Spikeshade developed strategies that denied the impact the ridicule had and justified the others' behavior. During our interview he explained the behavior of the "jocks" this way: "It could be that they were just brought up differently and not, now I don't want to call parenting into question but not properly disciplined and it could also be the fact that they get with their friends and they actually think that this is acceptable because their friends are doing it." Spikeshade justifies the bullying and harassment he experiences from the "jocks" because of parenting, being raised differently, and peer pressure. The locker room teasing has made Spikeshade, like many other boys, self-conscious, aware of his body and of thinness and the privilege extended to thin boys. He does not outwardly respond to the teasing because he refuses to "sink to their level." And while Spikeshade suggests he is not affected by the teasing, the opposite is evident. His bodily fears are best captured as he explains, "I'm afraid of what I look like and how other people perceive me and I know . . . it's kind of a gray area because I'm not sure what a healthy body weight for my height would be yet. I don't want to get too thin either from exercises. So what I'm really trying to do is lose the fat and build muscle. So I may weigh the same. I may end up weighing more but weight isn't really as important to me as physique." Spikeshade is concerned about his appearance and how others perceive him. He also understands that some bodies are privileged while others remain a pubic source for ridicule. And through his PE experiences, Spikeshade has learned that "weight isn't really as important to me as physique."

The polarized discourses of weak and muscular bodies are prevalent in many locker room spaces. Whether or not boys talk about or critically interrogate these discourses remains an area for ongoing research (Grogan and Richards 2002), but the relationship boys make among muscular bodies, physical abilities, and school sporting culture is evident. In the following interview excerpt Mythic further illustrates how changing room conversation influences his impression of his own abilities. The impact of social comparison among boys further reveals the kind of climate they endure coming and going to PE class. Mythic states, "Probably the most nerve-wracking thing would have to be is just people comparing me to themselves, maybe like 'God dude, you suck and gym is really bad for you' and you know they say that I'm not a team person and they say I'm not physical. They say I'm un-athletic sometimes, like it's a bad thing." Mythic illustrates the divisive manner in which boys compare one another based on athletic prowess. The changing room allows for uncensored conversation in which boys succumb to the verbal abuse of others who have become respected, regarded, and feared because of their athletic cachet both with peers and importantly oftentimes with teachers as well. The conversation, impressions, and experiences these boys have in school changing rooms contribute to how they define themselves, their bodies, and their relationship to physical activity in particular. The location provides a secluded, private, and unsupervised space in which masculinities and physical activity are seamlessly bound to youth identities. Unless this culture and the climate that prevails are more closely scrutinized, boys will continue to withdraw and decide that they "don't really want to be" good at gym.

Conclusion

In this chapter I have described how adolescent boys name and understand the relationship between adolescent bodies and masculinities in a PE context and offered a way of looking inward toward and outward from high school locker rooms, spaces that heretofore have been largely closed, private, or taboo within both research and school communities. The process of negotiating adolescent male bodies is not well understood, but is routinely accepted and interpreted within and among boys, viewed as simply "boys will be boys." People believe that the locker room towel whipping, ball tossing, wrestling, and banter are simply what happens when boys congregate. But research is starting to illuminate the costs of such "normal," taken-for-granted masculine culture.

High school locker rooms present a familiar and puzzling domain. Though they are regularly navigated and negotiated among boys, few scholars consider how bodily practices in those spaces intersect with boys' views of themselves as men and dominant masculine ideologies that underscore daily school interactions. As Mona-Iren Hauge and Hanne Haavind (2011) have argued, and as this study further illustrates, boys produce and reproduce various masculinities through their bodies. They impose their bodies through physical means on other boys and occupy physical space in ways that marginalize and oppress weaker bodies. Locker rooms and PE classes form a private space in which bodily practices among boys reveal a troubling geography of masculinities regularly enacted away from the supervision of adults. More vulnerable boys hide their bodies to protect themselves and secure their bodies from stronger, dominant, and aggressive others. Ordered by codes of masculinity and unspoken rules for maneuvering masculinities in school, locker rooms remain a forbidden and threatening space for some boys.

Messner and Musto (2014, 107) have argued the significance of studying "kids not simply as future adults, but as active subjects who create their own social worlds." They have prompted us to consider more closely those spaces and places where children play at sport. They also have acknowledged that there are challenges to conducting research on youth because of "a daunting gauntlet of gatekeepers," but that should not deter us from asking the deeper and critical questions required within sport sociology. There is space for ongoing research that could enhance and extend the work of others (for example, Diedrichs and Lee 2010; Gill, Henwood, and McLean 2005; Rich and Evans 2009; Sykes and

McPhail 2008). As I have shown in this chapter, adolescent boys are both concerned about their bodies and willing to talk about them. Our participants were incredibly attuned to the meanings associated with masculine bodies among men and the implications in the social context of their everyday relations. Until researchers engage with youth, sports, and particularly the cultures and changing rooms that are oftentimes restricted to understand youth identities and sport, these spaces will remain much the same, simply boys *doing* boy.

REFERENCES

Atkinson, Michael, and Michael Kehler. 2012. "Boys, Bullying, and Biopedagogies in Physical Education." *Thymos: Journal of Boyhood Studies* 6.1–2: 166–185.

Butler, Judith. 2004. *Undoing Gender*. New York: Routledge.

Connell, Raewyn. 1995. *Masculinities*. Berkeley: University of California Press.

Diedrichs, Phillippa, and Christina Lee. 2010. "GI Joe or Average Joe? The Impact of Average Size and Muscular Male Fashion Models on Men's Health and Women's Body Image and Advertisement Effectiveness." *Body Image* 7: 218–226.

Evans, John, Brian Davies, and Emma Rich. 2008. "The Class and Cultural Functions of Obesity Discourse: Our Later Day Child Saving the Moment." *International Studies in Sociology of Education* 18.2: 117–132.

Frost, Liz. 2003. "Doing Bodies Differently? Gender, Youth, Appearance, and Damage." *Journal of Youth Studies* 6.1: 53–70.

Gill, Rosalind, Karen Henwood, and Carl McLean. 2005. "Body Projects and the Regulation of Normative Masculinity." *Body and Society* 11.1: 37–62.

Grogan, Sarah, and Helen Richards. 2002. "Body Image: Focus Groups with Boys and Men." *Men and Masculinities* 4.3: 219–232.

Hauge, Mona-Iren, and Hanne Haavind. 2011. "Boys' Bodies and the Constitution of Adolescent Masculinities." *Sport, Education, and Society* 16.1: 1–16.

Hearn, Jeff. 2012. "Male Bodies, Masculine Bodies, Men's Bodies: The Need for a Concept of Gex." In *Routledge Handbook of Body Studies*, edited by Bryan S. Turner, 307–320. New York: Routledge.

Kehler, Michael. 2010. "Boys, Books, and Homophobia: Exploring the Practices and Policies of Masculinities in School." *McGill Journal of Education* 45.3: 351–370.

———. 2012. "Who Will 'Save the Boys'? (Re)examining a Panic for Underachieving Boys." In *Adolescent Literacies and the Gendered Self: (Re)constructing Identities through Multimodal Literacy Practices*, edited by Barbara Guzzetti and Thomas Bean, 121–130. New York: Routledge, 2012.

Kehler, Michael, and Michael Atkinson. 2013. "Examining the (Em)bodied Boundaries of High School Locker Rooms." In *Contemporary Debates in the Sociology of Education*, edited by Rachel Brooks, Mark McCormack, and Kalwant Bhopal, 112–130. Basingstoke: Palgrave Macmillan, 2013.

———. Forthcoming. "The Space Between: Boys, Bodies, and Negotiating Research Subjectivities in Physical Education." *International Journal of Men's Health*.

Krayer, Anne, David K. Ingledew, and Ron Iphofen. 2008. "Social Comparison and Body Image in Adolescence: A Grounded Theory Approach." *Journal of Health Education Research* 23.5: 892–903.

Martin, Jarred, and Kaymarlin Govender. 2011. "'Making Muscle Junkies': Investigating Traditional Masculine Ideology, Body Image Discrepancy, and the Pursuit of Muscularity in Adolescent Males." *Men's Health* 10.3: 220–239.

Messner, Michael, and Michela Musto. 2014. "Where Are the Kids?" *Sociology of Sport Journal* 31.1: 102–122.

Norman, Moss. 2011. "Embodying the Double-Bind of Masculinity: Young Men and Discourses of Normalcy, Health, Heterosexuality, and Individualism." *Men and Masculinities* 14.4: 430–449.

O'Donovan, Toni M., and David Kirk. 2007. "Managing Classroom Entry: An Ecological Analysis of Ritual Interaction and Negotiation in the Changing Room." *Sport, Education, and Society* 12.4: 399–413.

Paechter, Carrie. 2003. "Power, Bodies and Identity: How Different Forms of Physical Education Construct Varying Masculinities and Femininities in Secondary Schools." *Sex Education* 3.1: 47–59.

———. 2011. "Gender, Visible Bodies, and Schooling: Cultural Pathologies of Childhood." *Sport, Education, and Society* 16.3: 309–322.

Patton, Michael Q. 2002. *Qualitative Research and Evaluation Methods.* Thousand Oaks, CA: Sage.

Phoenix, Ann, Rob Pattman, Rosaleen Croghan, and Christine Griffin. 2013. "Mediating Gendered Performances: Young People Negotiating Embodiment in Research Discussions." *International Journal of Qualitative Studies in Education* 26.4: 414–433.

Pope, Harrison G., Katharine A. Phillips, and Roberto Olivardia. 2000. *The Adonis Complex: The Secret Crisis of Male Body Obsession.* New York: Free Press.

Pringle, Richard G., and Christopher Hickey. 2010. "Negotiating Masculinities via the Moral Problematization of Sport." *Sociology of Sport Journal* 27: 115–138.

Ricciardelli, Rosemary, Kimberly A. Clow, and Phillip White. 2010. "Investigating Hegemonic Masculinity: Portrayals of Masculinity in Men's Lifestyle Magazines." *Sex Roles* 63: 64–78.

Rich, Emma. 2010. "Obesity Assemblages and Surveillance in Schools." *International Journal of Qualitative Studies in Education* 23.7: 803–821.

Rich, Emma, and John Evans. 2009. "Now I Am NO-Body, See Me for Who I Am: The Paradox of Performativity." *Gender and Education* 21.1: 1–16.

Shilling, Chris. 2004. "Physical Capital and Situated Action: A New Direction for Corporeal Sociology." *British Journal of Sociology of Education* 25.4: 473–487.

———. 2010. "Exploring the Society-Body-School Nexus: Theoretical and Methodology Issues in the Study of Body Pedagogics." *Sport, Education, and Society* 15.2: 151–167.

Smolak, Linda. 2004. "Body Image in Children and Adolescents: Where Do We Go from Here?" *Body Image* 1: 15–28.

Sykes, Heather, and Deborah McPhail. 2008. "Unbearable Lessons: Contesting Fat Phobia in Physical Education." *Sociology of Sport Journal* 5.1: 66–96.

Taylor, Nicole L. 2011. "'Guys, She's Humongous!' Gender and Weight-Based Teasing in Adolescence." *Journal of Adolescence Research* 26.2: 178–199.

Wellard, Ian. 2007. "Inflexible Bodies and Minds: Exploring the Gendered Limits in Contemporary Sport, Physical Education, and Dance." In *Rethinking Gender and Youth Sport,* edited by Ian Wellard, 84–98. London: Routledge.

CHAPTER 11

Park "Rats" to Park "Daddies"

COMMUNITY HEADS CREATING FUTURE MENTORS

A. James McKeever

My earliest memory of my childhood was as a five-year-old boy living in our rundown two-bedroom home in Pacoima. There was a broken chain-link fence in the front yard, partially knocked down after a drunk driver plowed through it. I remember a large hole in the front mesh screen door, which led to the inside of the house that had a black-and-white tile floor. Sometimes at night, I could hear the claws of a rat scurrying across the floor, scaring my four-year-old sister and me so much that we were afraid to get out of bed. Pacoima was a low-income Black neighborhood back then. My mom worked as a job shopper in the aerospace industry and my father was a "hustler."[1] He also trained racehorses on the side, costing the family far more money than it ever brought in. My mother's intermittent checks barely covered our expenses.

My father was a large African American man with a violent temper and the physical and mental ability to inflict harm and terrorize our family. He would often come home late at night, drunk, and looking for a fight. Sometimes he would drag us out of our beds to beat us; most nights it was my mother who bore the brunt of his anger. I learned to sleep lightly and would awaken the moment I heard his keys opening the door. One night he began to beat my mother. My sister and I could hear her screaming and the sound of flesh hitting flesh. My sister climbed in my bed next to me and we both began to whisper only loud enough for each other, "please stop" over and over again. Eventually he did. When we heard him get in his car and drive away, we went out to the living room to find our mother curled up, crying, in the fetal position. She looked up at us, her face bloodied. She told us we were leaving.

We left the house my mother was paying for, never to return, and moved to a rundown apartment in El Lado Este,[2] a low-income Latina/o neighborhood, an area known for prostitution and drugs. Our Hungarian grandparents owned a house here, in a section of town that blended marginal middle-class homeowners with the low-income apartment dwellers. We escaped my father temporarily, but he had already scarred us all. My sister was fearful and tried to suppress the past; my mother was irritable, bitter, and becoming violent toward us. I lost my childhood and began on an unsuccessful path of self-parenting. I became resentful and angry, ready to lash out in violence against anyone who crossed me.

I began to go to the local park, People's Park, a part of People's Plaza. Like others in the neighborhood, I would come to see the park as a refuge from various personal and social issues facing both youth and coaches. Starting when I was nine years old, the park was a place where I could temporarily forget about the physical and emotional abuse I was experiencing at home, a relatively safe space to hang out with other kids under the loose supervision of adults. Every day I would go straight to the park right after school. When I was playing basketball, the only thing that mattered was my coach, my teammates, and the score. All other concerns faded away and I was momentarily free. When I wasn't playing ball, the park gave me plenty to do. I became a volunteer coach at thirteen, umpired baseball games, worked in the day care, handed out free lunches, and helped take children on field trips. All these activities gave me something positive to occupy my time, a sense of purpose, and a feeling of accomplishment and respect. On weekends and in the summer I would leave the house by nine or ten in the morning, not to return till the "street lights came on." I was what they used to call a "park rat." Though the park was in a rough neighborhood I felt safe and in control, which was in sharp contrast to the chaos of my own house.

As a nine-year-old in 1973, I began to play sports at People's Park—first tennis and swimming, then football. My football coach was Earl Smith, an African American man in his twenties from New York. He was the first positive Black male in my life; he was tall, thin, and good-looking, with that New York "cool" about him. Earl had played college basketball on the East Coast, which gave him a lot of credibility among the youth. I played wide receiver for Earl, and I was very successful. I was tall and quick, and I could jump, making it hard for defensive backs to cover me.

At eleven I tried basketball for the first time. I was horrible. I could not dribble the ball or shoot. I was afraid to go into the game. My coach was another African American named Mel Carter. Mel was a heavy-set, light-skinned Black man with freckles, who worked hard to help me improve. Two seasons later, I was playing basketball for Earl, winning a championship, and leading the league in scoring. I became pretty good and got respect for what I did on the court.

Mel was a friend of Earl and the park's athletic director, Bill Deuce. Bill was a thirty-year-old African American who had a brief stint as a professional football player. He was a tall, strong, charismatic Black man loved and respected by parents and youth alike. When I was thirteen, Bill asked me to coach T-ball, making me the youngest coach at People's Park, which was then largely white and marginally middle-class, with some working-class and poor African Americans and Latina/os.

I had a successful first season coaching, taking second place in our division and forging a new friendship with the family of one of my players, which has lasted to this day. Even with this success, many parents were not pleased to see a thirteen-year-old Black kid with a big Afro and facial hair coach their kids. When basketball season came around, Bill asked me to coach again, but this time the parents chose to call a community meeting in protest. Bill asked me to attend the community meeting and had me sit up front at a long table facing the crowd. The room was full of angry and annoyed parents demanding my removal as a coach. Bill sat with me and listened for about half an hour as the crowd vented. Then he pulled a metal cash box from the chair next to him and placed it on the table for all to see and said, "Thank you for your opinions, but James will be coaching here from now on. I have your checks and money here if you want to pull your child out of the program." I couldn't believe that someone was standing by me in this way; I knew I couldn't let Bill down. I have been coaching at People's Park ever since.

It was the mentorship and coaching of Earl, Mel, and Bill that led me to get more involved in the park. I wanted to experience this form of respect and admiration. I felt like they had trusted me and handed over a responsibility that I would have to take seriously. I knew there were other youth who were also trying to deal with issues of poverty and violence, who needed a coach, mentor, and friend. It was then that I began to transition from "park rat" to "park daddy," sharing mentoring responsibilities with others.

Park Daddy as Ethnographer

It is hard to say exactly when I started "studying" People's Park and Recreation Center, since I have been volunteering there for over thirty years. While my research includes traditional methods of participant observation and interviewing, it also draws on my past experiences and my insider's status. Some of my work, in other words, is autoethnographic and seeks to draw "directly from the fieldworker's own experiences and insights" (Emerson 2001, 125). Autoethnography gives researchers the ability to do field work among their own people and allows them to "produce field data that is sensitive to emotional and bodily experiences" (Emerson 2001, 125).

One of the hardest parts of having such an insider's perspective was experiencing the park as if it were my first time. I had become so accustomed to the site that I barely noticed things such as the graffiti around the pool area and rest rooms, the number of Latina/o families who came to the park early on a

Saturday to stake out a space for a birthday party, the way the restrooms were filthy at times and smelled like urine, and the rough appearance of the women and men who attended the Narcotics Anonymous meetings that were held there.

In order to try to see the space anew, I began to take walks around the park at different times during the day and evenings, snapping pictures as I'd go. I watched men young and old playing soccer with trash cans for goals. Younger Black, white, and Latina/o men and women played in softball leagues, while older Latino men played in hardball leagues against each other. On Sunday mornings, groups of Latino men had informal weekly basketball tournaments complete with tiny flip-top scoreboards, untrained referees, and barbeques after the game. Street vendors sold hot dogs wrapped in bacon, *pupusas* (a Salvadorian staple), *raspados* (flavored shaved ice), and fruit. I noticed women who would power walk around the park and the boys grinding their skateboards on the concrete benches by the pool. I would take the pictures home and just look at them. As I examined them, I looked not just at what I had focused my camera on, but more at the blurred background so that I wouldn't miss the periphery.

A central part of this research was the six months I spent volunteering about twenty hours per week at the park, coaching three basketball teams: a seven- to eight-year-old boys' and girls' team, a nine- to eleven-year-old girls' team, and a thirteen- to fifteen-year-old boys' team. I coached two hour-long practices and two games per team each week. This kept me in the park seven days a week. I was not the only coach who led multiple teams. I counted six other coaches who had two teams, five because they had children to coach at multiple age levels, the sixth because the director asked him/her to coach an additional team. Often the most reliable and dedicated coaches led multiple teams. I was also asked to coach the thirteen- through fifteen-year-old boys' team for the all-star tournament, which we won and which added a month to my volunteer service.

I also observed other African American coaches and staff as they worked with youth. I conducted formal interviews with four African American male coaches who had demonstrated multiple years of service to the park: Ricky Jackson, an eighteen-year-old, single African American male; Tyrell Jones, a divorced, thirty-four-year-old paraplegic; Marques Walker, a thirty-two-year-old, married father of two; and Charles Foreman, a forty-seven-year-old, married father of three. I conducted the interviews in the space of their choosing: a coffee shop or the park itself (two interviews each). Each interview took approximately an hour and twenty minutes. I also interviewed two Latino staff who grew up playing basketball and participating in the park program, to better understand how they transitioned from youth players to volunteer coaches to park employees. They elected to be interviewed together at a local Sizzler restaurant. One of the men, Andres Gamboa, is the thirty-year-old athletic director at People's Park, a single father of one and a talented volunteer coach whose teams have beaten mine more often than not. The other man, Juan Delgado, is a twenty-two-year-old Latino male whom I once coached when he was a teenager. He and I are very close, and he refers to me as "Pops."

In this chapter, I first discuss the larger context of shifting economic and race relations surrounding People's Park, posing questions about race, class, and youth. Next, I situate People's Park in the larger community, providing a detailed description of the park's social geography. Finally, I draw from my interviews and observations of the youth who are currently involved in the park and those who grew up there to reflect on the possibilities and limitations of intergenerational mentoring within community-park-based sport programs.

ECONOMIC DOWNTURNS AND THE DOWNTRODDEN

Elijah Anderson (1999, 102) argues that in the mid-twentieth century, an "old head"—a man living in a low-income African American community who had obtained some economic markers of success—frequently served as a mentor for boys and young men; the old head would follow "a youngster's career, may 'pull his coat tail,' intervening and warning him about what will happen to him if he does not change his ways." In the 1980s, however, middle-class Blacks began to move from previous middle-class African American neighborhoods to the suburbs, leaving behind an impoverished underclass (Wilson 1987).[3] Wilson (1987) argues that in fleeing the inner city, the Black middle class largely abandoned its traditional responsibility to provide a culture of success for other Blacks to emulate.[4] Middle-class flight from the inner city, coupled with an economic recession and the devastating impact of deindustrialization on the breadwinning possibilities of blue-collar Black men in the 1980s, created a crisis of intergenerational male mentoring for young Black boys. As "old heads" disappeared in the 1980s and 1990s, they were replaced by "new heads"—neighborhood gang members and drug dealers who possessed the economic markers of success, the relative material wealth that gave them credibility and led neighborhood youth to look up to them.

Things have not improved—perhaps have worsened today for boys growing up in conditions similar to those of the 1980s. Much of the sociological literature points to negative socioeconomic outcomes for Black and Latino males. Nationwide, while 86 percent of whites and 80 percent of Asians graduate from high school, only 72 percent of African Americans and a meager 52 percent of Latina/os graduate (Collatos et al. 2004). African American males' graduation rate is 47 percent, while that for Latino males is 57 percent (Jackson 2008). According to the US Department of Labor (2012), for twenty- to twenty-four-year-olds, the white male unemployment rate is 32.4 percent, while the rate is 50.5 percent for African American males. Those young African Americans who are lucky enough to find employment are largely relegated to minimum-wage jobs. Two-thirds of California's prison population are African American or Latina/o, the majority of whom are male and from the Los Angeles area.

El Lado Este

William Julius Wilson's (1996, 15) summary of the growth of minority popula-tions in low-income, inner-city areas is an apt description of how El Lado Este—the neighborhood I grew up in—became a low-income predominantly Latina/o suburb of Los Angeles. "The 1970s and the 1980s witnessed a sharp growth in the number of census tracts classified as ghetto poverty areas, and sharply divergent patterns of poverty concentration between racial minorities and whites. One of the legacies of historic racial and class subjugation in America is a unique and growing concentration of minority residents in the most impoverished areas of the nation's metropolis." El Lado Este is scarred by boarded-up businesses that serve as noticeable signs of the effects of the recession and a stalled attempt at gentrification. When I was growing up during the late 1970s and early 1980s, this was a thriving multiracial, predominately white community that featured Peo-ple's Plaza, spanning six blocks with a mixture of mom-and-pop shops alongside large chain stores including Macy's, Sears, and JC Penney. It even featured two multiplexes that at the time were considered revolutionary as they could each show six or seven different movies at a time. This plaza became a center for shop-pers, restaurateurs, and moviegoers. But as mega malls and theaters were built in Glendale, in Burbank, and across the west side of the San Fernando Valley, prom-ising bigger bargains, lower prices, and most of all a place to see and be seen, People's Plaza began to die. White flight began to take hold, and the neighbor-hood slowly transitioned from a marginally white middle-class neighborhood to a working-class Latina/o community.

This area survived on life support for much of the 1980s and 1990s. During the late 1990s, El Lado Este became infamous for the El Lado Este Shootout, a failed bank robbery just blocks from People's Park, which resulted in the killing of one robber and the suicide of another, all captured by television news footage. Busi-nesses began to close more rapidly, never to reopen. Some were bulldozed and replaced by a much-needed elementary and middle school. Some, like JC Penney, were replaced by a telemarketing business. Schaffer's Cafeteria became VIP Strip Club, which shares a parking lot with several other businesses, including Sears and a storefront church, all across the street from the new middle school and a block from People's Park.

The middle-class white, Black, and Latina/o flight coupled with the loss of industry resulted in a predominantly poor Latina/o community. Wilson (2009, 58) points out that this is not unique to El Lado Este but a national trend: "The number of whites living in high poverty neighborhoods declined by 29 percent (from 2.7 million people to 1.9 million), and the number of Blacks decreased by 36 percent (from 4.8 million to 3.1). Latinos were the major exception to this pattern because their numbers in high-poverty areas increased slightly during the 1990s, by 1.6 percent. However, this finding should be placed in the context of Latino population growth: the number of Latinos overall increased dramatically in the 1990s, by 57.9 percent, compared with 16.2 percent growth for African-Americans and 3.4 percent for whites." African Americans have been displaced from low-income communities all over Los Angeles. As Black population growth slowed, increased immigrant populations have swelled the number of Latina/o residents in previously low-income Black and white neighborhoods (Camarillo 2004).

Poverty has fueled an underground economy of drugs, prostitution, and gangs in neighborhoods like El Lado Este. Industry Avenue—a thoroughfare infamous for drugs and transsexual prostitution—dissects El Lado Este. Strip malls featuring 99-cent stores, laundromats, check-cashing businesses, pawnshops, Chinese takeout restaurants, taco stands, video stores, liquor stores, motels, and storefront churches dot the boulevard. The landscape is riddled with low-wage-paying fast-food chains like In-N-Out Burger, Subway, Taco Bell, Burger King, McDonald's, El Pollo Loco (which replaced Der Wienerschnitzel), and Jack in the Box. El Lado Este has several local gangs including 18th Street, Vineland Boyz, El Lado Este Boyz, Radford, Armenian Power, and loosely organized Crips and Bloods. Gang crime in this neighborhood rose 24 percent in 2007, while it dropped in the overall city of Los Angeles (Los Angeles Police Department 2007).

People's Park is nestled like an oasis within this troubled community, serving predominantly low-income Latina/o youth who share similar exposure to gangs and poverty. Law enforcement and park administrators perceive the youth as either relatively innocent or "at risk." The park staff and volunteers—such as old head African American men—see themselves as mentoring youth, trying to keep them out of trouble and offering them alternatives to gang involvement.

By examining African Americans today mentoring in majority Latina/o communities, this chapter challenges much of popular opinion and some of the academic work (Vaca 2004) that highlights conflicts between African Americans and Latina/os. I argue that race relations are more complex than outlined in Vaca's (2004) analysis, which predominately focuses on the Black-Latina/o conflicts so often highlighted in the popular press. I also observe, in contrast to Wilson's (1987) middle-class mentors and Anderson's (1999) "old heads," who lived in their communities, that this park acts as a "community hub" that draws coaches back long after they have moved from the surrounding neighborhood. I call these mentors "community heads" and argue for an expanded notion of community, beyond a place where people live to a place where they congregate and create relationships and community meanings.

This Ain't Daddy's Park Anymore . . . It's Ours

The multiple gangs that vie for territory in El Lado Este have left People's Park relatively untouched. The tagging that is evident around the pool area, bathrooms, and trash bins is the work of mostly "taggers," not "gang bangers."[5] I asked a young man from 18th Street gang why they don't "bang" in the park, and he explained, "We all grew up here, we played here. The way we look at it, we want to keep this park a safe place for our little brothers and sisters and our kids." Even in a gangster's life that can be hard and violent, People's Park provides an oasis of positive childhood memories and a repository of hope.

People's Park is not impressive in appearance. Its sixty-four acres are nestled against a freeway on one side and many apartments, houses, businesses, and vacant stores on the other. It begins with a thin strip of grass with a few concrete benches and tables and large green metal trashcans behind a combination of abandoned stores and struggling businesses. This area is seldom used, with the exception of the homeless who use the benches to eat, lovers who use the isolation to "make out," and an Aztec dance group that practices in the unoccupied space.

From here you cross the busy thoroughfare of Triumph Boulevard and pass a vocational school to come upon a lively corner of the main section of People's Park: the day care center. This center was built in 2005 to provide a safe and quality free preschool to the low-income community, but following the economic recession, the center started charging for its services. The day care center is in a brand-new red brick building next to four tennis courts that are often used to play soccer at night.

Two poorly groomed baseball fields sit at the center of the park. There are no raised pitching mounds in the middle of the rock-hard dirt infields, and the outfields are marked by gopher holes on the relatively green grass. During baseball season, numerous street vendors sell hotdogs wrapped in bacon, corn with mayonnaise and chili, mangos, watermelon, coconuts, and *doros* (small fried flaky treats that look like mini wagon wheels) with lemon and chili. Next to one of the diamonds is a playground with swings and slides embedded in the sand. An ice cream truck constantly parks nearby. On the weekends the benches are almost always adorned with balloons and signs saying "Happy Birthday" or "Feliz Cumpleaños."

Next to the playground is an older building that houses a small gym used for meetings and basketball for three- to six-year-olds. A bigger gym, built twenty years ago, connects to the small gym through a cold hallway with walls of thick concrete and a beige tile floor. Three soda machines and a candy machine line the hall. To the right of the gym is the staff office. To the left of the gym a short hallway leads to a small room that houses a piano for lessons. This room is next to a larger room for meetings and kids' arts and crafts, connected with a small room with a sign on it that reads "Teen Center." The door to the Teen Center is always open and you can hear the sounds of youngsters laughing and joking, running in and out. The room is so small it is hard to imagine it being a suitable meeting place, but it has a back door that leads directly to the outdoor basketball courts and then to the open fields. The gym is large and plain with worn hardwood floors with "dead spots."[6] Three rows of bleachers line one side of the gym and banners from "all-star" champion and runner-up baseball, softball, and basketball teams adorn the walls. Next to the large gym stands a parking lot that leads to a public pool, drained in the winter but teeming with life in the summer.

From here you cross another main street and immediately see a library that marks the park's far side, a clean and pleasant space with trees and tables that are seldom used. Travel west from the library and you will see some new but very used and worn soccer fields, home to Unidos Soccer League, and five baseball diamonds.

Community Heads Creating Future Mentors

My story of being a teen coach represents a common theme at People's Park: youth are now incorporated into every aspect of the park's functions. Juan Delgado is a young Latino man whom I coached as a youth. As I stated before, he saw me as a surrogate father; our difference in race was never an issue. Juan had come to me on several occasions asking for advice on a range of topics including dating, his parents, and school. Once Juan was having an issue with a local gang that was infecting the high school he was about to attend. Juan's parents were immigrants and their English was limited. Juan asked me to go to the school on his parents' behalf to advocate for him. With the parents' approval I visited Juan's school to seek a transfer to another local school. Although the transfer was denied, our bond grew. It didn't bother Juan that a Black man was taking him to school as his parent; he even introduced me as his "pops" to one of his friends.

Years later, Juan would serve as a role model to a young Armenian boy, the relationship again cutting across racial boundaries. In speaking about his role as a People's Park employee, Delgado said, "We wanna keep the youth teaching the other people, you know, whatever we teach them, keep them involved, keep them out of the street, stay out of trouble, they like being there, all our kids just gonna hang out." Delgado's words reflect an important dynamic at the park: the incorporation of youth into the park includes initiating them into mentorship roles, giving them something positive to do, keeping them involved and off the streets.

This tradition of cultivating future mentors from current park youth has been handed down from generation to generation and maintained by parents, youth, and employees who also grew up in the park. Regardless of who is serving as park director, they soon learn that they will not be allowed to disrupt this cultural pattern. Andres Gamboa, the thirty-year-old athletic director, describes the park's culture:

> It's the environment, it's the people that work with you, like the surrounding people that you work with, it's just different, um, there's expectations, they're respectful and stuff like that, and they like the glory, like, and there's things that we have and they want to be part of that, and I think a lot of the kids want to be a part of that, they want to coach because they see some good role models there at People's Park, we've had some really good coaches there in the past, a lot, and every coach gives, you know, their input and it allows the kids to take advantage of that and want to be like them too.

Andres describes an environment where the staff and the coaches create a culture of respect that stands in stark contrast to many youths' experiences in the larger El Lado Este community, where too often "respect" is really a form of fear, an intimidation that masquerades as respect. But here at People's Park, youth learn a respect where one's actions and commitment to the community earn praise and, as Andres says, "glory." Some youth see this—as I did—and want to be a part of something positive.

Like Family

The basketball program is the key component to incorporating the youth into the park. As Andres stated, "Look around, most of the youth in the teen center started out in basketball, the ones who work here too, and the ones who volunteer, same thing." He is right. Basketball is People's Park's heart, pumping life through its veins. Andres himself grew up playing basketball here. While football and baseball are played over a single season, basketball has winter and summer seasons. More youth sign up for basketball than the other two sports, and it is the only sport in which participation remains high even during youths' teenage years. In fact, it is the only sport that draws an audience of teenagers. Even after they are too old to play for People's Park and have gone off to play for their high school teams, some return to watch the Juniors (ages thirteen to fifteen) play, keep score, and referee. I asked a group of older youth who were watching a Juniors game why they continually return to the park. Jesus, a sixteen-year-old high school student, stated, "This is where we became friends and we know a lot of the kids who still play here, we also coached some of these kids, refereed their games, they ask us to come watch their games. This is our house, a place to hang with your friends and play some ball."

A prime example of this is Ricky Jackson, an eighteen-year-old Black man who grew up playing in the park. Ricky grew up in a small two-bedroom El Lado Este apartment, right around the corner from People's Park. His single father made a modest income. Ricky attended predominantly Latina/o elementary, middle, and high schools and still lives in the neighborhood. As he got older, he started keeping score at the park, later refereeing basketball games, and finally coaching. To Ricky, People's Park is like home: "I've been playing here since I was a kid. I grew up here. I used to come here as soon as I got out of school, played ball, hung out, went to the teen center. People respected me here, trusted me, and gave me a job. I mean it starts with basketball but then you see them asking you to do other things, makes you feel needed. It feels like home."

The respect Ricky initially gains on the court leads to respect off the court. He finds that young people listen to him because of his basketball skills. Ricky's story shows how the tradition of incorporating youth into the park continues. Most of the youth today are Latina/o, with a number of Armenian youth and a small but consistent group of African Americans. Many volunteer as coaches or scorekeepers, answer phones, and set up and clean up after events. Some of these youth eventually earn employment as referees, summer youth employees, and recreation assistants. Spaces like People's Park offer these youth an opportunity to earn legitimate money in an economic climate that has devastated the employment opportunities of Black and Brown youth, forcing more and more to seek illegal wage-earning activities. The youth are not the only ones who benefit from the arrangement at People's Park. With increasing numbers of low-income and single parents who are overworked and overstressed, volunteering has suffered. Youth, however, fill these holes. They serve as volunteer coaches when needed and act as low-wage scorekeepers and referees when possible. Juan stated the park "grabs" you:

> Um, at first it was just like a job when I used to work there, but the park kind of like grabs a hold of you. Like I don't know how to explain it really but like you say, "I'm just gonna go there for my hour shift, I'm on, I'm off," but then you kind of just like become part of [the park]. You kind of like helping out, when you're off the shift you help out, you just wanna, you understand. . . . I started playing there at first. I wasn't that good at basketball in the beginning so I started coaching because I saw everybody else doing it. Bill was my first coach and then after that, "I want to coach, I want to be like him," so I started doing it. Then it just becomes like a habit like you want to do it 'cause it makes you feel good, the kids you know, improving, and it makes you feel good you know. When I'm not there it's like I have all this spare time it's like, "what do I do now?" I'm so used to being at People's Park all the time, it's kind of like part of my life now, I just gotta be there, even when, even though I'm not working I go and still help out and stuff like that you know, because its, I been doing it forever, it's like a second home to me now, I guess.

I have felt a similar type of allegiance—a feeling like the park "grabs" you. Sometimes I would joke with Andres or Juan about my loyalty to the park by saying

"I got 'PP' tattooed on my chest next to my heart." The young men and women who work here contribute to the family income and are not simply "dependent" children (Zelizer 1985). Instead, they have the potential to transform traditional views of work-family relations (Estrada and Hondagneu-Sotelo 2011; Kwon 2014).

Keeping Our House Clean

Ricky's story illustrates another important reality about People's Park: here, kids are pulled into a multiracial, intergenerational mentoring system, where they learn that building a community is based on respecting others rather than building antagonistic boundaries based on racial categories. Ricky mentioned that he has always felt very comfortable around people of other races and has made friends easy among Black, white, Latina/o, and Armenian youth. Once, for example, some Black youth who weren't from the park had some issues with some of Ricky's Latina/o friends. The Black youth did not know Ricky and expected him to take their side in "racial solidarity." Ricky explained, "It wasn't like regular people that came to this park, these people that came here just to play, but it never affected me because I never took it personally. I never took it as if I needed to choose sides, 'cause I never knew them." He did not know these Black youth, so he sided with these Latinos who were his friends, which made his decision easy. Ricky had been a member of People's Park since he was a young, had coached there, and had won championships as both player and coach. When Ricky would come around some youth would run over to him and show off their new moves or shots they were practicing. Ricky's loyalty to other members of the park may have sprung from the commitment to and admiration of others at the park.

People's Park appears to have given Ricky and other youth the opportunity to transcend what Brett Berry (2008, 207), in his analysis of racial segregation dynamics, refers to as "spatial-opportunity distance (e.g., living in different neighborhoods) and social-psychological distance (e.g., avoidance, denying close relationships, selective membership, shared identities, and language)." Berry observes that one can live in an integrated neighborhood and still be racially segregated due to group "boundary work" that highlights and enforces racial divisions. If organizations, churches, and community centers operate racially exclusively, it matters little that the neighborhood is integrated.

Berry (2008, 207) argues that racial boundary work operates on three different levels: macro, meso, and micro. The micro level is most useful in explaining the interactions at People's Park: "'Micro-level' boundaries manifest themselves in situations based on contextual information and predisposition schemas. At this level actors are in physical proximity and even making superficial contact, but seldom share social and symbolic resources in the form of close ties or mutual feelings of membership or identification." In other words, when people share a common space and have casual contacts, there may be little shared resources or consciousness. An example of this is an urban mall where people of different races and faiths use the same space but remain mostly oblivious to each other, with little to no acknowledgment of each other's existence, let alone a recognition of community.

People's Park traverses this micro-level boundary. Here, as the following story illustrates, there is a shared consciousness of what it means to be a part of this space and what the space means to the surrounding community. While conducting this study, I was coaching a thirteen- to fifteen-year-old all-star team in a championship game against the Triumph Vines from a rival park. Enthusiastic fans from each side filled the stands. Walking to the court, I was greeted by youth and parents, some of whom I didn't know. Some young boys had constructed signs that read "People's Park" in marker on thin poster board. During the game, they ran up and down the sidelines, holding high their signs, exciting the crowd. I hadn't seen this type of support at my son's high school games, let alone a park league game. The park brought the community together: young and old, former and current players, past and current employees all wanted to be part of the moment, when we weren't Black, white, or Latina/os. We were fans and supporters of People's Park, nothing more, nothing less, united in support of our team.

A sense of community is often created through sport. In her study of Little League baseball in Philadelphia, sociologist Sherri Grasmuck (2005, 193) shows how recreational sports can affect race relations: "In changing neighborhood space, residents and outsiders who have lived most of their lives in racially segregated neighborhoods come together voluntarily to watch their children play together." Under certain conditions, sports can aid in the suspension of micro-level boundaries, as parents cross otherwise seemingly impervious racial divides and antagonisms to root for their child's multiracial team and children can develop friendships with those of other races.

In that championship game against Triumph Vines, my team won the second of two all-star championships, both of which were led by Black coaches at a mostly Latina/o park. Yet this seemed to go unnoticed by the populace of People's Park, who seemed only to acknowledge that the collective "we" had won. The community of People's Park cherished these championships; they vindicated "us" as a basketball program and elevated us beyond the image of being a "thug" park. They offered respectability for the community.

Grasmuck (2005) describes the "insider culture" of Fairmount Sports Association, where social ties were connected to the neighborhood and to continued service. Often this insider culture alienated "newcomers," many of whom hailed from a professional class and were gentrifying the neighborhood. Because most of the Little League parents in her study were white, when the outsiders were from another race they could confuse their marginalized treatment as racism. But as one African American newcomer stated, "It's not so much about race, it's about a group of people who may have grown up together, socialized together" (Grasmuck 2005, 71).

The same can be said of the "insiders" at People's Park. They form a group who has either "grown up together" or "socialized together." The system of Black-Latino/a intergenerational mentoring shows that, at least here in People's Park, insider status can trump race. Although the park is now a predominantly Latina/o space, being Latina/o doesn't by itself give one entrée into the club; one has to demonstrate continued service.

CONCLUSION

Gloria Anzaldúa (1999, 19) has asserted that "the space between two individuals shrinks with intimacy." People's Park is an intimate space that has carved out a common purpose for El Lado Este residents: provide community youth with safe and positive activities and, as Andres states, a place where racial problems "are to be left at the door." The race of the youth or coaches is insignificant to the program. Instead, a sense of class consciousness prevails; these are mostly working-class youth who are "at risk."

My research challenges simplistic and monolithic views of race relations between African Americans and Latina/os that emphasize across-group tensions, conflict, and violence, suggesting that social contexts can shape the degree to which these groups express racial antagonisms or cooperation and understanding. In the context of the youth sports programs in People's Park, these groups show a great deal of cooperation on a daily basis. This observation offers important lessons for future examinations of race relations, as Latina/o populations continue to grow, often in or near existing Black communities (Kun and Pulido 2014). This research also demonstrates the role sports can play in bringing multiple races and ethnic groups together for a common activity. But, as sociologist Douglas Hartmann (2001) has shown in his critical analysis of community efforts to use "midnight basketball" to reduce criminal activities among poor minority boys, it is important not to assume that "sports" alone can play this democratizing and integrative role. Instead, sports in People's Park is as an important *vehicle* through which connections are made; however the key *mechanism* for these connections is the system of intergenerational and multiracial respect that connects community heads with kids. This institutionalized mentoring process infuses kids with a commitment to the place and to each other, ultimately recruiting them to serve this system as volunteers and occasionally as paid employees.

This research has important policy implications. The recent economic recession resulted continuing slashes to public services, including discussions by LA Recreation and Parks administrators about the possibility of privatizing park services. Private companies would run these public leagues for a profit and would have to raise the prices of participation. This would be devastating to a community that needs low-cost services that can give youth alternatives to negative and criminal activities. In addition, privatization of this system could undermine what I have shown is the key mechanism of cross-racial community building: the informal system of intergeneration mentoring and the practice of creating paying jobs that meaningfully integrate youth into this system. There are political decisions to be made here, decisions that will shape the sort of communities and the sort of nation our children will live in: either we will invest in cheaper upstream solutions like intervention programs or more expensive downstream solutions such as incarceration. In this case, the choice seems simple: social investments in youth sports and mentorship programs can provide income to both youth and adults, thus benefitting families and communities while building cross-racial understanding. If the economic downturn has overwhelmingly harmed low-income communities, then mentorship and jobs may be one avenue out of the crisis: providing adults with purpose, youth with hope, and both with jobs.

NOTES

1. Neighborhood "hustlers" are individuals who help people acquire things legal and illegal. They act as intermediaries between people.

2. The park name, city name, and names of all participants are pseudonyms.

3. While Wilson described this pattern correctly, he likely overstated Black middle-class unity with the Black underclass, and falsely implied that Blacks are unique in this respect. Many groups, including whites, have experienced middle-class flight to the suburbs (Waters 1990).

4. Wilson's view of Black middle-class responsibility to the Black "underclass" is similar to traditional ideas of "racial uplift," grounded in part in W.E.B. Du Bois's (1903/1994) concept of the "talented tenth."

5. Taggers participate in a form of graffiti art. Generally they work alone and are not associated with a group. However, there are tagging crews that sometimes participate in marginal illegal activities to get money for paint and other tagging supplies. In contrast, gang bangers are members of a group that is associated with a particular area. They often participate in minor and serious crimes to support themselves and the gang. They also "tag" areas to mark their territory.

6. Dead spots are places where the floor is particularly worn, where the ball doesn't bounce well.

REFERENCES

Anderson, Elijah. 1999. *Code of the Streets, Decency, Violence, and the Moral Life of the Inner City*. New York: Norton.

Anzaldúa, Gloria. 1999. *Borderlands: La Frontera*. San Francisco: Aunt Lute Books.

Berry, Brent. 2008. "Indices of Racial Residential Segregation: A Critical Review and Redirection." In *White Logic, White Methods: Racism and Methodology*, edited by Eduardo Bonilla-Silva, 203–216. Plymouth: Rowman & Littlefield.

Camarillo, Albert M. 2004. "Black and Brown in Compton: Demographic Change, Suburban Decline, and Intergroup Relations in a South Central Los Angeles Community, 1950 to 2000." In *Not Just Black and White: Historical and Contemporary Perspectives on*

Immigration, Race, and Ethnicity in the United States, edited by Nancy Foner and George M. Fredrickson, 358–376. New York: Russell Sage Foundation.

Collatos, Anthony, Ernest Morrell, Alejandro Nuno, and Roger Lara. 2004. "Critical Sociology in K–16 Early Intervention: Remaking Latino Pathways to Higher Education." *Journal of Hispanic Higher Education* 3: 164–179.

Collins, Patricia Hill. 2006. *From Black Power to Hip Hop: Racism, Nationalism, and Feminism* Philadelphia: Temple University Press.

Du Bois, W.E.B. 1903/1994. *The Souls of Black Folk*. New York: Oxford University Press.

Emerson, Robert M. 2001. *Contemporary Field Research: Perspectives and Formulations*. Prospect Heights, IL: Waveland Press.

Estrada, Emir, and Pierrette Hondagneu-Sotelo. 2011. "Intersectional Dignities: Latino Immigrant Street Vendor Youth in Los Angeles." *Journal of Contemporary Ethnography* 40.1: 102–131.

Grasmuck, Sherri. 2005. *Protecting Home: Class, Race, and Masculinity in Boys' Baseball*. New Brunswick, NJ: Rutgers University Press.

Hartmann, Douglas. 2001. "Notes on Midnight Basketball and the Cultural Politics of Recreation, Race, and At-Risk Urban Youth." *Journal of Sport & Social Issues* 25.4: 339–371.

Jackson, John H. 2008. "Given Half a Chance: The Schott 50 State Report on Public Education and Black Males." Cambridge, MA: Schott Foundation for Public Education.

Kun, Josh, and Laura Pulido. 2014. *Black and Brown in Los Angeles: Beyond Conflict and Coalition*. Berkeley: University of California Press.

Kwon, Hyeyoung. 2014. "The Hidden Injury of Class in Korean-American Language Brokers' Lives." *Childhood* 21.1: 56–71.

Los Angeles Police Department. 2007. "Blog Site." http://lapdblog.typepad.com/lapd_blog/2007/week35/index.html. Accessed September 1, 2007.

US Department of Labor. 2012. Bureau of Labor Statistics. http://www.dol.gov/. Retrieved June 2011.

Vaca, Nicolas C. 2004. *The Presumed Alliance: The Unspoken Conflict between Latinos and Blacks and What It Means for America*. New York: HarperCollins.

Waters, Mary C. 1990. *Ethnic Options: Choosing Identities in America*. Berkeley: University of California Press.

Wheelock, Darren, and Douglas Hartmann. 2007. "Midnight Basketball and the 1994 Crime Bill Debates: The Operation of a Racial Code." *Sociological Quarterly* 48: 315–342.

Wilson, William J. 1987. *The Truly Disadvantaged: The Inner City, the Underclass, and Public Policy*. Chicago: University of Chicago Press.

———. 1996. *When Work Disappears: The World of the New Urban Poor*. New York: Vintage.

———. 2009. *More Than Just Race: Being Black and Poor in the Inner City*. New York: Norton.

Zelizer, Viviana A. R. 1985. *Pricing the Priceless Child: The Changing Social Value of Children*. Princeton, NJ: Princeton University Press.

Afterword

KIDS, SPORT RESEARCH, AND SPORT POLICY

William A. Corsaro

In recent years we have seen the beginnings of a new sociology of childhood, one that breaks free from the individualistic doctrine that regards socialization as the child's private internalization of adult skills and knowledge. In this new approach the focus is on childhood as a social construction resulting from the collective actions of children and youth with adults and each other. Childhood is recognized as a structural form (Qvortrup 2009) and children and youth as social agents who contribute to the reproduction of childhood and society through their negotiations with adults and through their creative production of a series of peer cultures with each other (Corsaro 2015). This new view of childhood as a social phenomenon replaces the traditional notion of socialization with the concept of interpretive reproduction. Interpretive reproduction reflects children's evolving membership in their culture, which begins in the family and spirals outward as children and youth create a series of embedded peer cultures based on the institutional structure of the adult culture. Overall, the notion of interpretive reproduction challenges sociology to take children and youth seriously and to appreciate their contributions to social reproduction and change (Corsaro 2015).

In the chapters in this volume we see a myriad of ways children and youth engage adults and each other in sports activities in various formal and informal social and community settings. The chapters are varied in scope and topic. I focus on several interrelated themes that pervade the chapters that particularly interested me as someone who has stressed the agency of children and youth and of incorporating their voices in our study of their lives. These themes are threefold: first, how children and youth sports participation emerges and unfolds in important transitions in the lives of children and youth; second, how children and youth sports participation is related to the intersectionality of gender, race, class, and age; finally, how children and youth sports participation is intertwined in adult marketing and consumer culture.

Sports Participation and Life Transitions

In sociology most research on life transitions is grounded in life course theory. A major strength of life course research is its insistence on situating the developing individual in historical time and structural or cultural place. Glen Elder (1994, 5) defined the life course as a "multilevel phenomenon, ranging from structural pathways through social institutions and organizations to the social trajectories of individuals and their developmental pathways." However, work to date on the life course has seldom addressed the life transitions of young children and youth (except for transitions related to paths to adulthood; see Elder 1974; Furstenberg et al. 2000).

My notion of interpretative reproduction is in line with what Elder (1994, 5) terms the four themes of the life course paradigm: "the interplay of human lives and historical times, the timing of lives, linked or interdependent lives, and human agency in choice making." I have used interpretive reproduction to study children's life transitions, most especially their transition from preschool to elementary school (Corsaro and Molinari 2005). When studying life transitions it is necessary to move beyond a focus on the individual child. Children do, of course, develop individually, but throughout this development the collective processes, which they are always part of, are also changing. These processes are best viewed as occurring in the interwoven local cultures forming children's worlds (Geertz 1973). When we discuss these collective processes developmentally or longitudinally, we must consider the nature of children's *membership* in these local cultures and the changes in their degree or intensity of membership and participation over time. We also must consider how different structural and institutional features constrain and enable the collective processes of interest (e.g., from transitions related to schooling or children and youth participation in sport or their sport careers).

Crucial to the nature of membership is participation in collective routine activities that signify that one is part of a group and collective action. At the same time, cultural practices in these routines prepare, or prime, members for future transitions. Along these lines, I with my colleague Luisa Molinari developed the notion of *priming events* (Corsaro and Molinari 2000, 2005; Corsaro et al. 2003). Priming events involve activities in which children and youth, by their very participation, attend prospectively to ongoing or anticipated changes in their lives. Such events are crucial to children and youths' social construction of representations of temporal aspects of their lives (including important life transitions) because these social representations arise not from simply thinking about social life but rather from children and youths' collective practical activities with others (see Corsaro and Molinari 2005).

We can look at children and youth participation in sports or their sport careers through the lens of interpretive reproduction and priming events. Regarding sport careers, Peter and Patricia Adler (1998) laid out a sequence of types of after-school activities that often involved physical or sports participation from spontaneous or informal play to recreational activities, competitive activities, and elite activities. Their analysis, based on observations and interviews of their own elementary-school-age children and their friends, loosely described what can be seen as sports careers in a sort of funneling frame from wide participation in spontaneous play to narrowing participation in the other activities with many children not entering or opting out of elite activities. Although the Adlers' analysis is interesting, a weakness is the lack of depth of the ethnographic observations and their reliance on a small sample with little variation by race, class, and ethnicity.

Several chapters in this volume transcend these weaknesses and provide important insights in what I call transitions in sports careers. In chapter 1 Don Sabo and Philip Veliz draw on national surveys that not only identify variation in sports participation by race, class, and gender but also hint at patterns in children and youth sport careers. They generally find that a large percentage of children and youth participate in sports from an early age but that participation rates are higher for white middle- and upper-class males, with males entering at an earlier age than females. They also find "that children leave organized sports in droves as they age—a pattern that is especially prevalent among girls and kids of color." While it is difficult to tease out underlying explanations for these patterns (without more direct observations or interviews), they use their survey data to point to things like girls' growing interests in other activities with age, working- and lower-class girls (especially of color) facing demands of helping with child care and other family work (a factor also noted by Cooky and Rauscher in chapter 3 and by Thul, LaVoi, Hazelwood, and Hussein in chapter 8 for Muslim East African immigrant girls), and a lack of support and sports mentoring of girls compared to boys by parents, especially fathers. The latter two findings are especially interesting regarding interpretive reproduction and priming events as we see how boys (especially the more wealthy) have structural advantages to pursue sports careers and receive more encouragement, mentoring, and priming to engage in sports over longer periods of time and possibly at more elite levels.

In chapter 2 Douglas Hartmann and Alex Manning, who focus on racial and ethnic inequalities in sports participation, report findings that mirror those of Sabo and Veliz. Their findings show again how the sports careers of lower-class and minority youth start later and often end earlier than those of middle- and upper-class white youth. They show especially how economic and structural factors limit poor minority youth (especially in sports outside of school) from beginning and sustaining sports participation. Especially relevant is their finding of how minority youth participate in certain sports like basketball and football (especially in school venues) in somewhat equivalent rates to white youth while others like tennis and soccer are out of reach largely for economic reasons, but also due to lack of mentoring and priming. Furthermore, the authors point to cutbacks in publically funded athletic opportunities and facilities, which most directly affect all but the most gifted of poor minority youth from the opportunity to enjoy and develop their sports skills and careers.

Several of the chapters report on longitudinal or quasi-longitudinal studies that capture temporal aspects of youth engagement with sport activity. In chapter 6 Michela Musto insightfully captures the importance of context in cross-gender relations on a youth swim team, which I discuss in more detail later. Here I note that her longitudinal design was essential in capturing what she notes as a spillover effect in which the boys' in-pool experiences of losing to the girls contributed to a baseline of respect, making them less inclined to invade the girls' space and provoke antagonistic relations outside pool time. In chapter 7 Murray Drummond's longitudinal focus group interviews capture how boys' meanings of masculinity, sport, and health shift over time. Of particular interest are the boys' developing perceptions of muscles, men, and masculinity. "Regardless of age," Drummond found that "the majority of boys had a comprehensive understanding that they are not capable, at present, of attaining a highly muscular physique, as some boys stated, 'like my dad.'" But they were not concerned about these perceived bodily inadequacies because they anticipated becoming muscular as they progressed through adolescence and toward adulthood. There was a sense of inevitability in the boys' beliefs that they would become big and muscular simply by becoming men. Here we see that the boys in a sense primed themselves by prospecting to a future where they would attain muscularity in line with adult role models like their fathers or stereotypic muscular men. In a related study in chapter 10, Michael Kehler looks inside boys' locker rooms, where he finds a division of muscular athletic boys who take center stage in bodily display, sometimes taunting and bullying less muscular and athletic classmates. Interestingly, Kehler focuses more on the less athletic boys (a tack that is different from many researchers who study the negative aspects of hypermasculinity—a point well made by Messner and Musto in the introduction to this volume). His longitudinal design enables him to capture a set of strategies or secondary adjustments (Corsaro 1990; Goffman 1961) these boys collectively develop including strategic use of space, time, and dress that enable them to avoid a good deal of harassment and even develop a sense of dignity and superiority over their often bullying and much less empathetic counterparts.

Two other chapters with quasi-longitudinal designs (chapter 9 by Ann Travers and chapter 11 by A. James McKeever) are quite different in topic, with the latter holding promise in its positive findings of community support and the former showing where such support and understanding are so lacking in the sometimes heartbreaking analysis. Travers, relying primarily on reflective interviews of mothers of transgender children and youth, captures the challenges and struggles these kids face when structural aspects of community sports programs attempt to force them into binary gender identities. Her narrative analysis is a trope of creative but frustrating navigation and negotiation by the children and mothers. Unfortunately despite some limited successes most of the youth decide in the end to opt out of the struggle for acceptance in organized sport. McKeever's autoethnography is beautifully written and totally lacking of the self-indulgence that can and often does typify this method. McKeever is everywhere in his story, but the tale is always about community where people, places, and activities come to inspirational life. The temporal aspects highlight mentors and mentoring (first those who mentor McKeever and then in turn those he mentors). Mentoring creates interactive spaces that fuse past, future, and present, capturing who one was, who one is, and who one can be. It is the essence of what I refer to as priming events, which McKeever captures in impressive detail in the moment and over time for himself and others.

Youth, Sport, and the Intersectionality of Gender, Race, and Class

Many of the chapters of this volume are about youth sports participation and how it intersects with gender, race, and class. In particular, chapters by Cooky and Rauscher; Drummond; Hartmann and Manning; Kehler; Musto; Thul, LaVoi, Hazelwood, and Hussein; and Travers integrate their analyses in important recent theoretical work on gender, race, and class far beyond my expertise, and I learned much from their discussions. Also each of these chapters adds to the conversation, debate, and advocacy of equality in this field in new and interesting ways—in ways that often bring the worlds and voices of children directly into the discussion. Thus, they are important contributions to the new sociology of children and youth.

However, I do want to discuss a few of the chapters that I feel add an important addition to the intersectionality literature with their focus on age and intergenerational relations. According to Leena Alanen (2009, 161), interactions "taking place between members of existing generational categories" are what produce and reproduce generational order. Alanen argues that investigation of the generational order from the perspective of children and youth "should focus on revealing (1) those *structures* that can be identified as specifically generational;

(2) the interdependent *positions* that these generational structures define for generational groups to take and to act from; and (3) the social and cultural *practices* of positioning—both self- and other-positioning—through which the current generational structures, and the generational order as their composite structure, are generated, maintained, and (occasionally) transformed" (2009, 170, emphasis original). In most of the chapters in this volume the intergenerational relations that are discussed are primarily those between youth and adults as most of the activities related to sport are primarily age-segregated. This factor may be due to the overwhelming focus of the chapters on organized sports participation rather than unorganized or spontaneous play among children and youth in neighborhood or after-school settings where mixed-age groups are common. Only McKeever's study hints at children of various ages participating in and supporting sports activities in a highly communal venue. However, a number of the studies touch on the importance of interactions between youth and adults in sports activities, and these interactions are mixed regarding their patterns of neglect or support between generations.

Looking first at studies where intergenerational relations were lacking or basically unsupportive we see in chapter 10 by Kehler that even though physical education was mandatory in the school he studied, adult supervision was absent. When one teacher did respond to the perceived problems by suggesting boys could have the option of wearing swimsuits in the showers, it was clear that neither he nor the students felt this was really a viable solution. Kehler argues that "the teacher was aware of the discomfort among his students and offered a coping strategy but failed to actually address the insecurities. There is a deeply held belief that boys can navigate, participate, and enter highly masculinized places such as boys' and men's locker rooms because of an assumed acceptance of and comfort with normative masculine ideology." This type of benign neglect also seems to run through the adult coaches' or supervisors' reactions to the problems of transgender youth in Travers's chapter. On the other hand, the unswerving support of the mothers in Travers's study is uplifting, and it is clear that their children were appreciative of such support and knew they could always count on their mothers in challenges they were sure to face in the future. We also see a mixture of positive and negative intergenerational relations in Jeffrey Montez de Oca, Jeffrey Scholes, and Brandon Meyer's chapter regarding the NFL and its Play 60 program to promote physical activity and health. While youth may be thrilled with the attention of their football heroes and have the opportunity to engage in or watch their peers engage in physical activities with their favorite players, the underlying aim of the program is grossly commercial. As the authors note the prime motive is to recruit youth as fans and as consumers of NFL products as well, of course, as those of their sponsors (such as fast food and alcohol), which are antithetical to a healthy lifestyle.

We see clearly positive intergenerational relations in three other chapters. Musto documents the importance of the high-achieving swim team coach who sets exacting standards and encourages strong performance without reference to the gender of her swimmers. Given her background as an Olympic swimmer and her clear dedication to bringing the best out of her swimmers, it is clear she is a respected role model for both the female and male youth she trains. In chapter 8 Thul, LaVoi, Hazelwood, and Hussein, in establishing a community participatory action research partnership with a group of East African immigrant girls, nourish important intergenerational relations with the youth they study. Their work is an excellent example of research with rather than on children and youth as through their observations and interviews the researchers capture the voices and concerns of the girls. They went further as one of the authors, Hussein, established the Girls' Initiative in Recreation and Leisurely Sports (G.I.R.L.S.) Program, is a community-based physical activity program that provides strength-focused, youth-engaged, holistic, and positive youth development opportunities that are tailored to the specific interests and needs of East African girls. Finally, earlier I discussed the importance of mentoring in McKeever's study of his own and the experiences of others in a community recreational center. McKeever brings to life the interwoven positive intergenerational relations that existed over long periods among adult coaches, referees, parents, neighbors, and youth. Furthermore, given variation in age of the youth sports participants, their friends, and siblings, we see strong communal intergenerational relations among the youth themselves.

Youth Sports, Media, and Consumer Culture

As Daniel Cook (2009) has noted, merchants, marketers, and advertisers have engaged children as consumers for the better part of a century. This recognition of the child consumer, often mediated through parents, can be seen in the marketing and advertising of a wide range of products and images, including books, clothing, food, and lifestyle. Many critics bemoan the power of marketers and the media more generally and argue that they have co-opted children, parents, and even schools into their strategies to create "commercialized children" (Schor 2004). Others (Buckingham 2000; Cook 2009; Cross 1997; Sternheimer 2010) acknowledge the power of marketers, the commodification of youth culture, and the complexity of today's media culture, but also recognize the agency of parents and children to be insightful consumers. These authors, above all else, call for increased consumer literacy.

Several chapters in this volume insightfully address the power of media and marketing related to youth and sport. Using an epidemiological approach, Toben F. Nelson challenges assumptions that sports participation can automatically lead to better health and reduce obesity. Nelson puts such beliefs into the context of types of food youth athletes eat or drink (often unhealthy) and how this relates to marketing activities at sporting events. He cautions assumptions about the nutritional value of sports drinks and notes that sales of fast foods of various types are highly profitable at such sporting events. These observations can be expanded to sporting events at all levels, from Little League baseball to elementary through secondary school sports and to college and professional sporting events. Nelson's research implies that for many youth athletes, far from nutritious eating habits fostered at an early age may be maintained in sports contexts as fans long after their playing days have ended. A somewhat similar theme appears in the chapter by Montez de Oca, Scholes, and Meyer regarding the NFL and its marketing of its Play 60 program that I discussed earlier. While the NFL wants to be seen in a positive way to be promoting children and youth health, they also have the ulterior motive of combating recent perceptions of football as a highly dangerous sport, especially given growing concerns about concussions. Play 60 and similar programs are meant to keep youth interested in playing football (and their parents allowing them to do so), but perhaps more importantly remaining football fans in the present and future. Further here, as is the case for much marketing to children and youth, there is a type of intertextuality in which multiple messages are interwoven in different genres. While we see Play 60 logos on the field and in commercials during games, they are just one type of commercial product mixed with other NFL brands that promote fast food, sugar-loaded soft drinks, and alcohol. The marketing strategies of these commercials are so routine and insidious that the contradictions become nearly imperceptible.

Finally, in their insightful review of relevant literature and analysis of media portrayals of female athletes, Cooky and Rauscher demonstrate how female athletes are silenced, trivialized, or sexualized. To illustrate this point they offer the recent example of Mo'ne Davis, thirteen at the time, as being the first Little League player to appear on the cover of *Sports Illustrated*, but also one of only a handful of female athletes to grace the magazine's cover not wearing a swimsuit. They argue that the portrayal of Black female athletes is even more egregious, pointing to examples of media degradation like that of the Rutgers University women's basketball team. They also note the contradictions in portrayal of especially successful Black female athletes like the Williams sisters in ways that belittle and trivialize their achievements and sexualize them as both unfeminine yet hyperfeminine and muscular yet threateningly hypermuscular. In short, media messages of this sort surely must cause confusion and even disillusionment for Black female youth as sports participants or fans.

These chapters certainly raise concerns regarding negative media effects on youth in sports contexts. However, as with media effects and children and youth consumer culture in general, we must be careful not to assume that children and youth are cultural dopes with little or no agency. The documentation of such media messages and marketing is an important first step. However, more studies are needed that investigate how children and youth process and evaluate such messages. Children and youth can be consumer-savvy, especially when guided and supported by knowledgeable and caring adults. Examples such as those covered in these chapters can and should be turned into reflective educational opportunities in families and schools.

Some Policy Suggestions

In conclusion I offer some policy suggestion in line with each of themes I discussed earlier. In regard to life transitions, programs that engage children, youth, and adults in activities related to physical activity and sport while marking and celebrating specific transitions hold a great deal of promise. An example of one such event occurs regularly in cities in Italy, which I documented in my study of children in Modena as they made the transition first from preschool to elementary school and then from elementary to middle school (Corsaro and Molinari 2005). This yearly event was the special Scuola Sport (Sports School) that was held in a large park for all fifth-graders in the city. The Sports School was organized by groups of volunteers who ranged in age from high school students to retired senior citizens. The event began as all the fifth-graders gathered with their fellow students from each of the elementary schools in the city in front of a stage that was covered with colorful balloons. Once the children were all grouped together they were led in a group song with coordinated movements. Then the children were told they could go to join one of over twenty different areas. In each area a different sport was presented and described by volunteers representing various sports clubs. The children could then join in and participate in the particular sport. Sports that were represented included wind surfing, field hockey, fishing, judo, boxing, canoeing, and many others.

The Scuola Sport celebrated the children's lives at an important rite of passage, in this case the completion of elementary school. It was an activity the children looked forward to and very much enjoyed. It was also a priming event in that it impelled the children to look forward to their coming transition to a new stage in their lives and their participation in the Modena community while also introducing them to community sports organizations that many of the children would later join.

Other activities that I observed in Italian schools were end-of-the-year parties where parents organized a range of activities including competitive sports activities that involved mixed-gender and -age teams made up of students, teachers, parents, siblings, and relatives. These parties strengthened the already close bonds of the children, families, and teachers and celebrated their community in psychologically and physically healthy ways.

Regarding the second theme of youth sports participation as related to the intersectionality of gender, race, class, and age, a number of the chapters in the volume addressed policy needs specifically. Two in particular, chapters 8 (Thul and colleagues) and 11 (McKeever), discuss and bring to life programs and community centers that help overcome many of the obstacles especially lower-class minority youth both male and female face in finding safe and supporting places for sports participation and mentoring. At a time of many state and city government cutbacks, such programs, as well as safe parks and other places for sport and play especially in inner-city areas, are under threat. The survival of these programs is vital in serving the many needs of the children and youth (see Heath and McLaughlin 1993).

Regarding the third theme of how children and youth sports participation is intertwined in adult marketing and consumer culture, more recognition and education are sorely needed. Several chapters in this volume impressively supply needed recognition regarding the complexity of media marketing and consumerism regarding kids and sport. They also suggest or imply educational programs. I would argue for the need of parents to use quality time with their children to reflect on and discuss the intricacies and the intertextuality of media messages related to sports and health. Along these same lines such discussions should play an integral part in health classes in schools. Also it is my hope that at local levels there can be a push for sponsorship of children and youth sport from especially small businesses that supply products for healthy lives to at least supplant if not break down the hegemonic control of large corporations.

In closing, I want to suggest that in the study of kids and sport we must never forget that sport should bring excitement, fun, and better health, not anxiety, toil, or sadness, to children and youth. After observing and studying children for forty years, primarily as they engage in spontaneous play, I have learned the importance of enabling children to have and live their childhoods. As we propose policies with the purpose of improving the futures of children and youth, we must remember that their future is the present.

REFERENCES

Adler, Peter, and Patricia Adler. 1998. *Peer Power: Preadolescent Culture and Identity.* New Brunswick, NJ: Rutgers University Press.

Alanen, Leena. 2009. "Generational Order." In Qvortrup, Corsaro, and Honig, *Palgrave Handbook of Childhood Studies,* 159–174.

Buckingham, David. 2000. *After the Death of Childhood: Growing Up in the Age of Electronic Media.* Cambridge: Polity.

Cook, Daniel. 2009. "Children as Consumers." In Qvortrup, Corsaro, and Honig, *Palgrave Handbook of Childhood Studies,* 332–346.

Corsaro, William. 1990. "The Underlife of the Nursery School: Young Children's Social Representations of Adult Rules." In *Social Representations and the Development of Knowledge,* edited by Gerard Duveen and Barbara Lloyd, 11–26. Cambridge: Cambridge University Press.

———. 2015. *The Sociology of Childhood*. 4th ed. Thousand Oaks, CA: Sage.

Corsaro, William, and Luisa Molinari. 2000. "Priming Events and Italian Children's Transition from Preschool to Elementary School: Representations and Action." *Social Psychology Quarterly* 63: 16–33.

———. 2005. *I Compagni: Understanding Italian Children's Transition from Preschool to Elementary School*. New York: Teachers College Press.

Corsaro, William, Luisa Molinari, Kathryn Hadley, and Heather Sugioka. 2003. "Keeping and Making Friends in Italian Children's Transition from Preschool to Elementary School." *Social Psychology Quarterly* 66: 272–292.

Cross, Gary. 1997. *Kids' Stuff*. Cambridge, MA: Harvard University Press.

Elder, Glen. 1974. *Children of the Great Depression: Social Change in Life Experience*. Chicago: University of Chicago Press.

———. 1994. "Time, Human Agency, and Social Change: Perspectives of the Live Course." *Social Psychology Quarterly* 57: 4–15.

Furstenberg, Frank, Thomas D. Cook, Jacquelynne Eccles, and Glen Elder. 2000. *Managing to Make It: Urban Families and Adolescent Success*. Chicago: University of Chicago Press.

Geertz, Clifford. 1973. *The Interpretation of Cultures*. New York: Basic Books.

Goffman, Erving. 1961. *Asylums*. Garden City, NJ: Anchor.

Heath, Shirley Brice, and Milbery M. McLaughlin, eds. 1993. *Identity and Inner-City Youth: Beyond Ethnicity and Gender*. New York: Teachers College Press.

Marsiglio, William. 2008. *Men on a Mission: Valuing Youth Work in Our Communities*. Baltimore: Johns Hopkins University Press.

Qvortrup, Jens. 2009. "Childhood as a Structural Form." In Qvortrup, Corsaro, and Honig, *Palgrave Handbook of Childhood Studies*, 21–33.

Qvortrup, Jens, William Corsaro, and Michael-Sebastian Honig, eds. 2009. *The Palgrave Handbook of Childhood Studies*. Basingstoke: Palgrave.

Schor, Juliet. 2004. *Born to Buy*. New York: Scribner.

Sternheimer, Karen. 2010. *Connecting Social Problems and Popular Culture: Why Media Is Not the Answer*. Boulder, CO: Westview.

Notes on Contributors

CHERYL COOKY is an associate professor in Women's, Gender, and Sexuality Studies at Purdue University. Her research has been published in *Sex Roles, Communication & Sport, Journal of Sex Research,* and *Sociology of Sport Journal,* among others. She is president-elect of the North American Society for the Sociology of Sport.

WILLIAM A. CORSARO is professor emeritus in the Department of Sociology at Indiana University, Bloomington. His research interests are the sociology of childhood, children's peer cultures, and the sociology of education. He is the author of several books, including *The Sociology of Childhood* (fourth edition, 2015).

MURRAY J. N. DRUMMOND is a professor and the director of the Sport, Health, and Physical Education (SHAPE) Research Centre at Flinders University. His primary research interests are based around boys' and men's bodies and masculinities. His current research includes a longitudinal research project with boys from early childhood through to adolescence.

DOUGLAS HARTMANN is a professor of sociology at the University of Minnesota. He wrote *Race, Culture, and the Revolt of the Black Athlete: The 1968 Olympic Protests and Their Aftermath* (2003) and has been studying sport-based social programs. His forthcoming book is *Midnight Basketball, Race, and Neoliberal Social Policy.*

TORRIE F. HAZELWOOD is a master's student and a research assistant in the Tucker Center for Research on Girls & Women in Sport at the University of Minnesota. Her research focuses on political ideology's impact on media representations of female athletes and on policies using sport for integration of immigrants.

FATIMAH HUSSEIN, MA, LGSW, is a licensed social worker. She founded the all-female, culturally sensitive G.I.R.L.S. program in 2008. Her interests and

expertise include community building, strategic planning, partnership development, volunteering, fund-raising, program evaluation/outcome measurements,
youth empowerment, girls and women in sport, and health promotion.

MICHAEL KEHLER is an associate professor in the Faculty of Education at
Western University, Canada. His research examines the intersection of masculinities, body image, and physical health education as well as gender, literacies,
and secondary schooling. He has been funded by the Canadian Institutes of
Health Research.

NICOLE M. LaVOI, PhD, is the associate director of the Tucker Center for Research
on Girls & Women in Sport at the University of Minnesota. Her research focuses on
the effect of adult sideline behaviors in youth sport, barriers experienced by
female coaches, and media representations of females in sport.

ALEX MANNING is a PhD candidate in sociology at the University of Minnesota. He studies race, sports, youth, and parenting. His current research projects
include elite youth soccer in the United States, out-of-school organized youth
activities, and American understandings of diversity.

A. JAMES MCKEEVER has a long history of involvement in social justice work and
is a former American Sociological Association and National Institute of Drug
Abuse (NIDA) fellow. Currently he is an assistant professor and chair of the Philosophy and Sociology Department at Los Angeles Pierce College.

MICHAEL A. MESSNER is professor of sociology and gender studies at the University of Southern California. He is the author of several books, including *It's All
for the Kids: Gender, Families, and Youth Sports* (2009) and *Some Men: Feminist
Allies and the Movement to End Violence against Women* (2015).

BRANDON MEYER is an economics major and research assistant at the University
of Colorado, Colorado Springs. His doctoral research will use feminist theory to
analyze gaming and gamer culture. He writes about video games at http://gamer
-identify-yourself.tumblr.com/.

JEFFREY MONTEZ DE OCA studies sport, media, and political economy at the University of Colorado, Colorado Springs. He is author of *Discipline and Indulgence:
College Football, Media, and the American Way of Life during the Cold War* (2013),
winner of the NASSS Outstanding Book Award in 2014.

MICHELA MUSTO is a PhD candidate in sociology at the University of Southern California. Her work on gender, children, and youth, social stratification,
education, and sport has appeared in *Gender & Society* and the *Sociology of
Sport Journal.*

TOBEN F. NELSON, ScD, is an associate professor with the Division of Epidemiology and Community Health at the University of Minnesota School of Public

Health. He studies public policy, substance use, physical activity, obesity, motor vehicle safety, and the health impacts of participation in organized sport.

LAUREN RAUSCHER is an assistant professor of sociology and director of the Women's Leadership and Mentorship Program at Robert Morris University. Her research examines the intersections of gender, race, and ethnicity in the domains of health, the body, and work. She earned her PhD from Emory University.

DON SABO, PhD, professor emeritus in Health Policy at D'Youville College, codirects the Center for Research on Physical Activity, Sport & Health. He is senior health policy advisor for the Women's Sports Foundation. He studies links among youth sport participation, educational attainment, health, and the struggle for gender equity.

JEFFREY SCHOLES is an assistant professor of philosophy and the director of the Center for Religious Diversity and Public Life at the University of Colorado, Colorado Springs. He has written books and articles on American political theology as well as the relationship between religion and sports.

CHELSEY M. THUL, PhD, is an affiliated scholar of the Tucker Center for Research on Girls & Women in Sport and a faculty member in the School of Kinesiology at the University of Minnesota. Her research focuses on community-based participatory research methods and culturally relevant physical activity promotion among girls.

ANN TRAVERS is an associate professor of sociology in the Department of Sociology and Anthropology at Simon Fraser University. Her research and publications focus on gender, race, sexuality, and social inequality; sport and social justice; transgender issues; and sport and transgender children.

PHILIP VELIZ, PhD, is an assistant research professor at the University of Michigan's Institute for Research on Women & Gender. He studies substance use among athletes and examines the impact of sport within public education. He is currently engaged in several projects that examine how involvement in certain types of sports either encourages or deters substance use among adolescents and collegiate athletes.

Index